EDUCATING MILWAUKEE

EDUCATING MILWAUKEE

*How One City's History of Segregation
and Struggle Shaped Its Schools*

JAMES K. NELSEN

Wisconsin Historical Society Press

Published by the Wisconsin Historical Society Press
Publishers since 1855

wisconsinhistory.org

Photographs identified with WHi or WHS are from the Society's collections; address requests to reproduce these photos to the Visual Materials Archivist at the Wisconsin Historical Society, 816 State Street, Madison, WI 53706.

Front cover photograph: Robert J. Boyd/*Milwaukee Journal Sentinel*
Back cover photograph: WHi Image ID 4993

Maps created by Mapping Specialists, Ltd., Madison, Wisconsin

Printed in the United States of America
Designed by Percolator Graphic Design

19 18 17 16 15   1 2 3 4 5

Library of Congress Cataloging-in-Publication Data

Nelsen, James K., 1975–
    Educating Milwaukee : how one city's history of segregation and struggle shaped its schools / James K. Nelsen.
        pages cm
    Includes bibliographical references and index.
        ISBN 978-0-87020-720-4 (pbk.) — ISBN 978-0-87020-721-1 (ebook)
    1. Public schools—Wisconsin—Milwaukee—History.
    2. Discrimination in education—Wisconsin—Milwaukee—History.
    3. Segregation in education—Milwaukee—History.
    4. School choice—Milwaukee—History.
    5. African Americans—Education—Milwaukee—History.
    6. Milwaukee (Wis.)—Race relations. I. Title.
        LA390.M5N45 2015
        370.9775'95—dc23   2015013015

To Mom, for instilling a love of learning in me

CONTENTS

INTRODUCTION

Freedom of choice is a basic concept in America. In order to contribute fully and freely to our society, a citizen must be able to choose, from a wide range of occupational options, the career best suited to his or her needs. Education is an essential prerequisite in this process of choice. Children, as well as adults, have a variety of talents and needs. No single educational program can meet the needs of all students. Thus, freedom of choice as adults largely depends on the opportunity to choose educational settings best suited to development of the unique potentials of each child.

—ALTERNATIVE EDUCATION IN MILWAUKEE[1]

Americans cherish freedom of choice. They have fought for it, celebrated it, and declared their willingness to die for it. Freedom as an ideal and as a concept has defined the United States even more than equality has. As historian Eric Foner points out in *The Story of American Freedom,* the United States is known as the "land of the free" and the "cradle of liberty."[2] Foner also writes:

The Declaration of Independence lists liberty among mankind's inalienable rights; the Constitution announces as its purpose to secure liberty's blessings. The United States fought the Civil War to defend the Free World. Americans' love of liberty has been represented by poles, caps, and statues, and acted out by burning stamps and draft cards, running away from slavery, and demonstrating for the right to vote. If asked to explain or justify their actions, public or private, Americans are likely to respond, "It's a free country."[3]

Historians frequently divide US history into various eras based on the quest for freedom. The Pilgrims were searching for freedom. American patriots fought for freedom. The pioneers went west seeking freedom. The Civil War was fought between the forces of freedom and slavery. The rise of organized labor, the Progressive Era, and the New Deal represent

1

economic freedom. The civil rights movement and related movements of the 1960s were also about freedom, including the freedom to attend a racially integrated school.[4] Milwaukee was one of many US cities that operated a segregated school system at that time, but Milwaukee's story is unique in that its struggle for integration and quality education has been so closely tied to choice.

When one mentions the "school choice" movement, many people think of publicly funded tuition vouchers for students to attend private schools, but that is not how I define choice. Instead, I use the term "choice" in its broadest sense. Choice is the act of using freedom, and it is a common thread that runs through the history of education in Milwaukee since the 1960s. Although a number of scholars have examined school choice, some going so far as to trace its origins to Milwaukee, few have studied the deeper history of choice in Milwaukee. Yet an understanding of that deep history is essential if we are to grasp the context of the choice movement and improve the current state of Milwaukee Public Schools (MPS). Milwaukee's choice movement is rooted in the city's civil rights movement of the 1960s and its magnet school movement of the 1970s and 1980s, which attempted to give students quality educational opportunities in racially integrated schools. With this history in mind, I divide the evolution of Milwaukee's educational policies into three periods—the eras of no choice (prior to 1976), forced choice (1976–1995), and school choice (after 1987).

During the era of no choice, Milwaukee, like other cities, based school assignment on neighborhood boundaries. Students typically walked to school. Even after automobiles became widespread in the mid-twentieth century, the idea of riding a bus to a school outside of one's neighborhood was not popular. African Americans in northern cities were usually concentrated in a few neighborhoods, and that led to racially segregated schools. African Americans and liberal whites challenged the segregated system in the 1960s and 1970s. Milwaukee's African American activist community, according to historian Jack Dougherty, could be divided into three groups: an older black elite that advocated the hiring of African American teachers, a young movement that wanted to integrate schools, and a third movement that advocated community control of schools, which historian Bill Dahlk refers to as "educational proprietorship." The older group had been most active in the 1950s and early 1960s and wanted to cooperate with the white community, but the pro-integration group was larger and came to dominate Milwaukee's civil rights movement. The third group did not gain much traction in Milwaukee until the late 1980s.[5]

The Milwaukee school board received a judicial order to integrate its students in 1976. MPS developed magnet schools, under its new superintendent, Lee McMurrin. The magnet program was supposed to integrate the schools in a way that would avoid the problems that arose in Boston, which had integrated using involuntary busing and was rocked with protest and violence afterward.[6] Milwaukee's magnet schools offered specialized curricula designed to attract students from all parts of the school district or beyond the district.[7] The schools focused on particular areas, such as math and science, computers, trade and technology, or fine arts; or they used nontraditional teaching approaches, such as open classrooms, individualized instruction, or the Montessori method.[8] But Milwaukee faced unique challenges in its implementation of the magnet plan. Magnets were supposed to give students a wide variety of choices regarding where they would attend school, but students did not volunteer in the expected numbers. Thus, integration did not happen at the anticipated rate. Many students—both black and white—wanted to attend their neighborhood schools. Therefore, school administrators forced African Americans to choose white schools on the south side of Milwaukee. I call the period from 1976 to 1987 the era of forced choice. During that time, MPS relied on a complicated, inefficient, and expensive busing plan to integrate schools.

The magnet plan was not well received by many students, parents, or community groups. African American students sometimes faced outright hostility and violence in predominantly white schools. A group of African American activists, under the leadership of former Black Panther Howard Fuller, put forth a different vision of choice and urged an end to busing in the 1980s. Fuller believed that African Americans could educate their children more effectively if they had control of their neighborhood schools. Meanwhile, many white parents feared the quality of their children's education would suffer if their children attended school with low-income African American students. As a result, many white families left Milwaukee for more affluent suburban districts.

Despite the district's hopes for magnets, the schools did not reverse the demographic and economic changes Milwaukee was experiencing in the 1970s and 1980s. Like many American cities, Milwaukee experienced a reduction in the white birthrate and a migration of white families from the city to the suburbs. Milwaukee's economy also sharply declined in that period. It was no longer the manufacturing city it had once been. In fact, Milwaukee lost more jobs than almost any other city in the United States, leaving many of its residents in poverty. African American children were among the city's poorest inhabitants, and their academic achievement declined. Parents, community groups, and business interests responded by advocating for more choices in schools. Parents and community groups that were oriented toward black power and self-improvement believed education would improve if the district discontinued busing and educated students closer to their homes. Business interests supported market-driven reforms—the idea that choice in school would spur competition among schools and improve education while lowering costs. Howard Fuller emerged as the leading advocate for the end of busing and the increase in choice. He eventually became MPS superintendent and served from 1987 until 1995.

The period from 1987 to the present is what I call the era of school choice. My definition of choice is broad. It includes charter schools, vouchers, open enrollment in suburban districts, neighborhood schools, and small high schools. All these options are available in Milwaukee, which offers more choices in school selection than any other city in the United States. During this era, "choice" has morphed into a free-market ideology shared by people who support privatizing education. They believe that the public schools are broken and that the only way to improve education is by providing public schools with competition, which will force all schools, both public and private, to improve. But Milwaukee's academic progress has remained stagnant in the era of school choice. Competition has not helped. Evidence shows that the quality of education in Milwaukee's private schools is about the same or worse than in the regular public school system. Voucher critics say that poverty is what really causes achievement to decline and that vouchers siphon money away from financially strapped public schools and into unaccountable, poorly run private schools.

School choice is expanding all over the United States, despite mounting evidence that vouchers and other forms of choice do not improve education. For public schools to flourish rather than founder, it is important to understand the whole story behind the choice movement. And maybe, instead of offering a plethora of choices—which divide students, parents, communities, and money—Milwaukee and other school districts would be better off bringing people together and concentrating all their efforts into providing the best education we can for our children.

PART ONE

THE ERA OF NO CHOICE

CHAPTER 1

ETHNICITY, RACE, AND THE URBAN LANDSCAPE BEFORE 1967

The Milwaukee metropolitan area is often noted for being the most racially segregated urban area in the United States. Ninety percent of all Milwaukee-area African Americans live in the inner city, according to the 2010 census.[1] This segregation is not a new development. Since its founding, Milwaukee has been a divided city, first along ethnic lines and then along racial lines. African Americans in Milwaukee have faced discrimination in zoning ordinances, real estate sales, and mortgage lending practices throughout the twentieth century. Segregation in residence patterns led to segregation in schools. But segregation in Milwaukee was more severe than in other cities, due to a unique settlement pattern and an entrenched white power structure—specifically, the Milwaukee Board of School Directors—that refused to meet the demands of African American community leaders.

One thing that sets Milwaukee apart from other northern cities is that it was not founded as a single community but rather as three separate, rival communities. The original settlement, often referred to as Juneautown, after its founder, Solomon Juneau, a French furrier, was established as a trading fort on the east bank of the Milwaukee River in 1818.[2] Colonel George H. Walker, a transplanted Yankee, founded Walker's Point south of the Menominee River in 1833, and Byron Kilbourn, a government surveyor, came to the area in 1834 and picked out a choice piece of land on the west bank of the Milwaukee River, which he aptly named Town of

Milwaukee on the West Side of the River. The village, having an unwieldy name, was commonly referred to as Kilbourntown.[3] These three communities eventually became the east, south, and west sides of Milwaukee.

The residents of the three towns never really got along. For example, whenever either Juneau or Kilbourn offered to sell land to a particular individual, the other man often followed with a more attractive offer.[4] But the cost of maintaining separate city governments was prohibitive, so Juneautown and Kilbourntown merged in 1839 and were joined by Walker's Point in 1845. Each of the old villages became a ward in the new town, but the union of the villages did not put an end to their rivalries. Each ward still competed for settlers, and they were still physically separated by the rivers. Ordinances varied from ward to ward, and each ward was allowed to raise its own tax money and spend it on itself. Voting for delegates to the territorial legislature was split across ward lines. Roads on one side of a river did not line up with the roads on the other bank in the rival community, which made bridge construction difficult. Bridges were finally built, only to be destroyed in 1845 when an armed conflict between Juneautown and Kilbourntown broke out. Visitors to downtown Milwaukee today will notice that the streets are still not aligned.[5]

When the city of Milwaukee was formally incorporated in 1846, it was divided into five wards—one for Juneautown, two in Kilbourntown, and two in Walker's Point. As more settlers arrived, the city created additional wards by annexing new lands or by splitting existing wards. Many early Milwaukeeans were from New England or New York. They tended to settle in the first ward, as it was the most developed and most affluent.[6] Germans arrived by midcentury. They were usually skilled tradesmen, and they established middle-class neighborhoods in the second, fourth, and sixth wards. Soon, Germans constituted a majority of the city's population.[7] Their children made up almost half the school-age population by 1851. The Irish came next and settled in the Third Ward, immediately south of the Menominee River.[8] They vacated the area in 1892 and moved north of downtown after a fire swept through their neighborhood, leaving it to the Italians, who were the poorest of Milwaukee's immigrants.[9] Poles immigrated to the south side in large numbers following the turn of the century.[10] Czechs, Slovaks, Russians, Hungarians, and Jews also had their own enclaves, but the Germans were still the dominant group.[11] According to the 1910 census, 17 percent of all Milwaukeeans had been born in Germany, and 53.5 percent identified themselves as being of German ancestry.[12]

The first public schools opened in 1836. These schools merged into the Milwaukee Public Schools (MPS) in 1846, when the city was incorporated.[13] After a few experiments in the 1850s and early 1860s,[14] the first permanent high school opened in 1867, when the state legislature authorized creation of Milwaukee High School (later East Side High School or Riverside) in Juneautown.[15] South Side High School opened in 1893 in Walker's Point, and West Side High School opened in 1894 in Kilbourntown. The schools were renamed East Division, South Division, and West Division in 1899. More high schools were built as the city's population grew and compulsory school laws were enacted.[16] The high schools included North Division on the near north side in 1907, Washington High School on the west side in 1912, and Bay View High School on the southeast side of the city in 1914. Milwaukee School of Trades (later Milwaukee Trade and Technical High School and now the Lynde and Harry Bradley Technology and Trade School), which had been an independent school in the Fifth Ward, became part of MPS in 1907. The city built several new junior high schools and elementary schools during this time as well.[17]

The city's governing body, the common council, originally appointed the school board with equal representation from the five wards, resulting in a board that was deeply divided along ward lines. In 1907 the state legislature attempted to unify the school district by taking away the common council's power to appoint the school board. As a result, Milwaukee's citizens began electing a new fifteen-member school board on an at-large basis. But the change did not dampen ethnic and neighborhood tensions. Members of the Masonic Order frequently voted together, and organized labor formed a bloc that was concerned about salaries, contracts, and the way the schools presented working-class issues. Protestant and Catholic board members argued over free textbooks and hiring practices, and each ethnic or group was concerned about the teaching of its language and culture.[18]

At that same time, the first substantial number of African American migrants began arriving in Milwaukee, most migrating from the South seeking jobs. Milwaukee was a leading city in flour-milling, meatpacking, brewing, and heavy manufacturing. In fact, the manufacturing industry was so prolific that Milwaukee earned the title of "machine shop

MAP 1

Milwaukee with Ward Numbers in 1883

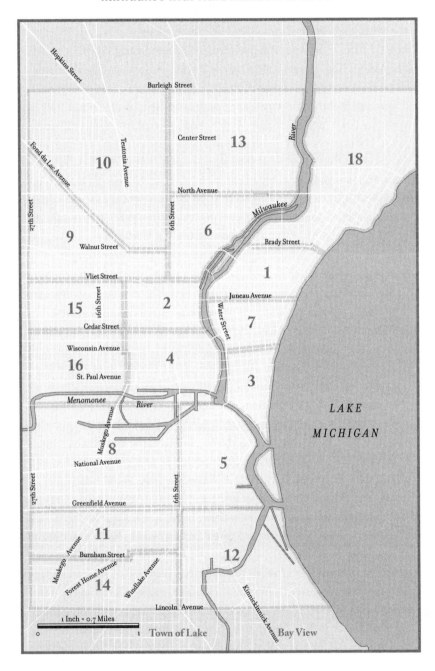

MAP 2
Milwaukee from 1957 Forward

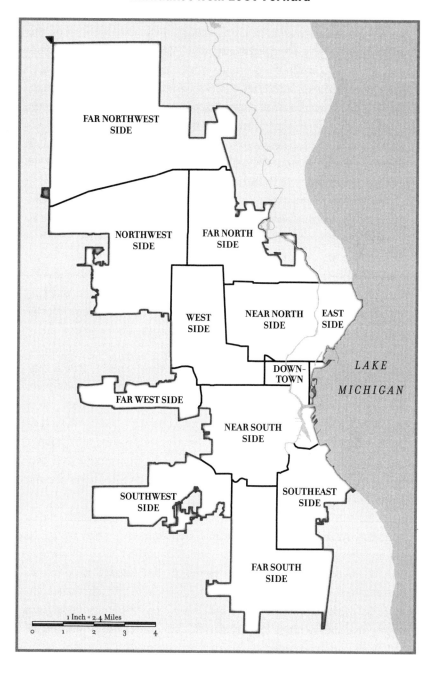

of the world."[19] But African Americans faced employment discrimination and were relegated to low-paying service-sector jobs, which forced them to rent homes rather than buy them. Most of Milwaukee's small African American population lived in a nine-square-block neighborhood on the north side of the city. The neighborhood had been populated by Germans until about 1900, when the Germans started moving north in search of better housing. Russian Jews and Greeks, being newer immigrant groups, then occupied the area until shortly before World War I, when they, too, began to move north, leaving what had become old housing stock to African Americans.[20] The neighborhood would become the hub of the city's African American community, which spread out as more migrants settled in Milwaukee in the mid-twentieth century.

In addition to housing and employment discrimination, African Americans were also excluded from public accommodations, such as theaters, hotels, and restaurants.[21] As in other northern cities, Milwaukee's African Americans turned inward, in the tradition of African American educator and orator Booker T. Washington, and developed their own black institutions, including churches, stores, and social clubs. But Milwaukee was different from other cities. As African Americans left the South in search of jobs at the beginning of the twentieth century, many skilled or semi-skilled laborers settled in Chicago.[22] This settlement pattern also meant that Milwaukee's African American population was very small until well after World War II. In fact, among the twenty-five largest cities in the United States, Milwaukee had the third-lowest percentage of African Americans as late as 1960.[23] The few that settled in Milwaukee lacked job skills and had a hard time finding well-paying jobs. Therefore, Milwaukee's black middle class grew very slowly, and it had to rely on close association with the white business community for economic support.[24]

As the city began to fill, Progressive leaders such as Socialist mayor Daniel Hoan, whose administration lasted from 1916 until 1930, and philanthropist Charles Whitnall became concerned about what they called "congestion" in the city.[25] Basically, they wanted residents to spread out, so they began a campaign to annex land and plan new communities with public parks and other services.[26] The city grew from twenty-five square miles to forty-four square miles from 1919 to 1932.[27] Talk of metropolitan consolidation surfaced during the Great Depression,

MAP 3
Milwaukee's African American Neighborhood Circa 1900

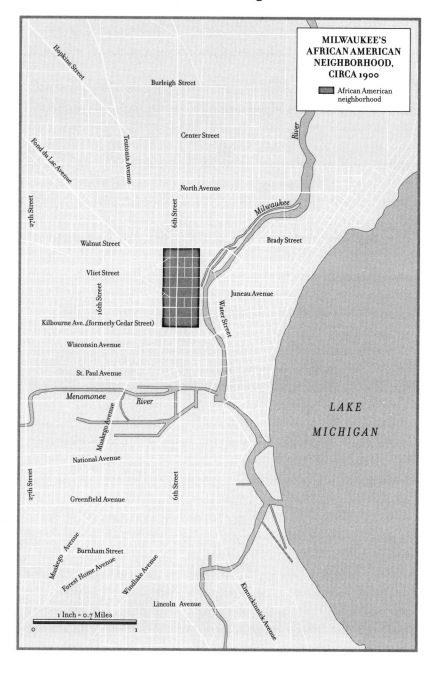

when local governments were looking to lower costs. This could have meant one countywide school district, which is common in southern states, but voters turned down referenda in almost every municipality, which historian John McCarthy attributes to a growing sense of consciousness among suburbanites that the suburbs should be different and separate from the city.[28]

The suburbs and newly annexed parts of Milwaukee were almost entirely white. Poverty continued to be a major impediment to African Americans finding better housing, but even when they could earn enough money to buy homes, Milwaukee real estate agents refused to sell property outside the central city to African Americans.[29] Additionally, banks promoted segregation by engaging in a practice called redlining—encircling poor black neighborhoods in red and denying mortgage loans to the residents within the red area. The federal government cooperated with the banks through the Home Owners' Loan Corporation, which did not guarantee mortgage loans to people who were in those redlined areas.[30] Restrictive covenants, clauses in deeds that prevented land from ever being sold to African Americans, were also used to keep African Americans out of the suburbs.[31] One study by an African American attorney in the 1940s found that 90 percent of the plats had these restrictions after 1910. Additionally, an ordinance was enacted in 1920 that zoned the area on the southern end of Milwaukee's black district for commercial and light manufacturing, instead of housing, effectively blocking African American migration until World War II.[32]

The World War II labor shortage and the postwar economic boom finally brought substantial numbers of African Americans to Milwaukee.[33] In fact, the city had the highest rate of African American emigration of any midwestern city in the period 1950 to 1959, averaging 2,552 per year during that decade.[34] When combined with live births, Milwaukee's African American population increased 186.9 percent, compared to a 16.3 percent population increase in the city overall.[35] This was the fastest African American growth rate of any US city in the 1950s.[36]

The increase in the overall population caused a renewed period of annexation under Frank Zeidler, a Socialist and the mayor of Milwaukee from 1948 until 1960. Zeidler added the Town of Lake (presently the far south side) to Milwaukee in 1953 and the Town of Granville (presently the far northwest side) in 1956.[37] He also annexed individual neighborhoods and houses in the Town of Greenfield (the southwest side) until the rest of Greenfield incorporated as its own city in 1957.[38] Zeidler, like Hoan before him, thought Milwaukeeans should spread out and believed that every man should be able to buy his own home. He tried to provide the poor with public housing at the edges of the city.[39] But he could not win enough support from the common council or the state, and he faced bitter opposition from suburbanites who feared African Americans might settle near their borders.[40] As a result of these policies, more than 98 percent of African Americans lived in the inner city in 1953.[41]

Residential segregation was further strengthened in the 1950s and 1960s. White suburbanites successfully lobbied the state of Wisconsin to change annexation laws in 1955 to prevent Milwaukee's expansion.[42] They also passed zoning laws that required lots that were larger than most African Americans could afford.[43] White families were able to get loans from the Federal Housing Administration (FHA) or the Veterans Administration (VA) to build single-family homes in the suburbs or on the edge of the city, but the FHA and VA did not grant loans to purchase multifamily units or to remodel older homes, which would have benefitted African Americans. The FHA also tracked racial information and used it to redline African American neighborhoods.[44] In fact, according to the FHA's own records, only sixty-six African American families lived in the twenty-five suburban communities surrounding Milwaukee in 1967, and eight suburbs had no African American residents at all.[45] As former Milwaukee mayor John Norquist commented, "[for] the FHA, creditworthiness was synonymous with whiteness."[46]

Father James Groppi, a white Catholic priest, led Milwaukee's campaign to end housing discrimination. Groppi had traveled to Selma, Alabama, in 1965 to participate in civil rights marches. Groppi, who was Italian American, felt that his fellow Italians had received unequal treatment from Irish church authorities in the Milwaukee Archdiocese. He therefore identified with the mistreatment of African Americans and took up their cause when he returned to Milwaukee.[47] Groppi is most known for leading African Americans and liberal whites in protest marches across the Sixteenth Street Viaduct to the south side in 1967 to demonstrate the need for an open housing ordinance in Milwaukee. During one peaceful march, the marchers were greeted by a crowd of five thousand angry whites when they reached Kosciuszko Park, some of whom held signs that said, "Polish Power" and "A Good Groppi Is a Dead Groppi." Others yelled, "Niggers go home!" "Go back to Africa," and "Sieg Heil," and some threw stones, bottles, garbage, and chunks of wood.[48]

Groppi's open housing marches were instrumental in passing open housing legislation and dovetailed with the movement to integrate schools. Milwaukee's segregated residence pattern led to a segregated school system, because students were assigned to schools closest to their homes. In the period between 1963 and 1975 the school board and Superintendent Harold Vincent took no steps to intervene and relieve segregation, preferring to deal with more traditional issues such as curriculum, appointment of administrators, the budget, school construction and repair, and legal matters. By the 1970s the board had also increased the amount of time it spent dealing with issues of student discipline, as fights and other disruptive behaviors had increased and the teachers union gained strength and demanded action. In some years, race was barely mentioned in the school board proceedings.[49] However, when race was mentioned, two factions of eight conservatives and seven liberals emerged throughout the 1960s and 1970s.

The school board was led by conservative president Lorraine Radtke from 1963 until 1965.[50] She prided herself on being "pure German [of] Prussian extraction," saying that all ethnic groups struggled when they first came to Milwaukee but were always able to overcome poverty. Radtke exemplified the paternalistic racism that was common at the time. She claimed to see "paradoxes in the Negro thinking," stating, "He says he hates the white man yet he wants to integrate with him. He wants to copy the white people, he wants the same standard of living, yet he says white people are all wrong." She also said African Americans should develop their own course in life:

> I would like to see him excel in areas which have not been thor-oughly developed by white people. I think that the Negro has a great deal to offer our culture in the fields of the arts—music, drama, painting, and sports. He should develop his skills to the ut-most. He should be original in his approach to living. He should re-alize that he need not imitate the white man to fulfill his culture.[51]

These conservative and liberal factions worked in the traditional sense of their titles, not the connotation prevalent in the early twenty-first

School Board Factions, 1963–79

TERM	LIBERALS	CONSERVATIVES
1963–65	Clare Dreyfus, Cornelius Golightly, Elisabeth Holmes, Lloyd Larson, Frederick Mett,[a] John Pederson, Evelyn Pfeiffer	President Lorraine Radtke, Thomas Brennan, Margaret Dinges, John Foley, Edward Krause/Patrick Fass,[b] Frederick Potter, Milan Potter, Harold Story
1965–67	Clare Dreyfus, Walter Gerken, Cornelius Golightly, Elisabeth Holmes, Lloyd Larson, Frederick Mett, Evelyn Pfeiffer	President John Foley, Thomas Brennan, Margaret Dinges, Patrick Fass, Frederick Potter, Milan Potter/Lillian Sicula,[c] Lorraine Radtke, Harold Story
1967–69	Clare Dreyfus, Walter Gerken,[d] Frederick Mett, Lloyd Larson, Donald O'Connell, Evelyn Pfeiffer, John Stocking[e]	President Margaret Dinges, Russell Darrow,[f] Thomas Brennan, Patrick Fass, John Foley,[g] Adele Horbinski, Frederick Potter, Lorraine Radtke, Lillian Sicula, Harold Story
1969–71	Clare Dreyfus, Harold Jackson,[h] Lloyd Larson, Frederick Mett, Donald O'Connell, Evelyn Pfeiffer, John Stocking	President Patrick Fass (to Sep. 1, 1970), President Thomas Brennan (after Sep. 1), Russell Darrow, Margaret Dinges, John Foley,[i] Adele Horbinski/ Virginia Stolhand,[j] Frederick Potter, Lorraine Radtke, Harold Story

[a] Frederick Mett was elected to fill a vacancy left by George Hampel Jr., who resigned October 31, 1963.

[b] Patrick Fass was elected after Edward Krause died on April 17, 1965.

[c] Lillian Sicula was elected on April 5, 1967, after Milan Potter resigned.

[d] Resigned November 30, 1967.

[e] Elected to fill John Foley's position.

[f] Elected to fill Walter Gerken's position.

[g] Resigned June 4, 1968.

[h] Elected to fill a vacancy created by the resignation of John Foley.

[i] Resigned October 27, 1969.

[j] Virginia Stolhand was elected after Adele Horbinski resigned on July 11, 1969.

School Board Factions, 1963–79 *cont'd*

TERM	LIBERALS	CONSERVATIVES
1971–73	President Harold Jackson (to Nov. 22, 1972),[k] President Ronald San Felippo (after Nov. 22), Anthony Busalacchi, Clare Dreyfus/James Wojciechowski,[l] Lloyd Larson, Frederick Mett/Doris Stacy,[m] Donald O'Connell, Evelyn Pfeiffer, Robert Wegmann	Thomas Brennan, Russell Darrow, Margaret Dinges, Frederick Potter, Lorraine Radtke, Virginia Stolhand
1973–75	President Ronald San Felippo[n] (to Sep. 24, 1974), President Donald O'Connell (after Sep. 24), Anthony Busalacchi, Lloyd Larson, Maurice McSweeny, Evelyn Pfeiffer, Doris Stacy, Robert Wegmann/Clara New[o]	Thomas Brennan, Arlene Conners, Russell Darrow/Stephen Jesmok,[p] Margaret Dinges, Gerald Farley, Edward Michalski,[q] Frederick Potter, Lorraine Radtke
1975–77	President Donald O'Connell (1975–76),[r] Joseph Koneazny,[s] Marian McEvilly, Maurice McSweeny, Clara New, Lois Riley, Doris Stacy, Leon Todd	President Evelyn Pfeiffer (1976–77), Thomas Brennan, Anthony Busalacchi, Margaret Dinges, Gerald Farley, Stephen Jesmok, Edward Michalski, Lorraine Radtke
1977–79	Joseph Koneazny, Marian McEvilly, Maurice McSweeny, Lois Riley, Doris Stacy, Leon Todd	President Evelyn Pfeiffer (1977–78), President Anthony Busalacchi (1978–79), Thomas Brennan, Margaret Dinges, Gerald Farley, Stephen Jesmok, Edward Michalski, Lawrence O'Neil, Lorraine Radtke

[k] Resigned November 24, 1972.
[l] Clare Dreyfus died on November 8, 1971; James Wojciechowski was elected March 8, 1972.
[m] Frederick Mett died on May 17, 1972; Doris Stacy was elected June 6, 1972.
[n] Resigned as president on September 24, 1974. Resigned from the board on January 7, 1975.

[o] Robert Wegmann resigned on May 31, 1974; Clara New was elected on September 3, 1974.
[p] Russell Darrow resigned on February 6, 1974; Stephen Jesmok was elected on May 6, 1975.
[q] Elected May 6, 1975, to complete the term of Ronald San Felippo.
[r] Resigned on December 15, 1976.
[s] Appointed to replace Donald O'Connell.

African American Factions

INTEGRATIONISTS	COMMUNITY CONTROL ADVOCATES
Lloyd Barbee, Cecil Brown, Marcia Coggs, Gary George, Cornelius Golightly, Leon Todd	Jake Beason, Spencer Coggs, Howard Fuller, Robert Harris, Larry Harwell, Marlene Johnson, Gloria Mason, Michael McGee, Marvin Pratt, Polly Williams

century. For the most part, conservatives resisted change, while liberals advocated for change. Steven Baruch worked in the MPS human relations office in the 1970s and described Radtke as "a conservative in the good sense of the word," saying that she preferred slow or little change and wanted to give programs a chance to work. Radtke and the other conservatives believed the school board should not alter the neighborhood school system.[52] The seven liberal board members disagreed, saying racial integration was a key to quality education. School board meeting agendas from that era show that the views of the liberals were largely ignored.[53]

The board also continued to employ the conservative Harold Vincent as superintendent. Vincent was most known for concentrating on school construction to accommodate the city's rapidly growing school-age population, which had increased 50 percent between 1950 and 1960.[54] He also introduced new curricula, paid teachers fairly well, and kept taxes low in his seventeen years in office. School board members, fellow administrators, the *Milwaukee Journal*, and the all-white Eagles Club praised him for his professional and personal conservatism. He did not drink alcohol nor smoke tobacco, and he refrained from using profanity.[55] Nevertheless, African Americans scorned Vincent and called for change.[56]

Lloyd Barbee was Radtke's and Vincent's most vocal opponent. A native of Memphis, Tennessee, and graduate of the University of Wisconsin Law School, Barbee joined the National Association for the Advancement of Colored People (NAACP) at age twelve and remained active in it his entire life. He moved to Milwaukee in September 1962 and began researching racial segregation in MPS almost immediately, partly because he experienced discrimination while attending law school.[57]

Until Barbee arrived in Milwaukee, not much organized resistance to school segregation had emerged. Surveys conducted by Bisbing Business Research, the *Milwaukee Journal*, and the University of

Wisconsin–Milwaukee in the early 1960s showed African Americans were most concerned with finding access to jobs and housing, while less than a third of the respondents listed education as the most crucial problem they faced. There was some speculation at the time that this may have been because many African Americans had only recently arrived in the city.[58]

Additionally, Milwaukee's African American leadership was divided on the best strategy to combat segregation, and this division impeded organization of a resistance movement. Three distinct groups of civil rights advocates existed in Milwaukee in the 1960s: a middle-aged, middle-class African American elite; a young group of integration activists; and an emerging group of Afrocentric activists. The middle-class elite had been around the longest and had lobbied MPS to hire African American teachers beginning in the 1930s. Primarily interested in financial success, the elite were conservative, included a fair number of entrepreneurs, frequently lived in white neighborhoods, and did not want to harm their relations with white business owners. The integrationists, led by Barbee and Groppi, wanted swift change. Finally, the Afrocentrists advocated for changes in curriculum and school governance, which in some circles involved state-supported vouchers to attend private schools.[59]

Barbee and the NACCP tried to work with the school board to integrate the schools. The board responded by creating a seven-member Committee on Equality and Educational Opportunity in 1963 to study racial problems in MPS. Radtke appointed attorney Harold Story, another conservative, as chairman. Story had strong ties to the business community and had been vice president and general counsel to the Allis-Chalmers Corporation when the United Auto Workers, its chief employee union, sued the company as part of a bitter labor dispute.[60] Story said the school board should take a "color-blind" approach, and that any kind of integration plan would be "in complete violation of the law."[61] Radtke appointed three other conservatives to the committee: John Foley, Margaret Dinges, and Ed Krause. She also appointed three liberals: Cornelius Golightly, Elisabeth Holmes, and John Pederson.[62]

Golightly, a philosophy professor at UWM, was the only African American on the board due to the at-large electoral system. Five school board members were elected every three years. African Americans, because of their small population, had a hard time placing in the top five in the elections. Golightly presented evidence of the harmful effects of de facto segregation, including a study of the school system by the Wisconsin Department of Public Instruction that, among other things, compared Fulton Junior High and North Division Senior High (both of which were more than 90 percent African American) to Audubon Junior High and Pulaski Senior High (both of which were more than 90 percent white) and found that the white schools had a wider array of courses and better programs for adult education. The conservative majority, however, disregarded most of what Golightly said, claiming the district had made improvements to black schools since the state report had been published, though they did not point out any specific examples.[63]

The integrationists, including representatives from the NAACP, the Congress of Racial Equality (CORE), and the local Near Northside Non-Partisan Conference (NNNPC), met with Harold Story's Committee on Equality and Educational Opportunity when hearings opened in 1963.[64] Barbee, representing the NAACP, told the committee that activists would stage a school boycott unless plans were put in place by January 30, 1964, to integrate the schools.[65] Barbee's statement marked the beginning of the movement that swayed Milwaukee's African American community away from the older elite and toward the younger integrationists. Barbee again met with Story's committee on January 21, but the meeting broke down quickly when Story refused to allow representatives from CORE and NNNPC to sit with Barbee. Barbee stormed out of the meeting with about twenty-five other people; the group sang "We Shall Overcome" in the lobby. Barbee left the building after a few minutes of singing, and Story went ahead and presented evidence that there was no intentional segregation in MPS. He was arrogant enough to direct questions at Barbee's empty chair and began each question with "Mr. Barbee . . ." Outside the meeting, Barbee reiterated the plans for a school boycott,[66] and he and his supporters launched a series of pickets at segregated schools that lasted about two weeks and drew support from some white Milwaukeeans.[67]

Finally, on March 1, 1964, Barbee and other members of the NAACP, CORE, and NNNPC joined with some Milwaukee parents and ministers who were concerned about racial segregation and formed the Milwaukee United School Integration Committee (MUSIC), of which Barbee was elected chairperson. Its purpose was to organize a grassroots movement against school segregation.[68] The organization demanded Story's committee be dissolved, and it organized two marches in support of the proposed boycott.[69] MUSIC planned "freedom schools" at churches and other sites, modeled after a successful boycott in New York City.[70]

Board president Lorraine Radtke, Harold Story, and Superintendent Harold Vincent refused to meet MUSIC's demands.[71] They thought of Barbee as something of a joke and actually welcomed a lawsuit, almost goading him into filing one.[72] Radtke published a 247-page "bibliographical digest" of newspaper and magazine articles detailing problems in the African American community, intending to show why integration would not be beneficial to Milwaukee.[73] Liberal board members Elisabeth Holmes and Cornelius Golightly blasted the document as racist, one-sided, and embarrassing.[74] John E. Pederson, another liberal board member, demanded Radtke's resignation.[75]

MUSIC went ahead with its boycott on May 18, 1964. Thirty freedom schools opened in African American churches.[76] They offered a curriculum centered on black history and culture along with many typical classroom activities, including reading, essay writing, attendance at lectures and films, small-group discussion, and singing. They even posted fire drill routes. Volunteers from the black community and a few whites served as teachers and principals.[77] The volunteers included three ministers, two attorneys, a county supervisor, a social worker, and Marilyn Morheuser, a white woman who had been a teaching nun until 1963, when she moved to Milwaukee and became Barbee's chief lieutenant and editor of the *Milwaukee Star*, a black community newspaper. She was chosen to write the freedom school curriculum because of her teaching background.[78] According to MPS attendance figures, about 14,000 of the district's 20,000 African American students were absent that day, which was about 11,500 more than usual. Perhaps as many as 60 percent of all African American students participated in the boycott.[79]

White Milwaukeeans still resisted change. A group calling itself the Citizens named Harold Story "Citizen of the Month" in May 1964 and sent a petition with 732 signatures to the school board to "uphold and support the neighborhood school system as it now exists under law."[80] The neighborhood school system itself was still something that Story described as "sacred," and any proposals to change it died in committee.[81] The mainstream media opposed the boycott, calling it a violation of truancy laws.[82] They encouraged the NAACP to cooperate with the

Story committee and advocated self-improvement as the only way for minorities to solve their problems.[83] Carl Zimmerman, director of news and public affairs for WITI-TV Channel 6, called the NAACP's complaints about segregation "unjustified" and said it was simply "a matter of geography," ignoring evidence that the school board promoted segregation.[84]

But criticism from the media was not very important to Barbee. The purpose of the boycott, in his view, was not to change whites' minds but to galvanize Milwaukee's black community, in the way boycotts had galvanized people throughout the South and in some other northern cities. With a school board election a year away, MUSIC started to mobilize candidates. Five seats, including Story's, were at stake. When MUSIC-backed candidates claimed integration would improve academic success for African Americans, Story countered with a claim that ineffective parenting skills were responsible for black students' low levels of achievement.[85]

The election produced mixed results, and only two of the five MUSIC candidates were elected.[86] Conservatives Milan Potter, John F. Foley, and Story placed first, second, and third, with Frederick Mett and Walter Gerken, both of whom were endorsed by MUSIC, placing fourth and fifth. Following the election, the board approved, with a nine-to-four vote, $1 million for compensatory education programs for African American students. The programs included funding for lowering student-teacher ratios, tutoring, reading centers, full-time prekindergarten teachers, welfare and psychological counseling, and special orientation programs.[87] Radtke stepped down as president in July, and the board elected attorney Foley to fill her position. Foley promised to continue all of Radtke's policies, and he appointed her to take his place on the Story committee.[88] The *Milwaukee Star* condemned the new president as a continuation of dictatorship and paternalistic racism.[89] The *Milwaukee Journal*, on the other hand, published a major study in September 1965 called "Reading, Writing, and Race" that stood squarely by the neighborhood school system.[90] White parents filed petitions in support of neighborhood schools after the survey results were published.[91]

Undeterred, CORE and MUSIC continued their peaceful protests. They led sit-ins at school board meetings and picketed Harold Vincent's office, Harold Story's home, and new black schools.[92] Activists staged a second boycott during the week of October 18, 1965.[93] Father Groppi, nineteen other priests, thirty-five nuns, and four Catholic parishes volunteered to aid the boycott.[94] Several other Catholics, some of whom were African American, also volunteered because they appreciated the peaceful nature of the first boycott.[95] The second boycott, however, attracted only 7,300 students, compared to the previous 11,500. Forty-nine guidance counselors were dubbed temporary truant officers and were sent to the freedom schools to seize students.[96] By the second day of the boycott, the number of participating students declined to 4,300. On the same day, Auxiliary Bishop Roman Atkielski, the top Catholic official in the absence of Archbishop William Cousins, gave the priests and nuns a direct order to desist, invoking their vow of obedience, which compelled them to comply.[97] A third boycott in March 1966 focused solely on North Division High School. But participation in this boycott was even lower than before, despite a high number of absentees at North, which suggests many absent students used the boycott as an excuse to take the day off rather than attend a freedom school.[98]

As the protests continued, Barbee filed suit against the school board on June 17, 1965, on behalf of the parents of thirty-two African American students and nine white students in *Amos et al. v. the Board of School Directors of the City of Milwaukee*.[99] Because the US Supreme Court had only overturned de jure segregation—that is, segregation by law—in public schools in *Brown v. the Board of Education of Topeka, Kansas*, Barbee was faced with the difficult task of proving that segregation in MPS was caused by more than just residence patterns. Barbee, therefore, argued that MPS deliberately promoted segregation in five ways: (1) the school board established school boundary lines that produced segregation; (2) it approved construction of predominantly black schools; (3) it allowed white students to transfer but restricted African American pupils to segregated schools; (4) instead of taking a "color-blind" approach to staff assignment, it preferred placing African American teachers and other African American staff in black schools and allowed white staff to transfer out of such schools; and (5) it failed to integrate classes of black students who were bused as one unit with the white students at receiving schools.[100]

MPS divided the city into several elementary school districts.[101] Those schools fed into specific junior high schools, which in turn fed into specific senior high schools.[102] Arthur Kastner, head of the MPS Department of School Housing Research, adjusted school district boundaries when a new school was built or an existing school became overcrowded, which was common in the 1950s and 1960s because of the tremendous growth in the central city population.[103] Kastner claimed that race was never a factor in his decisions, saying he did not care whether the students were "colored, white, Mexican, or polkadot."[104] But Barbee presented memos from Kastner's office that showed that Kastner considered neighborhood school districts that were 30 percent black to have reached their "tipping points." Kastner predicted rapid African American population growth and rapid white out-migration in those districts and recommended adjustments in district boundaries to reduce overcrowding.[105]

Barbee demonstrated that these boundary changes had caused segregation. For example, the Center Street School district experienced rapid growth in its African American population in the late 1950s, so the school board detached the eastern end of the district, which had mostly white students, and added it to the neighboring Pierce district, which also was mostly white. Thus, the Center Street School district went from being racially balanced to being primarily African American, while the Pierce district remained primarily white. The same thing happened to the La-Follette district when its white area was assigned to the Keefe Avenue School district. However, the boundaries of the Fratney School district, a predominantly white neighborhood adjacent to the central city, curiously were never changed to make room for African American students.[106]

These selective boundary changes continued as late as 1970, when the school board voted to alter the boundaries of forty school districts on the northwest side of the city to relieve overcrowding at Custer and Madison High Schools and at Peckham Junior High, which was a black-majority school. The school board proposed assigning Peckham's ninth grade to Washington Senior High, making it a four-year high school instead of a three-year school. This action would overcrowd Washington, so many of its white neighborhoods would be reassigned to Marshall Junior-Senior High (grades seven to twelve), which would also become a four-year high school.[107] This action was part of a general trend toward four-year high schools in the United States in the 1970s, but some parents, both black and white, predicted that Washington would go past "the tipping point" and quickly become a black school, while Marshall would remain all-white.[108]

Simply adjusting these boundaries, however, was not enough to meet the growing population of the city. MPS began a rapid building program in 1947 to accommodate baby boomers in outlying (white) areas of the city, while most schools in the central city were simply remodeled or repurposed.[109] Walnut Street School, for example, was remodeled and reopened as a "new" school in 1951 after being closed for several years. Two years later the Milwaukee Girls' Junior Trade School became the "new" Garfield Avenue Elementary School.[110] Storerooms and gymnasiums were converted into classrooms in several other schools.[111] The selective building of schools was the subject of the second part of Barbee's case.

In the mid-1960s, Milwaukee built and opened three new schools in the city: Parkman Junior High School, Holmes Elementary, and MacDowell Elementary. But the construction of McDowell caused problems.[112] It was three stories high with fortress-like towers and a dark, foreboding exterior. Kindergarten classes were held in the basement on the opposite side of the building from the nurse's office, which upset some parents who wanted the youngest children to have access to natural light and a nurse. Barbee compared MacDowell to the new Louisa May Alcott School, which was on the south side and was just one story surrounded by a large lawn. The exterior was a soft, red brick, and kindergarten classes were held in a separate wing that adjoined a grassy play area and was near the school nurse. In simple terms, the black students received the "bad" school, while the white students received the "good" school.[113] Barbee said the school board should bus African American students to south side schools instead of building schools in black neighborhoods.[114]

The board's third method of enforcing segregation was to selectively deny student transfers. The school board adopted a "free transfer" or "open transfer" policy in 1964 in an attempt to avoid litigation from the NAACP and other civil rights groups.[115] The policy allowed students to transfer for any reason, provided parents paid the cost of transportation. However, Barbee presented evidence that African Americans had a difficult time getting transfers, while white students could simply cite "fear" or "harassment" from African American students to get out of black schools.[116] Also, because parents had to provide transportation, getting to a white school on the south side of the city would have been difficult for low-income African American children.

The school board also discriminated in teacher assignment. The board had resisted hiring African American teachers: it took until 1930 for Milwaukee to hire its first two, and by the 1950–51 school year, only nine out

MAP 4
Composition of Central Area, 1940

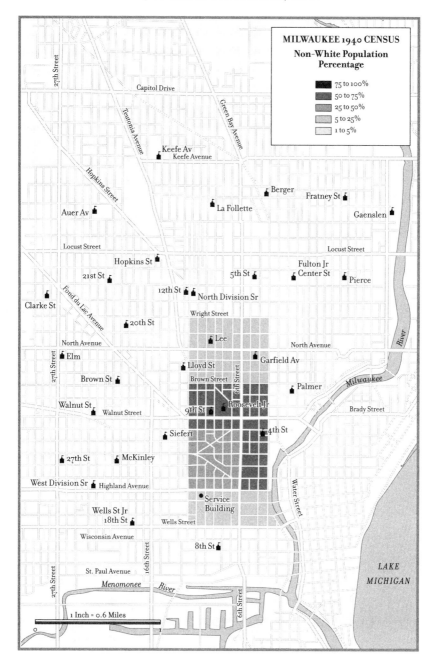

MAP 5
Composition of Central Area, 1950

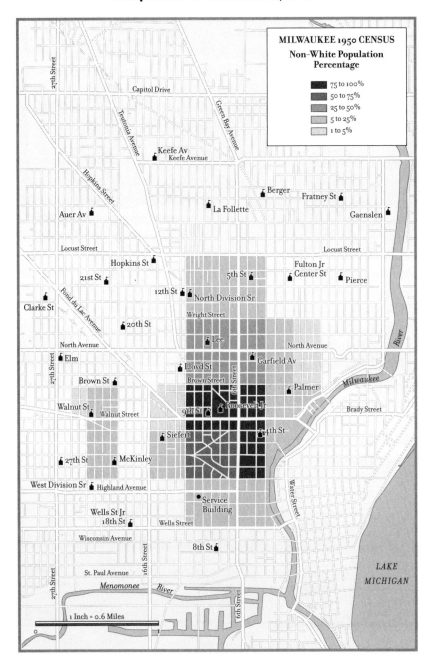

MAP 6
Composition of Central Area, 1960

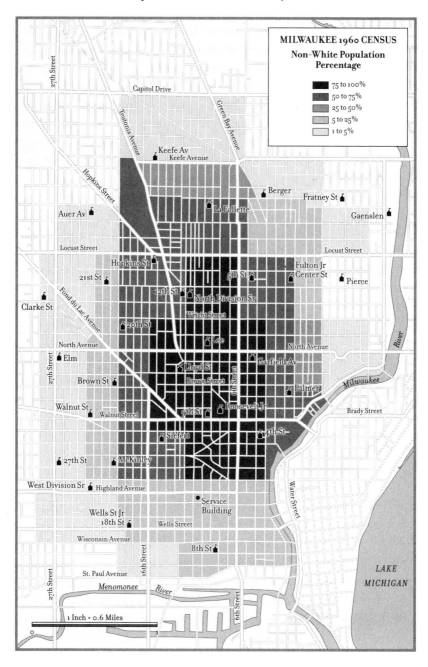

MAP 7

School District Changes—Central Area, 1943–63

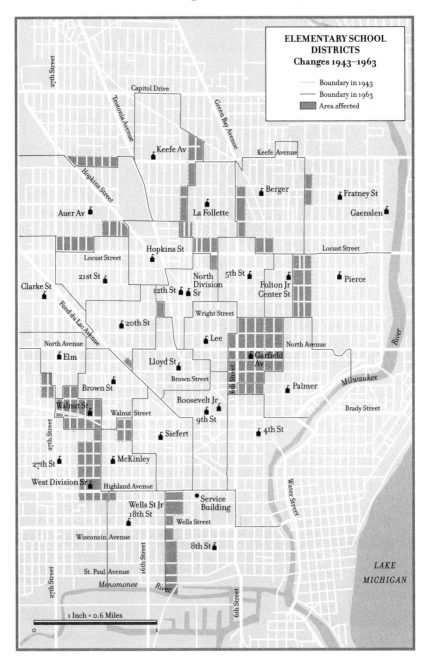

ELEMENTARY SCHOOL
DISTRICTS
Changes 1943–1963

‑‑‑‑‑ Boundary in 1943
——— Boundary in 1963
▨ Area affected

MAP 8
Milwaukee Senior High School Districts, 1970

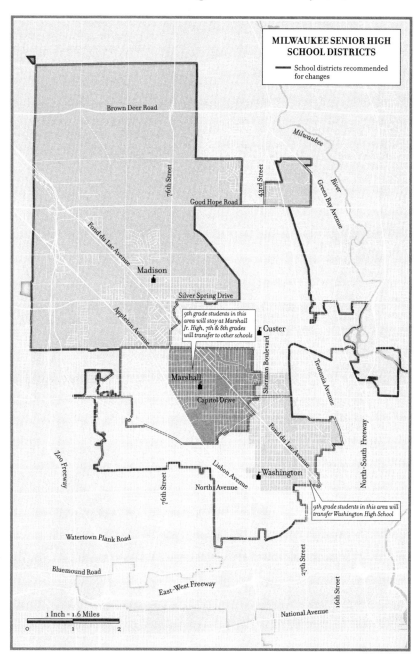

MAP 9
MAP 9
Percentage of Census Tracks Black, 1975

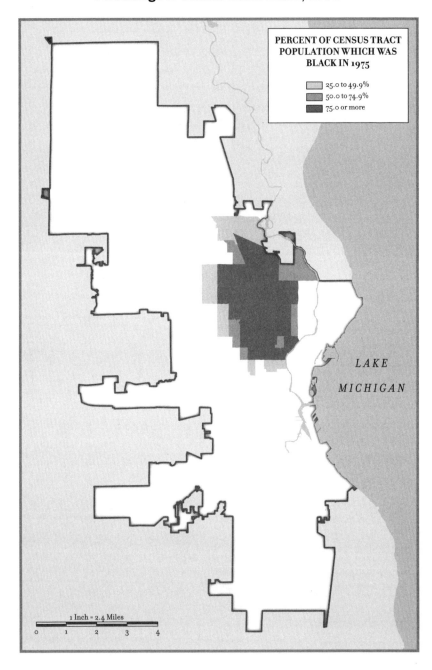

PERCENT OF CENSUS TRACT
POPULATION WHICH WAS
BLACK IN 1975

25.0 to 49.9%
50.0 to 74.9%
75.0 or more

LAKE

MICHIGAN

1 Inch = 2.4 Miles

0   1   2   3   4

of its 1,749 teachers were African American.[117] Eight of those nine were assigned to Fourth Street and Ninth Street Schools, which were black elementary schools. The remaining teacher taught at the only junior high school in Milwaukee where African American students were a majority. The number of African American teachers increased to 193 in the 1960–61 school year, but 64 percent of them were assigned to schools with at least 90 percent black enrollment, and another 19 percent were assigned to other black-majority schools.[118]

Teacher transfers were related to assignment. Teachers, like students, could request a change in schools for any reason.[119] "Environmental" reasons became an increasingly popular excuse among white teachers for getting out of black schools.[120] Others came right out and cited an inability to teach African American students.[121] Discipline problems and hostility from students were the most common reasons cited for transferring out of inner-city schools. Many teachers said they were physically and mentally exhausted and no longer saw themselves as teachers. Some teachers even reported being physically assaulted or having personal property, including automobiles, damaged.[122] Most of the transfers went to white teachers, as most of them had more seniority than African American teachers.[123]

Finally, "intact busing" was, in Barbee's view, the most blatant tool used to maintain segregation. Intact busing meant a class of African American students assigned to an overcrowded elementary school would board a bus at their school with their teacher and arrive "intact" at a different school. Students were not allowed to integrate at the receiving school and were bused back to their neighborhood school at the end of the day and, often, for lunch as well.[124] From the 1958–59 school year through the 1973–74 school year, 509 classes were bused intact for all or part of a semester (counting semesters separately).[125] Superintendent Howard Vincent claimed it would not be fair to integrate students at the receiving school and then break up their friendships when space became available again at the sending school. He also said the policy against integration made administration of the program easier because busing could be implemented any time during the semester without disrupting the daily routine at the receiving school. He said the students from the sending school still had their own teachers and were under the jurisdiction of their original principal, as if the bused students had never left their

original school.[126] He stated that intact busing was a notable improvement over programs in other cities that reduced overcrowding through
part-time or staggered scheduling, which disrupted normal school operations.[127] MUSIC countered Vincent by forming human chains around
"intact" buses.[128]

Barbee surveyed teachers who participated in intact busing and introduced the results as evidence at the trial. Teachers who taught in white
classrooms reported either positive or mixed experiences with intact busing. In some schools, the bused students were allowed to mix with the
other students and had full use of the facilities, including the cafeteria,
playground, audio-visual equipment, reading center, and library. They
also participated in school activities, and their parents were included
in the receiving school's parent-teacher association (PTA). But teachers
from black schools almost always reported negative results. Many reported their students felt isolated and not fully accepted, even when they
were allowed to participate in school activities. They also said students
needed a stable environment if they were to learn and that intact busing
created instability. Teachers of both races said students missed valuable
class time because the bus rides took too long, and they reported their
students did not feel they were a part of either the sending or the receiving school. A few complained also that their students were bused for
more than the one semester recommended in the intact busing plan.[129]

Based on this evidence, Barbee argued that intact busing was psychologically damaging. It branded African American students as inferior,
as they were physically separated from white students. Barbee also said
intact busing was not temporary, as Vincent claimed. For example, two
classes at Seifert School were bused intact while the building underwent
expansion, but the African American population increased so quickly
that when the project was completed, six classes still had to be bused.
This practice violated the school board policy mandating that if a group
of students needed to be bused for more than one year it was not temporary and that they should be permanently assigned to the white school.[130]

The *Amos* case lasted until 1976, and by then a third group of African
American activists had emerged. They were part of the growing national
black power movement and became active in April 1967, through Groppi's Youth Council. The Youth Council had distributed leaflets at North
Division, King, Riverside, and Lincoln High Schools urging students to

turn in their textbooks because they did not adequately reflect African history and culture.[131] Black power advocates also formed the United Community Action Group (UCAG) in 1967 on a platform of cooperation with MPS; but they ended up advocating for self-determination after becoming frustrated with MPS's reluctance to change.[132] In their view, African Americans needed to take charge of their own course in life. Integration was fine, but if that was not going to happen, then it was better to give African American families another choice, which was community control over schools.

Robert Harris and Jake Beason, both teachers at North Division, were two such advocates. Harris was head football coach, a physical education teacher, and a member of Groppi's parish, and Beason was a newly hired social studies teacher who advocated black pride and Pan-Africanism, rejected white leadership—even if it was duly elected—and took students on field trips to Islamic sites in Chicago.[133]

Harris, Beason, and other black power advocates inspired young people to take action in the 1967–68 school year. Students at Fulton Junior High staged a boycott of the school lunch program in December to protest the absence of African American cooks. According to Fulton's principal, all but two or three of the school's fourteen hundred students opted to bring lunches from home rather than buy food.[134] Students at Rufus King staged a walkout the following February to demand black history be taught.[135] About a week later, about eight hundred students walked out of North Division.[136] They were aided by NAACP Commandos, a sort of civilian defense force organized by Groppi.[137] Students at Wells Junior High conducted a lunch boycott in March 1968.[138] That April they staged a protest when the school failed to hold a memorial service for Martin Luther King Jr. after he was assassinated.[139] In May, parents petitioned the school board to remove the principal at Ninth Street Elementary for lack of sensitivity to African American students, parents, and culture.[140] Some African American students at West Division staged a walkout the following October because their principal refused to allow them to start an African American club. Ironically, his decision was based on the fact that the club would not be integrated. At about the same time, some African American students at West Division refused to take a standardized test because, they claimed, it did not relate to them.[141]

These protests achieved some success, and the district took steps to promote cultural awareness.[142] For example, MPS introduced a ninety-two-page booklet called "The Negro in American Life" in November 1967 to supplement junior and senior high school history courses.[143] A year later, Jake Beason was allowed to teach African American History at North, and a similar class began at Wells.[144] Fulton's administration tried to recruit African American cooks, and MPS appointed several new African American principals.[145]

It was in this context that racial integration unfolded in Milwaukee. Milwaukee was sharply divided along racial lines in the 1960s. The white power structure resisted change and was hostile to reform at times. African American resistance was hard to organize due to divided leadership, but those who favored integration stood firm in both belief and action. The Milwaukee school administration hoped that a voluntary integration plan that relied on magnet schools would ease tensions in both the black and white communities and end the era of no choice.

CHAPTER 2

PLANNING FOR MILWAUKEE'S MAGNET SCHOOLS, 1967–1976

T he story of the desegregation of America's public schools is well known. Most eighth-grade students know the story of Linda Brown, the girl who wanted to attend her neighborhood elementary school but was not allowed to because it was a "white" school. Segregation supposedly ended in 1954 when the US Supreme Court ruled in *Brown v. the Board of Education of Topeka, Kansas* that school districts could no longer segregate students according to race. "Separate but equal" was declared inherently unequal because it marked African American children with a "badge of inferiority" that hindered their performance. Southern states and schools reluctantly began to desegregate. But *Brown* and the Civil Rights Act of 1964, which followed it, mostly addressed de jure segregation, or segregation by law. De facto segregation, or segregation by residence pattern, was totally different. Because there is nothing inherently illegal about people of different races choosing to live apart from one another, attorneys had to prove that school districts deliberately chose to segregate students. Many school officials feared a white backlash. If courts ruled that white students could be forced to attend school with African Americans, then white families might choose to move out of the city.

School officials in some districts hoped that a new policy trend—magnet schools—might be an effective way to integrate schools without causing white flight. Magnet schools offer specialized curricula designed to attract students from all parts of a school district in hopes of achieving racial integration on a voluntary basis. Some magnet schools specialize in fine arts, while others focus on math and science, technology, or business skills. Magnet Schools of America, a national association of magnet schools, estimates that approximately four thousand magnet schools were operating across the United States in 2012.[1] Magnet schools represent the first crack in the era of no choice.

Milwaukee did not invent magnet schools, but it made greater use of them than any other city in the United States. Magnet schools actually began in Tacoma, Washington, in 1968 when McCarver Junior High School, which had a student body that was 84 percent African American, reopened in fall with an innovative curriculum, some of the best teachers in the district, and a popular principal. The effort was successful: McCarver reopened with a minority enrollment of less than 64 percent. By 1970, African Americans made up less than half the school, and there was a waiting list for white students.[2]

Other school districts soon followed in the 1970s. Magnet schools were set up in Minneapolis in 1972 and Houston and Cincinnati in 1975.[3] Houston's program initially featured thirty-four magnet programs at thirty-one campuses, the most prominent of which was the High School for the Visual and Performing Arts. Eleven more programs were added the following year, including foreign languages, ecology and outdoor education, music, science and petrochemicals, aviation, engineering, literature, art, and remedial course work.[4] Cincinnati offered fourteen different programs at thirty locations, including high school programs in college preparation and skilled trades. Its magnet elementary schools focused on bilingual and language immersion programs, the Montessori method, and multi-age classrooms.[5]

Those cities integrated peacefully, though sometimes they were pushed into it by lawsuits and public protests. The same cannot be said about Boston, a city with several parallels to Milwaukee. Boston, like Milwaukee, was a city divided into very specific ethnic enclaves in the early twentieth century.[6] As with the Germans in Milwaukee, the Irish controlled local politics in Boston, and as African Americans came north during the Great Migration, they moved into the former Irish ghettoes.[7] Again, as in Milwaukee, Boston had a neighborhood school system at the elementary level and a feeder system for the upper grades that created "black schools" and "white schools."[8] Similarly, Boston's school board manipulated district lines, restricted transfers, and discriminated in the hiring and promotion of staff, all to maintain segregation.[9]

Fearing a lawsuit, local officials decided to implement a magnet program before a judge imposed mandatory busing. The Boston School Committee designated two elementary magnet schools and one magnet high school in 1968.[10] This limited degree of integration was acceptable to most white citizens, but integrationists pressed for a stronger remedy. The Harvard Center for Law and Education filed suit against the Boston School Committee in 1972 on behalf of fifteen parents and their forty-three children. Judge W. Arthur Garrity ruled in favor of the plaintiffs in 1974. Garrity took over the school system and appointed a special master to monitor implementation of a multipart desegregation plan that included changes to student, faculty, and administrative staff assignments; changes in school capacities and program locations; construction, renovation, and closing of school facilities; changes in special education, bilingual education, and vocational and occupational education; and changes in school safety, security, and student discipline. Garrity ordered a massive busing plan that paired schools in white parts of the city with schools in black parts of the city.[11] He also ordered Boston Latin, known to be the best school in the city, to enroll at least 35 percent African American and Latino students.[12] The Boston School Committee created fifty-five magnet schools, which Garrity predicted would be an "enormous safety valve" that could mitigate the white community's anti-busing anger.[13]

Garrity was wrong. Whites rioted in the Boston streets and high schools in 1975, the first year of desegregation. Some riots lasted several days. Molotov cocktails flew through windows, and some African Americans were afraid to leave their homes. Hundreds of students were suspended for rioting at South Boston High School. When white students and residents tried to block the buses, the police were called, and when the officers arrived, the white mob turned on them. African American students were openly beaten in the streets for months. White racists threatened to blow up bridges to keep buses from crossing into white territory. Some African Americans responded with violence of their own, throwing stones at white buses and beating up white students. Leaders of both the black and white communities tried to calm people, to no avail. Just being a person of a different race in the wrong place was enough to incite an assault. Innocent motorists were attacked, their cars overturned and burned. Civil officials and law enforcement had lost control. Pandemonium reigned.[14] The white student population declined 17 percent in Boston public schools from 1974 to 1976 as white families left the city.[15]

The Milwaukee desegregation lawsuit had been in court since 1965, two years before the Boston lawsuit had begun. By 1967, many people believed federal judge John Reynolds would rule in favor of Lloyd Barbee's clients. Reynolds had a long history of liberal activism and opposition to segregation as state attorney general and governor of Wisconsin.[16] But Reynolds took a different, more gradual approach, than the judge in Boston had. He appointed Irvin Charne, a friend of his and a moderate Democrat, as Lloyd Barbee's co-counsel. According to people who were close to the case, Reynolds did this because he believed Charne could help control Barbee's temper and make desegregation more palatable to Milwaukee's white community.[17] A majority of the school board believed Reynolds's actions indicated a strong possibility that he would rule against them, but they still did not want to integrate. The board majority, therefore, decided to take a two-pronged approach to integration. One part was to engage in a limited amount of reform to try to demonstrate goodwill to the judge and possibly win a victory in court, while not actually doing anything to integrate schools. The other part was to quietly lay the groundwork for integration so Reynolds would not impose a plan if he ruled in favor of Barbee's clients.

There are several examples of the first approach, but one example from 1967 stands out. The school board paid the New York–based Academy for Educational Development (AED), a nonprofit educational think tank, to conduct a study on school problems. AED made several recommendations to improve the schools, including changes in curriculum, an increase in counseling and psychological services, expansion of Advanced Placement (AP) classes, professional development for teachers, decentralization of supervision and decision making, an increase in school spending of more than double by 1972, and steps to end de facto segregation.[18] AED described the board's highly touted "compensatory education program" as "nice" but lacking "the necessary air of emergency and urgency."[19] Some of the programs were inadequately funded, understaffed, or aimed at groups of students instead of focusing on individual needs. None of them provided college preparatory opportunities to students with high potential, nor did any provide interracial experiences.[20] The conservative majority on the school board refused to make any comments on the report and referred it to a study committee that did not do anything with it.[21] Thus, the board majority appeared to be taking action; in reality, it was engaging in a stall tactic.

The second part of the board majority's plan was to lay the groundwork for integration in case it lost the court case. Its first step was to hire a superintendent in 1967 who would work better with the black community, and later, it allowed citizens and parent groups at each school to formulate reform plans. The board ultimately rejected these plans due to white opposition, but those discussions provided a foundation for a much larger, citywide discussion about integration in 1976 and helped cultivate community support for the integration plan that the district eventually adopted.

Superintendent Richard Gousha assumed office on July 1, 1967, after a thirteen-to-one school board vote in May. Gousha was more progressive than his predecessor, Harold Vincent. He was willing to work with diverse groups of people to accomplish goals and had experience with desegregation, as he had been state superintendent of public instruction in Delaware, which had implemented a desegregation plan.[22] Historian Bill Dahlk has said Gousha kept quiet on controversial issues, like busing, and did what he could to reform the system the school board had given him.[23] Gousha assumed office during a civil disturbance that conservative whites described as a race riot. Though their assessment of the situation may have been overblown, Mayor Henry Maier put the city under curfew and called in the National Guard to keep the peace for a few days in the summer of 1967. The freeways were closed, and National Guard tanks rolled down Wisconsin Avenue, which nearly bisects the city.[24] Given this context, Gousha believed the city was not ready to desegregate the schools, so he compromised.[25]

Gousha took a number of steps to try to improve the quality of education for African Americans and prepare the city for integration. He spoke to community groups in black churches, recruited more African American teachers and administrators, and engaged in curriculum reform to address the needs of African American students. Most significantly, Gousha was the architect of the North Division subsystem, which gave an unprecedented degree of autonomy to the African American community surrounding North Division High School and its feeder schools. The subsystem included a community relations specialist; advisory councils made up of parents, teachers, principals, and high school students; special federal funding; and an innovative curriculum with its own curriculum specialists.[26]

Gousha planned to eventually decentralize the district's fourteen high schools into seven subsystems, called "program service areas," each of which would have included one inner-city high school and related feeder schools and one outlying high school and related feeder schools. The program service areas would have shared curriculum specialists, supervisory personnel, and support service personnel such as psychologists and social workers. Gousha's plan was designed to improve continuity in teaching and learning from elementary school through high school, to foster greater understanding between families and schools in the inner city and the outlying areas, and to promote community and parent involvement in the schools.[27] Some proponents hoped that if the program service areas led to greater understanding between the races, students might integrate voluntarily.[28]

Any pairing or integration plan would need a stable population to be successful, but Milwaukee experienced radical demographic shifts in the 1960s. Milwaukee's black population increased 68.3 percent between 1960 and 1970, while the white population declined 3.2 percent.[29] Part of this change can be attributed to continued black migration from Chicago and the South, but Milwaukee also had a young black population and an aging white population, which caused a change in birth rates—young families have more children; old families have few children.[30] People were also moving from the city to the suburbs: Milwaukee County's white population actually increased 6.3 percent in the 1960s, even though the number of whites in the city decreased.[31]

Rufus King High School is a perfect example of that change in demographics. Its minority population grew slowly in the 1960s, finally reaching 33 percent—the "tipping point"—in 1964. Once minority enrollment reached that level, a large number of white families left the school, leaving King 70 percent African American by 1967. Thus, true integration, which is supposed to be voluntary, never happened at King; it went straight from white to black.[32] West Division, Riverside, and Washington high schools experienced similar demographic shifts, although they were more gradual.[33]

Many schools embarked on plans to slow the swift demographic shift that occurred at King. Riverside High School is particularly interesting. The school is situated in Milwaukee's politically liberal east side, and a significant number of Riverside parents wanted their children to attend integrated schools. But as more inner-city students transferred to Riverside under the school board's open transfer policy, more white students from conservative families left. The remaining liberal white parents wanted to prevent the white flight that had happened at King, so on January 10, 1972, after a sometimes-heated two-and-a-half-hour debate, the Riverside parent-teacher-student association (PTSA) recommended a plan to the school board that would have capped black enrollment at 25 percent. Any other African American students desiring transfers to Riverside would have to go elsewhere. In this way, they hoped to keep Riverside from reaching the tipping point and becoming a black-majority school. School board member Anthony Busalacchi said he would introduce the plan to the school board, with the intention that it would apply to King and Washington as well, but African American parents were outraged. Some said it denied their children due process, others cited the fact that it violated the district's open enrollment policy, and others simply blasted it as racist.[34] The school board did not approve the plan, but it established a precedent for community involvement in integration plans.

Washington High School's attempt to integrate became more volatile, but it also showed that the board was willing to start a dialogue on integration. The African American population in the neighborhood surrounding Washington—known as the Sherman Park neighborhood—increased by 1,076.8 percent between 1960 and 1970 due to migration from the central city.[35] Washington had once been considered one of the best high schools in Wisconsin, but its new African American students did not perform as well as white students. According to teachers, they also caused more disruptions, and their attendance was poor. The English Department added fifteen new courses in topics they hoped would arouse student interest in reading, but the additional offerings did not improve behavior or attendance.[36] White and black students initiated racial fights at Washington and at Peckham Junior High, which was one of Washington's two feeder schools. Some white students at Washington said they were afraid to go into school restrooms alone.[37] African American students also complained about the lack of an Afrocentric curriculum, saying white teachers were out of touch with the needs of African American students.[38]

Harold Jackson, the only African American member of the school board since Cornelius Golightly, decided to get involved before the situation got worse. Jackson was part of a liberal coalition named the Young Turks, which challenged traditional school board stances on issues and criticized Superintendent Gousha for his quiet leadership style. The group included Anthony Busalacchi, Ronald San Felippo, and Robert Wegmann, all of whom were in their twenties and thirties. In voting, they were frequently joined by Donald O'Connell and, after the 1973 election, new board members Doris Stacy and Maurice McSweeny. The Young Turks were instrumental in the election of Jackson as president of the school board.[39] Jackson visited Washington several times to talk with students, staff, and parents, asking them to help him identify the problems in the school.[40] Jackson decided the best way to stop the racial violence was to increase the number of security aides. He also wanted adjustments to the curriculum to give African American students more input into what they learned and an open discussion of racial issues to build long-term understanding and stability.[41] But many people, including Lloyd Barbee and some of Washington's African American students, criticized Jackson's plan as repressive, because it centered on security aides.[42]

The interracial Sherman Park Community Association (SPCA) tried to come up with its own plan. Like the Riverside PTSA, the members of the SPCA wanted to stabilize racial integration and minimize white flight.[43] They believed two things were necessary to make this happen. First, the school board's open transfer policy had to end in order to stop whites from fleeing to other schools. Second, they wanted to introduce African American and white children to each other at an earlier age.[44]

At their urging, the school board created a multiracial study committee composed of parents, school staff, and community members from the areas around Washington's two feeder schools: Peckham Junior High School, which was mostly African American, and Steuben Junior High School, which was 80 percent white.[45] After several months of discussions, the Peckham-Steuben committee came up with a plan. All seventh-graders in the Washington district would be assigned to Steuben, all eighth-graders would be assigned to Peckham, and the ninth grade would be moved to Washington. The plan would integrate students prior to their entrance into high school and would reduce severe overcrowding at Peckham. Some committee members from Steuben objected to what they called "forced busing" in the plan,[46] but the plan went to the school board anyway.[47] The board voted it down thirteen to one, due to the opposition from the Steuben parents.[48]

As the school board cautiously engaged the community, other elected officials took note of the city's changing demographics and began to offer plans for metropolitan desegregation. State representative Dennis Conta's plan was the most well known. Conta proposed that the suburban Whitefish Bay and Shorewood school districts merge with Milwaukee's Riverside and Lincoln neighborhood districts.[49] This plan was based on an earlier plan devised by Robert Wegmann, who had proposed cutting the Milwaukee metropolitan area into eight wedge-shaped districts.[50]

Virtually no one supported Conta's plan. Suburbanites predicted they would lose control of their schools and worried it would divert their local property taxes to the city. Some people speculated that suburbanites simply did not want their children attending school with African Americans.[51] The Milwaukee Teachers Education Association (MTEA), the local teachers union, did not support the plan because removing two districts from MPS would have diluted the union's bargaining strength when engaged in contract negotiations.[52] Larry Harwell, of the Organization of Organizations (Triple O), criticized the Conta plan and all other plans that would have involved metropolitan desegregation as "lessen[ing] the number of blacks that whites have to deal with." Harwell represented the growing sense of black consciousness in Milwaukee.[53] He had helped organize the North Division subsystem, organized parent groups at Rufus King High School and several other black schools, and lobbied MPS to hire more African American aides.[54] The school board eventually voted seven to three against Conta's plan.[55]

Milwaukee's demographics continued to shift dramatically in the 1970s. The city's African American population increased 17.7 percent between 1970 and 1975, while the nonblack population decreased by 10.9 percent.[56] The rate of decrease in the white population in 1970–75 was more than three times the rate of decrease in the entire decade of the 1960s.[57] Birthrates changed due to the continued influx of young African Americans into the inner city.[58] The black birthrate was six times that of the white birthrate in some neighborhoods,[59] while an estimated

18.1 percent of Milwaukeeans left the city between 1970 and 1980.[60] The school board recognized the difficulty of integrating schools without a stable white population. Thus far, all the proposed desegregation plans had been rooted in the old ideology of "no choice." They attempted to limit the number of African American students, as had been planned at Riverside, or they used involuntary busing, as had been planned at Washington, or they forced people to accept metropolitan integration, as Dennis Conta had proposed. Some board members believed magnet schools were a better alternative, and some local precedents existed. Several neighborhood "specialty schools," mostly for language immersion or special teaching methods, had operated at the elementary level for decades.[61] And Milwaukee already had one citywide high school: Boys Trade and Technical High School had carried the designation since 1941.[62]

Magnet schools appealed to both liberal and conservative board members. Cornelius Golightly, a liberal and the only African American school board member in the 1960s, had proposed magnet schools in 1963,[63] and conservative Margaret Dinges had been talking about magnet schools since 1970.[64] The board also considered converting three neighborhood high schools to citywide magnet schools in 1973: Lincoln Junior-Senior High School would have focused on business and trade and technical education, another school would have become a school for the visual and performing arts, and long-troubled Washington would have included a magnet program of some sort.[65] Gerald Farley, a conservative, floated a plan in 1973 and 1974 that would have left each of the high schools as neighborhood schools but would have established citywide magnet programs within five schools. If a student lived outside of the high school's neighborhood, he or she would have to enroll in the magnet program. All other students would have been neighborhood students. Thus, busing would have been kept to a minimum and Boston-like violence avoided.[66]

Change finally came in 1975. The city's African American population had increased to the point that three African Americans were elected to the school board: Marian McEvilly, Leon Todd, and Clara New.[67] Milwaukee had been without a permanent superintendent since 1974, when Richard Gousha departed to assume the position of dean of the School of Education at the University of Indiana.[68] The new board members supported voluntary integration and formed a temporary coalition with

moderate conservatives.[69] They chose Lee McMurrin, deputy superintendent of Toledo, Ohio, to be the new superintendent in July 1975.[70]
Board members found it easy to work with McMurrin. Leon Todd, for
example, said McMurrin borrowed ideas from him. Doris Stacy, also on
the board, said he was a lovely man.[71] Anthony Busalacchi was another
big supporter and was something of a swing vote on the board, so his
support was essential.[72]

McMurrin was chosen for his experience in racial integration, con-
genial personality, and smiling disposition. He knew the desegregation
suit would be decided during his tenure and was aware of the volatile
nature of race relations in Milwaukee, so he immediately began building
links to the community. He went on a whirlwind speaking tour to civic,
political, and religious groups.[73] He attended PTA meetings, chatted
with parents in his office, listed his home phone number in the phone
book, and even wore a button that said "Everything is Beautiful."[74] Mc-
Murrin said he received a warm welcome from most Milwaukeeans, but
he also said uniformed representatives of the Ku Klux Klan and the Nazis
greeted him at his first school board meeting to silently oppose the coming integration.[75]

McMurrin wrote and encouraged the school board to adopt his "Statement on Education and Human Rights," which declared, in part, that
"[o]ur multi-ethnic population is potentially one of the richest resources
available in our schools" and that "[a]ll school districts have the responsibility to overcome within their capabilities any [racial] barriers that may
exist and to maximize the achievement potential of the children under
their care." He also said that schools had a responsibility "to work to [sic] a
more integrated society" and that schools must "carefully consider . . . the
potential benefits or adverse consequences that [their] decisions might
have on the human relations aspects of all segments of society."[76] Milwaukee's Nazis condemned McMurrin's statement, but it brought accolades
from the League of Women Voters and other civic organizations.[77]

McMurrin sought to develop a desegregation plan that was acceptable
to the board, the court, and the community, calling it an opportunity for
Milwaukeeans to "roll up their sleeves" and "get into the act." He also said
he was hoping to implement a set of alternatives rather than a singular
approach to education.[78]

McMurrin submitted a statement on "alternative schools" to the board.

(At the time, magnet schools were still called alternative schools in some circles. The term should not be confused with the modern-day connotation of alternative schools as schools for "at-risk" students.) It outlined plans for community involvement in developing a magnet school plan, which would rely heavily on busing.[79] He made these statements despite the fact that few Milwaukeeans supported magnet schools at that point.[80] According to Deputy Superintendent David Bennett, McMurrin was aware of the fractured nature of the school board and was willing to craft a plan without the board's active involvement.[81]

McMurrin proposed a plan similar to the one he had implemented in Toledo. Bennett assisted him and was responsible for the day-to-day implementation of the plan.[82] McMurrin called the concept "High Schools Unlimited," saying it would offer Milwaukeeans more choice regarding schools than any other US city. Instead of sponsoring just a few magnet schools, each of the fifteen high schools would offer some kind of specialized program. Two or three schools would offer college preparatory programs, and each of the remaining schools would specialize in some sort of job-training classes. These specialties would be unique to each school and could include aerospace and astronomy, business and computer technology, communication arts, distributive education (which includes both classroom education and on-the-job training), energy and power, fine arts, performing arts, and medical and health occupations. McMurrin believed the plan would give students an unprecedented level of choice in their curriculum and foster voluntary integration. For example, if North Division High School offered a medical specialty, the unique focus might draw white students from the south side. A curricular need would be met, and North Division, a high school that approached 100 percent black enrollment, would become more integrated.[83]

The plan McMurrin and Bennett crafted for Milwaukee also placed some magnet schools at the elementary and junior high school levels. The elementary school program, called "Options of Learning," would include "basic" (also known as "fundamental") education, open education (a program in which individual students choose their own topics of study), Montessori (a system of self-directed study), bilingual, year-round, and "multi-unit individually guided education."[84] The junior high school program, called "Schools for the Transition," would bridge the elementary schools and high schools. The junior high schools would continue to offer exploratory classes in different careers and fine arts but would do so in innovative ways so that parents and students could choose the learning style that best fit them.[85]

The plan won high praise from local media and many elected officials. The *Milwaukee Sentinel* said it "deserve[d] the wholehearted support of the board and the community at large" because it addressed racial integration and improved academics by offering specialized curricula not available in other school districts.[86] The *Milwaukee Journal* was a bit more cautious, endorsing the plan but also pointing out that magnet schools had not been effective at desegregating other school systems in other parts of the country.[87] The television news departments of WTMJ and WITI said it was the best plan that could be devised and that people should support it.[88] State Representative Conta and state Senator Sensenbrenner introduced legislation to give MPS money to help fund busing expenses, demonstrating bipartisan support.[89] Milwaukee school board members liked the voluntary aspects of the plan.[90] Some suburban superintendents indicated their students would also be attracted to magnet schools like the ones McMurrin proposed.[91]

The general public nominally supported integration. The *Milwaukee Journal* conducted a major public opinion study in 1975 in conjunction with Harvard University and the University of Wisconsin–Milwaukee.[92] The study concluded that slightly more than half of all county residents supported the goal of racially integrated schools, but few could agree on how to achieve that. Seventy-two percent of all African American respondents and 53 percent of whites said racial integration of schools was a desirable goal. Two-thirds of all respondents said they would be willing to let their children ride a bus into another neighborhood if it was to take specialty classes, but only one-third of all respondents said they would send their children to a school where more than half the students were a race other than their own. Seventy-five percent of the respondents opposed using busing for integration.[93] The *Milwaukee Journal* report also acknowledged that about half of Wisconsin's schoolchildren were already riding buses to school in 1975, including twenty-eight thousand MPS students who were bused to relieve overcrowding.[94] Firsthand accounts from reporters showed no problems at U.S. Grant Elementary, an integrated school on the south side, or Grantosa Elementary, an integrated school on the northwest side.[95] The study also pointed out a high level of parent and student satisfaction at Jackie Robinson Junior High School, a racially integrated open education magnet school.[96]

The turning point finally came on Monday, January 19, 1976, when federal judge John Reynolds ruled against the school board. He said that segregation was present in MPS due to decisions various school officials had made over a twenty-year period.[97] Having lost the court case, the school board approved McMurrin's plan with a ten-to-five vote on April 15, 1976.[98] Judge Reynolds appointed his friend John Gronouski as the special master to oversee desegregation. Gronouski had a strong background in diplomacy and legal matters. Although Gronouski was not from Milwaukee, Reynolds hoped Gronouski's Polish ancestry would appease south side residents, most of whom were Polish American.[99] The special master was to solicit input from the plaintiffs, the defense, the community, and desegregation experts to formulate a plan for the court by May 1, 1976. If Reynolds approved the plan, Gronouski would supervise the plan's implementation and evaluate its effectiveness.[100]

McMurrin hoped to work cooperatively with Gronouski, and plans for magnet schools accelerated as a result of Reynolds's decision. McMurrin formed the Committee of 100 (C/100) to solicit community input and make integration palatable to white Milwaukeeans. Each of the fifteen high schools formed a cluster committee with its feeder middle and elementary schools. The committee chose two parents or citizens, one high school student, and one staff member from each cluster committee, giving the schools sixty representatives. Thirty-six representatives were drawn from business and industry, civic groups, community organizations, educational agencies, government, labor, media, MPS employee groups, religious groups, and veterans' organizations. McMurrin appointed the remaining four representatives himself. After obtaining community input, he would forward his plan to the school board, which would approve it and send it to Gronouski, who could make whatever changes he saw fit. Finally, Gronouski would give the plan to Reynolds for final approval.[101]

A majority of C/100's membership was moderately liberal. According to a survey conducted by local desegregation scholar Ian Harris, 90 percent of C/100 members supported desegregation, and 53 percent were willing to use involuntary busing to do it. Harris admitted, however, that a survey by the *Milwaukee Journal* in the mid-1970s, as C/100 was forming, showed that only 29 percent of C/100 members supported involuntary busing.[102] Harris also found that most of the members of C/100 were fairly well educated: the average member had a college degree, while the majority of Milwaukeeans had only high school diplomas.[103] Forty-one percent of its membership consisted of white-collar workers, compared to 16.8 percent of Milwaukee's total population.[104]

The school board's conservative majority gave nominal support to C/100 but also made plans to appeal Reynolds's decision. If students had to be integrated, the board majority supported magnet schools, but if the conservatives could get away with not integrating students, they sought to keep neighborhood schools in place.[105] They believed the district could improve African American education through compensatory education programs, such as the Superior Ability program, the Upward Bound college preparatory program, and the school for unwed mothers.[106]

Although a majority of white Milwaukeeans told the *Milwaukee Journal* survey they supported integration, their actions showed otherwise. The first cluster committee meetings were held at each cluster's local high school on March 16, 1976. Nearly six thousand people attended the meetings, viewing a presentation about magnet schools and desegregation on closed-circuit television. The tone of the meetings varied from school to school. The two hundred parents at Washington were generally supportive of integration but wanted more time to submit an integration plan. According to newspaper accounts, most of the 431 people at Marshall were concerned about white flight. Slightly more than one hundred parents and teachers attended North Division's meeting. Many of them reflected Larry Harwell's black power philosophy and were less concerned about integration and more concerned about quality of education and constructing a new school to replace their existing building, which had been damaged in a fire. The 275 parents at the South Division meeting were strongly opposed to busing. One man said, "The blacks are scared to go into our neighborhoods, and we are scared to go into their neighborhoods." Perhaps most alarming was the tone at the meeting at Hamilton, the newest, whitest, and farthest south of the high schools. Some of the thirteen hundred parents in attendance at the meeting said Reynolds had violated the Constitution, and they complained about the tax increase that busing would bring. One man likened involuntary busing to Nazi war crimes and predicted a race war if "our kids [were bused] into that colored area, that high crime area."[107]

So volatile was the Hamilton situation that Gronouski personally addressed Hamilton-area parents at a meeting across the street at Bell Junior High School a few days after the initial meeting. Parents questioned his lack of familiarity with the city and his fifty-dollar-per-hour pay rate. Several parents claimed academic standards would decline if African American students were bused to the city's south side and did not want their children taking long bus rides to the north side. Ten uniformed members of Milwaukee's Nazi party requested speaking time but were turned down. They hurled insults at the people in charge of the meeting and did not leave until the police arrived.[108]

Despite the opposition, the cluster committees elected representatives to the planning committees on March 18, and the committee elected representatives to C/100 on March 30.[109] C/100 had its first meeting on April 2 and elected cochairpersons, one black and one white. The African American representative was Cecil Brown, a state assemblyman and member of MUSIC and CORE, and the white representative was Grant Waldo, an attorney and political liberal who had unsuccessfully run for city, state, and national offices.[110] According to Harris, C/100 started out as a mix of upper-middle-class and working-class individuals, but the working-class (both black and white) members felt "alienated by the formal proceedings, by Robert's Rules of Order, and by the endless haggling over parliamentary procedure." As a result, the number of working-class people who participated in C/100 meetings—which was already low— declined after the first few months.[111]

Harris was very critical of C/100's composition and agenda. According to Harris, affluent, well-educated, liberal representatives controlled the debate. They pushed out the few middle-class people who sat on the committee and refused to listen to the concerns of conservatives. In other words, C/100 represented only a fraction of Milwaukeeans, and without broad community support, any desegregation plan would be difficult to implement. Furthermore, by not directly connecting C/100 to Judge Reynolds or Special Master Gronouski, C/100 could be only advisory; neither the school board nor the superintendent had to accept its recommendations.[112] The administration may have wanted it that way. According to an analysis written by Deputy Superintendent David Bennett, one of the administration's main goals "was to maintain control of the school system in the hands of the board and administration."[113]

John Semancik was a parent on the Hamilton cluster committee. He said he and the other parents on the committee expected to have input into the desegregation plan but that Gronouski was unwilling to listen to their concerns. According to Semancik, many of the parents were open-minded about African Americans attending Hamilton, but they were concerned that money would be diverted from classroom teachers to busing, which would increase class size. Some board members, such as Margaret Dinges, were willing to listen to parental concerns, but ultimately, Gronouski was going to do what he wanted to do. According to Semancik, "It was just a big smokescreen."[114]

The Hamilton cluster asked for a medical specialty as part of the school's curriculum in addition to the word-processing and marketing specialties it had been assigned. But Superintendent McMurrin turned Hamilton down; instead, he assigned the medical specialty to North Division in an attempt to attract white students to the north side of the city. Hamilton then requested a performing arts specialty, but that program was assigned to Bay View High School in 1977.[115] The Hamilton cluster committee became frustrated and declared it would not participate in the planning process until the school board issued new guidelines and new elections were held for C/100.[116]

The liberal majority of C/100 asked the school board to drop its appeal of Reynolds's decision and asked Gronouski for more time to formulate a desegregation plan. The voting was contentious: the student representative from South Division, who voted along with the majority to halt the appeal, was grabbed by a woman who called him a traitor and warned him to not go to school if he valued his life. At the same meeting, Claire Riley, the student representative from Riverside and daughter of Lois Riley, a member of the school board and ardent integration supporter, encouraged C/100 to develop its own independent plan.[117] The clusters went to work on school-specific desegregation plans and submitted them to C/100. Some clusters supported McMurrin's plan more than others. Marshall, a racially diverse cluster on the north side, for example, endorsed magnet schools and asked that the district build a technical school in each quadrant of the city.[118] South Division's plan, on the other hand, barely mentioned integration, preferring to stick with traditional talk of compensatory education programs, including extended-hour day-care for children of working parents, more kindergarten and tutoring, work-experience centers in the high schools, and expansion of Spanish classes. It also explicitly stated that busing should be kept to a minimum. Interestingly, the plan from the cluster representing Pulaski High School, also on the south side, was fairly progressive. Though its plan was most concerned with establishing "human relations committees," it did support voluntary integration, including magnet schools, consolidating or closing schools with low enrollment, redistricting, changing feeder patterns, pairing schools, and busing, where necessary.[119]

Washington and Riverside presented much more aggressive plans. The Washington cluster supported the McMurrin plan for magnet high schools but argued that genuine integration would be possible only if it began at the elementary school level and believed it should be done by midyear, even if it disrupted the education process. Boundaries would have to be adjusted. No school would be allowed to have less than 30 percent or more than 60 percent minority enrollment. Faculty, staff, parents, and community members would participate in human relations programs, and MPS would implement an affirmative action program and hire a black and/or female deputy superintendent. Riverside's cluster, with its active PTSA, suggested a high degree of parental and student involvement in desegregation, including an interracial car pool and a student advisory committee. It also wanted a racial quota system similar to what was in Washington's plan, but it would have included Latinos. All "tracking" (placing students in classes based on ability level) would have ended, and the curriculum would have been revised to include improved math instruction, bilingual education, and the cultural histories of African Americans, Latin Americans, Native Americans, and women. Finally, the Riverside plan called for more minority representation on the school board.[120]

The North Division cluster, on the other hand, completely rejected all of McMurrin's ideas. At one point, McMurrin suggested closing North Division and other dilapidated black schools and busing their students into white areas, something North Division's parents and staff rejected on the grounds that it was "one-way" busing.[121] According to a 1995 interview with Cecil Brown, C/100 was caught in the middle of an ideological dispute between McMurrin and Howard Fuller, who not only wanted to keep North Division a neighborhood school, but actually wanted to pull North Division and its feeder schools out of MPS to form a separate school district. Brown criticized Fuller's movement and accepted one-way busing for integration.[122]

Despite the grand vision behind C/100 and the plans of the superintendent and the school board, Gronouski's opinion mattered most. He favored the superintendent's plan for the 1976–77 school year but made some modifications to individual specialties.[123] Gronouski also declared that white students would not be allowed to transfer to schools that were less than 35 percent African American and that African American students would not be allowed to transfer to schools that were more than 35 percent African American. He announced that North Division High School would be phased out and its students allowed to choose magnet schools, a suggestion that would prove to be very controversial. Gronouski also proposed in-service training for school personnel to prepare them for integration and included a plan for teacher desegregation that MTEA had submitted to him.[124] But Gronouski also wanted to implement involuntary busing, to which the conservative majority of the board objected. Some conservatives submitted a purely voluntary plan to Judge Reynolds.[125] Gronouski gave up in frustration and withdrew his plan.[126] Reynolds then ordered the board to give him a new plan.[127]

The new plan, crafted primarily by McMurrin, would phase in desegregation through magnet schools at the high school level, beginning with Washington and Hamilton in 1976 and expanding to all high schools by September 1978.[128] In 1977, Milwaukee would be divided into three zones, each of which would contain a portion of the central city. The zones would be divided into four noncontiguous leagues, each of which would contain a magnet high school and about twelve elementary schools.[129] McMurrin said that he had one of the best curriculum staffs in the United States and that they could develop curricula that would make students want to choose magnet schools.[130] The school board approved McMurrin's plan, probably out of fear that Judge Reynolds might impose a plan that mandated involuntary busing. Reynolds accepted the plan after Gronouski made a few modifications.[131] The final plan was about three hundred pages long and included a budget for personnel, training, travel, and equipment for magnet schools, as well as enrollment figures and an evaluation tool, as the judge wanted.[132] The board also voluntarily created a "human relations" office that sponsored mandatory workshops for staff, optional workshops for parents and community groups, and

MAP 10
Leagues, 1976

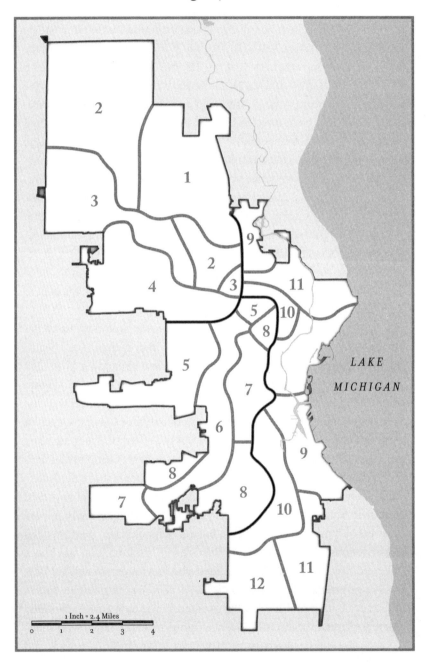

MAP 11
Option Elementary Schools, 1976

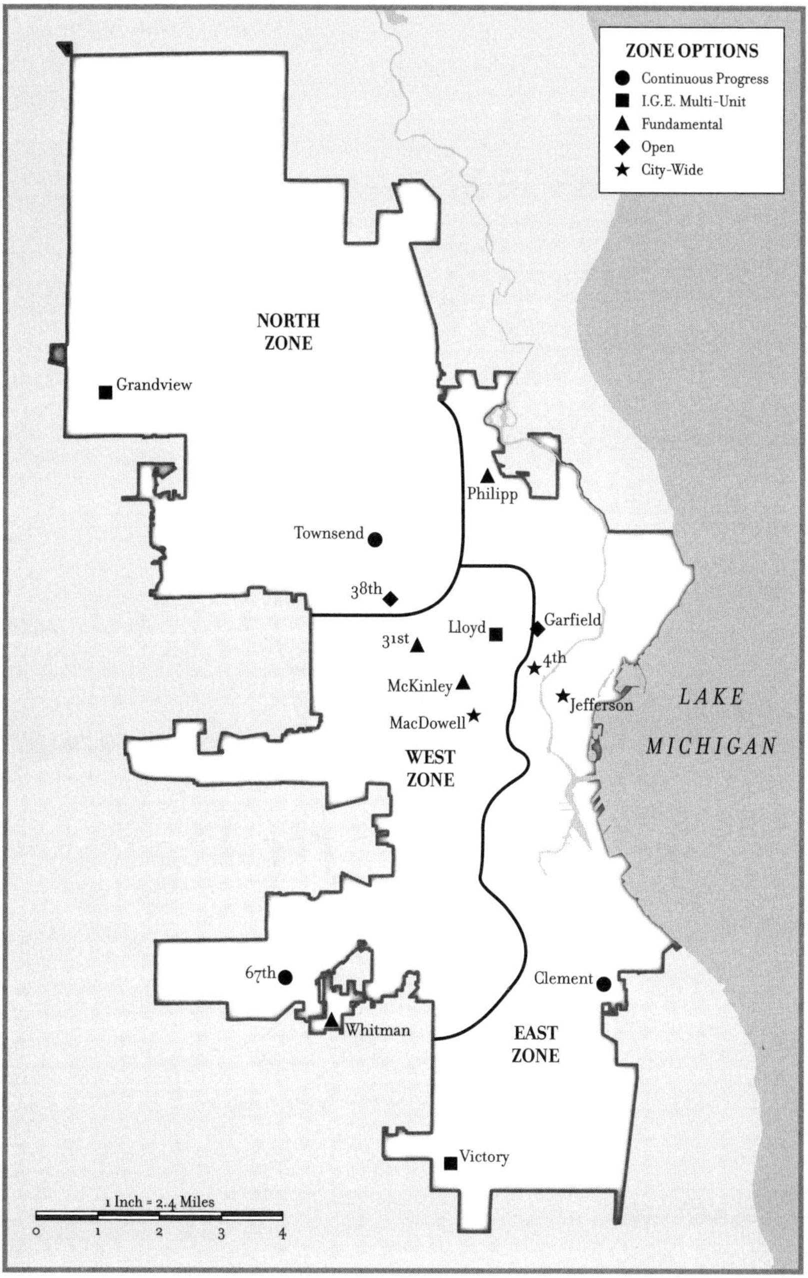

ZONE OPTIONS
- ● Continuous Progress
- ■ I.G.E. Multi-Unit
- ▲ Fundamental
- ◆ Open
- ★ City-Wide

NORTH ZONE

■ Grandview

▲ Philipp

Townsend ●

38th ◆

31st ▲   Lloyd ■   ◆ Garfield

McKinley ▲   ★ 4th

MacDowell ★   ★ Jefferson

WEST ZONE

LAKE MICHIGAN

67th ●   Clement ●

▲ Whitman

EAST ZONE

■ Victory

1 Inch = 2.4 Miles

0   1   2   3   4

MAP 12
Three School Districts Proposed, 1976

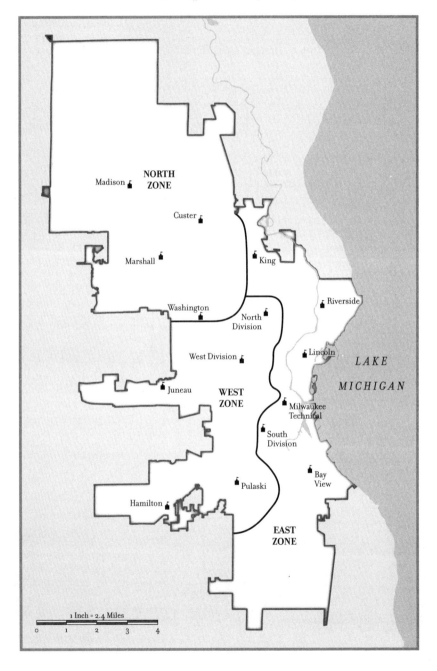

curriculum guides on cultural awareness. Each high school appointed a human relations coordinator and student committee to sponsor multicultural activities and provide mediation in racially charged conflicts.[133]

Thus, the labyrinthine planning process was concluded. The school board and Judge Reynolds approved the magnet plan, even though the superintendent had designed it with only marginal input from C/100. It seemed like a compromise that most people could accept, even if they did not like it. McMurrin won—at least temporarily. Students would have a wide array of choices in schools, as long as enough of them did not choose their neighborhood schools. This one restriction on a fundamental choice, which was cherished by so many Milwaukeeans, both black and white, would stick in the craw of many parents, but implementation began in 1976 anyway. Meanwhile, the conservative majority on the school board appealed to the US Court of Appeals of the Seventh Circuit and the US Supreme Court to have the program terminated.[134]

PART 2

THE ERA OF FORCED CHOICE

CHAPTER 3

IMPLEMENTING MILWAUKEE'S MAGNET PLAN, 1976–1986

Superintendent Lee McMurrin could not stop smiling on September 7, 1976, the first day of desegregation. Milwaukee Public Schools desegregated fifty-four schools, one more than required by Judge Reynolds's order, which defined racial balance as 25 percent to 45 percent black enrollment. McMurrin used phrases like "this is a miracle," "this is beautiful," and "doggone it, this was hard work but it is paying off." He also remarked, "A year ago many people were saying we couldn't do this. Now we're doing it and the next two years of this are going to be smoother because of this success. Success will breed success." School-level administrators also universally reported positive results. Elementary students laughed and played and made new friends who had different skin colors. Older students were more cautious, but there were no disruptions the first day.[1]

But careful examination of the evidence indicates that the magnet program was a mixed success. For the most part, the public supported the curriculum changes. There were several challenges, however, that did not become apparent until later in the school year, including problems with teachers, students, and transportation. And when too few students volunteered to attend schools out of their neighborhoods, MPS decided to bus them against their will, which a student at North Division High School referred to as a "forced choice."[2] Various advocacy groups raised issues regarding the scale of integration. For example, on a micro scale,

even supposedly "integrated" schools still experienced racial stratifica-
tion; administrators rarely placed African American students in superior
ability classes. And on a macro scale, the school board struggled with
white migration to the suburbs and proposed metropolitan integration as
a corrective measure. What looked like voluntary choice in the mid-1970s
appeared to be forced choice to some people by the mid-1980s.

Surveys showed that most Milwaukeeans professed support for integration but resented busing as a mechanism for achieving this goal. No
one has published more research on this issue than Christine Rossell, a
political scientist at Boston University. Rossell found—and other social
scientists have agreed—that white families were more likely to accept
integration if a certain set of conditions was met. For example, the African American population needed to be kept low at the white school.
Also, white parents were willing to accept African American students
into "white schools," but they did not believe their children should be
required to ride a bus, especially if the bus had to travel a great distance.[3]
Survey data from parents and school personnel in 119 districts across the
United States found that voluntary integration programs were superior
to mandatory programs in equity, efficiency, and effectiveness. Rossell
found that mandatory assignments usually resulted in white flight from
the city, which ultimately increased segregation. Rigorous curricula were
also important. Using sampling data, Rossell determined that magnet
schools in heavily minority neighborhoods had white enrollments of 37
percent, on average, if they had college preparatory programs. White enrollment declined to 32 percent if students were forced to choose the
school, and white enrollment declined even further, to less than 10 percent, in schools that offered career/vocational specialties instead of a
college preparatory specialty.[4]

Rossell did not study Milwaukee, but Belden Paulson, a professor
of political science at the University of Wisconsin–Milwaukee (UWM)
and chair of the Center for Urban Community Development of the UW–
Extension, studied Rossell's early work and concluded that Rossell's
theories fit Milwaukee.[5] Additionally, a detailed study of demographics
prepared by Maria Luce, also from the Center for Urban Community Development, showed that MPS's enrollment was declining, particularly
among whites and in schools in impoverished neighborhoods. Luce
therefore concluded that a magnet school, even a high-quality one,

would not attract whites to a poor neighborhood.[6] There was also a consensus among school board members that a school had to have both a good academic reputation and a substantial number of white students if it was going to attract other white students.[7]

Milwaukee Public Schools operated only three magnet high schools (Hamilton, Washington, and Milwaukee Trade and Tech) in 1976, the first year of integration. To increase white enrollment at Washington, MPS allowed any junior or senior enrolled at any of its high schools to apply for full- or half-time status at Washington, where they would be able to use computer equipment not available at any other school in the district, including eight computer connections, several (then) high-speed computer terminals, a data entry video terminal, key-to-disk units, and key-to-tape units. The school offered four computer classes: computer applications in business and industry, keyboard data training, introduction to computer science, and advanced programming.[8] In his unpublished manuscript, McMurrin recounts that a student at Washington won a national computer science competition that carried with it a four-year scholarship to the Massachusetts Institute of Technology worth forty-eight thousand dollars. McMurrin lamented that the media overlooked this and other magnet success stories.[9]

Hamilton, located on the far southwest side, was entirely white but had space available for African American students. Two courses were offered in word processing and marketing. The word-processing classes emphasized (then) modern technologies such as electric typewriters, transcribing machines, dictation units, and text-editing devices. The other course, Opportunities and Techniques in Marketing, was a double-period class and included training on personnel counseling, public relations, advertising and sales promotion, and purchasing. The curriculum was designed in partnership with the Sales and Marketing Executives Club, the Milwaukee Advertising Club, and the Kiwanis Club. An intern program was scheduled to start in the summer of 1977.[10]

The opportunities at Washington and Hamilton sounded excellent, and Hamilton's program was well received, but few white parents were willing to put their children on a bus to Washington or any other north side school. As Rossell reported, white parents were willing to send their children to magnet schools if the curriculum was rigorous, the bus ride was short, and a substantial number of other white students were enrolled at the school. In the case of Washington, the school was not perceived as good or safe, it was an hour away from Hamilton by bus, and the student body was racially mixed. Hamilton, on the other hand, was viewed as a good school, it was within walking distance for most of its students, and it was very white. According to a report from the Milwaukee Urban Observatory at the UWM, only 3 percent of MPS's white population opted to transfer to specialty schools in 1976, and most inner-city magnet schools were more than 40 percent empty.[11]

The district established five satellite centers, in addition to the magnet high schools, to accommodate 250 juniors and seniors. Students were transported from their schools to the satellite centers for half a day of instruction and received credit for two classes. They attended their regular schools the other half of the day. The Milwaukee Art Center hosted an art studio center where students met notable Wisconsin artists. Junior Achievement hosted the other four satellite centers. Students enrolled in the American Legal System Satellite Center met and learned from city, county, state, and federal court officials; law enforcement officers; and law students. Students enrolled in the Broadcast Communications Satellite Center studied broadcasting law, radio and television production and engineering, and sales and business aspects of broadcasting. The satellite center on the US economy in the Milwaukee area had students visit banks, stock-exchange offices, factories, and distribution centers to gain an understanding of Milwaukee's businesses and industries, meeting with business executives and labor leaders. Students in the fifth satellite center, which focused on state and local government, were split into small groups and discussed topics and job potential with various public officials.[12]

In addition, four magnet junior high schools were operating in Milwaukee. As many as 345 students could attend Eighth Street School in downtown Milwaukee. Students were organized into units by grade level in a format that is now referred to as a middle school.[13] The small size was supposed to help the students and faculty get to know one another, and the downtown location was to provide students with learning experiences at Milwaukee's central library, YMCA, and Marquette University, which were all nearby. Meanwhile, open education continued to be the sole mode of instruction at Jackie Robinson Junior High School, which expanded and moved into the old Peckham building near Washington High School. Because students choose their own course of study in an open environment, it was possible to find one student working on mathematics, another one reading, and others listening to records or watching a movie. Steuben Junior High School, also near Washington, continued to follow the middle school model it had used for years but with a new innovation—each unit emphasized one of four teaching techniques: open classroom, traditional, individually guided instruction, or science. Finally, Wilbur Wright Junior High, on the northwest side of Milwaukee, became a "fundamental school," emphasizing the "basics" of reading, writing, mathematics, science, and social studies. Students were expected to adhere to a strict dress code and complete all homework assignments, unlike in some urban schools where homework was optional. Students were grouped according to ability, and promotion to the next grade level was supposed to be based on academic achievement rather than age.[14] As with the other magnet schools, the intent behind the junior high locations was never stated, but it appears that all of them were placed in black or transitional neighborhoods in the hope of attracting white students.

Finally, Milwaukee had fifteen magnet schools at the elementary level. Three of the schools were citywide, enrolling all students regardless of where they lived. The schools included a gifted and talented program at Fourth Street Elementary (renamed Golda Meir Elementary in 1979), a Teacher-Pupil Learning Center at Jefferson, and a Montessori program at MacDowell. The other twelve magnet schools were each assigned to one of the twelve elementary school leagues and had programs similar to the ones at the three citywide schools. Although the citywide schools were popular with both black and white students, the twelve league schools, which were usually in African American neighborhoods, lagged behind in white enrollment—only 219 whites filled the 1,630 seats set aside for them by mid-August, compared to 721 whites who occupied 1,198 seats in the citywide schools. White enrollment in the four magnet junior high schools was also less than half of what Judge Reynolds and Special Master Gronouski wanted.[15]

Experts were not surprised by the disparity between black and white enrollment. Herman Goldberg, associate director of the US Office of Education, spoke at a symposium at UWM in the summer of 1976 and said voluntary desegregation plans, such as magnet schools, were usually ineffective because too few students volunteered to make the plans work.[16]

Robert L. Green, dean of the College of Urban Development at Michigan State University and an expert on more than a dozen desegregation cases, advised Milwaukee teachers that white students would not attend black schools no matter how good they were: "Black magnet schools . . . could have Beethoven teaching music and Einstein teaching math, and they still aren't going to attract whites."[17]

Also, despite what sounded like innovative curricula, some schools could not fully implement their specialty programs. According to magnet school expert Gregory Strong, not all principals provided adequate leadership. Successful principals created cultures that fostered acceptance of all students and emphasized elimination of stereotypes, individualized curriculum, heterogeneous classroom groups, consistent discipline, intra- and extracurricular activities, appropriate training for staff, and parental input and participation. Those principals usually had excellent human relations programs coupled with tutoring and other academic supports. Unfortunately, not all principals led their schools effectively through the transition.[18]

Likewise, not all teachers and students were ideally matched for their schools. Judge Reynolds had ordered MPS to increase its number of nonwhite teachers. The district was short seventy-one African American teachers, so it left their positions unfilled and temporarily hired substitute teachers instead.[19] Additionally, some teachers did not like the schools' specialties and made little attempt to implement them. At the time, seniority determined teaching assignments, and senior teachers usually received their desired schools, even if they were unwilling to implement the school's new curriculum.[20] The district also admitted that some students signed up for schools that did not fit their personalities or skills. For example, some students with severe attention problems registered for open education programs when they likely needed more supervision and regimented activity.[21]

Major problems arose with transportation, and the costs were high. For example, the district transported four thousand junior and senior high school students in the first year—a small number compared to future years—at fifty cents per day, or ten thousand dollars per week for the entire program. Most of these students had to crowd onto existing Milwaukee County Transit System bus routes during rush-hour traffic, while elementary school children took regular yellow school buses. The county transit system had to create twenty special bus routes for hard-to-reach schools, such as Hamilton and Vincent. The new routes forced the county to press spare buses into service, which increased the county expenditures on maintenance, fuel, and drivers.[22] African Americans were reluctant to join athletic teams at Hamilton because the buses did not run late enough after school, so some team practices were rearranged to accommodate the bus schedule.[23]

Seventy-three bus routes were planned at the elementary school level, fifty-three of which were contracted to Schoolways Transportation, which did not have enough drivers. Some drivers dropped their first group of students off at school and then picked up a second group of students, who would be an hour and a half late for school. They would also be two or more hours late in the afternoon, which meant students could be at school twelve hours per day.[24] Taxis were used for emergency work, which cost a minimum of six dollars per ride. MPS paid for more than one hundred rides on some days in the first three weeks.[25] Although Schoolways eventually hired more drivers, the company charged the school district twice the $2,108 bid in the original contract.[26]

In some cases, "double busing" occurred when students who volunteered for the new magnet schools were already attending integrated schools. When these students transferred to the magnet schools, they created vacancies at their original schools, and replacement students of the same race had to be bused to fill the vacant seats. Thus, the school was not any more integrated than it had been before, but one student was bused out, another was bused in, and MPS paid for two bus rides to keep the status quo.[27] Conservative taxpayers—both black and white—later criticized this practice for financial reasons.[28]

Superintendent McMurrin ordered planning for the 1977–78 school year in the fall of 1976, despite the unexpected problems. Meetings were conducted in each league and coordinated by the C/100. The specialties launched in 1977 were as follows:

- Marshall—communications and media

- Riverside—community, human services, and education

- West Division—law, law enforcement, and protection services

- Juneau—small business management

- South Division—tourism, food service, and recreation
- Four new satellite centers—environmental science, "Exploring the Consumers' 3Rs: Role, Rights, and Responsibilities," library media, and "Writing Laboratory in Advertising"[29]

South Division High School, the school with the highest percentage of white students on the preceding list, was assigned the specialty that was least likely to require a college education, while the most demanding specialty went to Rufus King, a majority-black school. The intent was obvious, although not spelled out in any of the board documentation—King's program would attract students from the south side and would integrate the school. The low-skill program at South Division was supposed to attract African Americans to the south side school.

Milwaukeeans showed nominal support for the plan. According to a survey by the Social Science Research Facility at UWM, 60 percent of all Milwaukeeans supported integrated schools, including 77 percent of African Americans polled and 57 percent of white respondents.[30] But that did not mean Milwaukeeans supported involuntary busing. Ian Harris's 1977 survey of Milwaukeeans showed 74 percent of all respondents opposed involuntary busing. The racial breakdown was 78 percent for whites and 65 percent for African Americans. These data fit well with the work of Rossell and others, showing that parents support integration when the program is voluntary, schools are good, and the bus rides are short. Data from Harris's poll also showed that 61 percent of the white respondents wanted the school board to continue its appeal of Reynolds's decision to the US Supreme Court, though only 38 percent of African American respondents felt the same way.[31]

The appeal became the major issue in the spring school board elections. Six of the fifteen seats were open. Anthony Busalacchi, who was something of a swing vote, ran for reelection and was very vocal. He said he supported integration and magnet schools, but he also believed involuntary busing would cause "middle and upper income families [to] abandon the cities."[32] He also said he believed that Judge Reynolds's 1979 deadline for full integration did not give whites enough time to change their minds about sending their children to school with African Americans. Busalacchi preferred a much longer timeline that would have given residence patterns time to change, believing that if more neighborhoods became integrated, schools would be able to integrate without involuntary busing.[33]

Most of the other fifteen candidates, including two other incumbents and newcomer Lawrence O'Neil, who lived in the all-white Hamilton High School neighborhood, also said they thought the city needed more time to integrate schools.[34] But according to Jeff Kartz, the student representative of the Hamilton cluster within C/100, many parents were opposed to any kind of integration, with or without busing. He recalls that he was often the only representative from the Hamilton cluster who voted in favor of integration policies and that an angry mother actually hit him at a C/100 meeting because she did not agree with his votes. He said some whites expressed concern that integration would increase crime.[35]

Not surprisingly, when voters went to the polls they reelected Busalacchi and two conservative incumbents. They also voted for O'Neil. Therefore, the conservative majority widened from a two-vote majority to a three-vote majority.[36] The new, larger board majority vowed to continue the appeal, and McMurrin vowed to go ahead and desegregate the schools, regardless of the outcome of the appeal.[37] However, newspapers and interviews do not indicate a strained relationship between the board and the superintendent. Everyone still seemed to think McMurrin was a nice, easygoing man.[38]

The US Supreme Court issued a ruling on June 29, 1977. It agreed with the plaintiffs that MPS was deliberately segregated, but it also sent the case back to the Court of Appeals in Chicago to determine whether Reynolds's remedy exceeded the scope of the segregation.[39] Lloyd Barbee and his associates asked the appellate court to remand the case to Reynolds, which it did in early September.[40] The appellate court also eliminated the special master position, which cleared the way for McMurrin to implement whatever program he wanted, as long as he could get it approved by the school board and the judge.[41]

The second year of integration proceeded while both sides prepared their legal cases. The use of yellow school buses for elementary school students expanded, and McMurrin asked the school board for additional personnel to minimize the busing-related problems from the year before. Instead of one transportation director and a secretary, the district employed a director, an assistant director, three secretaries, a rider supervisor, a route specialist, twenty staff who would ride the buses and monitor efficiency, and a three-hundred-thousand-dollar-per-year consulting firm to help monitor progress.[42] The final plan for the fall of 1977 called for busing for more than fourteen thousand of the one hundred thousand students in MPS to 102 schools. Half the elementary schools started at 8:35 A.M., and the other half started at 9:35. All high schools began at 7:45, and all middle schools and junior highs began at 8:30. The purpose of this staggered schedule was to allow school bus drivers to pick up students and drop them off at schools that began early, then double back and pick up students who attended schools that started later, which was supposed to save money.[43] Bus routes changed constantly to accommodate changes in enrollments or mistakes—an average of twenty changes per day in September. As a result, students were never quite sure of where or when their buses were going to pick them up, and some were left stranded.[44]

Transportation costs for integration increased to $6.8 million—or more than 5 percent of the MPS budget in the 1977–78 school year—a significant increase from $894,000 in the 1975–76 school year and $3.6 million in 1976–77. If transportation costs not related to integration, such as busing for special education students and taxis for students who were marooned at school without a bus, were included, then transportation costs rose to $12.1 million. Bus companies were paid $62,050 per day for 668 buses traveling 1,437 routes. At least one elementary school, MacDowell, was served by as many as thirty-two buses. The overwhelming need for buses resulted in contracts with bus companies that had to be negotiated at the last minute, which led to price gouging.[45] Shortages of drivers, fluctuating routes, and increasing costs continued into the 1978–79 school year.[46]

A few suburban schools also volunteered to enroll some African American students. Busing to the suburbs went much more smoothly than busing within the city. Buses were still late, but the Milwaukee students and the suburban administrators reported that students were friendly to one another and that teachers treated the Milwaukee students as they would any other students.[47] Again, these were mostly unilateral ("one-way") transfers. Nicolet High School, for example, took in fifty-three Milwaukee students in 1977–78 but sent only five students to Milwaukee schools.[48] However, those suburban students who did transfer to the city reported mostly positive experiences after an initial period of adjustment.[49]

To ensure true integration, Gronouski established a monitoring board in 1977 to watch for problems. The board included fifteen volunteers, many of whom were chosen by C/100, and targeted twenty-five schools during the first week of school: three high schools, five junior highs, and seventeen elementary schools. They went to other schools after the first week and were required to make at least one school visit per month. The monitors, most of whom were white, expressed concern about the treatment of African American students in white schools. As longtime education activist Bob Peterson explained, "Equal education and quality education aren't limited to what's going on in the school statistic books. It goes into curriculum and attitudes."[50]

Peterson was a member of People United for Integrated and Quality Education and a paraprofessional in MPS at the time. He would later become a teacher at Fratney Elementary School (now known as La Escuela Fratney) and a founding editor of *Rethinking Schools*, a magazine focused particularly on issues of race and social justice.[51] He was elected president of the Milwaukee Teachers Education Association in 2011.[52] Peterson said the monitors were trained to look for problems with late buses and were supposed to make sure that African American students were not improperly assigned to classes or unfairly labeled for special education. They also checked for language barriers with Spanish-speaking students, accessibility of extracurricular activities for bused students, and curricula geared to "the white male majority viewpoint." He offered Riverside High School, where the superior ability classes were nearly all white, while the rest of the school was of mixed ethnicity, as an example of racial inequality.[53]

Peterson said the monitoring boards were a mixed success. Teachers often viewed the monitors as suspicious outsiders, and "principals would lock themselves in their offices" rather than work on race relations.[54] According to Ian Harris, the last thing the school board wanted was "citizens snooping around the schools."[55] Plans did not always work out the way the monitoring board wanted. At Pulaski High School, for example, the student-run human relations committee wrote a multicultural handbook and made plans for a newsletter, a "rumor control center," and interracial dances and clubs.[56] But few of these planned activities actually happened, and the racial composition of clubs remained overwhelmingly white, except the drill team, which was predominantly African American.

All the student hall monitors were white, which contributed to racial tension. Perhaps most startling, the integration monitors intervened when a group of African American students and a group of white students exchanged money for drugs at a bus stop on Twenty-Seventh and Oklahoma, near the school. The groups almost turned violent when the buyers realized there were no drugs, but the monitors got the money back without alerting the principal.[57]

Judge Reynolds defined a school as integrated if it was 15 to 75 percent African American for the 1977–78 school year. He wanted 102 schools to meet that requirement by September, but only 73 did.[58] All schools were supposed to be integrated by 1978, but several were still nearly 100 percent African American, including Auer Avenue Elementary, Parkman and Fulton Junior Highs, and North Division and Rufus King High Schools.[59] Planning for the third year of integration continued undeterred. The complete magnet program, as it would stand for several years, is presented below.[60]

Options for Learning program (one of each of these in elementary schools in every area of the city)

- Multi-unit, individually guided education (IGE)
- Basic/fundamental
- Open education
- Creative arts
- Gifted and talented
- German language[61]
- Montessori education
- Bilingual-bicultural (Spanish) centers

Schools for the Transition program (junior high schools)

- Middle schools
- Multi-unit, IGE
- Basic fundamental
- Open education

- Gifted and talented
- Career orientation
- Bilingual-bicultural (Spanish) centers

High Schools Unlimited program

- Bay View—visual and performing arts
- Custer—applied technology
- Hamilton—marketing and business communication
- Juneau—small business management (citywide beginning in 1979–80)
- Rufus King—college preparatory academy (citywide)
- Lincoln—finance and commerce
- Madison—earth, energy, and environment (eventually electronics)
- Marshall—communication and media
- Milwaukee Trade and Technical High School (citywide)
- North Division—medical, dental, and health
- Pulaski—truck transportation
- Riverside—community human services and education (replaced with a citywide college preparatory program in partnership with UWM in 1984)
- South Division—tourism, food service, and recreation
- Washington—computer data processing
- West Division—law, law enforcement, and protective service
- Vincent—agribusiness and natural resources[62]

King and Milwaukee Trade and Technical were the only high schools on the preceding list that were initially designated as citywide. In other words, any student in any part of the city could attend those schools, and all students were required to take classes in the specialty.[63] King was (and still is) the flagship of the magnet schools. King had been a neighborhood school of nine hundred students, only one of whom was white, in 1977. But MPS removed the neighborhood population in 1978, when it instituted an entrance exam. Only sixteen former students returned when King reopened as a citywide magnet school for college-bound students in September. There were 345 students in its high school program, about 52 percent of whom were white, and 410 students in its middle school program, about 56 percent of whom were white. Principal William Larkin reported students were eager to learn, and students said they liked their new surroundings. It was a fully integrated magnet school succeeding in the mission for which it was designed: to prepare all its students for college. Students were expected to take four years of English and two to three years of mathematics, science, social studies, and foreign language.[64]

The other schools had neighborhood status instead of citywide status, which meant they were required to accept neighborhood students even if the students did not enroll in their specialties. Neighborhood schools were also required to accept any student who enhanced racial diversity at the school, even if the student did not enroll in the specialty. Likewise, some elementary schools and junior high schools on this list were citywide, while others were neighborhood specialty schools. This arrangement was set up to please parents who wanted their children to attend neighborhood schools and still participate in a magnet program.

Meanwhile, as planning got under way, so did the retrial. All the evidence from the first trial was reexamined. More attention was focused on the racially biased teacher transfer system from the 1960s.[65] The past practice of intact busing also came under close scrutiny. Almost a thousand new pieces of evidence were introduced.[66] Assistant Superintendent Robert Long testified that African American students who were bused intact were not allowed to mix with white students, although when he had taught in the 1950s and 1960s, white students had mingled freely with the population of the host school.[67] African American teachers and a white union representative testified about the administration's intent to segregate, and administrators testified about private conversations held with school board members in which the administration was told to keep the schools segregated.[68]

Reynolds ruled against the school board again on June 1, 1978, and ordered desegregation again, finding the actions of the school board had been so pervasive that a district-wide remedy was the only possible option to correct violations of the Fourteenth Amendment to the Constitution and the Civil Rights Act of 1871.[69] Further hearings were held from July until October to determine the details of the final desegregation plan, but most of the integrationists' goals had already been achieved.[70] Intact busing had stopped in 1971, most students were attending integrated schools by 1977, and the teachers' union decided to allow partial restaffing of magnet schools by 1978.[71] A new monitor, US Magistrate John C. McBride, was named to replace Gronouski. McBride was not expected to advocate for the plaintiffs as Gronouski had. In fact, McBride publicly announced, "I don't plan to be telling [MPS] what to do," and told reporters he would prefer to let the plaintiffs' attorneys provide the actual enforcement of the integration plan.[72]

Reynolds received a major boost from the state legislature in February 1978, when it approved the restructuring of the Milwaukee school board, reducing it from a fifteen-member board elected on an at-large basis to a nine-member board with eight members elected by local districts and one chosen at large between 1979 and 1983. By restructuring, the legislature sought to make the board more accountable to the voters.[73] The phase-in had a noticeable effect on the 1979 election: minority-dominated neighborhoods that had not been able to meet the threshold to elect representatives under the old system were able to concentrate their votes and win an election. The new liberal majority advocated for more integration and raised the possibility of busing white students to the north side of Milwaukee.[74]

Judge Reynolds issued his final ruling on February 8, 1979, although the details were negotiated in an out-of-court settlement between the plaintiffs and the school board in May—almost fourteen years after Lloyd Barbee had filed the initial lawsuit.[75] Seventy-five percent of all students—kindergartners exempted—had to attend schools that were racially balanced, which was now defined as 25 to 60 percent black at the elementary level and 20 to 60 percent black at the high school level. Students were allowed to attend neighborhood schools if it enhanced the racial balance at the receiving school. Schools in African American neighborhoods were closed to induce transfers, voluntary or not. Two-thirds of the schools were required to hire staffs that were 11 to 21 percent African American, and the remaining third had to employ staffs that were 6 to 26 percent African American.[76] The settlement was set to expire on

July 1, 1984, at which point MPS should have been completely integrated, assuming a static demographic.[77]

According to historian Bill Dahlk, Barbee realized MPS had achieved many of his integration goals and a settlement was the best he was going to get. He also knew that he had used up all his political and social capital and was losing control of the black school reform movement to black power advocates such as Howard Fuller (see chapter 4).[78] McMurrin and most school board members accepted the settlement because it would not require involuntary busing of white students and would allow for some desegregated white-majority schools.[79] This time, with a settlement in place, there would be no chance of appeal. The board's new liberal majority would not have appealed anyway.

The administration and school board created many new innovative magnets in the 1980s. Lincoln High School, which was a small high school in downtown Milwaukee, was closed in 1979 due to declining enrollment.[80] It reopened as a citywide fine arts middle school in 1982, a designation that Roosevelt Middle School also received in 1983.[81] West Division High School's law and law enforcement specialty did not attract enough white students, so Bay View High School and West Division switched specialties in 1984, with the latter becoming Milwaukee High School of the Arts, a citywide school.[82] Elm and Tippecanoe elementary schools were also assigned arts specialties.[83] Thus, a kindergarten–to–twelfth grade fine arts education became possible in MPS. Other innovations included a citywide gifted and talented program at Samuel Morse, which became a feeder school for Rufus King High School;[84] an international studies specialty at Webster Middle School;[85] and additional citywide magnet elementary schools that focused on Montessori education, environmental studies, and language immersion in Spanish or French.[86]

Initial reports showed that magnet schools were achieving their goal of integrating African Americans and whites. A news article from 1981 reported that more than twenty-five thousand MPS students, or close to 30 percent, were enrolled in magnet schools, and fifty-three of the district's 143 schools were citywide magnet schools or were neighborhood schools that offered magnet programs.[87] Washington High School had managed to slow white migration and held the African American population to only 52 percent by 1982.[88] Its computer specialty grew from seventy-five students in 1976 to six hundred in 1984.[89] The word-processing and marketing specialty at Hamilton was very popular, requiring a waiting list to get into it.[90] Juneau High School's business program was also successful in teaching students how to write business plans and market products and services.[91] South Division, meanwhile, had simulated hotel and restaurant facilities. Hamilton, Juneau, and South all released students from school for part of their day so they could work in actual job settings for both pay and academic credit.[92]

Rufus King was perhaps the biggest success story, with an attendance rate of 94.2 percent in March 1983, compared to 85.5 percent for all MPS high schools. King garnered national praise for its college-bound program. The White House recognized it as one of the best 144 high schools in the United States, and its Academic Decathlon team won third place in a national competition in 1983, after a string of first-place championships at the state level.[93]

French Immersion Elementary, located on the city's northwest side, also was very popular. It exceeded its capacity to enroll students in 1985, partially because of participation from families in the northern suburbs. The school board chose to move the school to the old 88th Street School on the far south side, prompting an outcry from north side and north-suburban parents who did not want their children to ride a bus far from home.[94]

These and some other schools proved to be so popular that by 1985 there were waiting lists to get into them. The district had to implement a lottery to admit students, which prompted criticism from parents whose children were not admitted, though MPS claimed that 93 percent of students were admitted to one of their top three choices when applying for a school.[95] In 1985 the federal government rewarded MPS with a $4 million grant to support magnet schools, which was more money than any other city received except New York City. Superintendent McMurrin said, "The money will make Milwaukee schools more attractive, not only to our children, but to suburban parents."[96]

Students enrolled in the magnet programs reported positive experiences. Jeff Hauser, who lived in Hales Corners, was one of about eight hundred suburban students who attended Milwaukee schools in 1985 to take advantage of the magnet programs. Hauser was drawn to the truck transportation program at Pulaski. He said he really wanted to be a veterinarian or zoologist but thought it was important to have a skill as a backup plan. Jeanne Laurenz of Oak Creek said she wanted to study theater and that Milwaukee High School of the Arts had a much better program than Oak Creek. Her friends were not supportive: "Many of the people I knew said: 'You're crazy. There are a lot of crime and drug problems [in Milwaukee]. Besides, you're a white girl. You'll get raped.' I think they've been living in Oak Creek too long. There are no cliques here. There is very little drug use, because everyone wants to take care of themselves." She admitted she did not like waking up between 5:30 and 6 A.M. to catch a 7 A.M. bus, but said she was willing to make that sacrifice.[97]

One of the more curious magnet programs was at Vincent High School. Although one might question the practicality of establishing a magnet school for agribusiness and natural resource management in an urban context, Vincent's program thrived. The school opened in 1979 on eighty acres on the far northwest side of the city, which still had farms at the time. Two hundred ten students enrolled in its specialty after only one year. Classes involved genetic research, horticulture, and veterinary science. One student, Steve Fischer, wanted to be a state fish and game warden: "Not many people can become one—usually only six are hired a year. But this might give me a head start." Students planted trees on the property—800 spruce and pine trees, 150 oaks, 100 tamaracks (99 of which were eaten by small animals in the school's vicinity), 50 poplars, and, in the 1979–80 school year, 1,200 ornamental shrubs. Students also planted seventy garden plots, the proceeds from which were used to defray the costs of field trips.[98] As the program grew, students were allowed to take increasingly advanced classes and also studied business management. The US Forest Service even started a program at Vincent in 1984, and it hired some students for summer jobs.[99] A handful of graduating seniors went on to study at the Milwaukee Area Technical College or the University of Wisconsin system, which the school administration saw as a victory, even though most of its students did not pursue post-secondary education.[100]

Although the magnet programs were popular, many students were not prepared for their desired careers. The Milwaukee Area Technical College and area employers reported that many graduates of MPS vocational programs were not prepared for technical college or the workplace. According to Superintendent McMurrin, half of all MPS graduates did not enroll in college and half of those that did dropped out before graduation.[101]

The Medical College of Wisconsin criticized North Division's program for "set[ting] its sights too low" because it trained students for careers as medical technicians and nurses' aides instead of preparing them to be doctors or nurses.[102] The magnet schools also did little or nothing to reduce the dropout rate, which remained about 25 percent between 1980 and 1982.[103]

The scale of integration was another problem. For example, many students at the middle school and high school levels attended segregated classes in 1980, even though they were in schools that met the court's standard for integration. Specifically, fifteen of the nineteen middle schools met the desegregation criteria from the settlement, but only 65 percent of their classes were integrated. And thirteen of the fifteen high schools were desegregated, but only 61 percent of their classes were.[104] African Americans were more likely to be placed into special education classes, and many students who rode buses could not participate in after-school activities because they had no way to get home if they did not board the bus immediately after school.[105] African American students made up only 7 percent of students in Hamilton's Program for the Academically Talented. Furthermore, students chose racially homogeneous groups in cafeterias and physical education classes. African American students were frequently late to school because of long bus rides and as a result faced suspensions for repeated tardiness. When interviewed by a reporter, two African American high school students downplayed the importance of race, but they acknowledged that many African American students could not participate in after-school activities and parties because they lacked private transportation. A few other students reported racial slurs or being ignored by white students when they tried to participate in extracurricular activities.[106]

Metropolitan segregation involved another problem of scale. MPS covered only the city of Milwaukee, and while the city was multiracial, the surrounding suburbs were not. According to the US Supreme Court case *Milliken v. Bradley* (1974), a court cannot mandate interdistrict busing unless the school district lines were established to promote segregation. The state of Wisconsin tried to encourage voluntary integration through its Chapter 220 program, which provided financial incentives to what would eventually be twenty-three suburban school districts. The program began in 1976 and was hailed by suburban superintendents as a way to bring about voluntary integration and supplement school funds, but it was never very popular with suburban parents, some of whom worried that MPS students lagged behind and might slow the academic achievement of their own children.[107] Other suburbanites were concerned about long bus rides or believed the state money would not cover all costs.[108]

Many more Milwaukee students volunteered for Chapter 220 than did suburban students. The West Allis–West Milwaukee school district, for example, accepted fifteen Milwaukee students in the fall of 1983, but only eleven West Allis–West Milwaukee students volunteered to attend Milwaukee magnet schools.[109] The Whitnall school district, which encompasses the village of Hales Corners and parts of Greenfield and Franklin, exchanged seventeen of its students for thirty-five Milwaukee students that same school year.[110] Likewise, Greendale admitted seventy-eight students for only sixteen students it sent to Milwaukee, and Brown Deer took just over one hundred students from Milwaukee but sent only twenty into the city. The disparity was worse in the Maple Dale–Indian Hill district, where fifty-four Milwaukee students attended school compared to the four it sent to MPS. Nicolet, the most affluent district in southeastern Wisconsin, accepted 123 Milwaukee students but traded only five of its students to the city.[111] When suburban freshmen were asked why they chose Nicolet over Milwaukee high schools, they responded that the Milwaukee specialties looked good but that they wanted to attend school with their friends.[112]

Suburbs in Waukesha County, to the west of Milwaukee, were eligible for Chapter 220 but sent few or no students to Milwaukee. Waukesha County has been one of the most politically conservative counties in Wisconsin since the mid-1970s, and this history was reflected in the community's reaction to the government-funded desegregation programs.[113] Parents and district officials cited underachieving Milwaukee students, school violence, and long bus rides as concerns.[114] In the words of one Brookfield parent: "No way on God's green Earth am I going to send my children to Milwaukee." Or, as another parent said, "You're living in a fantasy land if you think we'll send our children to Milwaukee." One parent predicted that "[i]f we go with the plan it will be the beginning of the end as we know it today." Another parent believed Chapter 220 was nothing but a way to siphon off Brookfield tax money for Milwaukee's purposes: "The City of Milwaukee would like nothing better than to dip into our checkbooks. I pay my property taxes to my school district. Let's keep them [the taxes] here." And as an MPS teacher who lived in Brookfield said, "I deal every day with children who can't read. [We will] fight this [plan] right down the line. We don't have to have it forced upon us."[115] Thus, despite early interest in magnet schools from suburban superintendents, metropolitan integration did not occur.

If the suburbs would not voluntarily integrate, then the Milwaukee school board would force the issue. The board had been considering a legal challenge since 1980, and it finally voted to join with the Milwaukee Integration Research Center (MIRC) in suing the suburban districts after pro-integration candidates were reelected to the board in 1983.[116] The board and MIRC sought to reorganize Milwaukee and twenty-nine suburban districts into several districts, each of which would include a portion of the city and some suburban territory.[117]

Not surprisingly, suburbanites opposed metropolitan integration. Waukesha parents, for example, said they opposed long bus rides and a tax increase that would probably be necessary to fund the buses. They also resented what they perceived as Milwaukee's interference in their schools. McMurrin told suburban residents that he wanted to place magnet schools in their municipalities, but Wauwatosa's superintendent said that if magnet schools were all Milwaukee had to offer, he would prefer to create his own, rather than lose self-governance.[118] Even Dennis Conta, who had urged a merger of Shorewood, Whitefish Bay, and the east side of Milwaukee just a few years earlier, could not accept a plan as radical as the proposed merger, saying, "It is insulting, demeaning, and patronizing to tell blacks that the best way for them to at least receive a basic education is for them to attend school with whites." He also said that expecting schools to fix racism, a societal ill, was folly and that the magnet schools were improving education only for children who "attend specialty schools such as Golda Meir, Rufus King, and a small number of others."[119]

The lawsuit did not have universal support in Milwaukee's black community either. By the 1980s, African Americans had begun turning away from the assumption that integration was the key to solving school problems, rejecting the *Brown* premise and embracing one of black self-determination. Only 68 percent of African American survey respondents said they supported a metropolitan school district.[120] Most African Americans who objected to the lawsuit said they would prefer that the school board concentrate on improving education in the inner city. Several black officials spoke out publically against the lawsuit. State representative Polly Williams, an outspoken critic of busing, said she would fight any lawsuit and that the proposed city–suburban merger had nothing to do with improving the quality of education. Williams, a former welfare recipient and single mother of four, originally from Bezloni, Mississippi, had worked her way out of poverty and was elected to the state legislature in 1980. She stated that she did not accept "the notion that a black student must be sitting next to a white student in order to learn."[121]

Some people speculated at the time that the school board knew it would lose but was hoping that it could provoke the suburban districts into increasing participation in Chapter 220.[122] Indeed, Brown Deer superintendent Kenneth Moe tried to broker a compromise that would have created teams of advisers to visit Milwaukee schools and suburban schools, assess the strengths of each, and recommend integration plans.[123] Twenty-four superintendents endorsed his idea at a conference in January 1984.[124] The Milwaukee school board voted to postpone the lawsuit one month in an attempt to cooperate with the suburbs and give Moe more time.[125]

But the hope for voluntary metropolitan integration lasted less than three months. Lois Riley, an ardent supporter of integration, was unanimously elected president of the Milwaukee school board in April.[126] She immediately proposed a new plan that would have merged the city with twenty-four suburban districts into six districts. Riley's goal was to have an approximate mix of 45 percent white, 45 percent African American, and 10 percent "other" in Milwaukee schools by fall 1985.[127] The school board approved her plan on a six-to-three vote. Joyce Mallory, the only African American on the school board in 1984, was one of the three votes against Riley's plan, reflecting the new trend toward African American self-determination. The vote was largely symbolic, because the state legislature and governor would have needed to approve it anyway, and of course, no suburban district approved the plan.[128]

Riley said Milwaukee's specialty schools had a lot to offer to the suburban students and admitted the city needed suburban money: "The Milwaukee schools have to broaden their financial base. That's part of what this is all about. You can't just have your inner-city schools with kids who come from poor families." She said if the suburbs did not agree "the only alternative is to go to court."[129] And that is exactly what happened. The board voted six to three to pursue a lawsuit, independent of MIRC, against twenty-four suburban districts on June 27, 1984.[130]

The school board stood on tenuous legal ground, as it needed to prove that the suburban districts and the state of Wisconsin had intended to discriminate against Milwaukee children.[131] But the lawsuit encouraged suburban districts to come to the bargaining table rather than take the risk of having a desegregation plan imposed on them. A number of integration plans were discussed and debated over the next few years.[132] Eventually the city and suburbs agreed to set integration goals that were to be filled over a period of years, and the legislature agreed to increase aid to MPS to reduce class sizes.[133] The final settlement was reached in 1986–87. The districts of Shorewood, Whitefish Bay, Brown Deer, Menomonee Falls, Mequon–Theinsville, Greenfield, Greendale, and St. Francis agreed to open two thousand seven hundred spots for Milwaukee minority students, and Milwaukee would take in about nine thousand suburban students. This agreement represented a small increase in the number of students participating in Chapter 220.[134]

Thus, implementing desegregation had mixed results in Milwaukee. The magnet programs appeared to be academically sound on the surface, but some lacked substance. Busing was extremely complicated and expensive, and students were often not integrated within schools. When metropolitan integration was proposed, suburban school districts resisted it, and Chapter 220 emerged as a compromise. The most vigorous challenge to desegregation, however, would not be curricular issues, busing problems, or opposition from the suburbs. Parent opposition, from both the black and white communities, would be the main obstacle to reform. Some parents objected to busing, others wanted to control their own neighborhood schools, and none of the parents supported "forced choice," as the next chapter shows.

CHAPTER 4

REACTION TO MILWAUKEE'S MAGNET PLAN, 1976–1986

Public reactions to Judge Reynolds's desegregation decision were calm at first but later became volatile. They revealed some of Milwaukee's underlying racial politics. Craig Amos, who was thirteen years old in 1965, when the case was filed on behalf of him and forty other children, was twenty-three years old and attending the University of Wisconsin–Milwaukee when Reynolds handed down his decision. He felt that so much time had passed that the ruling no longer seemed relevant. Amos explained that he was supposed to attend Lincoln Junior–Senior High School, but his parents sent him to Morse Junior High, a white school, so he could receive a "quality" education. He said, "It wasn't worth it. I got nothing out of it. Nothing but fights and name calling." He remembered some white students yelling, "Nigger, go home. Go back to Africa."[1] Threats of physical violence eventually wore him down. He transferred to Lincoln, as he had originally wanted, and graduated from its senior high school program in 1970.[2]

Some whites, as Amos indicated, were racist, while others were open-minded about integration and supported magnet schools but did not want low-achieving students bused into their neighborhoods. Virtually no white parents were enthusiastic about their children being bused into what they perceived as unsafe, low-achieving schools. Therefore, African Americans shouldered most of the busing to minimize disruption in the white community. The choice some African Americans really wanted—

to attend their neighborhood schools—was denied to them. As a result, some African Americans and liberal whites lobbied for two-way busing, while the black power movement continued to gain strength under Howard Fuller and the Coalition to Save North Division. White migration from the city also increased as busing did.

Anthony Busalacchi, who was school board president from 1978 to 1979, predicted the busing would accelerate white flight. "In reality, this plan will only segregate the city of Milwaukee," Busalacchi said. "I envision a white migration to private and parochial schools and, where financially possible, a flight completely out of the county."[3] Busalacchi even threatened Gronouski with a restraining order. Liberal board members criticized Busalacchi for opposing busing, but he pointed out that his children attended integrated schools, whereas some other board members sent their children to private schools. To this day, he holds firm to his conviction that breaking up neighborhood schools and requiring students to ride buses caused white flight.[4]

Busalacchi may have been correct about whites departing for the suburbs and parochial schools, but white parents looking to evade integration received no help from the Milwaukee Archdiocese, which declared that Catholic schools would not be havens for racists. The archdiocese hired a consultant to work on integration, teacher in-services, and curriculum. It also proposed that the archdiocese accept African American students at public expense, articulating an idea that would become part of the "school choice" voucher plan of the 1990s. In return, the white students at parochial schools would participate in public school specialty programs for part of the day. Relations between the archdiocese and Milwaukee Public Schools soured in spring 1976, however, when one thousand eighth-graders graduated from Catholic elementary schools and enrolled in MPS high schools. MPS considered them new students, which meant they were given low priority in school assignment. About two hundred of them were assigned to schools that were far from their homes or were once predominantly African American.[5] The MPS–archdiocesan exchange plan never materialized.

Few elected officials supported desegregation if it involved busing. State senator Monroe Swan, an African American and professed black nationalist, said he was more interested in quality education than integrated education and said he hoped some black schools would be left intact.[6] White elected officials, including Milwaukee Mayor Henry Maier, state senators James F. Sensenbrenner and Wayne Whittow, and US Representative Clement J. Zablocki staunchly defended the neighborhood school system.[7] Zablocki said he was so upset by Reynolds's ruling that "it makes my blood boil every time his name is mentioned." He claimed it was a waste of time for children to endure long bus rides that may have involved three or four hours of transportation time and questioned Reynolds's objectivity, stating, "Federal judges are supposed to be removed from politics, but I have yet to see one who doesn't have politics on his sleeve."[8] Circuit court judge Christ Seraphim sharply criticized his judicial colleague. Although he claimed he did not support segregation, speaking at the racially exclusive Eagles Club, Seraphim chastised Reynolds for taking too long to reach a decision and for exceeding his constitutional authority, saying the decision "would tear down the fabric of our society."[9] Governor Pat Lucey was more moderate and simply said he would comply with the ruling and hoped there would be a peaceful transition, unlike what had happened in Boston.[10]

The *Milwaukee Sentinel* polled nearly 400 Milwaukee households, 115 of which had school-aged children, in 1976, at the time of Reynolds's initial decision. Of the 115, 72 percent said they would prefer to have their children attend integrated schools, but 61 percent opposed busing. A racial divide was evident; 65 percent of African American respondents supported busing. Some of the other 35 percent articulated fear for their children's safety at white schools in the city. Half the white parents who were against busing said they would put their children in private or parochial schools to avoid involuntary busing. Another 10 percent said they would leave the city for the suburbs, and 34 percent said they would take other steps, including protests and keeping their children at home. Most concerned parents cited safety issues in north side schools, and some referenced the violence in Boston. But 17 percent of white parents admitted they wanted their children to attend all-white schools.[11] Some busing critics opposed a tax increase that would be necessary to pay for the buses.[12] Other survey data showed Latinos generally supported desegregation, but Native Americans worried they might lose their racial identity if busing was forced on them.[13] Residents of the Sherman Park community, a racially diverse part of Milwaukee, were divided: 31 percent thought integration would have a positive effect on the quality of education, 26 percent thought it would have no effect, 27 percent thought it would have a negative effect, and 16 percent did not know.[14] According to another *Milwaukee Sentinel* poll, 56 percent of city residents believed the suburbs should be part of integration, and 64 percent of suburbanites said they supported busing African American students to their schools.[15]

Many Milwaukeeans revealed in interviews that they liked the voluntary nature of McMurrin's magnet plan but they doubted it would actually achieve racial integration. They expected involuntary busing would soon follow.[16] An African American woman told a reporter that personal freedom should not be sacrificed in the name of desegregation: "If my son wanted to go to Fox Point, no one should tell him he can't. But if he doesn't want to go, he shouldn't have to." Several white parents said busing was unfair to people who had purchased homes in the middle-class parts of the city. One remarked, "You're paying taxes to live in a better area. If your children have to be sent to a school outside their district . . . it's Communist." White parents expressed fear that their children would be removed from their neighborhood schools and sent to areas of the city they perceived as unsafe. A white woman said, "I guess I'm the type of person who doesn't care who gets bused in, but I don't want my kids bused out." One white man, whose wife was a substitute teacher at Lincoln High School, called Lincoln a black prison, saying, "Now what's going to happen when they bus a whole lot of black students over the viaduct to the South Side? The people aren't going to accept that. You know what I mean by that."[17]

That last quote is key to understanding the white mind-set. It was spoken in a kind of code; no one wanted to admit it, but even though many white Milwaukeeans publicly said they favored integration as long as their children were not bused, they privately did not want any integration at all. White Milwaukeeans simply could not accept their children going to school with African American children, whether for racial reasons or out of a fear of a decline in educational standards.

Reaction in Milwaukee's black leadership was mixed. Lawrence Harwell, director of Triple O, feared for the safety of black children in white schools. He also questioned the benefits of integration and said it "somehow covers up the key issue, which is how to make every school in this city a quality school."[18] According to the *Milwaukee Courier*, an African American newspaper, many African Americans agreed with him.[19]

Milwaukee Urban League president Wesley Scott, on the other hand, took the more traditional integrationist viewpoint, saying busing was necessary to achieve equality. Frederick Carr, chair of the Black Administrators and Supervisors Council in the Milwaukee Public Schools, supported Reynolds's decision. He also said he liked McMurrin's magnet plan but predicted that involuntary busing would be necessary. O. C. White, a popular Milwaukee radio personality and head of an inner-city youth group, encouraged parents to get involved in formulating the desegregation plan. Both he and Carr believed countywide integration was necessary; otherwise white flight would result in the city becoming entirely African American.[20]

Students' reactions to integration varied. According to newspaper accounts, white students harassed African Americans at Hamilton High School. Hamilton's enrollment increased from 92 African American students (3.6 percent of all students) in 1975 to 538 (20 percent of all students) in 1976. A carload of white students hurled objects at a bus carrying African American students home after school on September 21, resulting in at least one minor injury.[21] Rumors spread about African American students carrying guns. Violent clashes took place between African Americans and "greasers," a white subculture that prized rebellion against authority. Several African American students said they felt unwanted at the school. As student Lisa Mann lamented, "Why can't you respect us the way we respect you?" Principal Robert Temple, several assistant principals, and security guards patrolled the hall and grounds trying to ease tensions.[22]

White students at Hamilton complained about the lack of self-discipline among African American classmates. For example, a story circulated that African American students urinated on the wildcat mascot mosaic on the floor of the main entrance. Some white students claimed that Africans Americans behaved badly at school dances.[23] Whites also said African Americans were not punished for their actions, and about fifty white students staged a walkout in protest at the beginning of the 1983–84 school year. They claimed that black gangs fought without the serious response from school officials, and that white students were afraid to go to school. Some white students actually called the *Milwaukee Journal* to explain their reasons for protesting. They accused the school administration of covering up racial problems. "They say we are prejudiced, but we are plain scared," said one junior girl. A freshman boy added, "If people can't walk by black people without putting their heads down, that is not a school, that is a hangout." A third student said the purpose of the walkout was to alert the public to what was "really going on" at Hamilton, claiming that white students "don't want to be pushed around anymore."[24]

But former Hamilton teachers report that stories in the *Milwaukee Journal* and *Milwaukee Sentinel* were overblown. Arlo Coplin, who was chairperson for the Physical Education Department in the 1970s and became a guidance counselor in the late 1980s and early 1990s, recalled few problems among students. He said the white students were apprehensive at first because they had limited contact with African Americans prior to integration. He acknowledged that some fights had occurred between black groups and white groups. But fights had taken place between white students prior to integration, so nothing had really changed other than skin color.[25]

A guidance counselor who requested anonymity agreed with Coplin, saying integration did not seriously alter the climate at the school. One problem she did recall, however, was that African American students were added to Hamilton in the middle of summer, which overloaded some classes. She said the whole school had to be reprogrammed three weeks into the school year and that some white students resented being removed from classes where they were earning A's. But the counselor said she thought the anger was about grades, not about race.[26] Scott Hirsch, who attended Hamilton from 1975 until 1978 and who worked as a safety aide at Hamilton in the 1990s, remembered a lot of anger and confusion over the reprogramming.[27] Some classes remained overcrowded despite the reprogramming, and some students wanted to transfer to less crowded suburban or parochial schools.[28]

James Jones was an art teacher who came to Hamilton in 1976. Jones, an African American, grew up in Rockford, Illinois, and attended Buena Vista University in Iowa. He said he always had a lot of white friends and was used to multicultural groups. His first job in Milwaukee was at Robert Fulton Junior High in 1969. He said he went to see the principal after the first day of school and asked where all the white children were, because he did not realize how segregated Milwaukee was. Jones said Fulton was at least 90 percent African American. He said he enjoyed his time there but realized he had to leave after seven years after his car was vandalized. He ended up at Hamilton in the first year of integration and was surprised to find out that even though many African American students were bused to Hamilton, few, if any, neighborhood students were bused out. Robert Temple, Hamilton's principal during much of the 1970s, asked him to take over the school's newly created human relations position. Jones accepted it and worked to improve relations between students and faculty through multicultural activities and a student–faculty advisory committee. He returned to the classroom after a few years and became chair of the Art Department and head basketball coach.[29]

Former Hamilton students also reported positive experiences with integration. Jeff Kartz said most white students accepted African American classmates.[30] Dena Platow agreed, saying she hadn't been concerned about racial violence, although she acknowledged a noticeable change in student behavior after integration: "We never had to worry about vandalism in the bathrooms until then."[31] Hirsch, who served on the human relations committee, remembered some fights over territory—for example, one of the doors to the school was the "greaser door"—but territorial conflicts had always existed. He also said the white students and teachers were unprepared for low-achieving African American students. The teachers were used to higher-achieving students and did not have much training on working with students who were below grade level and had learning styles that were different from those of middle-class students. He believes teachers might have had an easier time adjusting their pedagogy for the new students if the students had been phased into the school, perhaps starting at the elementary level.[32]

Eventually, some white parents took their children out of Hamilton and put them in parochial schools or suburban schools, but they claimed their decisions had nothing to do with race. John Semancik, for example, sent his two sons to Martin Luther High School, which was both parochial and suburban, to attend smaller classes with fewer disruptive students. One of his daughters also left Hamilton for the same reason, but he said she had gotten a fine education there before she left, and she went on to become a successful artist.[33]

Kenneth Knoll, who was also on the Hamilton cluster committee, agreed that the onset of integration was generally successful. Knoll had been a teacher and a principal in Greenfield and in the rural Milwaukee County school district that had preceded the modern suburban districts.

He said he remembered some fights and assaults at Bell Junior High School and Hamilton but said they were not race-based. In his view, lax discipline and tolerance of fighting was simply a sign of the times. Knoll never tolerated fighting, profanity, or other negative behaviors in his own school, and he eventually took his children out of MPS when he saw increases in these problems.[34]

As MPS entered its second year of desegregation in 1977, white students needed to volunteer for integration to clear out space in south side schools for African Americans. Many white parents did not want to remove their children from neighborhood schools and became angry when their children were bused to the north side. That year, more than a thousand such cases existed. Keith Malkowski is one example. Keith and his parents lived a few blocks from Lake Michigan and, along with fifty-five thousand other families, received information packets on desegregation in May 1977. These families were informed that they would face possible mandatory reassignment if they did not fill out transfer forms. The form allowed parents to list their top three choices, and the Malkowskis wrote "Fernwood" for all three and added the following message: "The above choice is our *one* and *only, positively without a doubt.*" The Malkowskis had sent Keith to Fernwood, which was only four blocks from their home, since he was in first grade, with the exception of one year at a Catholic school. Keith was in sixth grade in 1976–77, and his parents wanted him to complete seventh and eighth grades at Fernwood, where he could easily walk back and forth to school and come home for lunch. By listing Fernwood three times on the application, Keith risked being involuntarily assigned to a school if he was not readmitted to Fernwood, but Christine Malkowski did not care. "If I have to carry a folding chair and take my child into the seventh grade class at Fernwood next year and sit him down in it, I'll do that," she said. She also admitted that she and her neighbors did not believe the desegregation order applied to them: "We kept hearing how voluntary it would be and we thought that meant we'd never really have to become involved."[35]

Parochial students had even less choice. As previously stated, students in Catholic schools were given the lowest priority in school assignment if they chose to enroll in public school. Diane Duncan, for example, graduated from eighth grade at St. Florian's school in 1977. Faced with the prospect of paying tuition at a Catholic high school, Diane and her parents chose to fill out an application to enroll at Walker Junior High, the public junior high school closest to their home, for grade nine, after which she would attend a senior high school for grades ten to twelve. Audubon Junior High School and Bell Junior High School, also close to their home, were their second and third choices. But MPS assigned her and at least three other St. Florian graduates to Edison Junior High School on the north side of the city to integrate it. When interviewed, Diane's father said he did not mind his daughter attending school with African Americans but objected to the half hour bus ride his daughter would face: "I think it's fine to integrate the school system if they could do it without busing the kids. I've been paying property taxes here for 21 years, even though my daughter was attending parochial school. Now when I want her to go to public school down the block, they say she has to take a bus all the way across town, just because she's white."[36]

About a hundred white parents went to the school board shortly before the 1977–78 school year began to try to have the board rescind the mandatory assignments. Some parents demanded that McMurrin be fired. "The things that were once important in our schools—reading, writing, and arithmetic—are now forgotten. That's what this school system was set up for, not integration," said Frank Augustine. He received loud applause when he said "the biggest mistake ever made was in hiring McMurrin." Another parent claimed that his twelve-year-old son still could not read and that desegregation was doing nothing to help him. Other parents described mandatory school assignments as "a communist plot," "a Soviet scheme," and "akin to a three-ring circus."[37]

But not all white Milwaukee residents objected to mandatory busing. The *Milwaukee Journal,* for example, said integration was proceeding much more smoothly than in other cities, and a 1979 *Milwaukee Sentinel* survey found that about 60 percent of all parents and more than 70 percent of all teachers agreed with the statement "Children of different races get along at my school."[38] Parents hailed the Montessori schools for their innovative programs, and Washington High School, once the site of race riots, was singled out as a model for integration by the Sherman Park Community Association, which recognized the school at a fine arts celebration attended by more than four hundred people.[39]

Joel McNally, a white reporter for the *Milwaukee Journal* and a long-time liberal activist, enrolled his children in Lloyd Street School. He said he was watching the television news in July 1976 and was appalled and a bit frightened when they announced the small number of white students who had chosen to enroll at Lloyd. According to McNally, "The MPS administration hadn't done a thing to recruit people."[40] To rectify the problem, McNally and his wife organized a group of parents who recruited white families through house meetings, phone banks, potluck dinners, and school tours. He also complained about the lack of an adequate library at Lloyd: "We raised hell immediately, and a library was created. I don't believe for a minute that black parents weren't upset about the library before integration. But until white parents started yelling and screaming, the administration didn't care."[41]

Gronouski and some members of C/100 made public statements against "one-way busing," in which African Americans were bused in disproportionately larger numbers than were whites, and People United for Integrated and Quality Education (or simply People United) organized around the issue.[42] A total of 12,700 African Americans were scheduled for busing—either voluntary or involuntary—in the 1977–78 school year, compared to a mere 1,800 whites. That was one out of three black students, compared to one in thirty-eight white students.[43] People United advocated for pairing and clustering of schools. For example, students at a black elementary school and white elementary school would attend grades one through three at the white school and grades four through six at the black school. The organization's ambitious platform also called for more multicultural education, more bilingual education, an end to tracking (assigning students to classes based on ability level), changes in the way discipline referrals and suspensions were handled, counseling for students with substance abuse problems, use of affirmative action, and a boycott of corporations that did business in apartheid South Africa.[44]

People United criticized what it saw as overuse of suspensions as a means of disciplining students. It cited a study by the Social Development Commission that found African American students who were in white-majority schools in Milwaukee were suspended five to ten times more often than white students, compared to a rate triple that of whites nationwide.[45] One of the fliers from People United addressed the issue of suspensions this way:

Do you care about suspensions? . . . For every one white suspension
there are three black suspensions. Part of the reason there are so
many suspensions is because they're not teaching in a more modern way than just old-fashioned teaching methods. The MPS does
not have uniform rules defining what students can be suspended
for. Suspensions are not used as a last resort but as the typical
method of discipline—students can be suspended for breathing
out of turn! Racist administrators and administrators who tolerate
racism make it even more difficult for minority students.[46]

People United attempted to organize the black, white, and Latino
communities through meetings, pickets, and "speak-outs," which were
gatherings where individuals could approach a microphone and "speak
out" their concerns about a specific topic.[47] It also emphasized student involvement and issued a high school students' bill of rights, which called
for, among other things, a discipline appeal board with equal numbers
of teachers, administrators, and students; a truancy council run by students; freedom of speech and press; expanded tutoring and counseling
opportunities; an increase in minority and social history; the right to
grade teachers; the right to leave campus during the day; and the right to
smoke cigarettes.[48]

When Bob Peterson, cofounder of People United, was asked thirty
years later about why the organization was largely unsuccessful, he said
MPS refused to adopt two-way busing and reforms due to the "white
power structure" in the community and "spineless" white leadership. He
was particularly critical of Superintendent McMurrin, whom he referred
to as "Mr. Smiling Face." From Peterson's point of view, McMurrin was
unwilling to take the necessary steps to bring about bilateral busing and
curricular reform because such steps would have disrupted the white
community. Peterson accused the school board of "dragging its feet" by
accepting integration on the surface but delaying implementation while
it appealed Reynolds's decision. He also noted that specialty schools received extra funding to improve education but other schools did not.
According to Peterson, all schools should have received more funding
to improve curriculum and human relations work, both of which would
have encouraged whites to stay in them. Peterson also was disappointed
in the lack of leadership at the city, county, and state levels and said that

he considered John Gronouski to be "obnoxious" because he did not allow public hearings as he formulated his integration plan.[49]

African Americans also organized outside of People United. They were not unified in their opinion of integration. As explained in previous chapters, African Americans in Milwaukee were divided into three distinct groups.[50] Black business interests tended to oppose integration out of fear that it would upset the white business community. Others wanted voluntary integration without mandatory assignments, and the third group favored black community control over black schools and was adamantly opposed to magnet schools. The Black Administrators and Supervisors Council, Larry Harwell, and the *Milwaukee Courier* opposed one-way busing.[51] Joyce Mallory, who was on the school board and was a member of the local NAACP chapter, complained about long bus rides, white teachers' failure to teach African American students effectively, new discipline policies in white schools that were aimed at African Americans, and lack of opportunities for African American parents to provide input into how the white schools were run.[52] Former Urban League director Wesley Scott put it this way: "Blacks didn't have much input into the schools in the first place. This plan made it even worse."[53]

No one involved wanted to publicly admit it at the time, but the basic premise of busing was to bus only African American students and to leave white students where they were to minimize white flight. Deputy Superintendent David Bennett was the chief architect of Milwaukee's busing plan, and Bennett admitted this strategy in 1999 when he mentioned it twice at a forum on race issues. Anthony Busalacchi agreed, saying, "It was an issue of how do we least disrupt the white community."[54]

An organization named Blacks for Two-Way Integration formed in the spring of 1977 under the leadership of Larry Harwell.[55] According to their figures, 7,328 African American pupils were bused in 1976-77, the first year of integration, while only 985 whites were bused. African American students were removed from forty black schools to attend ninety-five white schools. It also said that 1,939 African Americans were "forced to volunteer" in 1977-78.[56] Blacks for Two-Way Integration found those statistics appalling. It recommended that some black schools be allowed to remain black, that busing be two-way (bilateral, instead of unilateral, black-only busing), that African Americans have more access to magnet schools, and that other schools receive new curricula.[57]

The school board's Committee on Community and Advisory Group Relations responded to Blacks for Two-Way Integration. The committee stated that no school would be allowed to have an African American population of more than 30 percent under the court order and two-way busing would be impossible without a completely mandatory system of school assignments. The committee ignored the fact that African American students were often denied admission to magnet schools in their neighborhoods in order to make room for whites and said it was doing all it could to reform curricula.[58] It also said it would like to devote more personnel to teaching but that it needed to prioritize having enough staff for discipline and security.[59]

Blacks for Two-Way Integration decided to take a vote in the black community. African Americans were given three options: follow the board's planned busing assignments, send their children to neighborhood schools, or boycott MPS altogether. Ballots also asked voters to decide whether they favored unilateral integration, as the school board did, or bilateral integration. A public forum was held prior to the vote, at which speaker after speaker talked about the "victims" of busing amid chants of "two-way or no way." "If we don't say 'two way or no way,' then we're saying Caucasians care more about their children than we do," said Marzuq Madyun, a Black Muslim. Marvin Echols, a former teacher, added, "This day hopefully marks the end of an era, an era when white folks tell us what happens to our kids." Future state legislator Polly Williams said that black communities were built around schools. In her view, losing control of the school meant losing control of the neighborhood.[60]

More than four thousand African Americans voted. The results were tallied, revealing that more than 60 percent of voters wanted to send their children to neighborhood schools, more than 30 percent supported a boycott, and fewer than 10 percent supported the school board's integration plan. More than 90 percent of all voters also said they favored bilateral busing over unilateral busing.[61]

Student opinion was at least as important as adult opinion. The students at Marshall High School had mixed reactions to integration. Although little violence had taken place, African Americans reported feeling isolated in what was still a mostly white school. Jill Gilmer, an African American student and member of Marshall's human relations council, observed that students were still self-segregated within the school and that whites still controlled the school's culture. She explained that students had problems in electing black class officers or having black music played at events in the white-majority school, saying, "Blacks might not feel that they are really wanted or belong [at Marshall]." She added, "We've got a mixture of kids from all sorts of schools. Some are coming from mainly black [schools,] and this is an entirely different setting. Many people feel uprooted." She said the human relations council tried to promote integrated events, but they sometimes turned into all-white or all-black occasions.[62] Larry Totsky, a white student, said change was coming slowly and that he could see that his younger brothers were more open-minded than his friends were. Cathy Pattillo, another white student, echoed similar sentiments about slow change:

> The black students who have been here for three years are just getting used to it and relationships are better, but for the 200 new black students, most are still acting like they did in their former schools. Many of them are still wearing T-shirts with the names of their old school, they don't identify with Marshall. It isn't so much a matter of black or white, it depends on the normal behavior of their group and what is expected of them. The teachers don't have time to change a whole lifestyle. We have to give the new black students a while—we can't expect them to catch up all at once.[63]

Reactions at King were a bit more positive. As indicated earlier, MPS removed the (black) neighborhood population from King so it could become the flagship magnet school with a college-bound program. In other words, all the students who attended King were there voluntarily and because they had passed an entrance exam; most people expected that King's highly motivated students would react positively to integration. Vanessa James, an African American student who had attended King both before and after integration, said the school had made slow progress, and Tarome Alford, another African American student, gave positive reviews: "Now that I'm here I'm proud of the school and my classmates. I have white friends too, and we all want the best education possible. I did find that the courses were harder . . . but we have more on the honor roll at King this year—it's become more than just a display of names and we want to keep it that way."[64]

Marshall had been in transition from white to black for several years, and King was voluntarily integrated, which meant students at both schools were fairly well prepared for integration. The situation at Bay View High School was much different. Bay View is a neighborhood on the south side of the city, near Lake Michigan. It was several miles from the African American part of Milwaukee. It has a long tradition of independence, and in fact, it was an independent village from 1879 until 1887. It is characterized by close-knit residents and locally owned businesses; even in the twenty-first century, Bay View has few chain stores.[65] Opinions on integration varied from mixed to hostile at Bay View High School. Elizabeth Dziennik, a white student, said the effort to integrate worked well when students worked together on an activity that was of interest to all, such as sports or music; but when students were not interested in an activity, perhaps something forced on them by school administrators, students were not likely to participate. One student, La Donna Goskowicz, stated that more students and parents had to get involved in activities that brought people of different races together if they were going to be successful.[66]

The examples above, while not entirely flattering, were not entirely negative either. They were, however, from an MPS-produced document, so they may not accurately reflect the opinions of the general student population. Some documentary filmmakers solicited other opinions at Bay View High School in 1980 and concluded that African American students were not really given a choice about where they would attend school. The filmmakers referred to it as a "forced choice," a term coined by an African American student who said he wanted to attend his neighborhood high school but was forced to make a different choice that would help with integration. He was not alone. An African American student at Bay View angrily said this about desegregation: "Hell, I got to go all the way out on South Kinnickinnic Avenue to get an education. I mean that was offered to me. I was told I couldn't go to Lincoln Junior-Senior High School [a black school]. I had to go somewhere else, and the only three choices I had was South, Pulaski, and Bay View," all of which were white schools.[67] In other words, this student's viewpoint was very much the same as that of Keith Malkowski's mother, whose only desire was to send her son to Fernwood Elementary School.

Some of the other African American students at Bay View were more open-minded about integration, but the white students appeared to be universally opposed to desegregation. Several of the white students casually used the word *nigger* in the interviews. Some girls who were passing by the camera crew yelled it out and laughed about it. Many said the African American students did not care about academic success: "They send the niggers here. Nine-tenths of them don't want to learn. All they want to do is just sit around in class and fuck around and stuff and screw up." Another student suggested taking all the "niggers" out in the ocean and drowning them or sending them back to Africa. Several students of both races recommended a return to segregated neighborhood schools. One white student said he would rather drop out than attend a school on the north side.[68]

Many African Americans felt the same way. Space had to be made available for white students at north side schools. Therefore, minority enrollment was restricted. For example, only one hundred neighborhood students were allowed to attend Garfield Elementary, which was a school of three hundred students with an open education specialty. The school had asked for the open education program two years prior to the court order, but the school board refused to grant the school's request. Vice Principal Lee Davis expressed her disappointment at the time: "We wanted [open education] for our neighborhood. We were not given it. But then when we got it, many of our neighborhood people had left, because they had to leave because of integration. It was hard to do anything positive without hurting someone, and it is unfortunate—it appears—that most of the uprooted population has been blacks."[69]

UWM professor Michael Barndt, a special consultant to the federal court during the desegregation proceedings, explained it this way:

> The specialty schools set up in white areas in most all cases were such that there was room in those schools for black students to come in without displacing those students. [In] specialty schools in black areas, the reverse was the case: There was no room in the school—it was usually overcrowded to begin with. Black students had to move to reduce overcrowding. Black students had to move to accommodate whites.[70]

Some African American parents complained when they needed to get their children on waiting lists to get into what had been their neighborhood schools. To enroll their children in the city schools of their choice, families would have had to move to the suburbs. Now that their schools had more desirable programs, they could no longer attend them.[71]

Most north side schools, however, failed to attract substantial numbers of white students from the south side or the suburbs. Logically, as African American families began enrolling in south side schools, north side schools began to lose enrollment, which increased the per-pupil cost of operating them. Therefore, the superintendent and school board decided to close some underenrolled north side schools to save money.[72] Sixteen black schools were closed between 1976 and 1980, the first four years of desegregation, displacing about forty-six thousand African American students and sixteen thousand white students.[73] These closures also had the effect of forcing African American students to "choose" south side schools.

The closures also provoked a strong reaction in the black community. Lincoln High School, for example, which had faced declining enrollment for years, still had strong alumni support and many people, including Mallory and Dwaine Washington of the Coalition of Peaceful Schools, spoke out against its closure.[74] The closing of Wells Street Junior High School, which had a gifted and talented program, was also controversial. But the board deemed it necessary because it wanted to send Wells's students to Rufus King, which housed the college-bound program for students in grades six through twelve.[75] The proposed closure of North Division High School in 1976, however, provoked the most controversy and represented a shift in black leadership in Milwaukee. No longer were Lloyd Barbee and middle-class African Americans in control of the civil rights movement. Rather, a grassroots movement, led by Howard Fuller and sustained by the lower class, grew to advocate for community control, not integration, of schools.[76]

North Division had several problems. The original building opened in 1906 and was in a sad state of disrepair by 1973, described by one teacher as "an archaic, depressing, dungeon-like building coming apart at the seams."[77] School board president Donald J. O'Connell, a member of the liberal faction, proposed that the school be closed and that its students be bused to white schools, an idea the community surrounding North Division strongly opposed. North Division was an important part of Milwaukee's black community, and residents said they would rather see a new building opened with an improved educational plan.[78] Eventually, the board voted to construct a new building, but debate went on for months over the location—the county refused to sell parkland to the school board for the favored site for the new school, and the community opposed another proposal that would have moved the school several blocks from its original site.[79] Then a fire burned a portion of North Division, closing it for a few days.[80] With repairs estimated to cost two hundred thousand dollars, it appeared that the board might reverse course, close the school, and divert its funds to the construction of the new South Division and Vincent high schools.[81] But the community surrounding North Division vowed to fight for a new school, even if it was not integrated.[82] Some even said they would rather keep the old school open and under neighborhood control if it was the only way to keep their children from being bused out.[83] Community activist Larry Harwell urged a walkout if North students were forced to leave.[84]

The board decided to go ahead with construction and, based on Superintendent McMurrin's recommendation, assigned North Division a medical and dental specialty.[85] The new $20 million building finally opened on September 5, 1978, at Eleventh and Center Streets.[86] It had state-of-the-art medical and dental laboratories and a field house that contained an Olympic-size pool, four basketball courts, and an indoor track. Each academic subject had its own resource center with reference books and special materials, and a computer that "looks like a television set" was installed with twenty student terminals.[87]

But despite the state-of-the-art facilities, the new North Division attracted only about 100 white students out of a student body of 1,700.[88] The racial disparity was probably the result of North Division's proximity to Rufus King High School, which was more attractive to white students.[89] King had become a citywide school with a competitive admissions process under the integration plan, which made it appealing to white parents, whereas most of North Division's students came from the surrounding neighborhood. Most of North's African American students treated their white classmates with respect, but some white students reported physical and verbal harassment, including racial slurs. As for academics, some students said classes were excellent, but others said the quality of learning suffered from the high truancy rate among African Americans.[90]

McMurrin suggested that integration would be more successful if the board converted North Division to citywide status, like King High School and Milwaukee Trade and Technical High School. But that conversion would have meant clearing the school of most of its neighborhood students. As could be expected, McMurrin's plan set off a firestorm,[91] despite the support of two African American school board members, Leon Todd and Marion McEvilly.[92] Five hundred students marched four miles from North Division to a school board meeting in a peaceful protest seeking to retain control of their school.[93] One junior said, in reference to white students, "We were here first."[94] Some of North Division's teachers—both African American and white—agreed and helped students stage a protest outside of the building at the end of the school year. As one teacher said, "Why can't the kids stay here? There's an undercurrent of racism here. The school board really feels they can't bring any white kids here until they move the black ones out."[95] Likewise, one North alumnus said, "When I look at integration so far, I see a bunch of black students depressed because they don't have anywhere to go except where the school board sends them. They are being forced to accept the blunt end of integration." Howard Fuller, another North alumnus, chastised the school board when it approved McMurrin's plan: "We exist. We have rights. We want North Division to be a special school, not a specialty school. You took Lincoln and Rufus King and now you want North. We say no!" Other speakers at the school board meeting pointed out that the board was willing to keep North Division a neighborhood school when it was in the old building. They felt cheated, as if white students were taking over their school. As one person said, "When the school was full of rats and rodents, nothing was said."[96]

McMurrin held firm: "Can North be racially balanced and still allow the present North Division students to remain in the school and be graduated? We believe the answer is no."[97] The following exchange between a North Division student and McMurrin from the documentary *Forced Choice* is enlightening:

STUDENT: I don't never hear you talk about going to the south side and making them integrate. See, but you make us go out, but you don't make them come in.

MCMURRIN: Because we tried. We are trying to do this, if we can, on the basis of choice.

STUDENT: But it's almost a *forced choice*. Everybody knows . . . back in
'75–'76, they pushed us. We didn't have no choice. You told us we
couldn't come to North. Can I ask you a question again? Custer is
perfect[ly integrated], ain't it?

McMURRIN: Do you know how we did it?

STUDENT: Oh, how did you do it? By forcing '75–'76 North out. It wasn't
no "open the door." You all opened it, but you pushed us through it
too. We didn't have a choice now. What I feel it was, was in '75–'76,
you all just cut up the black junior high schools and sent them all
where you wanted to.

McMURRIN: I think they [the white students] will come in.

STUDENT: No, you won't.

McMURRIN: You don't think white[s] will come in? To integrate, you
gotta have both black and white.

STUDENT: That's right. That's what I'm saying. . . . If you send all them
white kids that's gonna go to Vincent next year to these black schools
down here, you could even integrate Lincoln all the way. Integration,
as a whole, we ain't integrating. It's a one-way thing.

McMURRIN: It's gotta be two ways.

STUDENT: It's not two ways.

McMURRIN: If it's not two ways it won't work.

STUDENT: But see, they're not going to do this voluntarily. You gotta
make them like you did us in '75–'76. Everybody knows this.[98]

Fuller organized the Coalition to Save North Division. He was the perfect person for the job—tall, athletic, educated, eloquent, a North Division alumnus, and well connected in the black community. He had been
mentored by former Urban League director Wesley Scott and maintained
friendships with several black clergymen, community activists, and politicians, including Polly Williams. According to historian Bill Dahlk, Fuller's unique background enabled him to win support with some white
school board members and the editorial boards of the *Milwaukee Journal*
and the *Milwaukee Sentinel*.[99]

Fuller also was a passionate advocate for black nationalism and was
a natural leader. Raised Catholic, Fuller had attended St. Boniface grade
school, where he was the only African American in his third-grade class.
He was also one of the first African American students to attend Carroll

College in Waukesha, Wisconsin, where he was elected president of the student senate. He obtained a master's degree in social administration from Western Reserve University in Cleveland, Ohio, and became involved in Cleveland's school integration movement in 1964. He traveled to North Carolina in 1965 and founded and directed the Malcolm X Liberation University until 1973 and then went to Mozambique with the African liberation forces, which fought to overthrow Portuguese colonial rule. He eventually returned to Milwaukee to earn a doctorate in education from Marquette University and then held the position of associate director of Marquette's Educational Opportunity Program.[100] He began to organize in the black community in 1979 and was deeply concerned about the message that was sent to young African Americans when MPS converted black neighborhood schools to citywide specialty schools: "You're saying it makes it easier to get whites to come if you get rid of all those incorrigibles. Then you can say [to whites], 'You can come to school with blacks more like yourselves.'"[101]

Fuller was right. That was exactly what the school board was saying. The board felt it had to do something to make North Division a more attractive choice for whites. Leon Todd believed citywide specialty status was the best thing for all students. In his own words: "North Division is an academic cesspool. It is a cancer that manifests itself in severe below-average test scores. Five hundred per day are truant. The students are trapped there in concentration camps of underachievement."[102] He also said, "If it takes making North Division a citywide specialty to get it integrated, let's get on with the job."[103] Lois Riley, who was white and had a daughter at North Division, stated that such a busing plan was also in the best interest of underachieving African Americans: "The fact is North Division has the highest failure rate of any school in this system. Maybe it's true that they [underachievers] have to sit next to a higher achiever to succeed. Maybe they have to sit next to a white. I don't know. Just maybe, just maybe, if they see that kid taking books home and learning, they'll do the same."[104]

Fuller disagreed, saying he believed it was possible to teach underachievers, even if they were all in one school. Fuller blamed the failures of the students on the school itself. He said the secretarial and engineering staffs were too small and that many of the teachers were inexperienced and white.[105] Fuller and Michael Barndt both argued that the Milwaukee integration plan was psychologically damaging to African American students. It was as though the school board and superintendent were saying that black schools were bad and white schools were good, and that if any student attended a black school, he or she was a bad student.[106] Wesley Scott, president of the Urban League, predicted increased truancy if North Division's students were forced into long bus rides to south side schools.[107] North students said they felt as though they were mere pawns in desegregation. As student Lisa Smith said: "We are tired of being shuffled about with virtually no say in what goes on in our lives while the whites are still being given a vast number of alternatives."[108]

The school board ignored the community's pleas to keep North Division a neighborhood school and went ahead with the citywide medical specialty, which would have eliminated the neighborhood enrollment had it been fully implemented.[109] Fuller responded in a number of ways. He filed a complaint with the US Office of Civil Rights, claiming the school board was guilty of racial discrimination. And when McMurrin eliminated the North Division's ninth grade in the fall of 1979 to make room for white students in 1980, Fuller urged the students who would have been freshmen at North Division to skip the first day of school and attend a rally at the school instead.[110] About 250 students did so. Several parents also showed up, forced their way into the building, and tried to register their children.[111] Some students threatened to drop out of school if they could not attend North.[112] Fuller encouraged a boycott, and hundreds of African American students responded by walking out of North Division in the middle of the day. They walked to a nearby church, where they listened to a minister who criticized MPS for "a lackadaisical approach" to educating African American students.[113]

Public opinion began to swing toward Fuller. A national group called the Interreligious Foundation for Community Organizations supported his stance, as did the NAACP.[114] The Milwaukee Teacher Education Association; the *Milwaukee Journal* and *Milwaukee Sentinel*; and Milwaukee's two chief African American newspapers, the *Courier* and *Community Journal*, also came out against the plan for North Division.[115] US Magistrate Ruth Lafave ordered a hearing on the plan.[116] Alan Freeman, a well-known law professor from the University of Minnesota, argued that desegregation had come at the expense of the black community and that it was time for a reversal of policy to one that made integration voluntary and provided African American students with choices. In his own words:

> There's a time for new strategy. I call it the victim perspective on racial discrimination. The law is constantly trying to look at [school desegregation] from the perpetrator perspective. Something is very, very wrong. Somehow things have been twisted when kids other than those [at North Division] have more of a claim to the benefits of desegregation.[117]

Derrick Bell, the famous law professor from Harvard University, agreed and said that busing African American students away from their neighborhoods did nothing to address the inherent racism in the educational system. He further said that he preferred all-black schools to busing, but more important, African American parents should have a choice in where they send their children to school.[118]

Lloyd Barbee, now retired from his law practice, kept mostly quiet on the issue of forced choice but disagreed with Fuller, Freeman, and Bell. He told the *Milwaukee Courier* in 1978, "We should enjoy the same things as the white community. I don't care how we accomplish that. If students must crowd into a Volkswagen or take a helicopter . . . [these are] extremes that we must live through as long as we receive the same type of education the whites receive."[119] Later, in an interview with Jack Dougherty, he mused:

> The process of desegregation is undoing what has been done by the segregators. Sometimes that is hard on the people who have been segregated, like the Little Rock Nine or James Meredith. The burden many times is uneven. But when you get integration, that burden disappears.[120]

But Barbee was no longer the voice of the black community, and with the school board under pressure from Fuller and his allies—and only forty whites signed up to attend North Division in the fall—the board finally gave up in April 1980 and voted ten to two to pursue an out-of-court settlement with the Coalition to Save North Division High School.[121] The North Division community rejoiced.[122] The final plan for North Division allowed it to remain almost all black with a medical and dental specialty designed to draw in a small number of white students.[123]

But the fallout from the North Division fiasco continued for months. Leon Todd criticized the MPS administration's attempts to recruit whites to North Division as "pathetic."[124] He and the other two African American board members, Marian McEvilly and Peggy Kenner, continued to advocate for integration.[125] The administration briefly considered capping white enrollment in other schools to force whites into "choosing" North Division, but heavy criticism from white parents put a quick end to the proposal.[126]

Fuller continued to raise concerns about inequities in busing. He claimed the percentage of whites bused to black schools remained low (only 3 percent in 1983) compared to African American students bused to white schools (34 percent at the elementary level and 48 percent at the middle school level) and that this disparity broke up black neighborhoods by sending students to as many as a hundred different schools.[127]

Data from the Wisconsin Legislative Audit Bureau fit with Fuller's conclusions. According to a 1984 report, twice as many African American students were bused within the city compared to whites in the 1983–84 school year, and almost five times as many African American students were bused through the Chapter 220 program compared to whites.[128] In any given year, 50 to 75 percent of all African American students were bused out of their neighborhoods, while only 4 percent of white students were bused into black neighborhoods. A crazy-quilt-like pattern of busing resulted. The average elementary school attendance area had its students bused to twenty-six different schools, and in one extreme example, students from Auer Elementary's school attendance area were bused to 95 of the 108 elementary schools in the city. Deputy Superintendent Bennett himself admitted at the time that he had created a "transportation monster."[129] State senator and future Milwaukee mayor John Norquist agreed and urged the school board to reopen some closed neighborhood schools for students who wanted to attend them.[130]

Howard Fuller also criticized what he perceived to be elitism in the specialty schools. He said the specialties created a dual system in which a small group of the best and brightest middle-class students and teachers went to a small group of schools while other students, most of whom were poor, got what was left over. He especially did not like Rufus King High School. In his own words:

I can't believe they are getting away with claiming they have turned a "ghetto school" around. Sure, it's an excellent school, but what they don't say is that they took a school, stripped it of its attendance-area enrollment, and put in a different, an elite population. If the central administration had the same kind of commitment to educational excellence at North that they have in their little powerhouse [King], I'm sure North could be turned around and become a Top 10 school. Then, they would have something to brag about.[131]

Fuller continued to actively criticize involuntary busing into 1986. He and about forty other people testified at a public hearing in May of that year. One parent said his children were "shuffl[ed] . . . around like dominoes," and a minister exclaimed, "No longer will we tolerate you dictating to us."[132] Such criticisms did not seem to faze McMurrin, who insists to this day that many parents liked the fact that their children got to ride a "warm bus" that left them free from worry about Milwaukee's cold, unsafe winter roads.[133] He and some school board members considered mandating busing for some white students, but they were met with strong opposition from south side parents.[134] Karen Murphy, an African American mother of three, helped organize white south side parents because she believed children should have access to neighborhood schools.[135] Joyce Mallory urged resources devoted to busing be redirected to training teachers in new instructional techniques that would help them teach African American students.[136]

Polling data from the *Milwaukee Journal* continued to show opposition to involuntary busing in the mid-1980s. One survey of 607 residents of Milwaukee, Washington, Ozaukee, and Waukesha counties showed that 80 percent of all respondents supported voluntary integration, but only 25 percent supported buses. Eighty-four percent of the respondents opposed involuntary transfers.[137] A black–white gap was also evident—69 percent of black Milwaukeeans thought racial integration of any sort was a good idea, while only 51 percent of suburban respondents did.[138] When the question was narrowed further, and respondents were asked whether students should be bused into their neighborhoods, only 36 percent approved, while 58 percent disapproved.[139] In other words, integration was fine as long as it applied to someone else.

These data fit with a paper written by Ronald Edari, a sociology professor at UWM, in 1977. Edari tied opposition to five stages in the adult life cycles: marriage, establishment of a household, birth and rearing of children, marriage of children, and death of spouses.[140] All of these stages are tied to race: people often marry within their race, and according to Edari, when white couples looked for homes, they almost always wanted them to be in white neighborhoods. Such neighborhoods convey a sense of values and shared heritage and were believed to hold the promise of a good return on the purchase and sale of a house.[141] According to Edari, whites associated life in their neighborhoods with free choice, local autonomy, social status, social mobility, and aspirations for their children, all of which were the result of hard work. Edari said white suburbanites saw African American communities as representing the opposite of those values, even though many hardworking African Americans were denied loans for no other reason than race. Any attempt to integrate schools challenged ideas of free choice and local autonomy and was viewed as rewarding people who failed to maintain their own homes, schools, and neighborhoods.[142]

The shift from a white-majority school district to a "majority minority" district was due to a decline in the white birthrate and changes in immigration patterns, along with discrimination in housing and busing.[143] The district's white population declined by eight thousand students between the first and second years of desegregation, while white enrollment in south side parochial schools increased.[144] The number of African American students finally exceeded the number of white students by 1980.[145] A 1986 study by *Milwaukee Magazine* found that white families with children who were about to start school were moving out. Specifically, the city had lost 115,070 of its nonblack residents between 1975 and 1985, including about one-third of all non–African American children who were four years old or younger. A different study showed that the number of white elementary school students attending private schools had doubled between 1975 and 1985. By 1985, only 51 percent of white elementary-school-age children in the city attended MPS schools, compared to 94 percent of minority children.[146] Because not all families could afford tuition, some families (both African American and white) petitioned Superintendent McMurrin for vouchers to attend private schools, which he denied.[147]

As Christine Rossell and other scholars have pointed out numerous times, white flight and opposition to busing are caused by a combination of the quality of education in schools, the distance students must ride on a bus, and the number of white students in schools. J. S. Fuerst of Loyola University and Daniel Pupo of Chicago's Dunbar Vocational High School conducted a study of the Milwaukee experience in 1983. According to their report, the number of white students enrolled in MPS declined by 40 percent between 1976, the year of Reynolds's judgment, and 1979. It declined another 20 percent in 1980, to approximately twenty-nine thousand.[148] Fuerst and Pupo concluded the main cause of this white migration was the busing of African American students to white schools. However, like Rossell, they also concluded that the white exodus was not totally due to racial concerns. Rather, according to their findings, the African American students who were bused to white schools were not academically successful. Fearing a decline in educational quality, white parents removed their children from MPS, according to Fuerst and Pupo.[149]

When studying elementary and middle schools, Fuerst and Pupo broke the city into five regions—southwest, southeast, northwest, midnorth, and Hartford Avenue School. Five schools in the southwest region lost almost 60 percent of their white students between 1976 to 1979. Southwest principals said busing had been introduced too quickly, without giving white families a chance to adjust to African Americans. Fuerst and Pupo believed part of the problem was that most middle-class African American parents kept their children in their neighborhood schools. Impoverished students whose parents did not indicate a school preference on registration forms were then assigned to southwest schools. According to the principals at these schools, the new students did not do well in school because their parents were often not involved in their children's education and those students hurt the schools' overall performance. The principals said middle-class white families bailed out and fled to the suburbs to seek better schools—not to get away from African Americans.[150]

Fuerst and Pupo gathered more information from other schools that supported this conclusion. The decline in white enrollment in southeast schools, for instance, was only 35 percent. Fuerst and Pupo speculated this was because fewer poor African American students were bused there.

Thus, reading scores did not change significantly. The northwest schools also experienced a 35 percent decline in white enrollment, though little white migration occurred in schools with middle-class African American children—again because academic achievement at those schools remained unchanged. Indeed, some schools with stable racial levels in the midnorth, which included the Sherman Park neighborhood, showed improvement in some test scores, because many of the lower-income African American students were bused away from those schools.[151]

Finally, at Hartford Avenue Elementary School, white enrollment declined from 75 percent in 1976 to 50 percent in 1979, and test scores dropped by 25 percent. In Fuerst and Pupo's view, it seemed unlikely that parents of Hartford students would pull their children out of school for racial reasons, because Hartford is located on the UWM campus, which is in a well-educated and politically liberal neighborhood. The decline in test scores probably spurred white migration, according to the researchers, because these parents wanted their children to have the kind of education that would prepare them for college.[152]

After synthesizing all the studies on race and educational quality in Milwaukee, it appears that racism alone was not responsible for white migration from Milwaukee's schools; the decline in educational quality was a significant factor as well. Much anecdotal evidence supports this conclusion. African American parents viewed Catholic schools, for example, as a superior alternative to MPS. Catholic schools had tighter standards for discipline and academics. As one African American parent with children in a Catholic school said: "To most teachers in the public schools, [teaching is] a job. I wish my kids had come to [St. Agnes] sooner. There's more order, more homework."[153] Another African American parent said she was putting her children into St. Leo's Catholic School because it was the only way to avoid busing and keep them in the neighborhood.[154] These parents were not alone—St. Leo's maintained a racially diverse population and had strong parent involvement, with attendance at parent meetings, according to St. Leo's, approaching 95 percent. The waiting list grew to nearly double the enrollment, and the school added two additional classrooms in September 1978, even though 87 percent of the students in the school were not Catholic.[155] If academically talented minority students were not attending a parochial school, they were using Chapter 220 to leave the city. According to Nicolet High

School's dean of students, all sixty transferees in 1986 scored in the seventieth percentile or above on standardized tests, while only 6 percent of MPS's African American tenth-graders placed in the seventy-fifth percentile or above.[156]

Armed with all these facts, McMurrin's critics moved against him in the mid-1980s and orchestrated his departure from MPS. They claimed that McMurrin had let academic standards decline, and their solution was to introduce more forms of choice than ever before.

CHAPTER 5

RETHINKING MAGNET SCHOOLS AND INTEGRATION, 1987–1995

Magnet schools appealed to a lot of people. They appeared to be a way to voluntarily integrate students of different races while also providing innovative choices in education. The federal government set aside money for local districts to implement magnet schools. The Emergency School Aid Act appropriated close to $30 million between 1975 and 1981, and Milwaukee spent an additional $739 million in federal money between 1985 and 1994 through the Magnet Schools Assistance Program after *A Nation at Risk* was published in 1983. *A Nation at Risk*, a report published by President Ronald Reagan's Commission on Excellence in Education, alleged that American students were years behind their counterparts in the rest of the industrialized world, and some reformers thought magnet schools might be a way to improve academic achievement.[1] The average magnet school received 10 percent more public funding than a nonmagnet school in the same district in the 1990s, money that could be used to hire additional staff, reduce the student-teacher ratio, or give teachers supplemental training.[2]

By the 1991–92 school year, more than 230 American school districts had magnet schools and were enrolling more than 1.2 million students in them. Urban districts accounted for 85 percent of all magnet schools at that time. Most of these districts were "majority minority" and majority low income.[3] According to a 1999 report by the Department of Education, 76 percent of all districts with magnet schools had greater demand than available seats.[4] Proponents claimed magnet schools were part of an important package of choices for students and families and that competition among magnet schools resulted in higher academic achievement.[5] Magnet schools were also shown as an effective means to engage students in fine arts, technology, or Advanced Placement (AP) and could successfully matriculate students to college, if the schools also provided appropriate guidance counseling and other academic supports.[6]

But magnet schools, as good as they may be, are not enough to induce racial integration. Tacoma, Washington, the birthplace of magnet schools, was 44 percent white in 2011–12, but only 25 percent of McCarver Elementary, the first magnet school in the United States, was white that year.[7] Likewise, Houston's High School of the Performing and Visual Arts was 49 percent white in 2012, but it had fewer than seven hundred students, rendering it fairly ineffective as a means of citywide integration. Only 8 percent of the entire district was white in 2012, which means the rest of Houston's magnet schools did not do much to attract whites either.[8] Likewise, Boston Latin was 49 percent white in 2012, but only 13 percent of all Boston students were.[9]

Critics raise questions about who gets access to magnet schools. Magnet schools tend to attract middle-class students and, according to some, may promote economic segregation. According to a Vanderbilt University study of Cincinnati magnet schools in 1993, more than 33 percent of children in Cincinnati's magnet schools came from families with incomes of more than fifty thousand dollars, compared to 18 percent of nonmagnet school parents. Conversely, only 25 percent of magnet school parents had incomes below fifteen thousand dollars, compared with 44 percent of nonmagnet school parents. Parents of magnet school children were also more likely to have college degrees and be employed.[10] The study further found that school selection was largely based on social networking, which is closely related to economic class. An electronics engineer said, "When we first started, we talked to different people. There are a lot of people we know who are in the school system here. We know someone who works for the board of education, so we always deal with him." Other college-educated parents made similar comments. They knew people on the inside and could make better choices. Some upper- and middle-income parents even admitted having an advantage over poor parents: "I think that is why a lot of people stick with their neighborhood schools—because it is safe and they don't know that maybe sending them someplace else would be better. They don't have that frame of reference. I'm glad I have influence on my decisions."[11]

Chicago's Whitney Young High School provides a compelling example of segregation by socioeconomic class. At a cost of $31 million, Whitney Young was built to revitalize a portion of the central city that had once been a manufacturing hub. Three specializations were available in medical arts, science, and performing arts, and a rigorous admissions process was put in place. The experiment was a stunning success, drawing in white students and fostering academic success at a rate far above state average. *U.S. News & World Report* ranked it fourth in Illinois and 126th in the nation in 2013.[12] Thirty percent of Whitney Young's 2,177 students were white in 2012–13, compared to less than 9 percent of all students in Chicago. Approximately 98 percent of its students graduate in four years and demonstrate proficiency on standardized tests, while only 67 percent of all Chicago students do.[13] Whitney Young's 2013–14 course guide lists twenty-four AP classes and six foreign languages. Its fine arts program includes classes on sculpture, graphic design, video production, piano, guitar, music theory, drama, and dance, as well as the traditional fare.[14] The school also offers a full slate of athletic teams and boasts more than eighty clubs, including architecture, business professionals, cycling, debate, engineering, film, gymnastics, Habitat for Humanity, skiing and snowboarding, and Young Doctors League.[15]

But the club that Whitney Young is best known for is the Academic Decathlon, an academic competition involving ten different events: Art, Economics, Essay, Interview, Language and Literature, Mathematics, Music, Science, Social Science, and Speech. Many people view it as the premier high school academic team competition in the United States.[16] Whitney Young won the Illinois competition nine years in a row, only to be overthrown by Steinmetz High School in 1995. Steinmetz was a general enrollment high school. Its team practiced every day for two hours before school and five hours after school and on weekends, but the students believed they could not beat Whitney Young. As their coach, Dr. Gerald Plecki, says in the film based on the actual events, "They call [Whitney Young] a public school. It uses public money, but what it is, is a private school operating in the public system. [Their] kids get the best education your tax dollars can buy. You get to go to school [there] if your parents know how to work the system." Steinmetz challenged that system. One of the students stole a copy of the state exam and beat Whitney Young. The cheating was eventually exposed, and the team was stripped of its medals.[17] Steinmetz's team was widely criticized, but the incident also led some people to question how fair it is for a school board to give one public school more advantages than other public schools.

Other critics have said that magnet schools benefit their own students but do not improve school districts as a whole. Ian Harris provided evidence of this type of disparity in Milwaukee in 1983. Harris acknowledged that Milwaukee's magnet plan integrated some schools, but the schools that remained overwhelmingly African American had the lowest achievement levels in the district. Harris also found that African American students bore a much larger share of busing than whites did and that they were forced to choose schools outside of their neighborhoods if they were denied admission to magnet schools close to their homes. Finally, Harris said the Milwaukee integration plan did not provide adequate community involvement, as evidenced by white resistance and the Coalition to Save North Division.[18]

George Mitchell, a conservative businessman, was even more critical of MPS than Harris. According to a study authored by Mitchell, MPS spent $1,846 per pupil in the 1975–76 school year, but $5,351 in 1987–88, an increase of 190 percent during a period in which the rate of inflation was only 114 percent.[19] A lot of that money went toward busing and school construction in white neighborhoods. Schools in black neighborhoods were closed to encourage African American students to choose white schools on the south side. As a result, nine times as many African American students were bused compared to whites.[20] African American enrollment in MPS increased by more than 20 percent in the 1970s, while white enrollment declined by more than 50 percent.[21]

Mitchell also concluded that the magnet schools did not increase academic achievement. Although students at the four citywide high schools (Rufus King, Riverside, Milwaukee High School of the Arts, and Milwaukee Trade and Technical) had grade point averages that were higher than those of students at the other eleven high schools, the achievement gap between African American and white students did not vary much from the gap at other MPS high schools, and the overall grade point average of all MPS high schools was in the D range.[22] Standardized test scores declined in almost every MPS high school since integration started, and African American students failed almost one-third of their courses.[23] African Americans had a dropout rate of 12.5 percent in MPS in 1985, but it was substantially higher at three white south side high schools: Pulaski had a black dropout rate of 14.3 percent, Bay View's was 18.5 percent, and Hamilton—the whitest high school in MPS—had a black dropout rate of 23.6 percent.[24] African American students did well in citywide magnet schools, but they also did well in suburban schools when they were in the Chapter 220 program.[25] In other words, magnet schools were really no better than average suburban schools.

Worse yet, the quality of education was not good at most MPS schools. A survey conducted by the University of Wisconsin–Milwaukee asked a sample of MPS teachers and parents to grade the schools on an A-B-C-D-F scale. Close to 37.9 percent of teachers and 17.2 percent of parents graded their schools as D or F. Sixty percent of teachers said they would not send their own children to the schools where they taught.[26] Administrators admitted that education was compromised because their schools had attendance rates of less than 50 percent. Students might arrive to school to find their friends, and then go to a shopping mall or some other teen hangout. Students would return to school to get their free transportation home. Some students went to class only once per week, and it was to pick up a bus pass. Those who did attend class often did so without supplies and did not do any work. Many teachers gave up under the circumstances, lowered their expectations, and showed videos rather than teach.[27]

When these data were synthesized, Mitchell concluded that magnet schools had not improved academic achievement. He said that the reason magnet schools appeared more successful was that their students came from stable, middle-class families. Thus, black–white segregation was replaced by a system of segregation based on economic class, similar to the other cities cited in this chapter, with middle-class students getting into their desired Milwaukee magnet schools or suburban schools and poor students with low levels of parent involvement going to "traditional" MPS schools.[28] As school board member and former principal Larry Miller said in 2009, "We're creating two school districts. One district offers schools that select who can get in, and one takes everyone who applies."[29]

By 1987, Superintendent McMurrin faced an increasingly vocal coalition of critics that included Howard Fuller, elected officials, and white businessmen. Fuller continued to advocate for community control of education, elected officials were concerned about young people's lack of preparedness for the job market, and white businesspeople searched for a way to cut taxes by employing cheaper, nonunion teachers at private schools. This coalition of interests accused McMurrin of failing to improve the quality of education in MPS and eventually drove him from office. McMurrin's critics seemed to ignore the role that poverty played in student achievement, and his successors would do no better than he had.

Howard Fuller was one of McMurrin's sharpest critics. Fuller began putting together a coalition of African American community activists, white business leaders, and leaders of nonsectarian private schools in 1984, with the aim of setting up a voucher system in which parents would receive money from the state to use toward tuition at private schools. Voucher proponents believed such a system would appease African Americans who wanted community control over schools, business leaders who were looking for cheaper and higher-quality schools, and private schools in poor neighborhoods that needed money to continue operating.[30] Fuller also doubted that white teachers could effectively teach African American students. In his view, African American teachers could relate better to the experiences of their students, African American students would respond better to teachers of their own race, and those teachers would be excellent role models for what students could become.[31] He continued to oppose unilateral busing, and he criticized McMurrin's magnet school plan for improving only magnet schools, leaving all other students with low-quality education. He even called for McMurrin to resign in early 1987.[32] Some whites agreed with Fuller because they did not like the high cost of busing.[33] State representative Polly Williams, an African American, resented involuntary busing on the grounds that it broke up neighborhood schools and the communities those schools anchored.[34] She also supported the Fuller-endorsed voucher movement as a means of finally achieving community control of schools.[35]

The voucher idea was not new. Legendary economist Milton Friedman introduced the concept of market-based reform in 1955. His theory was that education would improve if schools were privatized and had to compete against one another for students and funding.[36] Social scientist Christopher Jenks modified Friedman's proposal in the 1960s and advocated vouchers for low-income students so they could attend schools of their choice.[37] Voucher proponents pointed to the decline in standardized test scores in the 1980s, as documented in James Coleman's famous report *Equality of Educational Opportunity*, and advocated an alternative to public schools that would use inexpensive nonunion labor.[38]

Locally, the Milwaukee voucher movement began when the parish school at St. Benedict the Moor reorganized as Urban Day School in 1967. Urban Day was the first of the Independent Community Schools (ICS) most of which had been Catholic schools that the Milwaukee Archdiocese closed when white Catholics moved out of inner-city neighborhoods. The poor non-Catholic African American families that remained in those neighborhoods needed tuition assistance. The movement involved more than a half dozen schools in the early 1970s. The ICS schools tried to find private funding when they could, but without public assistance, most ICS schools closed in the late 1970s. However, as Milwaukeeans became more aware of the low academic achievement in MPS in the late 1980s, some of them saw the Catholic schools as a viable alternative.[39] The movement toward a voucher system was stronger in Milwaukee than anywhere else in the United States, perhaps because MPS did more than virtually any other district to put students in magnet schools and disband neighborhood schools, thereby taking control of schools away from the black community.[40]

By 1987 several public officials joined Fuller in his criticism of McMurrin. County Executive William O'Donnell said that few MPS students could participate in a Milwaukee County summer jobs training program because most youths were at least three years below grade level.[41] Milwaukee Development commissioner William Drew said MPS was "crippling class after class of graduates" and joined the chorus of individuals asking for McMurrin's resignation.[42] McMurrin retaliated by calling Drew's comment racist.[43] He also pointed to "competency tests" in reading, writing, and mathematics, which the school board had recently added to the graduation requirements, as evidence of high standards.[44] Critics responded by saying the competency tests showed that only 74 percent of the class of 1987 was ready to graduate and that severe inequities existed between schools. North Division, for example, was the lowest-performing high school, with only 50 percent passing the competency tests, while Rufus King, the most well-known magnet school, had a 96 percent pass rate, which was the best in the district.[45]

McMurrin also faced opposition from former assistant superintendent Gloria Mason who, upon retiring, decided to run for the at-large seat on the school board. The seat was held by board president Doris Stacy, an ardent supporter of McMurrin, desegregation, and magnet schools. Mason wanted change.[46] Mason said she believed resources should be directed away from busing and toward academic achievement.[47] She pointed to declining graduation rates and standardized test scores as evidence of failure.[48] She recommended three methods by which MPS could improve: reviewing and toughening the competency tests required for graduation; allowing graduates to return to their high schools for further training if they lacked employment skills; and decentralizing schools so teachers would have more independence and responsibility, parents would have more choices in schools, and local schools would have more freedom from the MPS central office.[49] George Mitchell threw his support to Mason.[50] Mason lost the election by only 5 percent of the vote, but she won votes from all races and neighborhoods of the city, demonstrating that Milwaukee was primed for change.[51]

Criticism of McMurrin continued to mount after the election. Mitchell proposed a voucher system that would have provided funds to low-income parents so they could send their children to any public or private school of their choice.[52] Mitchell blamed McMurrin for low student achievement. McMurrin countered that the schools were doing the best they could considering the level of poverty in the city. The *Sentinel* basically said McMurrin was criticized for things over which he had no control. Mitchell also continued to make public statements about McMurrin, criticizing him for a new $100 million building plan, for allegedly not having any sort of education plan, for having a top-heavy administration, and for having low standards. He said, "As for results, the majority of students entering MPS high schools either will drop out or be graduated with less than a C average. A major reason for this, but not the only reason, is that the district is simply not well-run on almost any basic measure."[53] McMurrin's contract was set to expire at the end of June 1988, and Mitchell urged the board not to give him a two-year extension.[54] The *Milwaukee Sentinel* accused his critics of having a vendetta and deplored "sneak attacks" by his critics.[55] It lauded his desegregation efforts, as did the *Milwaukee Journal*, but criticism continued to mount.

Parents had several concerns. Some said that "regular" schools had larger classes and fewer resources than magnet schools and that white teachers lacked training in cultural sensitivity.[56] Others voiced concerns that the admissions criteria for some of the best magnet schools were too lenient. They said that the lottery system should be abandoned in favor of strict admissions criteria. Parents of high-achieving students who had lost the lotteries at Rufus King High School and Golda Meir Gifted and Talented Elementary were particularly vocal.[57] Others believed that many of the students who chose to attend Milwaukee Trade and Technical High School attended because it had a good reputation, not because they were interested in the curriculum. Thus, they were taking seats away from students who actually wanted to enter skilled trades.[58]

Doris Stacy remained on the school board but chose not to run for another term as president. David Cullen, twenty-seven years old in 1987, was then elected. Some people criticized the board for ceding too much power to McMurrin, who had been superintendent for twelve years. Cullen responded by saying, "The school board has to set its own agenda, and then determine whether McMurrin is the person to lead us in that direction."[59]

In July McMurrin began to hint that he was looking for another job.[60] He ultimately accepted the position of superintendent in Beechwood, Ohio, a wealthy suburb of Cleveland. McMurrin's decision was based on financial considerations: returning to Ohio, where he had been a teacher and administrator for twenty-three years, meant that he could complete enough years in the Ohio pension system to earn four thousand to five thousand dollars per month in retirement income, compared to about a thousand dollars per month in Wisconsin.[61] With a nine-to-nothing vote, the school board agreed to release McMurrin from his contract. Several board members, including some of his critics, such as Joyce Mallory, praised him for efforts at desegregation and the magnet schools he had championed. "He stood for integration, and he fought for it," Mallory said. McMurrin, ever the kind-hearted gentleman, replied that it was the school board and parents who made the magnet schools work: "What we attempted to do to integrate the school system in 1976, 1977, and 1978 wouldn't have worked if we didn't have the cooperation of the parents."[62]

McMurrin's critics ignored the fact that middle-class families were leaving the district, and they downplayed the negative effect this change in demographics had on the success of Milwaukee's public schools. According to Marc Levine and John Zipp of UWM, Milwaukee lost more than 80 percent of its manufacturing jobs between 1960 and 1985. That was a greater loss of manufacturing than any other US city, and it meant Milwaukee faced crushing poverty.[63] Unemployment increased as twenty-eight thousand jobs left the city between 1979 and 1986; the jobs that remained were low paying and in the service industry. Meanwhile, the suburbs added thirty-three thousand jobs in the same period.[64] The new jobs in the suburbs went to whites, because African Americans were confined to living in the city by various legal and illegal means, such as lack of affordable housing and discriminatory mortgage lending practices. African Americans and MPS students, therefore, sank deeper into poverty.[65] In fact, by 1980, more than 37 percent of Milwaukee's African Americans lived at or near the poverty line.[66]

Milwaukee was also the second most popular destination for poor African Americans in the period 1985–1990. According to demographer William Frey, many of the in-migrants were single mothers who relocated from Chicago, where workers were also getting laid off. They came to Milwaukee looking for assistance from friends and relatives who lived there.[67] Some people claimed African Americans came for Wisconsin's welfare benefits, which were better than Illinois's.[68] According to MPS data, 18.7 percent of its students were new to the district in 1987–88, and 59.8 percent of students transferred from other MPS schools. According to MPS administrators, highly mobile students, a frequent problem in poor communities, were harder to educate than students who stayed in the same school from year to year.[69]

MPS became identified with African American poverty. In the 1987–88 school year, 62.8 percent of MPS students were nonwhite, an increase from 55.7 percent in 1980.[70] The median black income was only two-thirds that of all families in metropolitan Milwaukee, and 48 percent of that income was derived from welfare.[71] Fathers were largely absent—approximately 60 percent of households with children were headed by single mothers living in poverty, according to the US Census Bureau.[72] Howard Fuller said such poverty created a feeling of hopelessness.[73]

Teen pregnancy was another obstacle to success for many MPS students. In fact, Milwaukee had the highest black teen pregnancy rate in the United States in the 1980s and 1990s. Although unplanned pregnancies accounted for the majority of teen pregnancies, some girls, hoping to take control of some aspect of their lives, chose to get pregnant.

According to community activist June Perry, girls felt "that getting pregnant [wouldn't] interrupt their lives, because they [did] not have anything to look forward to in the future."[74] According to historian Bill Dahlk, in the view of some observers, "having a baby gave a female teen something to love, to show off, and an entry into a young mothers' club. In a sense, a baby provided a proprietorship for many; education did not."[75] As Jewel Reed, an unwed mother of about age twenty, said, "I just wanted something of my own, something that's mine, that I could love. I just wanted a baby, just *wanted* one. Even though I wasn't working, I didn't have my own place, whatever—I still wanted a baby."[76] Sociologist William Julius Wilson and other social scientists said that a generation of urban African American children had grown up not knowing what it was like to live without crime, poverty, substance abuse, and domestic violence. Having experienced chaos and uncertainty more often than love and stability, these teen mothers lacked the parenting skills necessary to successfully raise children. Some scholars predicted the entire collapse of the urban black family structure.[77]

According to contemporary scholars, impoverished students are less likely than their middle-class peers to have parents who read to them, who teach them to pay attention and listen, and who supervise homework. Poor students may start school not knowing how to spell their names, they may direct profanity or violent behavior at teachers or peers, they may not be able to pay attention to lessons, and they are unlikely to complete homework assignments or study for tests. Older students may not even attend school regularly and may not face parental consequences for being truant.[78] Poor parents are also less likely than middle-class parents to enroll their children in after-school and summer programs that promote intellectual and character development. They may also have lower behavioral and academic expectations of their children, and poor children are more likely than middle-class children to have problems with uncorrected vision, asthma, poor nutrition, fetal alcohol syndrome, lead poisoning, and other health impairments.[79] As one might expect, all of these factors negatively affect students' level of academic achievement. This fact was evident in the test scores for MPS and contributed to McMurrin's reputation as a failed superintendent.

These students were not helped by a heavy turnover of teachers. According to MPS and the Milwaukee Public Policy Forum, an estimated

25–30 percent of teachers in inner-city schools requested transfers to other schools in the late 1980s, and nearly half of all teachers resigned within five years. MPS hired 315 first-year teachers in 1989–90. Union seniority rules required that they usually be assigned to the most undesirable schools, which meant the most inexperienced teachers taught the most difficult students.[80]

The problems children faced at home affected their behavior in the classroom. Clifford George, principal of Marshall High School, observed in 1982: "Youngsters come to school with so many problems, the least little thing, they fly off the handle. Our social worker says she's seeing family situations she hasn't seen in ten, fifteen years, terrible conditions of poverty." MPS social workers received more frequent calls to investigate allegations of child abuse and neglect, and Milwaukee County reported that incidents of child abuse increased 79 percent between 1986 and 1992.[81] As one fourth-grade teacher said, "I spend a lot of my time dealing with kids' emotions. We are supposed to be educating these kids, but we often end up as a dumping ground." She said she was trying to help a girl with some mathematics problems when the student looked up and said, "My mommy just cut my daddy last night." The teacher said she wondered how she was supposed to help a child who had those kinds of problems.[82]

Incidents of violence increased during the mid- to late 1980s, including violence among younger students. During the 1986–87 school year, 1,148 students were transferred from one MPS school to another for violent infractions of school rules. There were 138 reported assaults; 159 weapons possession charges, including six handguns; and twenty-five charges for sex offenses at the high school level. The middle schools had 143 reported assaults; 103 weapons possession charges, including six pistols; and thirty-four charges for sex offenses. Finally, there were ninety-four reported assaults; 110 weapons violation charges, including two pistols and four switchblades; and thirty-four charges for sex offenses in the elementary schools.[83] Two students raped a third student at Audubon Middle School, a pupil knifed another student at Burroughs Middle School, a student stabbed a teacher with scissors at Sholes Middle School, and two students accidently fired a gun at Mitchell Elementary School during the 1987–88 school year.[84]

Problems were especially acute in "regular" schools, so parents complained that they wanted more seats in magnet schools.[85] The *Milwaukee*

Journal compared a nonmagnet elementary school to a magnet elementary school in 1986, and it showed the disparity between the two. Palmer Elementary, the nonmagnet, had a poverty rate of 83 percent. Only about a dozen parents volunteered to help at school, and teachers referred about two hundred students to school support services. The population was transient—296 students left the school and 290 entered it during the 1985–86 school year, and teachers reported that their students read below grade level. Golda Meir Elementary, on the other hand, was a middle-class magnet school that was about half African American and half white. Its list of parent volunteers was four pages long, and teachers referred only ten students to support services. The population was stable, and its students were among the highest performers in the district.[86] Thus, it should not have been a surprise that magnet schools did well while nonmagnets did poorly.

Jeannie Ullrich's experiences in MPS in the 1980s reflected this dichotomy of schools. Ullrich, an African American who had been adopted by a white family, attended Elm Creative Arts School, one of the most popular magnet schools: "It was a wonderful school with wonderful teachers. It was everything I think a school ought to be." After graduating in the sixth grade, she attended Fritsche Middle School in the Bay View neighborhood, and she later described the school as "horrible." She said academic expectations were low and teachers did not assign homework. The students were disrespectful to teachers, and the school was on the verge of being out of control. She endured a lot of harassment from other African American students and transferred to a parochial school after one year at Fritsche. She applied to Rufus King for high school but did not get in through the lottery system. She then applied at Nicolet High School through the Chapter 220 program rather than attending a "regular" MPS high school. She left her house every day at 6:15 A.M. to take an hour-long bus ride to school. Finally, her family moved into the district when she was a sophomore. Ullrich said she received a wonderful education and never felt out of place at Nicolet. Class, not race, is what divided Nicolet students: "We were mostly middle-class blacks. The kids that were considered different, they were called burnouts. They wore black shoes, army clothes, they smoked. They were the 'other' kids, not the 220 kids."[87]

Ullrich's departure to the suburbs was part of a bigger trend. Flight from the city accelerated in the late 1980s as middle-class and affluent residents looked for better schools. In 1986, William Drew conducted a survey of Milwaukeeans who had moved to the suburbs and found that 23 percent cited concerns over schools as their most important reasons for leaving, while another 16 percent said schooling was their second most important reason.[88] The middle-class flight included African Americans who often relocated to the northwest side of Milwaukee or the nearby suburb of Brown Deer. Without African American doctors, lawyers, and other professionals, Milwaukee lacked black leaders, such as those who had helped bring about integration in the 1960s and 1970s.[89]

Without strong leadership, industrial jobs, education, and behavioral skills, many young African Americans ended up unemployed after leaving school. Some turned to gangs for economic support, selling drugs and committing other crimes. According to John Hagedorn, an expert on Milwaukee gangs of the 1980s, at least 70 percent of gang founders in the period 1979–83 were between the ages of eighteen and twenty-five and were unemployed. Less than a third of gang members had graduated from high school or earned a GED.[90] According to Joan Moore, another Milwaukee-based researcher, gang members were "aggressive young men who have no future and know they have no future." Schools, in her opinion, were "so boring, so defeating, so negative" that they did not help solve the gang problem. Moore and other experts agreed that gangs fostered a sense of community. According to Fred Blue, who worked for the city's Commission on Community Relations, "kids get involved in youth gangs because they are essentially trying to be heard but nobody's listening."[91]

Gangs created an "oppositional culture" among Milwaukee's black youth in the 1980s. Donald Sykes, executive director of Milwaukee's Social Development Commission, observed that the increase in black anger correlated with the deterioration of black–white relations.[92] Black students were more likely to get into fights with one another in school or on the streets and were more likely to disrupt classes and defy their white teachers. Schools served as recruiting grounds for gangs, and young African Americans, desperate for a sense of belonging and disconnected from education, sometimes found themselves trapped in gangs with no way out. And even though most African American students did not join gangs, the sense of anger toward authority could still be felt. African American youth viewed white teachers, social workers, and police officers with suspicion. Likewise, some whites assumed that all Africans Americans were potential criminals.[93]

Former civil rights advocate James Groppi, himself white, lamented the rise of gangs: "You can't look at these kids as an oppressed minority because they have become the worst kind of oppressors. They are terrorizing blacks and whites. They are really a negative force in that community." Groppi recognized the source of the anger: "They are angry, angry as hell at everything. They want things. They can't have them. Most of those kids don't even know where their next meal is coming from."[94] African American community activist Tony Courtney put it more bluntly: "Our youth are our executioners."[95]

MPS's magnet schools were designed to attract white students to the inner city and to provide an array of innovative educational choices. They were not designed to rescue an African American population devastated by unemployment, poverty, broken families, and gangs. In this context, there was little McMurrin could have done to improve MPS. His resignation invited competition between integrationists and the black nationalists for control of the district. The integrationists still supported magnet schools, but they lacked the leadership they had shown in the 1960s and 1970s, and Lloyd Barbee had retired to private life by 1987. That left the nationalists—referred to as separatists by some of their critics—as the dominant group. The nationalists tried to seize control of traditionally African American schools so they could rebuild their community.

Howard Fuller led the nationalists, as he had in the 1970s. Fuller began making public statements advocating community control of schools almost immediately after McMurrin left office. Specifically, he proposed that the state legislature create a new, separate school district for North Division High School, two feeder middle schools, and seven (later five) feeder elementary schools. Fuller and his followers argued that African American achievement would improve if students were taught by African American teachers and governed by a school board elected from the surrounding community.[96] They believed a return to neighborhood schools would increase parental involvement, improve teacher morale, and encourage the development of a focused curriculum that would reduce the dropout rate.[97] The plan was very similar to the experiment that took place at North Division from 1969 until 1972. African American state representatives Polly Williams and Spencer Coggs supported the new district, as did African American alderpersons Michael McGee Sr., Marlene Johnson, Marvin Pratt, and former assistant superintendent Gloria Mason.[98] Governor Tommy Thompson, Assembly Speaker Tom Loftus, and businessman George Mitchell, all of whom were white, also gave their support to an independent North Division district.[99]

Fuller and his supporters believed that integrated education was better than segregated education in the best of all possible worlds. But this was not that world; therefore, Fuller and his supporters preferred to have African American students attend their own schools, where they could participate in and benefit from their own community and unique American heritage.[100] The plan's supporters referred to MPS's busing program as "madness" and criticized it for breaking up the black community. They rejected metropolitan desegregation, arguing it would only exacerbate black underachievement by dispersing African Americans throughout the suburbs, as if they were not good enough to have their own schools. They also, however, strongly supported the right of parents to send their children to any Milwaukee-area schools of their choosing. Their manifesto was endorsed by twenty-seven locally prominent African Americans, including Mel Hall, president of the Central City Scholarship Organization; Wesley Scott, retired executive director of the Milwaukee Urban League; and former Wisconsin secretary of state Vel Phillips.[101]

Deputy Superintendent Hawthorne Faison, an African American, was named acting superintendent following McMurrin's resignation.[102] Many African Americans saw Faison's promotion as a big opportunity to raise standards, decentralize the district, and return to neighborhood schools, but Faison opposed the North Division plan.[103] He was not alone. Barbee's protégée, state representative Marcia Coggs opposed the plan, as did several other prominent African Americans, including state senator Gary George, school board members Joyce Mallory and Jeanette Mitchell, several clergymen, and Cecil Brown, former co-chairperson of the Committee of 100.[104] Grover Hankins, general counsel for the NAACP, called proponents of the plan "apostles of urban apartheid."[105] Among whites, Milwaukee School Board President David Cullen vowed to challenge the plan's constitutionality in court if it became law, and city attorney Grant Langley said the plan violated the equal protection clause of the Fourteenth Amendment and the *Amos* decision.[106] A *Milwaukee Journal* survey found that 62 percent of all likely Milwaukee voters were against the plan, only 27 percent supported it, and 11 percent were undecided. These findings cut across all age, gender, and racial lines.[107] The bill passed the state assembly on March 17, 1988, by a sixty-one-to-thirty-six vote, but a concerted effort by Gary George killed it in the Senate.[108] Though they lost the vote, black separatists continued to advocate for neighborhood schools and community control of public schools and for vouchers for private schools throughout the 1990s.

With the North Division scheme defeated, it was time for the school board to name a permanent superintendent. Faison was well liked by the teachers, especially African American teachers, and won the endorsement of the Milwaukee Teacher Education Association (the teachers union), but the school board wanted to conduct a nationwide search, believing that Faison did not have enough experience to run a school district as big as Milwaukee.[109] Dr. Robert Peterkin emerged as the frontrunner. Like Faison, Peterkin was African American, which appealed to the school board's three African American members and Mary Bills, who was a white reformer. Peterkin was the superintendent of the schools in Cambridge, Massachusetts, which had only about eight thousand students, compared to MPS, which had one hundred thousand students. But he had also been deputy superintendent in Boston, where he was credited with increasing standardized test scores.[110] The school board approved Peterkin's appointment with a nine-to-nothing vote. He received rave reviews from the school board and the general public.[111] As school board member Jeanette Mitchell said, "It's almost a dream come true."[112]

Peterkin faced several daunting challenges. He inherited a school system that had lost most of its white middle-class students. Test scores, attendance, and grades had declined to an all-time low. And the state legislature and Department of Public Instruction were threatening to reconstitute MPS into several smaller districts.[113] But Peterkin promised to raise academic achievement by breaking MPS into six "service delivery areas," each with its own deputy superintendent responsible for high schools, middle schools, and elementary schools.[114] By moving administrators out of the MPS central office, Peterkin hoped to put the administrators directly in touch with the parents and communities they served, which would lead to increased accountability. Once accountability was ingrained, achievement would improve.[115] Racial diversity would be achieved by incorporating a portion of the central city into each service delivery area.[116]

Peterkin's plan failed to improve MPS and lasted only two years. The plan essentially created two levels of bureaucracy, which was expensive and doubled the paperwork. It also slowed the system down in some cases. Reports surfaced that the community superintendents were reluctant to leave the comforts of their offices and get into the schools to help people.[117] The plan did nothing to reduce busing, and instead of making the bureaucracy more accessible to parents, it may have actually isolated them. As George Mitchell said:

> They [a family that lives in the Palmer Elementary School attendance area] live in one attendance area, which is part of a new Service Delivery Area headed by a new community superintendent. They are represented on the School Board by the member from District Four. Yet their child likely attends another school, in another Service Delivery Area, headed by another community superintendent, represented by another member of the School Board.[118]

The service delivery areas did not improve student achievement. In fact, student achievement continued to decline.[119] The average high school student had a 1.62 grade point average, the average daily attendance in all schools was around 90 percent in 1989, and 9,359 students were suspended from school in the 1988–89 school year.[120]

Peterkin proposed two solutions, both of which included magnet schools. The first solution was called the Long-Range Educational Equity Plan, or the Willie Plan, named after its principal author, Charles V. Willie, of the Harvard Graduate School of Education. The city would have been split into two zones—east and west—with magnet schools and other opportunities placed in both halves. Students would have to choose a school in their zone, which was intended to reduce busing. The exceptions would be Rufus King, Riverside, Milwaukee High School of the Arts, and Milwaukee Trade and Technical, which would remain citywide magnet schools. Busing would have been bilateral, and the schools would have been integrated.[121] Peterkin hoped to reduce feelings among parents that the district only offered a few good magnet schools.[122]

White parents, afraid of losing their magnet schools, opposed the Willie Plan. A crowd of about 175 parents and teachers assembled in the auditorium at Marshall High School on February 27, 1990, to complain about it. A parent of a Greenfield Avenue Elementary Montessori School student warned, "You will see what a revolt is really like."[123] White parents predicted more white flight and asked the school board to leave the school assignment process alone. Some African Americans whose children attended magnet schools had the same concern; others, who did not have children in magnet schools, worried that the Willie Plan would limit their choices and busing options.[124] A third set of African American parents at another meeting urged a return to neighborhood schools.[125] MPS did not approve the Willie Plan, mostly due to white opposition.[126] Peterkin lamented, "People didn't see what they were going to gain, only what they were going to lose."[127]

With the failure of the service delivery areas and the Willie Plan, the public was beginning to lose faith in Peterkin. As Jean Tyler, executive director of the Public Policy Forum, a local agency that studies public policies pertaining to metropolitan problems, said, "I'd give him an A for effort, for understanding the major kinds of changes that need to be taken to improve the Milwaukee Public Schools. But I'd also have to give him an incomplete for his accomplishments so far."[128]

Peterkin's last attempt to improve MPS came in the form of a new magnet school that would host an immersion program for African American males. Peterkin knew young black males were the largest "at-risk" group in MPS, making up roughly 27 percent of Milwaukee's student population in 1990. This cohort had a 19.3 percent dropout rate and an average grade point average of 1.35 in the 1989–90 school year, compared to the district average of 1.6. Only 2 percent of MPS's African American males had a 3.0 or higher. Eleven percent had flunked a grade, and 17 percent were suspended, compared to 7 percent of non–African Americans.[129] Peterkin hoped that an immersion program focusing on African culture and self-pride might help change these numbers. In his words, "A population is literally dying, both educationally and physically. We can wring . . . our hands or we can try something new."[130]

The immersion program set off a storm of controversy that garnered national media attention. Some people said targeting African American males for a "special" school would be a return to segregation. Others said it ignored much more complex issues involved in the lack of male achievement, such as poverty and the weakening of the family.[131] Dr. Kenneth Clark, who provided much of the social-psychological research on segregation's harmful effects on black students for the *Brown* decision, said, "I can't believe that we're regressing like this. . . . Why are we talking about segregating and stigmatizing black males?"[132]

Supporters of the plan disagreed. They saw integration as a means to an end—quality education for all of Milwaukee's children. Involuntary busing was not working in their view, so they wanted to try another method that might result in better schools. Joyce Mallory, who had a sixteen-year-old son, was one such person. She said she wanted to "create a climate and a culture that says to all children, particularly black boys, that you're OK."[133] Ken Holt, another African American and principal of Alexander Graham Bell Middle School, put it more directly: "The school system is going to have to be surrogate parents. These kids see despair in the community. Dope pushers, not role models. They don't know how to be a man."[134]

Peterkin, Mallory, Holt, and other supporters of the immersion plan were able to put together enough votes on the school board to get a plan approved. Two schools—Martin Luther King Elementary School (formerly Victor Berger Elementary) and Malcolm X Academy (formerly Fulton Middle School, which had had academic and behavioral problems for years)— were designated for the new program, but they were open to all children regardless of race or gender. All students would participate in the Afrocentric curriculum and daily counseling sessions, and uniforms would be required. Once approved, Peterkin set out to recruit a mostly black male staff; he wanted them to be role models as well as teachers.[135] But as the controversy deepened and Peterkin fell under closer media scrutiny, his desire to remain on the job waned. He announced in late 1990 that he would take a position at Harvard University the following fall.[136]

Malcolm X Academy did not do very well. Although its founders envisioned well-ordered classrooms where students would take rigorous courses and improve their self-esteem, what they got were students with some of the lowest attendance, grades, and test scores in MPS.[137] Leon Todd, an African American integrationist who had been on the school board in the 1970s, returned to the board in the 1990s and alleged that the school was teaching its students separatism and racism.[138] There were several attempts to close the school in the 1990s. Eventually, the enrollment at the middle school shrank to such a low level that a high school had to be added.[139] The middle school component was cut in the mid-2000s. After a few years the school became the African American

Immersion High School and merged with the small Metropolitan High School. It then moved into North Division, which itself had been reconfigured as three small high schools in 2005,[140] and it still had some of the lowest-performing students in MPS.[141]

Howard Fuller emerged as one of the top candidates for superintendent to replace Peterkin. He had put together an impressive résumé in the 1980s. Already known as a civil rights advocate, leader of the Coalition to Save North Division, and a proponent of vouchers, Fuller, who had a PhD, had served as dean of general education for the Milwaukee Area Technical College, as the director of the Wisconsin Department of Employment Relations, and as the head of Milwaukee County's Department of Health and Human Services. Thus, he was considered an expert in his field and had connections all over the state. He also had endorsements from Milwaukee Mayor John Norquist, County Executive Dave Schultz, and County Board Chairman Tom Ament. State law, however, required a minimum of three years as a classroom teacher to be superintendent, experience that Fuller lacked.[142]

The school board waited until after the spring elections to appoint a superintendent. Deputy Superintendent Deborah McGriff, the only other serious candidate for the job, grew tired of waiting so many months for an appointment and accepted a job as superintendent of Detroit schools instead. That left Fuller, and with the end of the school year drawing near, the state legislature and governor changed the law requiring teaching experience so Fuller could become Milwaukee superintendent.[143] Both the black and white communities rallied around him.[144] The school board, wary of the man who had been their sharpest critic, searched for other candidates but could find none.[145] The school board unanimously elected Fuller on May 29, 1991.[146] Fuller was also vested with more power than any other superintendent before him, because the school board eliminated the separate secretary–business manager position, giving Fuller complete control over district finances.[147]

Fuller had his work cut out for him. A report issued in 1992 by the Wisconsin Advisory Committee to the United States Civil Rights Commission indicated that Milwaukee-area schools remained very segregated. According to the report, 57 percent of MPS's students were African American in 1991; 27 percent were white; 10 percent were Latino; and the rest were Asian, Native American, or categorized as "other." These figures included

5,714 Milwaukee students who attended suburban schools through Chapter 220. Of those students, 71.5 percent were African American. Conversely, only 873 white suburban students attended city schools.[148] On a state level, more than 70 percent of all African American students attended segregated schools. Almost all of them attended MPS schools.[149]

According to research conducted at the University of Chicago, Milwaukee-area schools fit into three classifications. The first was white, middle class, and suburban. Their students were doing very well and were above the national medians in several standardized categories. The second classification was the college-preparatory MPS magnet schools. They were fairly well integrated and were also above national medians in several categories but were not doing as well as suburban schools. Most of their students were low to middle income. The third classification of schools, which the vast majority of MPS students attended, was traditional schools dominated by low-income, minority children. Their level of educational achievement was significantly below that of students in the other two types of school and was below the national median in most statistical categories.[150] The average grade point average in thirteen of Milwaukee's fifteen public high schools was less than 2.0. More than 25 percent of the courses taken in MPS high schools ended in failing grades, and in seven high schools, that number topped 30 percent.[151] Only about 40 percent of freshmen graduated from high school in four years. The rest dropped out or spent more than four years in high school.[152]

These facts caused several people, including the state assembly, the NAACP, and Mayor John Norquist, to question the success of desegregation.[153] In a survey by the *Milwaukee Community Journal*, only 55 percent of white parents, 55 percent of African American parents, and 52 percent of Latino parents believed the desegregation guidelines should be continued.[154] Howard Fuller, who had not yet become superintendent by the time of the survey, said, "Milwaukee pursued a discriminatory implementation of desegregation; and, in essence, what happened in Milwaukee was they stood the *Brown* decision on its head." In other words, *Brown* was supposed to improve educational opportunities for African American students, but in Milwaukee's case, desegregation had put a tremendous burden on the students it was supposed to have helped.[155]

When Fuller became superintendent, he put forth a number of innovative reforms to try to correct these problems. Almost immediately, he announced the closure of the six service delivery offices, calling the experiment "noble" but inefficient and expensive.[156] He also turned over most school functions directly to the principals, including budgeting and personnel decisions, so that MPS would be a "system of schools," rather than a school system.[157] Cutting administrative positions also made more money available to individual schools.[158] Fuller wanted high schools to be more rigorous, so he asked the school board to increase the high school graduation requirements, to require all ninth-grade students to take algebra, and to pass new policies to make schools safer and discipline standards stronger.[159] He also wanted parents to play a greater role in choosing their children's school and to get involved.[160] He planned to close schools and reopen them with new staffs and programs, possibly as charter schools, if they were chronically low achieving.[161] The MTEA interpreted Fuller's plans for school reconstitution and nonunion charter schools as an attack on teachers.[162] The union also resisted a wage freeze, which Fuller proposed in 1991–92 to help hold property taxes in check.[163]

Fuller also proposed changes in school funding. Citywide magnet schools received $2,297 per pupil in 1992, while the neighborhood schools received only $1,855 per pupil.[164] The magnet schools drew mostly middle-class students, who were often white, but the neighborhood schools served mostly poor students of color. Fuller, who never liked magnet schools, decided to equalize funding, which he felt would allow neighborhood schools to meet the challenges of poverty. His proposal also included shifting money from high schools and middle schools to elementary schools to try to raise achievement, even though high schools are more expensive to operate. Not surprisingly, the students, parents, and staffs of the magnet schools and high schools protested the cuts.[165] Fuller eventually restored 30 percent of the cut funding to the high schools and middle schools, but he did not restore funding to the magnet schools.[166]

Fuller also proposed a return to neighborhood schools, saying busing was a failure that "destroyed communities."[167] He divided the city into five elementary school districts and required students to choose an elementary school in their district if they were not going to attend a magnet school.[168] He also proposed a ten-year, $474 million building plan for neighborhood schools, of which $366 million would be financed by long-term borrowing. Fifteen schools would be constructed, and fourteen existing schools would be expanded. State law required a referendum to get the loans. Mayor Norquist and other public officials expressed doubt that the referendum would pass without MPS cutting busing and showing "a dramatic increase in the quality" of education.[169]

Early polling data made the chances of an affirmative vote look good, but citizens began to have doubts when the financial costs of the building plan were calculated.[170] Therefore, when not battling the teachers union, Fuller spent the rest of 1992 and part of 1993 promoting his building plan and seeking the support of voters.[171] County Executive Dave Schultz called it "a referendum on Howard Fuller."[172] Most African Americans supported the plan, but many whites, especially those who lived on the edges of the city, said they opposed the plan because it would increase their property taxes.[173] The voters rejected the referendum by a three-to-one margin.[174] Lee McMurrin's magnet school plan and the busing it required would remain in place for at least the next few years.

Fuller continued to push other reforms while he was superintendent, including a school-to-work program; a classification system of schools as "high achieving," "improving," or "in need of assistance"; and expanded school choice through nonunion charter schools.[175] Fuller said he preferred nonunion labor because the MTEA hamstrung his efforts to be innovative and to fire ineffective teachers. The MTEA fought back and forced Fuller to observe union rules at Edison Middle School, which was the one charter school he had been able to start.[176]

The school board and the public seemed to support most of Fuller's plans, but some people within MPS resented Fuller's disruption to the normal flow of MPS activities and felt alienated by what they perceived as a heavy-handed approach to school administration. Relations with the teachers union also continued to sour. When Fuller wanted to bypass seniority and appoint additional African American teachers to the two African American immersion schools, the union objected, but Fuller did it anyway. The MTEA filed a grievance and won.[177]

Fuller also introduced radical changes to the North Division administration. He fired Cecil Austin, North's principal, in April 1992 for being ineffective and replaced him with a committee of teachers, parents, alumni, and business leaders. The committee was given five years to turn North around and was given control over budgeting, scheduling, staffing decisions, and curriculum; but the MTEA charged that the staff members had not been elected to the committee and were under Fuller's direct control. This violated the teachers' contract and collective bargaining process. Maxine Hannibal, a North teacher whom Fuller had appointed as committee chair, told newspaper reporters the teachers on the committee lacked support from the union and central office administrators.[178] Fuller eventually named a new principal in 1993.[179] In return, the union agreed to the creation of a new advisory committee of teachers, administrators, and union representatives. It also waived portions of the contract, allowing North to hire additional African American teachers.[180]

The school board's support for Fuller waned in the wake of his defeats. Fuller had been hired on a unanimous vote in 1991, but two of his allies, Joyce Mallory and Jeannette Mitchell, resigned in 1993 and 1994, respectively. Mallory's position was filled by Leon Todd in a special election in 1994. Todd had been a Fuller foe when Todd was on the school board in the 1970s and had been particularly critical of Fuller's proposal that the North Division neighborhood be considered its own school district. Todd continued to criticize Fuller in the 1990s.[181]

But the conflict did not stop there. Fuller pushed for a big expansion of charter schools, which took money away from public schools (and union salary increases) and funneled it to nonunion public schools.[182] As a result, MTEA lobbied hard and helped elect Leon Todd and three other school board candidates, all of whom rejected the expansion of charter schools, in April 1995.[183] Fuller resigned in frustration two weeks after the election. He blamed the teachers union in his resignation statement, saying their "scurrilous messages" were designed to "smear any effort to bring genuine reform to the system."[184]

Fuller may not have accomplished as much as he thought he would, but he left a lasting legacy. Charter schools and the voucher program flourished in the decade following the Fuller administration, and MPS finally made a move back to neighborhood schools. These schools and suburban schools would compete with magnet schools for Milwaukee's best students. Thus, Fuller ushered in the third era of educational choice in Milwaukee—the era of school choice.

PART 3

THE ERA OF SCHOOL CHOICE

CHAPTER 6

FIVE MORE CHOICES, 1987–2013

M ilwaukee's magnet schools provided innovative curricula to the city's children. But they could not fix the economic devastation that the city faced, and they were never designed to do so. Critics in the business community and some segments of the African American community demanded change when Superintendent Lee McMurrin left office in 1987, but Milwaukee Public Schools did not drastically alter its integration plan, even while longtime magnet school critic Howard Fuller was superintendent. Some Milwaukeeans, therefore, began to look for educational options outside of MPS beginning in the late 1980s. These options included charter schools, vouchers, and open enrollment. MPS, facing increased competition from non-MPS schools, tried to make itself more attractive by adding two additional choices—neighborhood schools and small high schools. These five reforms would give Milwaukee parents and students an unprecedented level of choice in schooling.

CHARTER SCHOOLS

Charter schools are the most common alternative to traditional public schools in the United States. Charter schools operate under a special agreement (or "charter") with a chartering authority—often a school district, city government, or university. They are public schools but may be privately run and are exempt from most state and local regulations, such as particular graduation requirements, testing requirements, district-adopted textbooks, district-imposed schedules, and in some cases, union contracts.[1] Those exemptions allow charter schools more freedom to use innovative teaching methods.[2] The charter school movement began in 1992 with the first charter issued in Minneapolis–St. Paul.[3] By 2010, 4,600 charter schools were serving 1.4 million children in kindergarten through twelfth grade in the United States.[4] Criteria for receiving a charter vary from state to state, but generally speaking, the holder of the charter must exhibit some kind of commitment to educating children.[5] Some charter schools are sponsored by community groups, and others are sponsored by religious institutions or ethnic organizations seeking to preserve their values or cultural traditions. However, charter schools usually do not teach specific theologies, which would violate the principle of separation of church and state.[6] Charter schools are usually easier to close than traditional public schools, because the school closes automatically if the chartering authority does not renew the charter. However, if a chartering authority attempts to revoke a charter before the charter period has elapsed, it may face a lawsuit for breach of contract.[7]

Charter schools have expanded in Wisconsin since they were initially authorized in 1993. Originally, only ten school districts were allowed to charter up to two schools each, but in 1995 that expanded to an unlimited number of schools in all school districts. The City of Milwaukee, the University of Wisconsin–Milwaukee, Milwaukee Area Technical College (MATC), and the University of Wisconsin–Parkside have been allowed to charter schools since 1997. In addition to those charter schools, MPS operated twenty-five of its own in 2003, and about 22 percent of MPS students attended charter schools in 2011.[8] Some MPS charter schools and all non-MPS charter schools use nonunionized labor, but, as they are public schools, all teachers must hold some sort of valid teaching license.[9] They must also admit students with special education needs, but, unlike regular public schools, they are not required to make appropriate accommodations to meet those needs.[10]

Opinions on charter schools vary. Supporters argue that charter schools offer a superior education and force public schools to improve by making public schools compete for students and funding.[11] Charter schools garner high praise when they are academically successful and are run by school districts; but they create controversy when they use nonunion labor and when they are run by for-profit companies.[12] Charter schools have also been criticized for resisting enrolling students with educational or behavioral problems.[13] Although most charter schools are nonprofit, for-profit charters have been criticized for having inexperienced staff and high staff turnover due to low wages.[14] There is also some evidence that charter schools may contribute to racial segregation, as they do not typically provide transportation to students and therefore tend to exclude families that cannot afford transportation.[15] Gary Orfield, of the UCLA Civil Rights Project, says that almost a third of all African American students end up in "apartheid schools," which he defines as schools that have white enrollments of 0 to 1 percent.[16] In terms of academic performance, some studies show that competition between charter schools and regular public schools raises achievement in both types of schools.[17] Most studies, however, including studies of Milwaukee charter schools, show charter schools and regular public schools have no difference in achievement levels if they serve students of the same socioeconomic background.[18]

VOUCHERS

"School choice" is often used as a euphemism for a voucher program that is more radical than charter schools. Parents are issued a voucher, usually from the state, which they use to pay tuition at a private school. Supporters argue that vouchers give poor parents the same level of choice in schools that wealthy parents already have. Like charter schools, vouchers are supposed to spur public schools to improve by providing the public schools with competition. Voucher programs are active in Cleveland and Dayton, Ohio; Indianapolis; Milwaukee; New York City; San Antonio; Washington, DC; and several other cities.[19] The voucher concept has been around for decades but did not gain traction until the late 1980s.

The Milwaukee-based Bradley Foundation was one of the chief proponents of vouchers. The foundation was established in 1942 after Milwaukee businessman Lynde Bradley's death so that his heirs could shelter money from taxes and make philanthropic contributions to the Milwaukee community. Some of its founders supported the far-right John Birch Society.[20] The foundation's assets increased from less than $14 million to more than $290 million when the Allen-Bradley Company was sold to Rockwell International Corporation in 1985 for $1.65 billion. Investment income pushed the foundation's assets up to more than half a billion dollars by 2011.[21]

With so much money at its disposal, the foundation was able to recruit as its president Michael Joyce from the conservative Olin Foundation, headquartered on the East Coast, in 1985. Joyce led the foundation until 2001. The foundation gave away tens of millions of dollars per year under Joyce's leadership, including donations to the Milwaukee Art Museum, the Milwaukee Repertory Theater, Marquette University, and local charities. It was instrumental in securing funding for the Milwaukee Brewers' baseball stadium, Miller Park, and it funds educational initiatives in MPS and private schools. Milwaukeeans celebrate these philanthropic acts, but many appear to be unaware that the Bradley Foundation makes large contributions to conservative causes and think tanks that have not always aligned well with public education or teachers unions. It has donated money to the Heritage Foundation, the American Enterprise Institute, the Manhattan Institute, the School of Advanced International Studies, the Ethics and Public Policy Center, the Claremont Institute, and fellowships for research projects that further conservative causes. The Bradley Foundation has sought to shape public policy around free enterprise and other conservative ideas since 1985.[22] As the foundation's vice chairman, W. H. Brady, remarked to historian John Gurda, "It is not government, it is not dictators or presidents or generals or popes who rule the world. It's ideas."[23]

School vouchers were an integral part of the Bradley Foundation's conservative philosophy. The foundation's first direct involvement with vouchers occurred in 1986, when the foundation gave seventy-five thousand dollars to conservative scholars John Chubb and Terry Moe to support their research on privatized education. The foundation donated another three hundred thousand dollars to them in 1990, which led to the publication of their book *Politics, Markets, and America's Schools*. Chubb and Moe studied data from the Department of Education and concluded that public education would not be effective without competition from the private sector.[24] The foundation also paid nearly $1 million over an eight-year period to Charles Murray to research and coauthor *The Bell Curve*, a 1994 best-selling book that argued that some people, including many African Americans, had lower intelligence quotients because they were genetically inferior to other people. Murray and coauthor Richard

Herrnstein said that spending tax money on people who were incapable of significant learning was a financial waste and had resulted in a lowering of academic standards. They argued that public money should flow to private schools where gifted students could be held to higher expectations apart from their below-average peers.[25]

In addition to those contributions to conservative research, the Bradley Foundation donated $1.5 million to Partners Advancing Values in Education (PAVE), an organization founded in 1987 by Milwaukee businesspeople who were interested in providing scholarships to low-income students who wanted to attend Catholic schools.[26] PAVE was a way of keeping those schools open, and the Bradley Foundation's donation to PAVE was a key part of establishing an alliance between voucher advocates and the Milwaukee Archdiocese. With that alliance forged, Wisconsin Governor Tommy Thompson presented a voucher plan to the state legislature in January 1988 that would have allowed some low-income Milwaukee students to attend private schools, including religious schools. But Thompson did not work to gain bipartisan support, and the measure failed to gain approval.[27]

It was not until black Milwaukeeans joined that alliance that the voucher movement gained the strength it needed. The turning point came at a March 1989 educational reform conference at MATC. The conference featured a panel discussion on vouchers, which included voucher advocates John Chubb, Terry Moe, and Howard Fuller and voucher critic Walter Ferrell of UWM. Hundreds of African American parents attended and listened to both sides, but the crowd clearly favored the voucher advocates.[28] The following year, in 1990, Polly Williams introduced a bill into the Wisconsin legislature to create the Milwaukee Parental Choice Program. To get support from Democrats, Williams did not include religious schools in the program, although schools that had at one time been affiliated with the Milwaukee Archdiocese were included. Families could not earn incomes above a certain level of poverty, and schools were not allowed to have more than 49 percent of their students on vouchers. Thus, a majority of families were still paying tuition, and the schools could claim that they were still truly private schools. The program started out small—only a thousand students were allowed to participate.[29]

Wisconsin's private schools operate differently from public schools, even if they receive public money. For example, until 2010, private schools were not required to employ teachers with college degrees.[30] Private schools also do not have to obey Wisconsin's open meeting or open records laws, which means they are allowed to hold meetings that are closed to the public, and records of staff pay and certification, graduation rates and suspension rates, and staff and student demographics are not publicly accessible. They may suspend or expel students without a hearing and are not required to provide anything beyond minimum special education services, while public schools must enroll any student with any disability and must make all accommodations.[31] Private schools are often quick to say they admit students with special needs, but as Milwaukee Superintendent Gregory Thornton pointed out in 2011, just one MPS school—Hamilton High School—enrolled as many special education students as all 102 voucher schools combined.[32]

Finally, private schools did not have to comply with the No Child Left Behind Act, which required that every public school student, including those with special needs, severe behavior problems, or limited English fluency, be proficient on standards as measured by standardized tests. Under the law, a school could be declared "in need of improvement" if just one student demographic group did not perform well on the test. That provided another incentive for students to leave "failing" public schools and attend "successful" private schools—schools that could not fail because they never took the test that would declare them to be failures.[33]

Funding for vouchers does not work the way one might expect. The state takes the money for the vouchers out of MPS's budget, even if the students have not previously been enrolled in MPS schools. Essentially, MPS and Milwaukee property taxpayers pay the cost of private school tuition without being reimbursed by the state.[34] And if a private school expels a student after the third Friday in September, when the state school census is taken, the private school gets to keep the voucher money. It also keeps the money if any students leave voluntarily and return to public schools. The public schools are required to admit the students free of charge. This "funding flaw," as it is called, was apparent as early as 1991, when Juanita Virgil Academy, a voucher school, closed and kept all its funds.[35]

The voucher program started slowly but reached its enrollment cap (about a thousand students) by 1995, the year of Fuller's resignation.[36]

Parents overwhelmingly reported satisfaction with the voucher schools their children attended, and voucher proponents renewed the demand to include religious schools.[37] Nationally, the Republican Party had won control of the House of Representatives the previous year, under the leadership of Newt Gingrich, and conservative causes were gaining ground. The time was right for Wisconsin Governor Tommy Thompson to make a move.[38]

Thompson was joined by the Bradley Foundation, the Milwaukee Metropolitan Association of Commerce, Milwaukee Mayor John Norquist, and other public officials in his push to include religious schools in the voucher program.[39] Richard Abdoo, chairman of the commerce association, said there was no time to waste and that MPS was "creating an army of illiterates with no skills." He pointed to Messmer High School, a Catholic school where most of the students were not Catholic but were receiving PAVE scholarships, as an example of successful private education. "In the MPS system, [the Messmer students] would be in a gang somewhere. How can it hurt to give another five thousand kids a chance?"[40] Norquist, a Democrat, also supported expansion.[41] Norquist blamed MPS for its students' failures and went so far as to proclaim that he wanted to "get rid of a system that stifles choice by parents of students and a system that has virtually no accountability for the employees of the system."[42] Howard Fuller, himself Catholic and no longer working for MPS, endorsed expanding vouchers to religious schools.[43]

However, Polly Williams backed away from the voucher movement at that point, saying she suspected the chamber and others in the business community were using expanded choice as a pretext to eventually remove the income limits from the choice program. In Williams's view, making vouchers available to everyone, regardless of income, would lead only to further abandonment of poor African American children. "I didn't see where their resources really were being used to empower us as much as it was to co-opt us," she told reporters in 1995.[44] She also complained, "The conservatives made me their poster girl as long as it appeared I was supporting their case. And now I am the odd person out. They want the religious schools to be tax supported. Blacks and the poor are being used to legitimize [the conservatives] as the power group."[45] She later said, "In no way was it our intent, in any way, to harm the Milwaukee Public Schools. Our intent was always to show the Milwaukee Public Schools that, see, if parents had more to say, see how much better off the student would be. And to replicate that in the public schools."[46]

Expanded school choice became law on July 27, 1995. Enrollment at that time was limited to 15 percent of the enrollment in MPS, which worked out to a cap of about fifteen thousand students. MTEA and the American Civil Liberties Union sued on the grounds that the law violated separation of church and state.[47] Three years later, in 1998, the US Supreme Court ruled a similar program in Cleveland to be constitutional and refused to hear the Milwaukee case, effectively approving Milwaukee's voucher program.[48]

The rapid expansion of vouchers allowed for some unqualified schools to be admitted to the program. According to a major investigation of 106 voucher schools conducted by the *Milwaukee Journal Sentinel* in 2005, well-established private schools, such as Catholic and Lutheran schools, seemed to do at least as good a job as MPS—teachers worked hard, students learned, and parents reported high levels of satisfaction—but other schools were fraught with problems. Facilities were substandard. Interviews with parents showed that many of them were more inclined to choose schools based on word of mouth rather than academic data. Some schools would not let the reporters into their buildings. Some did not have licensed teachers or even teachers with high school diplomas, which was not a requirement for private schools at that time. Other teachers were not teaching or were teaching at levels below what their students should have been able to do.[49]

Some voucher schools lacked a curriculum or adequate staff. For example, when police investigated a fight at the Academic Solutions Center for Learning, they encountered more than a hundred unsupervised students fighting chaotically among themselves. When asked where the teachers were, students reported they had quit because they were not getting paid.[50] Teachers at Louis Tucker Academy did not have a written curriculum and did not have grades in grade books after three months of school.[51] Northside High School was thrown out of the voucher program because it did not comply with the state's requirement for a minimum number of instructional hours and because it did not have a written curriculum. One student said the pupils passed their time by "doing crossword puzzles and shooting dice."[52]

Some voucher schools faced charges of financial mismanagement. For example, the Ida B. Wells Academy took ninety-four thousand dollars in vouchers from the state, did not report what it did with the money, and then closed.[53] Worse yet, at the Mandella [sic] School of Science and Math, the school's founder reported artificially high enrollment, took three hundred thirty thousand dollars in public funds from the school, spent part of the money on two Mercedes automobiles (one for him and one for his wife), and did not pay the teachers.[54] Meanwhile, four hundred fourteen thousand dollars went missing from the Sa'Rai and Ziegler Upper Excellerated [sic] Academy, which was supposed to have eighty students but had only fifty and had barely any furniture or supplies. When questioned about the name of the school, the principal said "Upper" referred to "the upper room where Jesus prayed," and that "Excellerated" was "short for anything that starts with excel. It's a fusion word combining 'accelerated' and 'excellent.' It's spelled wrong on purpose."[55] Another school, the L.E.A.D.E.R. Institute, was removed from the voucher program when it was discovered that it had fewer students in attendance than it had reported to the state, it did not meet the requirement for minimum hours of instruction, and its leaders had misspent more than four hundred ninety-seven thousand dollars.[56]

Finally, there was Alex's Academic [sic] of Excellence, which is perhaps the strongest example of lack of oversight. James Mitchell opened the school in 1999. Mitchell had been convicted of raping a woman at knifepoint in 1971. He was sentenced to thirty years in prison but was paroled in 1980, only to return to prison in 1984 for committing burglary. He founded a state-funded juvenile treatment center in 1991 that went out of business in 1993. After opening Alex's Academic of Excellence, he was sentenced to six months in prison for tax evasion before the end of the first school year.[57] The school continued to operate but moved around because of numerous fire code violations.[58] Few books or computers were available, and teachers complained that they had not been paid their salaries and had to bring supplies from home. Bus companies and the landlord had also allegedly not been paid, and some staff members were accused of using illegal drugs on school grounds.[59]

Vouchers continued to expand despite these problematic schools. The state raised the enrollment cap from 15,000 to 22,500 in 2006, but it also

required that schools be accredited by a recognized agency.[60] The goal
was to eliminate weak schools while supporting Catholic schools, Lutheran schools, and other schools with good reputations. The Institute
for the Transformation of Learning at Marquette University, a Catholic
university run by the Jesuit order, was one such accreditation agency.
Howard Fuller founded the institute, and it was still under his direction
as of 2014.[61] The Bradley Foundation donated almost $4 million to it
between 1995 and 2010.[62] The voucher enrollment cap was finally eliminated in 2011. The income level was also raised to allow some lower-
middle-class families to participate, and any school in Milwaukee County
was allowed to accept the city's "choice" students in 2011.[63]

Meanwhile, the state shifted money from MPS's budget to voucher
schools.[64] Wisconsin also made a 10 percent cut to school district bud-
gets across the state in 2011.[65] These cuts required MPS to reduce funding for fine arts, physical education, vocational education, and social
services, making MPS look less attractive to parents than ever before.[66]
Some money had to be diverted from teachers' benefits to make up for
the shortfall. Union officials and some MPS administrators and school
board members said that there would have been enough money to fund
the pensions, reduce class sizes, and provide a variety of classes to students if money had not been diverted to vouchers.[67]

Proponents of vouchers believe that voucher schools encourage public
schools to improve through competition. They also hope voucher schools
will turn out a better product (students) at a lower price (nonunion teachers with lower pay and benefits compared to public school teachers).
Voucher schools were not required to report standardized test scores
until 2010, and even then, voucher students were not required to take
the Wisconsin Knowledge and Concepts Exam (WKCE) as public school
students did, which made comparing test scores difficult.[68] Nonetheless,
a couple of studies have been conducted based on whatever data have
been available. One study showed that MPS's test scores improved 3.0
percent to 8.4 percent in the late 1990s after the expansion of vouchers.
Voucher supporters said the public schools improved because of competition from choice schools.[69] Another study, ten years later, reached
similar conclusions,[70] but a third study found that schools that faced high
levels of competition did not perform much differently than schools that
faced little competition.[71]

Even if Milwaukee's schools have improved, the improvement has been slight. According to standardized test results, MPS has remained far behind the rest of Wisconsin. For example, according to the results of WKCE tests, only 62.0 percent of Milwaukee's third-grade students were proficient or advanced in reading in 2010, compared to 80.0 percent of third-grade students in all of Wisconsin. The gap widened as students aged—40.2 percent of Milwaukee's tenth-grade students were proficient or advanced in reading in 2010, compared to 74.7 percent of all of Wisconsin's tenth-grade students.[72]

The assertion that voucher schools turn out better students at a lower price is also only partly true. Few people dispute that private schools often operate at a lower cost than public schools, but a couple of studies have shown that private school students perform only slightly better—less than 10 percent—than public school students on standardized tests.[73] Studies have shown that voucher schools have higher graduation rates than public schools, but those studies did not disaggregate the data on students who were enrolled with vouchers from those who paid tuition and came from higher-income families. Also, those studies provided no evidence that voucher school students needed to meet the same standards as public school students for graduation.[74] Most other studies show no difference in outcomes between students in voucher schools and students in public schools.[75] For years, some voucher schools successfully resisted efforts to release standardized test scores, but when they were forced to do so in 2010, data revealed that MPS students outperformed voucher school students.[76] And even when individual choice schools did exceed MPS, that could have been due to the reality that voucher schools serve fewer special education students and students with behavior problems.[77]

Standards vary from state to state. What constitutes proficiency in one state may be far below proficiency in another state, which is why Wisconsin switched to new cut scores (the minimum score needed to achieve a certain level of proficiency), based on the National Assessment of Educational Progress (NAEP), in 2012. The NAEP requires students to score much higher on standardized tests than Wisconsin had previously. Based on the new standards, only 36 percent of Wisconsin students were proficient in reading, and 48 percent were proficient in mathematics. In Milwaukee, only 14 percent of MPS students were deemed proficient at reading, and 20 percent were proficient in mathematics, while 10 percent of voucher school students were proficient in reading, and 12 percent were proficient in mathematics.[78] The students at one voucher school, Atlas Preparatory Academy, were only 5 percent proficient at reading and mathematics. Meanwhile, students at Travis Academy, another voucher school, were only around 2 percent proficient. Atlas accepted $6.3 million in vouchers during the 2012–13 school year and $46.8 million since it opened in 2001. Travis took $4.5 million from the state in 2012–13 and $39.7 million since it opened in 1997. The Atlas owner/principal paid herself $192,433 in 2009, and the owner/principal of Travis paid herself $216,620 in 2010.[79]

OPEN ENROLLMENT

Vouchers are not the only form of school choice in Milwaukee. Open enrollment is the other main alternative to MPS. In 1997, the state of Wisconsin passed Act 27, which allows students to attend any public school in Wisconsin as long as the school or district is willing to take them.[80] Only 2,464 students took part in the open enrollment program in 1998–99, whereas 18,223 participated in 2004–05, and close to 26,000 students participated in 2008–09. If those students were in their own school district, they would have constituted the second biggest school district in the state.[81] State funding is adjusted to follow the students, and more than $88 million was transferred in 2004–05, including $32 million out of MPS's budget.[82] MPS initially resisted open enrollment, believing it had the potential to drain the district of its remaining white students, but the administration acquiesced after a group of conservatives was elected to the school board in 1999.[83] Three hundred seventy students left the district that year, and 269 of them were white.[84] Four years later, 6,310 students left the district through open enrollment or Chapter 220, leaving MPS only 13.3 percent white in 2005.[85]

Suburban districts like the program because the students who want to leave MPS usually have good grades and test scores. The suburbs also like the money. Twenty-three percent of the students at Greenfield High School, for example, lived in Milwaukee during the 2010–11 school year, generating $2.5 million in additional state aid. As Greenfield Superintendent Conrad Farner said, "Literally, it's keeping us alive. It's absolutely critical to us."[86] The Wauwatosa district, as another example, accepted more than seven thousand Milwaukee students through open enrollment or Chapter 220 in 2010–11. Those students yielded $10 million in state aid and a property tax reduction of about $2.5 million. St. Francis High School reaped an additional $2 million in state aid in 2010–11, because 48 percent of its 580 students lived in Milwaukee. The superintendent of St. Francis said that without the aid the school would probably have to merge with nearby Cudahy High School.[87] Meanwhile, Bay View High School, the MPS school closest to St. Francis, had a neighborhood population of only 7.5 percent in 2010–11. The rest of the students were bused in from other parts of the city.[88] Of the 5,781 Milwaukee students using open enrollment in 2010–11, 61 percent were white, while Bay View High School had a white enrollment of only 12.5 percent.[89] And like voucher schools, districts are not required to admit students with special needs if those needs would put an "undue financial burden" on the district.[90]

In 2011, many children who lived in Milwaukee did not attend MPS. In fact, only about 66 percent of all Milwaukee children attended a conventional MPS school, MPS charter school, or MPS partnership school (an independent "alternative" school contracted with MPS often working with students who are at risk of dropping out) by 2012.[91] Table 1 summarizes enrollment patterns.

TABLE 1: Milwaukee School Enrollments, 2008–09 and 2011–12

TYPE OF SCHOOL	ENROLLMENT, 2008–09	ENROLLMENT, 2011–12	PERCENT CHANGE
Traditional MPS	78,148	72,672	-7.0
MPS partnership	2,823	1,216	-56.9
MPS charters	2,503	4,573	+82.7
Non-MPS charters	4,947	7,365	+48.9
Voucher schools	20,113	24,941	+24.0
Open enrollment	4,688	6,696	+42.8
Chapter 220	2,300	1,792	-22.1
Total	**115,522**	**119,255**	**+3.2**

THE NEIGHBORHOOD SCHOOLS INITIATIVE

Charter schools, voucher programs, and open enrollment offer significant competition for MPS. Therefore, the district made two policy changes in the 1990s, both of which represented a reduction in magnet schools. Those two changes were the neighborhood schools initiative (NSI) and the small schools initiative.

The NSI was supposed to give parents the choice many of them really wanted—neighborhood schools. Advocates for neighborhood schools pointed to tremendous academic success at Hi-Mount Elementary, Clarke Street Elementary, Fratney Elementary, and Andrew Douglas Community Academy middle school, all of which served neighborhood populations that were traditionally thought of as underachieving.[92] Neighborhood schools had several potential advantages. Schools could once again inspire neighborhood pride, as North Division had when it was a neighborhood school. Neighborhood schools would be more convenient for families without automobiles, making it easier for parents to get involved in the schools. Logically, they would also reduce the transportation budget. White families might be more apt to stay in MPS if their local schools were only for children in the neighborhood and if magnet schools had tougher admissions standards.[93] More bluntly, when discussing the purpose of NSI, conservative school board member John Gardner allegedly said, "We need to insulate the wealthy and white students from the floaters."[94]

The school board voted unanimously to move back toward neighborhood schools in 1997, but it took little action to implement the NSI until 1999, when five conservative "reformers" were elected to the board.[95] The conservatives were led by Gardner, who spent more than one hundred ninety thousand dollars to win his seat, much of which came from out-of-state donors who supported privatizing education, including the Walton family, of Walmart fame.[96] Gardner, who was white, beat Theodoll Taylor, a retired principal, who was African American. Gardner won 57 percent of the overall vote and won 71 percent of the vote in the six whitest aldermanic districts.[97] The new board, with a conservative majority, endorsed vouchers, open enrollment, and the NSI. Crowds of whites cheered at the school board meeting as the NSI vote was taken.[98] The board also made the bold move of hiring Hi-Mount Elementary School's principal, Spence Korté, as superintendent, after the brief administrations of Fuller's former deputy superintendent Robert Jasna, Acting Superintendent Barbara Horton, and outsider Alan Brown, who had been superintendent in Waukegan, Illinois. Korté, who was white, had successfully run Hi-Mount as a neighborhood school for years and was well respected by parents and administrators.[99]

The school board approved Korté's radical plan for neighborhood schools. MPS would borrow $170 million to construct new elementary schools, build additions to overcrowded schools, and renovate non-MPS buildings for school use. MPS would make ten thousand new seats available for students who wanted to attend schools in their neighborhoods. Once those students were removed from the buses, that would leave open ten thousand seats at the schools in which they were currently enrolled, which would enable additional students to choose neighborhood schools, moving more students off buses. The effect would repeat several times until an estimated twenty-seven thousand students would be removed from the buses. The plan would create a 45 percent reduction in busing, saving almost $25 million at the beginning. If the students stayed in neighborhood schools through high school, even greater savings would be generated, and the new schools would be paid for in less than ten years. Some people said the plan was a return to segregation, but MPS had few white students left at that point.[100] Busing was not doing much to facilitate integration, and, as Polly Williams said, "We're transferring over 20,000 black children now from one black school to another black school."[101]

According to a poll conducted in 1999 by UWM and the Public Policy Forum, 73 percent of people in the Milwaukee metropolitan area favored neighborhood schools over busing, even when busing was used to promote racial integration, a percentage that was consistent with earlier polling data from the 1960s and 1970s. Seventy percent of all respondents said they supported the NSI. That included 61 percent of African Americans and 77 percent of Latinos. When asked to rate the importance of integration on a scale of 1 to 5, with 5 being very important, the respondents averaged only 3.41.[102] The legislature approved the necessary bond issue, and Governor Thompson signed it in October 1999, despite a warning from the Public Policy Forum that the poll data were inconclusive, which meant that the plan from MPS was not certain to work.[103]

The final plan received school board approval in August 2000 and was scaled down from Korté's original proposal.[104] It called for $100 million in borrowing and predicted a decline of twenty thousand bused students and savings of $15 million. The plan boosted the number of kindergarten-through-eighth-grade (K–8) schools from ten to forty-seven in MPS. Some of them would be converted from existing elementary schools, one would be converted from Edison Middle School, and the rest would be new schools. The shift to K–8 schools was prompted by parents' requests to keep their children in smaller schools.[105] The big boost in K–8 schools required closing several of the district's middle schools.[106]

But things did not work out as planned. Despite the polls showing support for neighborhood schools, parents did not sign up in the predicted numbers—only 15.7 percent opted to do so for the fall of 2001.[107] Seventy percent of all students were still bused.[108] Milwaukeeans also elected two new school board members who were opposed to the neighborhood schools plan.[109] The *Milwaukee Journal Sentinel* said Superintendent Korté's job was in jeopardy.[110] Korté, by most accounts, was an able administrator. But critics said he let the school board determine too many district policies, and the board had grossly miscalculated parents' desire to enroll their children in neighborhood schools.[111] MPS continued to be plagued by low test scores, a high school graduation rate of only 56 percent, and an African American graduation rate of only 34 percent.[112] Korté managed to hold out for two years before resigning under pressure from the board in 2002.[113]

William Andrekopoulos became the new superintendent that summer. He had been principal of Fritsche Middle School and was known as a maverick who pushed hard for more authority over his school. He promised to continue to decentralize the school district; to continue the NSI; and to raise standards for teachers, administrators, and students.[114] Construction of neighborhood schools continued to boom into 2003, and Andrekopoulos decided to nudge students into them by limiting students' choices at the elementary level to magnet schools and a few schools in the region where they lived.[115] Students whose parents did not meet enrollment deadlines were assigned to their neighborhood schools.[116]

Parents, however, still wanted a broad array of choices, so classrooms stood empty in many new schools as well as in the expanded older schools.[117] The *Milwaukee Journal Sentinel* visited every one of those schools in 2008, which is the first and, as of this writing, only comprehensive review of the NSI. The *Journal Sentinel* found that enrollment dropped at nearly half the schools that added classrooms. Reporters found that excess classrooms had been converted to storage and detention areas, recreation rooms, and teachers' lounges or just sat empty. Students near Auer Avenue School, for example, attended more than ninety different MPS schools, while its $2 million addition went unused. In another example, Hi-Mount School, where Spence Korté had been principal, added six classrooms when it expanded to a K–8, but Hi-Mount had an increase of only thirty-four students by 2007. The new construction included a science lab, but the school could not afford a science specialist because it did not have enough students.[118]

Clarke Street Elementary School experienced similar problems. The school had high test scores and had reached enrollment capacity, so MPS built a $4.1 million middle school addition for it. But as staff positions and before- and after-school programs were cut, the remaining teachers faced a workload increase, and the quality of instruction suffered. Test scores declined, and families left the school. Enrollment declined by 33 percent after the addition was built.[119]

One of MPS's biggest failures was a partnership with Holy Redeemer Institutional Church of God in Christ. MPS agreed to convert a warehouse near Thirty-Fifth Street and Hampton Avenue, a very poor area of the city, into a school complex with space to accommodate 405 district students. The complex would serve as a satellite for the Thirty-Fifth Street School two blocks away and would include a new Boys & Girls Club and a private school for Holy Redeemer, which was a voucher school. The building cost more than $15 million. Holy Redeemer owned it and built it. MPS paid $7 million upfront to lease space for fourth- through eighth-graders, essentially providing nearly half the construction money. The district spent $4.5 million more on a second addition for kindergarten through third grade at the original Thirty-Fifth Street campus. But enrollment was so low that by September 2007, after being open for three years and with twenty-one years remaining on the lease, MPS quietly moved out and consolidated the school in the original Thirty-Fifth Street building. Thus, the district gave a $7 million subsidy to a church to build a school that MPS was not even using, and it still had to pay $223,000 per year to provide building maintenance. Wilson Wells, a parent at Thirty-Fifth Street School, said, "It was a waste of a lot of resources and money.

Now they are paying for the space, and it's unoccupied. And they want to raise my taxes." MPS did not save money on busing, because parents near Thirty-Fifth Street School still chose schools outside their neighborhoods. MPS decided to recoup some of its losses by cutting art, music, physical education, and other electives, creating even more empty classrooms at Thirty-Fifth Street School.[120]

That was not the only time MPS partnered with a church. MPS paired LaFollette Elementary School with Rockhill Missionary Baptist Church in 2003 at school board member Charlene Hardin's urging. MPS gave the congregation seven hundred forty thousand dollars to build a new church with four attached classrooms. Rockhill used the money to make a down payment on construction and borrowed the rest. MPS planned to operate the school as an extension of LaFollette for twenty years, and Rockhill was supposed to recruit students from its congregation. MPS made this decision even though LaFollette's enrollment was declining. Environmental problems caused a delay, so MPS allowed the church to temporarily meet in LaFollette's new gymnasium, which cost nine hundred thousand dollars to build, while a second contractor was recruited. The church and classroom additions were finished in 2006, but the rooms were never used due to a further decline in LaFollette's enrollment. Rockhill's enrollment declined too; it was down to just twenty families.[121] The school board voted in 2011 to close LaFollette at the end of the school year.[122]

All told, the district spent $102 million on the neighborhood schools initiative from 2001 until 2005. Thirty million dollars of that sum was spent on major additions to schools where enrollment had actually declined, and an additional $19.5 million went toward construction at schools where enrollment gains had fallen far short of expectations. Interest payments will push the final cost past $175 million by 2024, because most of the money was borrowed. Just before the construction program was approved in 2000, MPS spent $57 million a year on busing, but in 2007–2008, the district spent $59.5 million. The percentage of MPS children attending their neighborhood schools actually declined during that interval, and even the expanded schools that gained students got less than 40 percent of them from their designated neighborhoods. The rest were bused to school.[123]

The district based its construction decisions on misleading data. MPS paid for phone and door-to-door surveys and held hundreds of community meetings, which were sparsely attended, before developing the plan. According to the survey, seven out of ten parents who sent their children to schools outside their neighborhood, mostly by bus, were very satisfied with their choice, and three out of four parents said they did not consider their neighborhood school a viable option. Parents were also asked to list what they wanted in their children's schools. Then they were asked whether they would choose a neighborhood school if it had all those attributes. Fewer than half the respondents said they would be "very likely" to do so. The *Milwaukee Journal Sentinel* implied that some board members, such as Charlene Hardin, may have ignored enrollment trends in order to secure construction contracts for their constituents. MPS chose to ignore the survey data and listened to the few vocal parents who attended the community meetings, a fact that surprised Craig Maher, who oversaw the survey and later became a University of Wisconsin–Oshkosh public administration professor: "MPS's outreach effort failed in the sense that the policy outcome did not accurately reflect the opinions of the citizens." Or as parent Tina Johnson, who was concerned about neighborhood safety, said, "You can't just build a facility and expect people to come when in between is a violent environment. That's why parents continue to opt for busing."[124]

MPS also failed to take other types of schools into account. Specifically, when MPS surveyed parents, it did not consider that some parents had already enrolled or were planning on enrolling their children in magnet schools, charter schools, and voucher schools. Charters and vouchers were growing at substantial rates in the early 2000s.[125] Simply put, the district acted as though it could stop students from leaving just by building schools. It cut its marketing budget and told its schools to recruit students on their own, but not all of them did. Reading scores declined at sixteen of the twenty-two schools with new buildings or additions, which hindered enrollment. At Thirty-Fifth Street School, for example, with all its empty classrooms, the percentage of fourth-graders who were proficient at reading fell from 56 percent in 2002 to 33 percent in 2007, and math scores declined from 40 percent to 33 percent. When interviewed, teachers cited disorganization in MPS, budget cuts, poverty, and the lack of strong principals as factors in the decline of student achievement. These are factors that cannot be addressed by new construction. In fact, the neighborhood schools that did show increases in test scores were frequently in white neighborhoods on the south side, which had higher numbers of middle-class students and had principals who were strong leaders. Parents flocked to those schools.[126]

In contrast to the middle-class south side schools that were thriving, McNair Elementary at North Twenty-Third Street and West Fairmount Avenue was a neighborhood school located in a residential African American neighborhood with a low crime rate and light traffic. The school was physically attractive and had lots of playground space, and a reporter from the *Journal Sentinel* observed that "teachers and students appeared focused on appropriate activities and hallways were orderly. Principal Willie Fuller was friendly, and so were teachers and students. A writing contest sponsored by an outside group seemed to encourage students to take extra steps aimed at achievement." But at least according to standardized measures, the school was declining. Reading proficiency scores slipped from 48 percent in 2002 to 42 percent in 2007, and math proficiency declined from 52 percent to 42 percent in the same period. The addition to the school did not attract more students. In fact, enrollment fell from 313 students in September 1999 to 243 in September 2000—even though the school added space for 162 more students. Funding from MPS decreased in proportion to the decrease in enrollment. The school completely eliminated art and music to save money, and cut physical education back to two days per week. The new library had a librarian only one day per week. Six of the nine new classrooms were not used for conducting classes, and six classrooms in the older sections of the building were also unused. The additions cost $2.7 million.[128] McNair closed in 2010 and reopened as a middle school and extension of Rufus King High School, which was less than two miles away.[127] Thus, a magnet school had won ownership over what was supposed to be a neighborhood school.

The failure of the NSI and persistent exodus of students to non-MPS charter, voucher, and suburban schools combined so that, by 2005, MPS had capacity for more than one hundred twenty thousand students but had about only eighty-six thousand. The school board then closed several elementary schools, most of the middle schools, and Juneau High School, despite the fact that it had built new schools and additions onto others.[128] The closure of Juneau was particularly contentious. Built in 1933 on Milwaukee's west side, the school had a capacity of 1,200 but had an enrollment of only 942. The staff and students protested the closure at a six-and-a-half-hour school board meeting to no avail. The school board voted five to four to shut it down. The projected savings from closing the school was $1.4 million.[129] People began to criticize the NSI, but Superintendent Andrekopoulos defended it: "When you build a school, you're building it for over 100 years. If we would have put up shanties and put up temporary buildings . . . that would have been very shortsighted."[130]

SMALL HIGH SCHOOLS

MPS pursued one last major reform strategy involving choice in the 2000s—the small high schools initiative. The movement began in the late 1980s in urban districts that were looking for innovative ideas to meet the needs of students who were not successful in traditional comprehensive high schools. Small high schools typically have fewer than four hundred students, and some have fewer than two hundred. A school may be in a stand-alone building, such as a former elementary school or a rented space, or it may be in a multiplex—a building that used to house a comprehensive high school but is reconfigured to accommodate three to six small high schools. Each school is supposed to have a particular theme, much like magnet schools, and the idea is that students will pick the schools for which they are best suited. Small schools are intended to foster a bond among students and between students and teachers. Classes may rotate from one teacher to another, as in a middle school. Because the enrollment is so small, students may have the same teachers for all four years of high school. Sports, clubs, and electives are harder to offer, however,[131] because small schools cannot take advantage of economies of scale.[132] The public took little notice in the small schools movement until 2003, when the Bill and Melinda Gates Foundation donated $51 million to New York City to start sixty-seven small high schools. The foundation gave millions more in subsequent years to other districts, including Milwaukee, to establish small high schools.[133]

After studying small high school designs in Baltimore and New York, MPS planned to create forty-five schools between 2003 and 2008 that would serve about sixteen thousand students, despite inconclusive research on the effectiveness of small high schools.[134] Originally, the district planned to convert seven of the fifteen high schools to multiplexes, effectively abolishing a large portion of the magnet school plan. The Gates

Foundation committed more than $17 million to the effort, intended to help MPS modify buildings and retrain staff.[135]

But the district converted only three high schools to small school multiplexes. North Division, once the medical and dental science magnet, was broken up into three schools in 2003: the School of the Humanities, the Truth Institute for Leadership and Service, and the Genesis School of Business Technology/Trade, Health, and Human Services. At the time, about half of North Division's entering freshmen read below a fourth-grade level, and the school's attendance level was only about two-thirds of students. District officials hoped the small schools would foster a sense of belonging and that achievement would improve.[136] Washington (the computer magnet) and Marshall (the broadcasting magnet) were broken up in 2004. South Division (tourism, food service, and recreation) and Bradley Tech were allowed to remain comprehensive schools but were reconfigured internally to create "small learning communities" in the schools, similar to the schools in a multiplex but with one administrative structure.[137]

Although most district officials praised the moves, there were a few dissenters. Tom Balistreri, a school board member and former principal of Rufus King High School, said the initiative involved too many schools and was rushed through without the opportunity to train new administrators and lead teachers. "The schools have not been set up for success, and there's no evidence that they are going to have a higher level of achievement," he said. John Schissler, who taught at Marshall for thirty-two years and coordinated the school's alumni association, predicted that the initiative would fail due to high costs: "I know they've tried it in New York and a few other large cities, but after thirty-two years teaching in MPS, all the new programs they've tried to implement, unfortunately, have gone awry, especially as soon as the money dries up."[138] Jay Bullock, an English teacher at Madison University High School, wrote a letter to the *Journal Sentinel* and explained, "We have heard, from colleagues at schools such as Marshall, Washington, and the erstwhile North Division, that the transitions are messy, support is insufficient, and the teachers are shouldering responsibilities that take away from teaching duties."[139]

Data on the freshman class from the 2004–05 school year showed that plans were not working out as expected. There were 9,857 students in ninth grade, but only 4,551 students in twelfth grade, or 46 percent of the ninth-grade total, in 2004–05. The rest dropped out or left MPS. Twenty-two percent of all freshmen were repeating the ninth grade. Some of the repeating freshmen would never graduate—more than 40 percent of the district's dropouts were in grade nine. The ninth-grade suspension rate (number of suspensions divided by number of students) was 48 percent, although that was because many students were suspended more than once. The ninth-grade attendance rate was only 77 percent. District officials pointed out that those startling numbers were why they were creating more K–8 schools and more small high schools, ignoring the facts that the percentage of students in K–8s had already increased from 9 percent to 29 percent and that the percentage of students in small high schools had increased from 2 percent to 23 percent from 1999 to 2005 with no noticeable improvement in achievement, attendance, or behavior.[140]

MPS opened more small high schools in 2005, including:

- Alliance School, a school for gay, lesbian, bisexual, or transgendered students and other students who felt bullied in their previous schools

- The Maasai Institute, which took its approach to education from the culture and philosophy of an African tribe

- Foster & Williams, which taught American Sign Language

- The Milwaukee Learning Laboratory & Institute, which was supposed to teach social justice, leadership, and service through participation in the community

- Three schools inside Washington: Washington High School of Expeditionary Learning (a project-based curriculum); Washington High School of Information Technology; and Washington High School of Law, Education, and Public Service (LEAPS)

- Three schools inside Marshall: W. E. B. Du Bois High School, which took over Marshall's communications specialty; Milwaukee Academy of Aviation, Science & Technology, where students were supposed to train in aviation, aerospace, and aeronautics; and Marshall Montessori, a college-prep school that used a variation of the Montessori system of education[141]

Almost none of MPS's plans worked out as intended. One problem was that students wanted sports, clubs, and electives, which the small schools did not have the resources to provide. Also, hundreds of students enrolled in schools they knew nothing about, then complained that they did not like the school's specialty; and other students were randomly assigned to schools that had low enrollments. Many of these students were so far behind academically that they could not take classes in their school's specialty. Some teachers who had spent a year planning curricula had to stop what they were doing so they could teach basic reading and mathematics. Test scores and attendance rates did not improve, and schools could not always meet the needs of special education students—some did not have the equipment, and others did not even hire special education teachers.[142] Teachers had to teach multiple subjects because the schools were too small to afford full-time teachers in every area. That meant teachers were not always licensed in what they were teaching.[143]

Many of the small high schools were not successful in other ways. The Alliance School received positive media attention for its efforts to make students feel comfortable in the face of bullying, but students did not perform well academically, and it was threatened with closure.[144] The Maasai Institute closed in 2008 with 150 students and four hundred thousand dollars in debt.[145] The school board voted to close Foster & Williams at the end of the 2009–10 school year.[146] The teachers at Milwaukee Language Laboratory & Institute had to change their curriculum completely when they found out most of their students lacked basic reading, writing, and math skills. The project-based classes they had envisioned never developed. Finally, escalating costs in the face of low enrollment and staff cuts caused the nine remaining staff members to request closure by the school board.[147]

The multiplexes could circumvent some of these problems by sharing resources, but none of the schools inside North Division worked out well. Of the twenty-four sophomores at the School of Humanities, only one was proficient in reading and none were proficient in mathematics, according to state test scores. Humanities had 189 chronically truant students even though it had an official enrollment of only 143, which indicates that it also had high student turnover. It had a 92 percent suspension rate in 2004–05, and there were eleven reported incidents involving weapons or drugs. The violence continued the next year until Superintendent

Andrekopoulos ordered the school closed in October for safety reasons. The school board ratified his decision at its next meeting.[148] The Truth Institute struggled along for three more years and was finally closed in 2009.[149] Metropolitan High School, another small school that moved in after Humanities closed, was also closed in 2009. Genesis was allowed to continue at a new location. The African American Immersion High School (formerly Malcolm X), another recent tenant, was allowed to take over the entire North Division building in 2009, despite the fact that the Department of Public Instruction had named it the lowest-performing school in the state that year.[150] African American Immersion was given the name North Division in 2011.[151]

The small schools inside Washington High School still did not show significant improvement either. Data from fall 2005 showed an attendance rate of only 45.5 percent at the School of Expeditionary Learning and 59.7 percent at the School of Information Technology, in contrast to a district high school rate of 72.5 percent.[152] Washington High School LEAPS was put on the state's list of lowest-performing schools in 2010, so MPS closed it at the end of the school year.[153] The School of Expeditionary Learning closed the following year, and Washington School of Information Technology was allowed to expand to fill the building, ironically returning it to McMurrin's original magnet specialty, although enrollment remained below capacity.[154]

The schools inside Marshall did not fare any better. The aviation school closed in 2009 due to budgetary shortfalls and chronic failures in required classes, which prevented students from taking aviation classes.[155] The Montessori school asked to be moved to the old Juneau High School to get away from Du Bois High School, which was plagued with violence.[156] But the Montessori school did not show enough improvement or high enough enrollment at Juneau, so the school board voted in 2011 to close it.[157] The board moved the MacDowell Montessori K–8 into Juneau as a K–12 school.[158] Du Bois ended up on the same list as Washington LEAPS in 2010 and closed a year later.[159]

One small school, Ronald Reagan High School, was actually very successful. Located in the old Sholes Middle School, on the far south side of Milwaukee, Reagan grew from 127 students in 2003 to more than 1,000 in 2011, offering the same rigorous academic program used at Rufus King High School. It was located in a safe neighborhood and had a dynamic principal who had a reputation of expecting the best from students, teachers, and district administrators.[160] By growing to more than a thousand students, Reagan may have demonstrated that big high schools are actually more effective than small ones.

The *Milwaukee Journal Sentinel* ran a series of articles in 2006 examining MPS high schools, both big and small. It found that, generally speaking, MPS graduates were not as well prepared for higher education or employment as their suburban counterparts. The average MPS ACT score was 17.5 in 2004–05, compared to a statewide average of 22.2. MPS students were not assigned as much homework as suburban students, and the assignments were usually shorter. Students who had attended suburban middle schools and MPS high schools reported that their middle school classes were more difficult than their high school classes. There was variation within MPS too. One student who transferred from Marshall High School to Riverside High School said, "A 4.0 in John Marshall is like the equivalent of a 2.5 at Riverside." The student successfully graduated and enrolled at UWM, but after seeing how well prepared suburban students were for college, he said, "I feel like [the MPS] kids have been cheated out of an education."[161]

MPS teachers said that they had to lower their expectations because students were reading very far behind grade level. They reported that students were no longer registering for advanced math or science classes and that teachers had to use low-level worksheets because students were disruptive during lecture and engaged in horseplay during group work.[162] But even then, students did not turn in their work. Reporters found students were disengaged, no matter how big or small the school. Large groups of students walked the halls all day long in the big high schools, and administrators and safety aides had to constantly patrol the halls, looking for students. Classroom doors were locked, and students were not allowed in the halls unless it was an emergency.[163] Reporters believed that small schools made better connections between teachers and students, but again, they believed the schools were not rigorous.[164] UWM officials agreed that MPS graduates were often unprepared for college. Seventy-two percent of MPS graduates who were UWM freshmen in 2004–05 required remedial math classes, compared to only 25 percent of graduates from other districts. Just 22 percent of UWM students who had graduated from MPS in 1999 earned bachelor's degrees within six years, compared to 43 percent of other students. When looking only at students in the top quarter of their high school classes, 36 percent from MPS graduated from UWM, compared to 59 percent of other students. MATC reported similar disparities, and the Milwaukee Metropolitan Chamber of Commerce reported that MPS graduates were often late for work and did not show much initiative.[165] When Gregory Thornton took over as superintendent in 2010, he promised big changes in MPS, including higher standards, a more uniform curriculum, better professional development for teachers, higher tests scores and graduation rates, more students enrolling in college after graduation, safer schools, lower suspension rates, better engagement with parents and community members, increased collaboration with teachers, and more fiscal responsibility.[166]

As other schools continued to decline in both enrollment and academic performance, MPS closed buildings under Andrekopoulos and continued to do so under Thornton. Of the forty-two small high schools that had opened under the small schools initiative, only twenty-three were still open in fall 2010.[167] Additionally, as the number of middle schools shrank due to competition from K–8 schools, MPS allowed five middle schools to grow into what it called 6–12 schools, or middle school/high school, giving students and parents even more choices.[168] Samuel Morse Middle School for the Gifted and Talented expanded to this format and moved into Marshall after the small schools inside Marshall closed or moved.[169] Custer High School closed after years of low achievement and reopened as a multiplex with two 6–12 schools and one K–8 school in 2011.[170] The schools consolidated into one program in 2014 and it is now known as the Barack Obama School of Career and Technical Education.[171]

Bay View High School merged with Fritsche Middle School as a 6–12 school, but the new configuration of Bay View did not improve academic achievement, and the school was plagued by a rash of violence between 2010 and 2012, including a riot in the cafeteria before school and a stabbing on a bus. The Bay View neighborhood, which is noted for its liberal values and commitment to the city and urban life, wanted a neighborhood high school. Parents asked that the current Bay View student body be removed and that the school introduce a rigorous college-preparatory curriculum and an admissions test for non-neighborhood students.[172] Some people have accused Bay View parents of being "elitist," but Bay View parents say they just want what is best for their children.[173] The school board approved a plan in 2013 to phase out the middle school program, reduce busing, and establish a program in science, technology, engineering, arts, and mathematics.[174] Only time will tell if the changes will be effective.

More changes occurred between 2011 and 2013. Each of the three original multiplexed high schools were occupied by a single school. There were only six middle schools and eleven big high schools left by 2011.[175] Superintendent Thornton also introduced a "Long-Range Facilities Master Plan," which aimed to close even more underused schools and to duplicate popular magnet programs, such as Montessori and gifted and talented, and spread them around the city to reduce transportation costs.[176] High school specialties were barely mentioned in the plan. The district website recommends that parents visit individual schools to find out about their programs, and the MPS school catalog describes many schools in vague terms—such as "college-prep," "at-risk," or "rigorous."[177] Even schools that are performing far below the state average are listed as "college-prep." With so many students failing required classes, high schools have had to eliminate the specialties that made them attractive. North Division, for example, no longer has its medical program, and the once-popular word-processing and marketing program at Hamilton had been reduced to fewer than three full-time teachers in 2012–13.[178] Rufus King, Ronald Reagan, Riverside, Milwaukee High School of the Arts, and Milwaukee School of Languages are the only schools that really stand out as being college preparatory in the catalog, and many of the other schools promote the fact that they have GED programs and "credit recovery options" for failing students.[179] Those options do not sound appealing to most middle-class parents.

Thus, the city of Milwaukee moved into an era of unprecedented school choice in the twenty-first century. It was far different from the school system that had existed a century before, with a neighborhood system and only a few citywide schools. It was also unlike anything Lloyd Barbee had envisioned, with its reliance on religious schools and suburban schools to provide choices to families. And it was also very much the opposite of Lee McMurrin's plan for schools, with the abandonment of most aspects of the magnet plan, the expansion of small high schools, the exodus of students from MPS, and many half-empty buildings.

CHAPTER 7

MILWAUKEE, CHOICE, AND U.S. EDUCATION POLICY

S cott Walker was elected governor of Wisconsin in November 2010. Walker, a Republican, ran on a platform of tax cuts and improved fiscal responsibility, including cuts to public employees' pay and benefits. That seemed to make sense to many Wisconsinites. After all, employees in the private sector had faced reductions in pay and benefits since Wisconsin's industrial base began declining in the 1970s. Public employees had largely been spared these sacrifices. Then, on February 11, 2012, Walker unveiled his "budget repair bill," formally known as Act 10, to the Republican-controlled state legislature. The budget bill required most public employees to contribute to their pensions, which was essentially a 5.8 percent cut in take-home pay. The bill also required most public employees to pay at least 12.6 percent of their insurance premiums. Although it was proposed as a fiscal measure, Act 10 also forbade most public unions from negotiating anything other than total base wages. They would no longer be able to bargain collectively for salary schedules or benefits packages, which meant school districts were free to raise employee insurance contributions. The government would dictate all terms of working conditions, including evaluation, promotion, dismissal, preference of assignment, safety, and grievance procedures. Act 10 also made union membership optional. Walker said he did that to save workers union dues, a gift to workers who would now have smaller paychecks. Liberal commentators believed Walker's true motive was to encourage workers to leave their unions by limiting unions' capacity to represent them. They also pointed out that Walker gave tax breaks to billionaires, while he essentially cut the pay of thousands of middle-class public employees.[1]

Thousands of teachers, other public employees, and supporters descended on Madison, the state capital. They occupied the capitol building around the clock. Some stayed there for as long as twenty-six days. By the end of the first week, private unions joined them, and crowds swelled to an estimated one hundred thousand. The protesters reasoned that if the public unions fell, the private unions would too, and Scott Walker admitted as much to Diane Hendricks, a billionaire who had financially supported his campaign.[2] The Walker campaign had also received contributions from out-of-state billionaires, such as Charles and David Koch, who frequently donate millions of dollars to antiunion political candidates. As a result of the US Supreme Court ruling in *Citizens United v. Federal Election Commission* (2010), corporations could spend unlimited sums of money on political activity, which meant the unions were some of the only organizations capable of raising significant funds for Democratic candidates, and even then, they were consistently outspent by corporate interests. Unions said that Act 10 was financially unnecessary and offered to make the concessions on benefits if they could maintain their other collective bargaining rights. Walker refused to compromise. Liberal commentators called him a union buster and reasoned that if Wisconsin succumbed to right-to-work laws, other states would not be far behind. The world was captivated by scenes from the demonstrations in Wisconsin. Thousands of supporters who could not be there donated food, water, and supplies for protesters. People from around the world, including Egypt, which was experiencing its own revolution, donated pizza via credit cards—at one point, more than twelve hundred pizzas per day.[3]

Things looked hopeful to the protesters for a while. All fourteen Democratic state senators fled to Illinois to prevent the Republicans from obtaining the necessary quorum to pass the contested budget bill.[4] But eventually, the Republicans removed the financial aspects of the bill, which meant they needed a smaller quorum. Eighteen of the nineteen Republican senators voted for Act 10.[5] Wisconsinites organized a recall of the governor but failed to remove him from office.

Wisconsin's experience is important for the other forty-nine states. The Wisconsin legislature and Governor Walker expanded vouchers from Milwaukee to the entire state in 2013—five hundred for the first year and one thousand for subsequent years. They also approved tax breaks for people who pay private school tuition, and they increased funding for private schools.[6] If Milwaukee's experience is any indication, then Wisconsin may be on its way to two systems of schools—one publicly operated and the other privately run with almost no accountability.[7] Vouchers and charter schools are spreading to other states under the mantle of "choice." According to the National School Boards Association, eight states and the District of Columbia have voucher programs, and all but nine states have charter schools.[8] According to the National Alliance of Public Charter Schools, only 12 percent of charter schools are unionized.[9]

According to liberals, the expansion of vouchers and charters, combined with limits on collective bargaining rights, indicate that Walker and the conservatives are part of a larger political agenda. It appears to them that an alliance of conservative educators, politicians, and business interests seek to empower the wealthy over the poor and middle class through a conservative takeover of schools and possibly every level of government.[10] Polly Williams certainly thought the purpose of vouchers changed. Williams helped forge the original voucher plan as a means of empowering African Americans, but she said in 2013 that she believed vouchers were "hijacked" by conservatives: "They have definitely undermined the intent of the [original] legislation. I could have never gotten that legislation passed the way it is now. The upper-income people, they push the low incomes out. It's as if the struggle we went through twenty-some years ago—now the upper crust have taken over."[11]

The struggle Polly Williams referred to seems far removed from the current state of education in Milwaukee. The expansion of choice has been the main theme since the 1960s. Lloyd Barbee sued the school board to integrate students. The result was a magnet school plan that was supposed to induce racial integration and increase academic achievement by giving students choices. But the plan was difficult to implement, was not well received by parents (African American or white), and did not meet its goals for most Milwaukee students. So choice was redefined in the 1980s and 1990s to include privatization of schools and, more broadly, new educational options in charter schools and suburban schools. And despite all the promised solutions, Milwaukee's public schools are not thriving. Only about two-thirds of Milwaukee children are enrolled in MPS, and increased choice has not yielded the promised results. It makes one wonder whether choice is really worth the price.

Psychologist Barry Schwartz explains it this way: Schwartz walked into a store and asked to buy a pair of jeans. The salesclerk asked, "Do you want them slim fit, easy fit, relaxed fit, baggy, or extra baggy? Do you want them stonewashed, acid washed, or distressed? Do you want them button-fly or zipper-fly? Do you want them faded or regular?" Schwartz was stunned—all he wanted was a "regular" pair of jeans. He ended up trying on all the styles and left with a pair that he liked, but he also left with feelings of wasted time, fatigue, self-doubt, anxiety, and dread.[12]

Schwartz concluded that although some choice is good, more choice is not necessarily better. In fact, Schwartz says an overabundance of choice can lead to bad decisions, stress, dissatisfaction, and even clinical depression. Schwartz writes that, by some estimates, depression rates in the United States in 2000 were ten times that of 1900, and suicide rates tripled between 1965 and 2000.[13] The standard of living in the United States was much higher in 2000 than it was a century before, and more choices are offered to people than ever before. But expanding choice does not necessarily make people happy.[14]

Likewise, the idea of having many choices in schools makes people feel good at first, but by most accounts, education has not improved substantially in Milwaukee in the past forty years. In fact, many people argue that the schools are worse than ever. Thinking about those educational problems makes people tired, frustrated, and depressed, as Schwartz found when he tried to buy a pair of jeans. It also leads one to consider whether Milwaukee and Wisconsin should offer only a couple of choices in schools and simply concentrate on providing a really good education to all students.

Furthermore, choice, in a school context, assumes that parents are well informed, but many parents are not. Consider, as Schwartz does, that most respondents to a recent medical survey claimed they would want to choose their own treatment if they were diagnosed with cancer, but an overwhelming number of cancer patients do not actually choose their own treatment. They defer to their doctors, assuming medical professionals know best.[15] Yet advocates of choice in urban education somehow think that parents, who oftentimes were not successful in school, can make the best choices for their children with almost no guidance.

Nonetheless, civic leaders and business interests often insist competition and choice are essential components of a business model for education.[16] According to the 2011 National Assessment of Educational Progress (NAEP), MPS had lower reading and mathematics scores in grades four and eight than seventeen or eighteen other urban school districts. Only 38 percent of fourth-graders and 47 percent of eighth-graders were reading at or above grade level, and only 57 percent of fourth-graders and 42 percent of eighth-graders were doing mathematics at or above grade level.[17] Furthermore, the MPS four-year graduation rate was only 62.8 percent in 2011, compared to a statewide rate of 87 percent.[18] Charter schools and voucher schools were supposed to be the answer to the problem of underachievement, but these schools perform about the same as MPS schools. It would appear, then, that competition and choice do not actually improve achievement. Therefore, people who advocate a "business model" for education should be mindful that methods of manufacturing (teaching), quality of management (administration), and competition (choices), while important, are not enough, by themselves, to significantly improve education for Wisconsin's most challenging students.

Educating Milwaukee becomes more of a challenge when taking into account the city's vast economic and racial disparities. Numerous studies have pointed to the link between poverty, family background, and student achievement.[19] Milwaukee was the fourth-poorest city in the United States in 2010, according to the US Census Bureau.[20] After checking the poverty list against the NAEP list, a strong correlation between poverty and student achievement is revealed. Both liberal and conservative scholars agree that family background has an important impact on education. For example, parents who were successful in school usually raise children who are successful in school, and parents with advanced degrees are more likely to have children with advanced degrees. Stable, middle-class families are more likely to have parents who monitor homework, get involved at their children's schools, and teach their children the values of hard work, good attendance, and school-appropriate behavior.[21] No amount of choice or competition can affect these family-related factors that contribute to a child's success in school.

Other evidence indicates that choice may harm some students by segregating students based on ability level. Specifically, magnet schools and private schools may want to enroll only the intelligent, motivated students and may try to prevent students with disabilities, behavior problems, and low test scores from enrolling. In 2009–10, for example, 20.1 percent of MPS high school students were classified as special education, but Custer High School's percentage was 30.8, while Rufus King High School's was 14 percent and Ronald Reagan High School's was 10.1.[22] The school board closed Custer at the end of the 2010–11 school year, while Rufus King and Ronald Reagan were named the top two schools in Wisconsin by *U.S. News & World Report* in 2012.[23] Certainly, one can understand why school administrators would want to restrict who can enroll, especially in light of the push to tie teacher pay to student test scores. And one can also understand why MPS allows certain schools to have admissions criteria. MPS needs academically talented students to stay in the city and not use the state's open enrollment law to attend suburban schools. When Reagan's principal, Julia D'Amato, was asked about enrolling more special education students at her school, she said that would mean she would have to take fewer regular education students who wanted to enroll in Reagan's college-bound program. She warned, "These children will leave the district."[24]

Milwaukee's movement toward more choice was intended to give students equal educational opportunities. Lloyd Barbee wanted integrated schools. Lee McMurrin attempted to achieve integration through magnet schools, Howard Fuller and business leaders countered with vouchers, and the state of Wisconsin also offered charter schools and suburban schools as options. All of these movements fall under the mantle of "choice." But while the choice of where to attend school is ostensibly vested in the students and their parents, the enrollment practices described here make one wonder who is doing the choosing, the students or the schools? These practices also raise questions about the fairness of setting up a hierarchy of schools—a hierarchy that runs counter to the notion of equal educational opportunity—and about the political motivations behind choice. Surely that was not what reformers intended.

NOTES

INTRODUCTION

1. "Alternative Education in Wisconsin," n.d. (but sometime after 1967 and probably around 1971) in Kathleen Mary Hart, Milwaukee Public Schools Desegregation Collection, 1975–1987, box 1, folder 5, UWM Manuscript Collection 90, Milwaukee Area Research Center, Golda Meir Library, University of Wisconsin–Milwaukee.

2. Eric Foner, *The Story of American Freedom* (New York: W.W. Norton, 1998), xiii–xiv.

3. Ibid., xiii.

4. See Alpheus Thomas Mason and Richard H. Leach, *In Quest of Freedom: American Political Thought and Practice* (Englewood Cliffs, NJ: PrenticeHall, 1972); Leon Whipple, *The Story of Civil Liberty in the United States* (New York: Vanguard Press, 1927; repr., New York: Da Capo Press, 1970) for classic works written under similar themes. See Michael Kammen, *Spheres of Liberty: Changing Perceptions of Liberty in American Culture* (Madison: University of Wisconsin Press, 1986); Lee Quinby, *Freedom, Foucault, and the Subject of America* (Boston: Northeastern University Press, 1991); and Richard Stivers, *The Illusion of Freedom and Equality* (Albany: State University of New York Press, 2008) for more recent histories of freedom in the United States. See John W. Danford, *Roots of Freedom: A Primer on Modern Liberty* (Wilmington, DE: ISI Books, 2000); and R. W. Davis, ed., *The Origins of Modern Freedom in the West* (Stanford, CA: Stanford University Press, 1995) if interested in comparing American intellectual history to the history of freedom in a European context.

5. See Bill Dahlk, *Against the Wind: African Americans and the Schools in Milwaukee, 1963–2002* (Milwaukee: Marquette University Press, 2010); and Jack Dougherty, *More Than One Struggle: The Evolution of Black School Reform in Milwaukee* (Chapel Hill: University of North Carolina Press, 2004).

6. Ronald Formisano, *Boston Against Busing: Race, Class, and Ethnicity in the 1960s and 1970s* (Chapel Hill: University of North Carolina Press, 1991; and J. Anthony Lukas, *Common Ground: A Turbulent Decade in the Lives of Three American Families* (New York: Knopf, 1985).

7. Grace Chen, "What Is a Magnet School?" *Public School Review*, last modified December 4, 2007, http://publicschoolreview.com/articles/2; "Fact Sheet," Magnet Schools of America, www.magnet.edu/ modules/info/who_we_are.html.

8. The Montessori method is a system of self-directed learning. See chapter 10 of William Hayes, *The Progressive Education Movement: Is It Still a Factor in Today's Schools?* (Lanham, MD: Rowman & Littlefield Education, 2006), for a biographical sketch of progressive theorist Maria Montessori, an explanation of her teaching methods, and how her approach differed from that of John Dewey.

CHAPTER 1

1. Daniel Denvir, "The 10 Most Segregated Urban Areas in America," *Salon.com*, last modified March 29, 2011, www.salon.com/2011/03/29/most_segregated _cities/slide_show. Denvir's article was based on a study of census data conducted by William H. Frey, the Brookings Institution, and the University of Michigan. For raw data, see "New Racial Segregation Measures for States and Large Metropolitan Areas: Analysis of the 2005–2009 American Community Survey," Census Scope, http://censusscope.org/ACS/Segregation.html. Denvir's article was followed by several others, including Richard Florida, "The U.S. Cities Where the Poor Are Most Segregated from Everyone Else," *The Atlantic Cities*, last modified March 24, 2014, www.theatlanticcities.com/neighborhoods /2014/03/uscitieswherepoolaremostsegregated/8655; Erica Ho, "Where Are the Top 10 Most Segregated Cities?," *Time*, last modified March 31, 2011, http:// newsfeed.time.com/2011/03/31/wherearethetop10mostsegregatedcities; Veronica Jones, "The Most Segregated City," *Milwaukee Magazine*, last modified November 28, 2012, www.milwaukeemag.com/article/11282012.

2. John Gurda, *The Making of Milwaukee*, 3rd ed. (Milwaukee: Milwaukee County Historical Society, 2008), 26–32; Bayrd Still, *Milwaukee: The History of a City* (Madison, WI: State Historical Society of Wisconsin, 1940), 5; and Robert W. Wells, *This Is Milwaukee* (Garden City, NY: Doubleday, 1970), 10, 15–16. These are the three best sources of Milwaukee history. See chapter 1 of Greg J. Carman, "Wall of Exclusion: The Persistence of Residential Racial Segregation in Metropolitan Milwaukee" (PhD diss., University of Wisconsin–Milwaukee, 2010) for a brief account.

3. Gurda, *The Making of Milwaukee*, 32–38; Still, *Milwaukee*, 12–13; and Wells, *This Is Milwaukee*, 21–23.

4. Still, *Milwaukee*, 19–23, 30–32.

5. Gurda, *The Making of Milwaukee*, 43–57; Still, *Milwaukee*, 35–41; and Wells, *This Is Milwaukee,* 48–53.

6. Gurda, *The Making of Milwaukee*, 24–26, 68. See maps 1 and 2.

7. Gurda, *The Making of Milwaukee*, 59–60; Still, *Milwaukee*, 112 and 265.

8. Still, *Milwaukee*, 80–81; Wells, *This Is Milwaukee*, 82, 143. See Gurda, *The Making of Milwaukee*, chapters 3–6; and Patrick D. Jones, *The Selma of the North: Civil Rights Insurgency in Milwaukee* (Cambridge, MA: Harvard University Press, 2009), 14–18, for more on immigration and settlement patterns.

9. Judith A. Simonsen, "The Third Ward: Symbol of Ethnic Identity," *Milwaukee History* 10, no. 2 (1987): 61–62; Gurda, *The Making of Milwaukee*, 175–176; Still, *Milwaukee*, 268; and Wells, *This Is Milwaukee*, 152.

10. Gurda, *The Making of Milwaukee*, 133–136; Still, *Milwaukee*, 267–270; and Wells, *This Is Milwaukee*, 151–152.

11. Gurda, *The Making of Milwaukee*, 66–69, 175–177; Still, *Milwaukee*, 275–278; and Wells, *This Is Milwaukee*, 152–153.

12. Still, *Milwaukee*, 259.

13. Rolland L. Callaway, *Formative Years, 1836–1915*, with Steven Baruch, vol. 1 of

The Milwaukee Public Schools: A Chronological History, 1836–1986 (Thiensville, WI: Caritas Communications, 2008), CDROM, 34–37; and William M. Lamers, *Our Roots Grow Deep*, 2nd ed. (Milwaukee: Milwaukee Board of School Directors, 1974), 4–5. Lamers wrote the most comprehensive history of MPS from 1836 to 1967. Though he lacks scholarly citations, Lamers had access to key personnel and primary sources necessary for writing the book. Lamers became an assistant superintendent in 1941 and worked with administrators whose tenure stretched back to before World War I, so he learned a lot of history from personal conversations. He also had access to their personal files, which, unfortunately, have been lost by MPS. Lamers also used the published *Proceedings of the Board* and articles from the *Milwaukee Sentinel*, both of which are also used in this book and other published reports from the school board and the superintendent. See Lamers, *Our Roots Grow Deep*, 171–173, for his list of sources. Excerpts appear in chapter 1 of Robert Tanzilo, *Historic Milwaukee Public Schoolhouses* (Charleston, SC: The History Press, 2012). Other sources of early MPS history include Patrick Donnelly, *History of Milwaukee Public Schools* (Milwaukee: Evening Wisconsin Company, 1892); Jas. M. Pereles, *Historical Sketch: The Milwaukee School Board, 1845–1895* (Milwaukee, 1895); and D. H. Schueler, *Milwaukee Public Schools, Historical Sketch* (Milwaukee, 1904).

14. Callaway, *Formative Years*, 45.

15. Milwaukee Board of School Directors, *Proceedings of the Board of School Directors* (Milwaukee: The Board of School Directors), August 23, 1867 (hereafter cited as *Proceedings*); and Lamers, *Our Roots Grow Deep*, 4–5.

16. James G. Cibulka and Frederick I. Olson, "The Organization and Politics of the Milwaukee Public School System, 1920–1986," in *Seeds of Crisis*, ed. John L. Rury and Frank A. Cassell (Madison: The University of Wisconsin Press, 1993), 15–16, 19, 78.

17. *Proceedings*, August 1, 1893; May 1, 1894; September 4, 1894; March 5 and July 8, 1907; August 28, 1911; May 17, 1912; and June 1914; Lamers, *Our Roots Grow Deep*, 10–13, 41, 153–159, 164–165.

18. Cibulka and Olson, "Organization and Politics of the Milwaukee Public School System," 75–77.

19. Gurda, *The Making of Milwaukee,* 160–169.

20. Joe William Trotter Jr., *Black Milwaukee: The Making of an Industrial Proletariat, 1915–45*, 2nd ed. (Urbana: University of Illinois Press, 2007), 24–25. See also Bill Dahlk, *Against the Wind: African Americans and the Schools in Milwaukee, 1963–2002* (Milwaukee: Marquette University Press, 2010), 12–14; Jones, *The Selma of the North*, 18–20; and Phyllis M. Santacroce, "Rediscovering the Role of the State: Housing Policy and Practice in Milwaukee, Wisconsin, 1900–1970" (PhD diss., University of Wisconsin–Milwaukee, 2009), 51–55. See map 3.

21. Jones, *The Selma of the North*, 20; Trotter, *Black Milwaukee*, 25.

22. Jones, *The Selma of the North*, 20–23; Trotter, *Black Milwaukee*, 28–31. See p. 28 of Trotter for comparisons to Chicago.

23. John M. McCarthy, *Making Milwaukee Mightier: Planning and the Politics of Growth, 1910–1960* (DeKalb: Northern Illinois University Press, 2009), 195.

24. Trotter, *Black Milwaukee*, 32–33.

25. McCarthy, *Making Milwaukee Mightier*, ix, 4.

26. Ibid., 45–55.

27. Ibid., 66.

28. Ibid., 106–112.

29. Ibid., 194–195; Santacroce, "Rediscovering the Role of the State," 138; and Trotter, *Black Milwaukee*, 71.

30. David L. Kirp et al., *Race, Housing, and the Soul of Suburbia* (New Brunswick, NJ: Rutgers University Press, 1995), 7, 26–27; Douglas Massey and Nancy Denton, *American Apartheid: Segregation and the Making of the Underclass* (Cambridge, MA: Harvard University Press, 1993), 51–52. See also Carman, "Wall of Exclusion," 119–122; Arnold R. Hirsch, *Making the Second Ghetto: Race and Housing in Chicago, 1940–1960*, rev. ed. (Cambridge: Cambridge University Press, 1983; repr., Chicago: The University of Chicago Press, 1998); Kenneth T. Jackson, *Crabgrass Frontier: The Suburbanization of the United States* (New York: Oxford University Press, 1985), especially chapter 11; and Thomas J. Sugrue, *The Origins of the Urban Crisis: Race and Inequality in Postwar Detroit* (Princeton, NJ: Princeton University Press, 1996) for what are considered the three classic texts on the federal government's role in promoting segregation.

31. Santacroce, "Rediscovering the Role of the State," 22, 231.

32. Jones, *The Selma of the North*, 25; Barbara J. Miner, *Lessons from the Heartland: A Turbulent Half Century of Public Education in an Iconic American City* (New York: The New Press, 2013), 12–13; McCarthy, *Making Milwaukee Mightier*, 194; and Trotter, *Black Milwaukee*, 71.

33. Gurda, *The Making of Milwaukee*, 310–311; McCarthy, *Making Milwaukee Mightier*, 195; and Charles T. O'Reilly et al., *The People of the Inner Core: North* (New York: LePlay Research), 1965, 2. 34. "Negro Population Shifts in Growth," *Milwaukee Sentinel*, July 13, 1965, 1:7. See also Carman, "Wall of Exclusion," 68–69; Dougherty, *More Than One Struggle*, 53.

35. Frances Beverstock and Robert P. Stuckert, eds., *Metropolitan Milwaukee Fact Book: 1970* (Milwaukee: Milwaukee Urban Observatory, 1972), 46.

36. Dahlk, *Against the Wind*, 53.

37. McCarthy, *Making Milwaukee Mightier*, 186–187, 191. The annexation was tied up in litigation until 1962.

38. Gurda, *The Making of Milwaukee*, 342.

39. McCarthy, *Making Milwaukee Mightier*, 129–131.

40. Jones, *The Selma of the North*, 26–28; McCarthy, *Making Milwaukee Mightier*, 198–200. See also Carman, "Wall of Exclusion," 69–74, 162; and chapters 3 and 4 of Santacroce, "Rediscovering the Role of the State."

41. McCarthy, *Making Milwaukee Mightier*, 198.

42. Ibid., 197. The legislation is commonly referred to as the "Oak Creek law" after a semirural area that was incorporated as a city in 1955.

43. Carman, "Wall of Exclusion," 167–169, 177–203; McCarthy, *Making Milwaukee Mightier*, 207–212. See also "Negro Population Shifts in Growth," *Milwaukee Sentinel*, July 13, 1965, 1:7; John L. Rury, "The Changing Context of Urban

Education: A National Perspective," in *Seeds of Crisis*, ed. John L. Rury and Frank A. Cassell (Madison: The University of Wisconsin Press, 1993), 11–14; and Trotter, *Black Milwaukee*, 24–25.

44. Massey and Denton, *American Apartheid*, 52–54. See also Carman, "Wall of Exclusion," 161–165, 170–171; Miner, *Lessons from the Heartland*, 111–112; Harold M. Rose, "The Development of an Urban Subsystem: The Case of the Negro Ghetto," *Annals of the Association of American Geographers*, 60, no. 1 (1970): 1–4; and Trotter, *Black Milwaukee*, 258–263. See Gurda, *The Making of Milwaukee*, 358–365, for a broad perspective on Milwaukee, and chapter 2 of Santacroce, "Rediscovering the Role of the State," for the development of postwar public housing in Milwaukee. See chapter 1 of Dahlk, *Against the Wind*, for a short synopsis of organizing efforts against segregated housing in Milwaukee.

45. Frank A. Aukofer, *City with a Chance* (Milwaukee: Bruce Pub., 1968), 57. See Frank A. Aukofer Papers, 1957–2000, boxes 7–8, 16, Milwaukee Manuscript Collection 16, Wisconsin Historical Society, Milwaukee Area Research Center, Golda Meir Library, University of Wisconsin–Milwaukee for a collection of news articles written by Aukofer, who covered James Groppi for the *Milwaukee Journal*. The articles form the basis of Aukofer's book.

46. Quoted in Carman, "Wall of Exclusion," 171.

47. See chapter 4 of Jones, *The Selma of the North*, and chapter 7 of Miner, *Lessons from the Heartland*. See Register of the James Groppi Papers, 1964–1978, Milwaukee Manuscript Collection EX and Milwaukee Tape 5, Wisconsin Historical Society, Milwaukee Area Research Center, Golda Meir Library, University of Wisconsin–Milwaukee, for biographical information on Groppi and his involvement in the NAACP Youth Council. See also Dahlk, *Against the Wind*, 106–125; Gurda, *The Making of Milwaukee*, 365–376; and Santacroce, "Rediscovering the Role of the State," especially 261–272, 302.

48. Quoted in Jones, *The Selma of the North*, 169–170; Miner, *Lessons from the Heartland*, 63.

49. Rolland L. Callaway, *Building Boom and the Winds of Change, 1946–1975*, with Steven Baruch, vol. 3 of *The Milwaukee Public Schools: A Chronological History, 1836–1986* (Thiensville, WI: Caritas Communications, 2008), CD-ROM.

50. Lamers, *Our Roots Grow Deep*, 87. Radtke evidently had broad support, as she was elected president on the first ballot. See *Proceedings*, July 2, 1963.

51. Quoted in "Miss Radtke Assails Churches on Rights," *Milwaukee Journal*, June 1, 1964, 1:1, 3. Couching race in terms of ethnicity was common among whites in the 1960s. See Stephen M. Leahy, "Polish American Reaction to Civil Rights in Milwaukee, 1963 to 1965," *Polish American Studies* 63, no. 1 (2006): 35–56; and Matthew Frye Jacobson, *Whiteness of a Different Color: European Immigrants and the Alchemy of Race* (Cambridge, MA: Harvard University Press, 1998) for a complete account of the psychological transition from ethnicity to "whiteness" among whites.

52. Steven Baruch, interview with author, Glendale, WI, July 9, 2010.

53. Doris Stacy, interview with author, Milwaukee, June 30, 2010; Leon Todd, interview with author, Milwaukee, June 28, 2010.

54. Callaway, *Building Boom*, 64. Percentages derived from Beverstock and Stuckert, *Metropolitan Milwaukee Fact Book*, 50.

55. "Supt. Vincent Plans to Retire at End of Next School Year," *Milwaukee Journal*, August 3, 1966, 1:1, 4; Roger W. LeGrand, WITI–TV, July 29, 1969; and Carl Zimmerman, WITI–TV, September 15, 1966. Both television editorials found in Lloyd A. Barbee Papers, 1933–1982, box 75, folder 3, Milwaukee Manuscript Collection 16 and Milwaukee Micro Collection 42, Wisconsin Historical Society, Milwaukee Area Research Center, Golda Meir Library, University of Wisconsin–Milwaukee (hereafter cited as Barbee Papers).

56. "Eagles Club Will Honor Supt. Vincent," *Milwaukee Journal*, September 25, 1966, 2:4; "MUSIC, Youth Council Protest Vincent Award at Eagles," *Milwaukee Star*, October 22, 1966, 6; "Rights Groups Join Protest at Eagles Club," *Milwaukee Sentinel*, October 14, 1966, 1:5; "2 Rights Groups, 4 Klansmen March as Eagles Fete Vincent," *Milwaukee Journal*, October 14, 1966, 2:10; and "Vincent's Award Called 'Slap in the Face' of Negroes," *Milwaukee Journal*, September 26, 1966, 1:16.

57. Barbee Papers register. See also "At the Heart of Barbee's Many Causes Was Education," *Milwaukee Journal Sentinel*, February 1, 2004; Dougherty, *More Than One Struggle*, 74–77; Jones, *The Selma of the North*, 60–61; and miscellaneous notes and documents in Barbee Papers, box 14, folder 12. Some notes and documents are dated as early as 1963.

58. Charles E. Friedrich, "Most Negroes Call Education Good Here," *Milwaukee Journal*, February 7, 1966, 1:1, 13; "Negroes Like It Here, but Seek Improvement," *Milwaukee Journal*, February 6, 1966, 1:1, 24; and O'Reilly et al., *The People of the Inner Core*, 150. See also editorials in *Milwaukee Journal*, September 18, 1965, 1:12.

59. Jack Dougherty provides the best analysis of these three groups, organizing his book around the idea that there was "more than one struggle." Bill Dahlk acknowledged and used Dougherty's framework. See Dahlk, *Against the Wind*, 17–30. See also interviews in Gayle Schmitz-Zien, "The Genesis of and Motivations for the Milwaukee Parental Choice Program, 1985–1995" (PhD diss., University of Wisconsin–Milwaukee, 2003).

60. See Stephen Meyer, *Stalin over Wisconsin: The Making and Unmaking of Militant Unionism, 1900–1950* (New Brunswick, NJ: Rutgers University Press, 1992). See Cibulka and Olson, "Organization and Politics of the Milwaukee Public School System," 90–91; and Dougherty, *More Than One Struggle*, 64–70, for the NAACP's 1957 request to integrate MPS.

61. Cibulka and Olson, "Organization and Politics of the Milwaukee Public School System," 92; William John Dahlk, "The Black Educational Reform Movement in Milwaukee, 1963–1975" (master's thesis, University of Wisconsin–Milwaukee, 1990), 40; and "11 Demonstrators Seized for Blocking School Buses," *Milwaukee Journal*, May 24, 1965, 1:1, 4.

62. Dahlk, *Against the Wind*, 63; "School Board Study Won't Halt NAACP," *Milwaukee Journal*, August 7, 1963, 2:1, 12.

63. "School Group Named on 'Equity,'" *Milwaukee Sentinel*, August 7, 1963, 1:1, 5.

64. Richard McLeod to Harold Story, October 4 and 24, 1963, Congress of Racial Equality, Milwaukee Chapter, records, 1963–1964, box 1, folder 1, Milwaukee Manuscript Collection 27, Wisconsin Historical Society, Milwaukee Area Research Center, Golda Meir Library, University of Wisconsin-Milwaukee. See also Richard McLeod, "Segregation in Milwaukee Public Schools" (Milwaukee Chapter of the Congress of Racial Equality, December 10, 1963), 2–5, in CORE records, box 1, folder 2.

65. "NAACP Threatens Boycott," *Milwaukee Journal*, January 12, 1964, 1:1.

66. "Rights Leader Walks Out of Meeting," *Milwaukee Journal*, January 22, 1964, 2:1, 14; and "Rights Groups Walk Out," *Milwaukee Sentinel*, January 22, 1964, 2:1. See also "Story Explains Stand: Barbee Best Qualified," *Milwaukee Journal*, January 24, 1964, 2:7; Harold Story to Richard McLeod, January 30 and February 3, 1964; and Richard McLeod to the Board of School Directors, January 28 and February 4, 1964. All four letters are in CORE records, box 1, folder 1.

67. "Community Action on the Issue of Intact Busing," 1–3, Barbee Papers, box 73, folder 44; "Negro Teachers Sent to All-White Schools," *Milwaukee Journal*, January 25, 1964, 1:3; and "Sherman School Site of Picket Line Again," February 5, 1964, 2:1.

68. Dahlk, *Against the Wind*, 74; Dougherty, *More Than One Struggle*, 104–105; Jones, *The Selma of the North*, 65–73; and Theodore V. Montgomery Jr., "A Case Study of Political, Social, and Economic Forces Which Affected the Planning of School Desegregation, Milwaukee, 1976" (PhD diss., University of Wisconsin–Milwaukee, 1984), 149.

69. "End Story Committee, Resolution Requests," *Milwaukee Journal*, April 26, 1964, 2:9.

70. "Facts About the Freedom Day School Withdrawal, May 18, 1964," CORE records, box 1, folder 2; and James Farmer to CORE contact list, CORE records, box 1, folder 1. See chapters 5 and 6 of Clarence Taylor, *Knocking at Our Own Door: Milton A. Galamison and the Struggle to Integrate New York City Schools* (New York: Columbia University Press, 1997) for information on the New York boycott. See also Dionne Danns, *Something Better for Our Children: Black Organizing in Chicago Public Schools, 1963–71* (New York: Routledge, 2003), 3, 37–84, 80–87.

71. "School Board Study Won't Halt NAACP," *Milwaukee Journal*, August 7, 1963, 2:1, 12; "Only One Negro Plan Legal on Schools, Atty. Story Says," *Milwaukee Journal*, April 24, 1964, 2:1, 18.

72. "Welcome Lawsuit, School Board Told," *Milwaukee Sentinel*, July 1, 1964, 1:1–2.

73. "Negro Study Raises Ire of School Group," *Milwaukee Journal*, May 8, 1964, 2:1, 12; "Value Seen in Rights Digest," *Milwaukee Journal*, May 11, 1964, 1:12; "Negro Digest Out, Stirs Flap," *Milwaukee Sentinel*, May 8, 1964, 2:1, 9; and "Taylor Rips Digest," *Milwaukee Sentinel*, May 11, 1964. The bibliographic digest is in Lorraine Radtke Papers, 1947–1981, box 1, folder 2, UWM Manuscript Collection 64, Golda Meir Library, University of Wisconsin–Milwaukee (hereafter cited as Radtke Papers).

74. "Negro Digest Out, Stirs Flap," *Milwaukee Sentinel*, May 8, 1964, 2:1, 9.

75. "Rights Groups Asks Radtke Resignation," *Milwaukee Sentinel*, May 9, 1964, 1:6.

76. "11,500 Boycott Public Schools to Protest de Facto Segregation," *Milwaukee Journal*, May 18, 1964, 1:1, 12.

77. A "Program of Activities" for three grade levels (primary, intermediate, and junior/senior high) and a "Teachers' Guide for Freedom Schools" dated May 1964 are found in Helen I. Barnhill Papers, 1963–1965, box 1, folder 6, Milwaukee Manuscript Collection 4, Wisconsin Historical Society, Milwaukee Area Research Center, Golda Meir Library, University of Wisconsin–Milwaukee.

78. "School Boycott Group Invites Atty. Story," *Milwaukee Journal*, April 19, 1964; "Boycott Team Includes Ex-Nun," *Milwaukee Journal*, May 18, 1964, 1:4; Marian McBride, "Former Nun Directs Freedom Schools," *Milwaukee Sentinel*, May 18, 1964; 1:4; and "Negro History Makers in Milwaukee," *Milwaukee Star*, February 26, 1966, 2.

79. Ralph D. Olive, "Issue Is: Do School Leaders Refuse to Tackle Problem?" *Milwaukee Journal*, May 11, 1964, 1:1, 13; "11,500 Boycott Public Schools to Protest de Facto Segregation," *Milwaukee Journal*, May 18, 1964, 1:1, 12; "Schools Try to Go On in Usual Way" and Barbara Schmoll, "Equality Promoted at Freedom Schools," *Milwaukee Journal*, May 18, 1964, 2:1, 11; and "Barbee: Boycott Data False; Vincent: Figures Accurate," *Milwaukee Journal*, May 19, 1964, 1:1, 11.

80. *Proceedings*, May 5, 1964.

81. Quoted in "Story Committee OK's Easing Transfer Rules," *Milwaukee Journal*, May 22, 1964, 2:1. See also *Proceedings*, May 15, 1964; June 2, 1964; and December 2, 1965.

82. Bob Heiss, WTMJ–TV, February 25, 1964; Rod Synnes, WTMJ–TV, May 19, 1964; and Carl Zimmerman, WITI–TV, March 31, 1964 (all three editorials from Barbee Papers, box 195, folder 4); and "Wrong Target," *Milwaukee Sentinel*, May 2, 1964, 1:12.

83. Bob Heiss, WTMJ–TV, August 12, 1963, Barbee Papers, box 195, folder 4; and Carl Zimmerman, WITI–TV, September 15, 1966, Barbee Papers, box 75, folder 3.

84. Barbee Papers, box 195, folder 4 (July 17, 1963).

85. "Candidates for School Board Give Views," *Milwaukee Journal*, March 29, 1965; 1:14.

86. "Gerken, 4 Incumbents to Sit on School Board," *Milwaukee Journal*, April 7, 1965, 1:1, 15.

87. "Schools Spend Millions on Poor, Foley Says," *Milwaukee Journal*, September 7, 1965, 2:1.

88. "School Board Picks Foley on 3rd Vote," *Milwaukee Journal*, July 7, 1965, 2:1, 10.

89. "More of the Same," *Milwaukee Star*, July 10, 1965, 4. Foley was reelected in 1966. He defeated the pro-desegregation Elisabeth Holmes, eight to seven, confirming that the board was split on racial questions. See *Proceedings*, July 5, 1966.

90. Charles E. Freidrich, "Reading, Writing, and Race," *Milwaukee Journal*, September 1965.

91. *Proceedings*, November 2 and December 7, 1965.

92. "Barbee Threatens School Boycott," *Milwaukee Sentinel*, May 4, 1965, 2:1; "Sit-In Staged at Vincent's Office," *Milwaukee Sentinel*, May 6, 1965, 2:1; "Rights Group May Hike Activities" and "CORE Members Picket Story," *Milwaukee Journal*, May 22, 1965, 2:8; and "Construction of School in Negro Area Approved," *Milwaukee Journal*, September 8, 1965, 1:28.

93. Charles E. Freidrich, "Reading, Writing, and Race," *Milwaukee Journal*, October 16, 1965; *Milwaukee Journal*, September 16, 1965; Letter to the Citizens of Milwaukee, Milwaukee United School Integration Committee Records, 1964–1966, box 1, folder 1, Milwaukee Manuscript Collection 5, Wisconsin Historical Society, Milwaukee Area Research Center, Golda Meir Library, University of Wisconsin–Milwaukee.

94. "4 Parishes to Aid Boycott, Despite Orders by Bishop," *Milwaukee Journal*, October 17, 1965, 1:1.

95. Dahlk, "Black Educational Reform," 58; "Barbee Leads Picketing at Palmer School," *Milwaukee Journal*, June 1, 1965, 1:26; "School Defends Bus Policy," *Milwaukee Journal*, June 1, 1965, 2:2; "Women at School Bus Seized," *Milwaukee Journal*, June 3, 1965, 2:1; "Law Proves Rather Disorderly in Civil Rights Case," *Milwaukee Journal*, June 5, 1965, 1:7; "CORE Calls 2 Week Halt to Protesting," *Milwaukee Journal*, June 8, 1965, 1:4; "5 Sit-Ins Arrested in Schools Office," *Milwaukee Sentinel*, May 29, 1965, 1:1, 7; "Picketing on School Bus Fails," *Milwaukee Sentinel*, June 3, 1965, 1:9; and Walter Jones, "Support MUSIC Protests," *Milwaukee Star*, June 12, 1965, 1, 4.

96. "Extra 7,300 Students Out, Officials Say," *Milwaukee Journal*, October 18, 1965, 1:1, 12.

97. "School Boycott Goes On," *Milwaukee Journal*, October 19, 1965, 1:1–2.

98. "North High Boycott Doubles Absences," *Milwaukee Journal*, March 28, 1966, 2:1, 8.

99. Barbee Papers, register, ix; Michael Stolee, "The Milwaukee Desegregation Case," in *Seeds of Crisis*, ed. John L. Rury and Frank A. Cassell (Madison: The University of Wisconsin Press, 1993), 245. See Santacroce, "Rediscovering the Role of the State," 249–259; and the register of the Barbee Papers for information on Barbee's career in the state legislature prior to the *Amos* lawsuit. The case was *Armstrong v. O'Connell* from 1976 until 1979.

100. *Amos et al. v. The Board of School Directors of Milwaukee et al.*, Civs. A. No. 65–C–173 (United States District Court, E.D. 1976), 780; Dahlk, *Against the Wind*, 33–41; "Sherman School Site on Picket Line Again," *Milwaukee Journal*, February 6, 1964, 2:1; "Suit Here Charges School Segregation," *Milwaukee Journal*, June 18, 1965, 2:1; "Three Say Bias Study Is Going to Slowly," *Milwaukee Journal*, February 1, 1964, 1:9; "Vincent Maps Plan for Equal Schooling," *Milwaukee Journal*, February 6, 1964, 1:1, 4; and "Vincent to Place Teachers by Needs—Not by Race," *Milwaukee Sentinel*, July 17, 1963, 1:2. Caroline Goddard, "Lloyd A. Barbee and the Fight for Desegregation in the Milwaukee Public School System" (master's thesis, University of Wisconsin–Milwaukee, 1985) is the best legal history of the case.

101. Office of the Superintendent, "Report of School District Changes in Central

Area of Milwaukee 1943–1953–1963" (Milwaukee: Milwaukee Public Schools, January 1964), 2, Barbee Papers, box 114, folder 9.

102. "An Analysis of the Impact of School District Boundary Changes on the Pattern of Racial Imbalance in Central Area Schools," October 4, 1966, 18–20, Barbee Papers, box 114, folder 10. The report does not list an author but appears to be written by Barbee or a member of his staff.

103. Goddard, "Barbee and the Fight for Desegregation," 54; Office of the Superintendent, "Report of School District Changes in Central Area of Milwaukee: 1943–1953–1963," 2–5, Barbee Papers, box 114, folder 9.

104. "Integrate Schools? He'd Give Up," *Milwaukee Sentinel*, February 8, 1967, 1:8.

105. See "Analysis of the Impact of School District Boundary Changes," Barbee Papers, box 114, folder 10; Barbee's notes in folder 11, and "support evidence" in folder 12; and "Report of School District Changes in Central Area of Milwaukee, 1943–1953–1963," January 1964, Barbee Papers, box 114, folder 9. See also *Proceedings*, June 1 and 30, 1950; September 6, 1955; and January 10 and June 5, 1956.

106. "Analysis of the Impact of School District Boundary Changes," 11; Office of the Superintendent, "Report of School District Changes in Central Area of Milwaukee: 1943–1953–1963," 2–5; and Office of the Superintendent, "Report on Visual Count of Pupils by Schools," in *Background Papers on Equality of Educational Opportunity* (Milwaukee: Milwaukee Public Schools, 1964), Barbee Papers, box 158, folders 8 and 9. See maps 4–6 depicting the racial breakdown of Milwaukee's central city in 1940, 1950, and 1960. See map 7 for elementary school boundary changes affecting the central city, 1943–1963.

107. David I. Bednarek, "Boundary Shift at Washington Termed Extension of Ghetto," *Milwaukee Journal*, April 14, 1970, 2:1, 3; David I. Bednarek, "Boundary Right: School Board Can't Win," *Milwaukee Journal*, April 28, 1970, 1:1, 14. See Dougherty, *More Than One Struggle*, 131–133, for more on the changing demographics of Washington High School. See map 6 for racial composition of Milwaukee's central city schools.

108. David I. Bednarek, "Boundary Shift at Washington Termed Extension of Ghetto," *Milwaukee Journal*, April 14, 1970, 2:1, 3; and David I. Bednarek, "Boundary Right: School Board Can't Win," *Milwaukee Journal*, April 28, 1970, 1:1, 14. See William M. Alexander and Paul S. George, *The Exemplary Middle School* (New York: CBS College Publishing, 1981), 11–12; and chapter 12 of William Hayes, *The Progressive Education Movement: Is It Still a Factor in Today's Schools?* (Lanham, MD: Rowman & Littlefield Education, 2006) on the national shift to middle schools in grades 6–8 and four-year high schools in grades 9–12.

109. *Proceedings*, August 6, 1947; June 5, 1951; January 13 and September 1, 1953; and April 4, 1956.

110. "Analysis of the Impact of School District Boundary Changes," 5; and Office of the Superintendent, "Report of School District Changes in Central Area of Milwaukee: 1943–1953–1963," 2–5. See map 7.

111. Goddard, "Barbee and the Fight for Desegregation," 87.

112. "Construction of School in Negro Area Approved," *Milwaukee Journal*,

September 8, 1965, 1:28; and "New Black Jr. High Approved," *Milwaukee Courier*, September 7, 1968, 1:2.

113. "Separate Is Not Equal," *Milwaukee Courier*, June 22, 1968, 1:1.

114. Barbee Papers, box 114, folder 10; and Office of the Superintendent, "Report of School District Changes in Central Area of Milwaukee: 1943–1953–1963," 2–5.

115. Goddard, "Barbee and the Fight for Desegregation," 83–84.

116. See transfer requests in Barbee Papers, box 109, folders 15–18, 22; box 110, folders 1–6; and box 155, folders 7–13.

117. William J. Kritek and Delbert K. Clear, "Teachers and Principals in the Milwaukee Public Schools," in Rury and Cassell, *Seeds of Crisis*, 148. See chapter 1 of Dougherty, *More Than One Struggle*, for detailed information on the struggle to force MPS to hire African American teachers. These were important middle-class job opportunities for African Americans.

118. See assignment documentation in Barbee Papers, box 98, folders 1–3, and box 101, folder 8; "Nonwhite Pupils in More Schools," *Milwaukee Sentinel*, March 3, 1965, 2:1, 12; and Stolee, "The Milwaukee Desegregation Case," 237–238.

119. Goddard, "Barbee and the Fight for Desegregation," 84–85.

120. See transfer requests in Barbee Papers, box 111, folder 26; box 112, folders 15–16, 18; and box 157, folders 1–13.

121. See transfer requests in Barbee Papers, box 111, folder 2; box 112, folders 9–12; box 132, folder 25; and box 157, folders 1–13.

122. See transfer requests in Barbee Papers, box 111, folder 26.

123. Goddard, "Barbee and the Fight for Desegregation," 84–85.

124. *Proceedings*, December 2, 1959.

125. See untitled charts, graphs, and tables in Barbee Papers, box 73, folders 43–44; Goddard, "Lloyd A. Barbee and the Fight for Desegregation," 90.

126. Stolee, "The Milwaukee Desegregation Case," 251.

127. Office of the Superintendent, "Policies and Procedures Relating to Pupil Transportation" (Milwaukee: Milwaukee Public Schools, 194), 1, Barbee Papers, box 122, folder 1. See Amanda I. Seligman, *Block by Block: Neighborhoods and Public Policy on Chicago's West Side* (Chicago: University of Chicago Press, 2005), 125–127, for double shifting in Chicago.

128. Barbee Papers, box 73, folder 44; "7 Chained in Front of Bus Arrested," *Milwaukee Journal*, May 28, 1965, 1:1, 11; "11 Demonstrators Seized for Blocking School Buses," *Milwaukee Journal*, May 24, 1965, 1:1, 4; "Civil Rights Workers Halt Bus, 11 Seized," *Chicago Tribune*, May 25, 1965, A:2; and "Rights Group Drops Plan to Disrupt Circus Parade," *Milwaukee Sentinel*, July 6, 1965, 2:7. See chapter 6 of Miner, *Lessons from the Heartland,* for a first-person account of intact busing and the protests against it.

129. See interviews in Barbee Papers, box 117, folder 8.

130. Goddard, "Barbee and the Fight for Desegregation," 89; "Mrs. Dinges Likely to Head School Board," *Milwaukee Sentinel*, June 26, 1967, 1:1, 9.

131. "Textbook Turn-In Called For," *Milwaukee Sentinel*, April 29, 1967, 1:5. See Dougherty, *More Than One Struggle*, especially chapters 6 and 7, for more information on the Afrocentric movement in MPS. Pages 142–148 provide useful

information on Beason, North Division, and Afrocentrism. See also chapters 5–9 of Dahlk, *Against the Wind*; and chapter 8 of Patrick Jones for more on black power.

132. Dahlk, *Against the Wind*, 143–144.

133. Ibid., 155–164; Dahlk, "Black Educational Reform," 125–133.

134. "Parents Vow to Empty Fulton Jr. High School if Demands Aren't Met," *Milwaukee Courier*, December 23, 1967, 1:1, 3; "Lunch Protest to Continue at Fulton School," *Milwaukee Journal*, December 15, 1967, 2:1–2; and "Fulton School Faces Student Boycott," *Milwaukee Journal*, December 20, 1967, 2:1.

135. "King Students Stage Walk Out [*sic*]; Demand Negro History," *Milwaukee Courier*, February 3, 1968, 1:1. This was a popular topic in the *Milwaukee Courier*, and many other articles can be found on the subject in the *Courier* archives.

136. Ray McBride, "Your Letter from Home," *Milwaukee Journal*, February 10, 1968, The Green Sheet:1.

137. "Groups Invited to Rally for Negro History," *Milwaukee Sentinel*, February 26, 1968, 1:5. See chapter 5 of Jones, *The Selma of the North,* for a history of the NAACP Youth Council and the Commandos.

138. "Wells Hit by Food and Table Dumping as Students Revolt for Black Books, Cooks," *Milwaukee Courier*, March 2, 1968, 1:1; "Wells St. School," *Milwaukee Star*, March 2, 1968, 5.

139. "No King Memorial; Students React," *Milwaukee Courier*, April 13, 1968, 1:1.

140. "Group Charges Students Bribed to Frame Ninth Street Principal," *Milwaukee Courier*, May 11, 1968, 1:1.

141. "Black Students Walk Out of West Division High," *Milwaukee Courier*, October 5, 1968 1:1.

142. *Proceedings*, January 31, 1967.

143. Gerry Hinkley, "City Schools Get History of US Negro," *Milwaukee Sentinel*, November 2, 1967, 1:5. A copy is available in Radtke Papers, box 2, folder 15.

144. "North Seniors Get African History," *Milwaukee Courier*, October 5, 1968, 1:1–2; Mary Spletter, "Heritage Course a Difficult Sounding Board," *Milwaukee Sentinel*, December 25, 1969, 3:1.

145. "Fulton School Faces Student Boycott," *Milwaukee Journal*, December 20, 1967, 2:1; "OOO Eyes Election," *Milwaukee Courier*, December 23, 1972, 1:3.

CHAPTER 2

1. "About MSA," Magnet Schools of America, www.magnet.edu/about.

2. Alex Sergienko, "How a Small City in the Pacific Northwest Invented Magnet Schools," *Education Next* 5, no. 2 (Spring 2005): 49; US Commission on Civil Rights, *School Desegregation in Tacoma, Washington: A Staff Report of the U.S. Commission on Civil Rights* (Washington, DC: The Commission on Civil Rights, 1979), 1–4.

3. Charles B. McMillan, a national expert on magnet schools, said Minneapolis was the first district to use magnet schools, in 1972. See Charles B. McMillan, *Magnet Schools: An Approach to Voluntary Desegregation* (Bloomington, IN: Phi

Delta Kappa Educational Foundation, 1980), 9. However, documentation from Tacoma shows it was using magnet schools in 1970.

4. John Brandstetter and Charles R. Foster, "Quality Integrated Education in Houston's Magnet Schools," *Phi Delta Kappan* 57, no. 8 (April 1976): 502–506; Connie Campbell and John Brandstetter, "The Magnet School Plan in Houston," in *The Future of Big-City Schools: Desegregation Policies and Magnet Alternatives*, ed. Daniel U. Levine and Robert J. Havinghurst (Berkeley, CA: McCutchan Publishing, 1977), 124–137; and Pamela J. Sampson, *Options, School Desegregation*, foreword by Miriam G. Palay and Lois Quinn (Milwaukee: Milwaukee Urban Observatory, University of Wisconsin–Milwaukee, 1976), 26–27.

5. Brandstetter and Foster, "Quality Integrated Education," 503; Joseph L. Felix and James N. Jacobs, "Issues in Implementing and Evaluating Alternative Programs in Cincinnati," in Levine and Havinghurst, *The Future of Big-City Schools*, 105–115; Virginia K. Griffin, "Desegregation in Cincinnati: The Legal Background," in Levine and Havinghurst, *The Future of Big-City Schools*, 87–88, 96–100; and Sampson, *Options, School Desegregation*, 27–28.

6. George R. Metcalf, *From Little Rock to Boston: The History of School Desegregation* (Westport, CT: Greenwood Press, 1983), 205; Steven J. L. Taylor, *Desegregation in Boston and Buffalo: The Influence of Local Leaders* (Albany: State University of New York Press, 1998), 14–15, 168. See also chapters 2–7 of Ronald P. Formisano and Constance K. Burns, eds., *Boston, 1700–1980: The Evolution of Urban Politics* (Westport, CT: Greenwood Press, 1984).

7. Taylor, *Desegregation in Boston and Buffalo*, 18–19.

8. Metcalf, *From Little Rock to Boston*, 197–198; Taylor, *Desegregation in Boston and Buffalo*, 44–45.

9. Taylor, *Desegregation in Boston and Buffalo*, 48–49, 52–53. See J. Anthony Lukas, "All in the Family: The Dilemmas of Busing and the Conflict of Values," in Formisano and Burns, *Boston, 1700–1980*, 241–; J. Anthony Lukas, *Common Ground: A Turbulent Decade in the Lives of Three American Families* (New York: Knopf, 1985); and Jeanne Theoharis, "I'd Rather Go to School in the South": How Boston's School Desegregation Complicates the Civil Rights Paradigm," in *Freedom North: Black Freedom Struggles Outside the South, 1940–1980*, ed. Jeanne Theoharis and Komozi Woodard (New York: Palgrave Macmillan, 2003) for more on black activism, boycotts, and the very violent white reaction. See chapter 3 of Adam R. Nelson, *The Elusive Ideal: Equal Educational Opportunity and the Federal Role in Boston's Public Schools, 1950–1985* (Chicago: University of Chicago Press, 2005) for an analysis of segregative methods in Boston.

10. Scott Gelber, "'The Crux and the Magic': The Political History of Boston Magnet Schools, 1968–1989," *Equity & Excellence in Education* 41, no. 4 (December 2008): 456.

11. "Morgan vs. Hennigan Working Files," finding aid, City of Boston, www .cityofboston.gov/Images_Documents/Guide%20to%20the%20Morgan%20Case %20working%20files_tcm3-23345.pdf; Peter W. Cookson and Barbara L. Schneider, *Transforming Schools* (New York: Garland, 1995), 477; "Desegregation-Era Records Collection," finding aid, City of Boston, www.cityofboston.gov

/images_documents/guide%20to%20the%20desegregation-era%20records%20
collection_tcm3–23340.pdf David H. Rosenbloom and Rosemary O'Leary,
Public Administration and Law (New York: M. Dekker, 1997), 284–285; "School
Committee Secretary Desegregation Files," finding aid, City of Boston, www
.cityofboston.gov/Images_Documents/Guide%20to%20the%20School
%20Committee%20Secretary%20Desegregation%20files_tcm3–23346.PDF;
and Lauri Steel, Roger Levine, and the American Institute for Research,
*Educational Innovation in Multiracial Contexts: The Growth of Magnet Schools
in American Education* (Washington, DC: US Department of Education, 1994), 4.

12. Nancy Conneely, "After PICS: Making the Case for Socioeconomic Integration,"
    Texas Journal of Civil Liberties and Civil Rights 12, no. 1 (2008): 113–114;
    "Desegregation-Era Records Collection."

13. Quoted in Gelber, "'The Crux and the Magic,'" 456. See also "Education:
    Integration by Magnets," *Time*, June 16, 1975; chapters 6 and 7 of Nelson, *The
    Elusive Ideal*; and Charles B. McMillan, "Magnet Education in Boston," *Phi
    Delta Kappan* 59, no. 3 (November 1977): 158–163.

14. Metcalf, *From Little Rock to Boston*, 207; Arthur L. Stinchcombe and D. Garth
    Taylor, "On Democracy and School Integration," in Walter G. Stephan and
    Joe R. Feagin, eds. *School Desegregation: Past, Present, and Future* (New York:
    Plenum Press, 1980). 164–169; and Taylor, *Desegregation in Boston and Buffalo*,
    135–145.

15. Gelber, "'The Crux and the Magic,'" 456.

16. Barbara Dembski, "Judge No Stranger to Tough Decisions," *Milwaukee Journal*,
    January 19, 1976, 1:1, 9; "Wisconsin Governor John W. Reynolds," The National
    Governors Association, www.nga.org/cms/home/governors/pastgovernorsbios
    /page_wisconsin/col2content maincontentlist/title_reynolds_john.html.

17. Bruce Murphy and John Pawasarat, "Why It Failed: Desegregation 10 Years
    Later," *Milwaukee Magazine*, September 1986, 36–37. Reynolds did not com-
    ment on why he appointed Charne co-counsel but said it was not a negative
    reflection on Barbee. See US District Court (Wisconsin Eastern District), *Craig
    Amos [and Other] Plaintiffs v. Board of School Directors of the City of Milwaukee
    (and Others) Defendants: Decision and Order / John W. Reynolds Presiding*
    (Milwaukee: The Court, 1976), 11–12 (hereafter cited as *Amos*).

18. Academy for Educational Development, *Quality Education in Milwaukee's
    Future: Recommendations to the Citizens Advisory Committee to Comprehensive
    Survey of Milwaukee Public Schools and the Milwaukee Board of School Directors*
    (New York: Academy for Educational Development, 1967), especially pages 83–91.

19. Quoted in David Bednarek, "Race Mixing Called Duty of Education," *Milwau-
    kee Journal*, September 17, 1967, 1:1, 26.

20. Ibid. See related articles on page 22 of the *Journal*.

21. "Proposals on Schools Get Mixed Reaction," *Milwaukee Journal*, September 18,
    1967, 2:1–2.

22. *Proceedings*, May 17, 1967.

23. Dahlk, *Against the Wind*, 171; Dahlk, "The Black Educational Reform Move-
    ment," 130.

24. Gurda, *The Making of Milwaukee*, 371–376. See also chapter 4 of Carman, "Wall of Exclusion"; McCarthy, *Making Milwaukee Mightier*, 218–219.

25. Richard Gousha, telephone interview with author, May 17, 2011.

26. Dahlk, *Against the Wind*, 172–180; Gousha interview; and "What Is the North Division Cluster?," Milwaukee Urban League Records, 1919–1979, box 23, folder 5, Milwaukee Manuscript Collection EZ, Wisconsin Historical Society, Milwaukee Area Research Center, Golda Meir Library, University of Wisconsin–Milwaukee (hereafter cited as Urban League Papers).

27. "Board Hears Praise of Decentralization," *Milwaukee Journal*, March 18, 1971, 2:2; "Cluster System Reviewed Before School Board," *Milwaukee Sentinel*, March 18, 1971, 1:5; "Decentralization Developments in Milwaukee Public Schools," Urban League Papers, box 23, folder 5; Gousha interview; "Gousha Asks for Decentralization," *Milwaukee Sentinel*, May 18, 1968, 1:1, 18; "Gousha Proposes Massive Revision," *Milwaukee Journal*, May 18, 1968, 1:1–2; and "A Plan for Improvement of Milwaukee's School Operations" (Milwaukee Public Schools, undated but written in 1967, according to Gousha), in author's possession.

28. Steven Baruch, interview with author, Glendale, WI, July 9, 2010; Office of the Superintendent, "A Subsystem Approach to the Problems of a Large City School System: An Application for a Title III Grant" (Milwaukee: Milwaukee Public Schools, March 1968), Barbee Papers, box 74, folder 22, and Urban League Papers, box 23, folder 5; and *Proceedings*, July 1, 1969.

29. Beverstock and Stuckert, *Metropolitan Milwaukee Fact Book*, 46.

30. Ibid., 44.

31. Ibid., 28.

32. David F. Behrendt, "Transition Is Swift on Edge of Core," *Milwaukee Journal*, April 16, 1967, 2:1, 13; "Nonwhite Pupils in More Schools," *Milwaukee Sentinel*, March 3, 1965, 2:1, 12.

33. Donald Pfarrer, "Is Racial Balance Only a Precarious Pause?" *Milwaukee Journal*, December 26, 1971, 1:1, 18.

34. "Plan to Stabilize Schools Backed," *Milwaukee Journal*, January 11, 1972, 2:2; "Quota System at Riverside Rejected," *Milwaukee Courier*, January 29, 1972, 1:1, 8.

35. Beverstock and Stuckert, *Metropolitan Milwaukee Fact Book*, 190–191. See also Michael Kirkhorn, "What's Ahead for Washington Area?" *Milwaukee Journal*, December 27, 1971, 1:1, 8.

36. Donald Pfarrer, "Is Racial Balance Only a Precarious Pause?" *Milwaukee Journal*, December 26, 1971, 1:1, 18.

37. "'Get Whitey Day' Declared at Peckham Jr. High," *Milwaukee Courier*, May 30, 1970, 1:1, 6; Donald Pfarrer, "Is Racial Balance Only a Precarious Pause?" *Milwaukee Journal*, December 26, 1971, 1:1, 18; Gregory D. Sandford, "Judge Hears of Ills of High School," *Milwaukee Journal*, January 16, 1972, 1:1, 10.

38. Florence I. Bryant, letter to the editor, *Milwaukee Courier*, February 19, 1972; "Racial Battle Erupts," *Milwaukee Courier*, November 22, 1969, 1:1. See Dahlk, *Against the Wind*, chapter 7; and Dougherty, *More Than One Struggle*, 133–137, for additional information on racial problems at Washington High School.

39. Dahlk, *Against the Wind*, 274–275; Doris Stacy, interview with author, Milwaukee, June 30, 2010. Wegmann was a professor at the University of Wisconsin–Milwaukee. He and his graduate students developed a metropolitan integration plan that would become the basis of the Conta Plan, which is described later in this chapter. See "Mrs. Stacy's Stands Win Friends, Foes," *Milwaukee Sentinel*, April 1, 1977, 1:5, for a profile of Stacy, including her position on several educational issues.

40. "Board President Outlines Progress at Washington," *Milwaukee Journal*, February 8, 1972, 2:6; Marilyn Kucer, "School Officials Try Distinct Tacks," *Milwaukee Sentinel*, January 29, 1972, 1:5; "Washington Security Discussion Continues," *Milwaukee Journal*, February 9, 1972, 2:2; and Tom Wyatts, "Pupils at Washington Talk, Listen During Jackson Visit," *Milwaukee Sentinel*, January 29, 1972, 1:1, 14.

41. "Board President Outlines Progress at Washington," *Milwaukee Journal*, February 8, 1972, 2:6; Marilyn Kucer, "School Officials Try Distinct Tacks," *Milwaukee Sentinel*, 1:5,14; Marilyn Kucer, "Test Plan OK'd for High School," *Milwaukee Sentinel*, March 28, 1972, 1:1,10; "Plans OKed for Washington," *Milwaukee Courier*, April 1, 1972, 1:1, 3; "School Security Planned," *Milwaukee Courier*, February 5, 1972; and "Washington Security Discussion Continues," *Milwaukee Journal*, February 9, 1972, 2:9.

42. Lloyd Barbee, "From the Legislature," *Milwaukee Courier*, March 4, 1972; Edward H. Blackwell, "In the Inner City," *Milwaukee Journal*, April 28, 1972, Accent on the News: 1, 10; Tom Watts, "Pupils at Washington Talk, Listen During Jackson Visit," *Milwaukee Sentinel*, January 29, 1972, 1:1, 14; and Lauri Wynn, "Armed Guards in Schools Won't Fit," *Milwaukee Courier*, January 29, 1972, 1:1, 4.

43. Dahlk, *Against the Wind*, 282; Dahlk, "Black Educational Reform," 184–185; "Group Criticizes 'Open Enrollment,'" *Milwaukee Sentinel*, June 15, 1972, 1:5; Michael Kirkhorn, "What's Ahead for Washington Area?," *Milwaukee Journal*, December 27, 1971, 1:1, 8; Donald Pfarrer, "Is Racial Balance Only a Precarious Pause?," *Milwaukee Journal*, December 26, 1971, 1:1, 18; and "Race Issue Ends Meeting," *Milwaukee Journal*, December 3, 1971, 2:6.

44. Education Committee of the Sherman Park Community Association, "Educational Recommendations," April 21, 1976, in Kathleen Mary Hart, Milwaukee Public Schools Desegregation Collection, 1975–1987, box 1, folder 1, UWM Manuscript Collection 90, Golda Meir Library, University of Wisconsin–Milwaukee (hereafter cited as Hart Papers); Sherman Park Community Association, "Recommendations re: Desegregation/Integration of Milwaukee Public Schools," A Collection of Papers Relating to the Desegregation/Integration of the Milwaukee Public Schools, Milwaukee Public Library Humanities Room, 1976; and *Sherman Park News* 3, no. 3 (March 1973), 5, in Sherman Park Community Association, Sherman Park Community Association Records, box 6, folder 1, UWM Manuscript Collection 72, Wisconsin Historical Society, Milwaukee Area Research Center, Golda Meir Library, University of Wisconsin–Milwaukee (hereafter cited as SPCA Papers). The SPCA would later

advocate a quota of no more than 50 percent African Americans at Washington in an effort to stabilize enrollment and slow white migration. See also "McMurrin, Critics Meet on '78 Plans," *Milwaukee Journal*, June 9, 1972, 2:1; "Washington High to Be 49% Black," *Milwaukee Journal*, July 17, 1978, 2:2.

45. Michael Kirkhorn, "OK on School Study a Victory for Citizens," *Milwaukee Journal*, February 1, 1973, 2:6; "Peckham-Steuben Panel Asked," *Milwaukee Journal*, January 31, 1973, 2:2.

46. The term *forced busing* was probably adopted from national media coverage of the Boston case. Although casually used in the vernacular of the 1970s, it is considered highly controversial today because it was used as a tactic to scare whites. In light of this troubling connotation, I have chosen to use the term *involuntary busing* when describing situations in which children were assigned to ride buses against their parent' wills.

47. Barbee Papers, box 74, folder 26; Dahlk, *Against the Wind*, 283–285; and Dahlk, "Black Educational Reform," 186–187. See Dougherty, *More Than One Struggle*, 137–142, for additional background information on the SPCA and the Peckham-Steuben Plan.

48. Dan Carpenter, "Blacks Nix School Site," *Milwaukee Courier*, July 7, 1973 1:1, 4; Rick Janka, "New Plan Submitted for North Division," *Milwaukee Sentinel*, June 6, 1973, 1:1, 11; and "Washington Committee Adopts Plan to Achieve Racial Balance," *Milwaukee Courier*, June 16, 1973, 1:1. Wegmann was the only affirmative vote.

49. Dennis J. Conta, "The East Shore District Plan: A City-Suburban School Merger Proposal," Barbee Papers, box 24, folder 8, and many other locations. Additional support documents are in folders 8–9. See also David I. Bednarek, "Area School Chiefs Cool to Conta Plan," *Milwaukee Journal*, March 24, 1975; 2:1, 3; "Integration Bill Expands," *Milwaukee Journal*, March 19, 1975, 2:1, 12; "City-Suburb Model Proposed for Schools," *Milwaukee Journal*, January 6, 1975, 2:1, 3; "Conta Defends His Plan Against Attack," *Milwaukee Journal*, March 28, 1975, 2:3; "Conta Stirs Up a Hornet's Nest," *Milwaukee Journal*, January 14, 1975, 2:1, 4; and "School Merger Proposal Scores Flat Zero in Bay," *Milwaukee Journal*, January 9, 1975.

50. Linda B. Malman, "New School Board Members: New Ideas," *Milwaukee Journal*, April 6, 1975, 2:1, 16; "Transfer Options at School Asked," *Milwaukee Journal*, January 17, 1975, 2:1.

51. Rick Janka, "Blacks Hear Attack on School Merger," *Milwaukee Sentinel*, July 21, 1975, 1:5; Janka, "Peril of 'Do Nothing' Led to Integration Planning," *Milwaukee Sentinel*, September 11, 1975, 1:5; and miscellaneous correspondence in Barbee Papers, box 24, folders 8–9. Kathryn M. Kubacki, "An Attempt at Metropolitan Desegregation in Milwaukee County: The History of the East Shore District Plan" (master's thesis, University of Wisconsin–Milwaukee, 2005), chapter 4; Miriam G. Palay, *Chapter 220, Student Exchanges Between City and Suburb: The Milwaukee Experience* (Milwaukee: Milwaukee Urban Observatory, 1978), 7; and Nancy Sidon Smuckler, "Chapter 220: A Study of the Academic Achievement of Minority Interdistrict Transfer Pupils" (PhD diss.,

University of Wisconsin–Milwaukee, 1984), 25, also detail the opposition to the Conta plan. See Special Committee to the Shorewood School Board, Peter Barry, Chairman, *Report of the Special Committee Established by the Shorewood School Board to Prepare an Analysis of the Educational, Financial, Legal, and Community Implications of the Proposed Merger of the Schools in Whitefish Bay, Shorewood, and Certain Areas in Milwaukee* (April 7, 1975) for the opinions of Shorewood's school board. The report is thirty-seven pages long. The page preceding page 1 has a short summary of arguments. See Mikel Holt, *Not Yet "Free at Last": The Unfinished Business of the Civil Rights Movement; Our Battle for School Choice* (Oakland, CA: Institute for Contemporary Studies Press, 2000), 33–34, for an acerbic response to the Shorewood school board from an African American viewpoint.

52. Kubacki, "An Attempt at Metropolitan Desegregation," 65–66.

53. Quoted in Rick Janka, "Blacks Hear Attack on School Merger," *Milwaukee Sentinel*, July 21, 1975, 1:5

54. See chapters 9 and 12 of Dahlk, *Against the Wind*; and Dougherty, *More Than One Struggle*, 159–163, for more on Harwell. See Santacroce, "Rediscovering the Role of the State," 294–295, 305–309, for background information on Triple O.

55. "School Appointees Give Conservatives the Edge," *Milwaukee Journal*, May 7, 1975, 2:1, 10.

56. Percentage of African Americans derived from Miriam G. Palay, *Census Update, City of Milwaukee, 1975* (Milwaukee: Milwaukee Urban Observatory, 1977), 15; percentage of whites derived from Palay, 17.

57. Beverstock and Stuckert, *Metropolitan Milwaukee Fact Book*, 46.

58. Palay, *Census Update,* 50–54.

59. Ibid., 55–56.

60. "Milwaukee Urban Atlas Population Characteristics" (Milwaukee: Milwaukee Public Library, 2003), 8, http://city.milwaukee.gov/ImageLibrary/Groups /cityDCD/planning/data/pdfs/UrbanAtlasPopulation.pdf. See also Palay, *Census Update,* 17–18, and Miriam G. Palay, *Census Facts: Milwaukee Areas and Neighborhoods, 1970–1980 Statistics Compared* (Milwaukee: University of Wisconsin–Milwaukee and University of Wisconsin–Extension, 1984). See Belden Paulson, "School Segregation and the Metropolitan Issue," 1978, Barbee Papers, box 216, folder 22, for an early study on demographic changes and metropolitan integration.

61. Rick Janka, "Specialties Preceded Busing," *Milwaukee Sentinel*, August 31, 1977, 1:1, 16. See also Steven A. Baruch, "Factors Affecting the Process of Curriculum Formation in the Milwaukee Public Schools, July 1955 to June 1976" (PhD diss., University of Wisconsin–Milwaukee, 1982).

62. *Proceedings*, May 6, 1941, and April 5, 1961.

63. "Integration Proposals Lag Here," *Milwaukee Journal*, August 24, 1967, 1:4; "Stronger Schooling, Dispersal of Pupils Is Urged for Core," *Milwaukee Journal*, September 5, 1963, 2:1; and "We Are Losing a Major Social Resource," *Milwaukee Courier*, February 25, 1967, 1.

64. David I. Bednarek, "School Idea Rooted in Toledo," *Milwaukee Journal*,

October 21, 1975, 2:1, 6; *Proceedings*, June 2 and 22, 1970; and "McMurrin's Aim on Target," *Milwaukee Journal*, October 22, 1975, 1:16.

65. *Proceedings*, September 4, August 7, and June 5, 1973; "Board to Weigh Plans for Schools," *Milwaukee Journal*, March 24, 1974, 2:3.

66. David I. Bednarek, "Race Plan for Schools Modified," *Milwaukee Journal*, March 5, 1974, 1:1, 8; Bednarek, "School Board Isn't Leaping into Integration Plans," *Milwaukee Journal*, March 12, 1974, 2:1, 5; Bednarek, "School Transfer Plan Rejected," *Milwaukee Journal*, March 7, 1974, 2:1, 3; and *Proceedings*, March 6 and October 30, 1973.

67. Rick Janka, "3 Blacks Win School Board Jobs," *Milwaukee Sentinel*, February 28, 1975, 1:1, 7.

68. Baruch, "Factors Affecting the Process," 303.

69. "Candidates Speak Out on Busing," *Milwaukee Journal*, February 28, 1975, 2:1, 4.

70. David I. Bednarek, "School Lunch for New Boss," *Milwaukee Journal*, May 17, 1975, 1:1, 22; Rick Janka, "School 'Boss' Lends Ear, Smile to Inquisitive Pupils," *Milwaukee Sentinel*, May 17, 1975, 1:5; and "Our New Superintendent," *Milwaukee Journal*, May 8, 1975, 1:22.

71. Stacy interview; Anthony Busalacchi, interview with author, Milwaukee, July 7, 2010; and Leon Todd, interview with author, Milwaukee, June 28, 2010. See also "Desegregation Ruling Comes 10 Years after School Suit is Filed," *Milwaukee Courier*, January 24, 1976, 1, 6.

72. Busalacchi interview.

73. Baruch, "Factors Affecting the Process," 415.

74. Murphy and Pawasarat, "Why It Failed," 38.

75. Lee McMurrin, "Big City Rookie," in untitled, unpublished manuscript in author's possession, 1–2. My thanks to Dr. McMurrin for sharing his manuscript with me.

76. *Proceedings*, September 2, 1975.

77. Lee McMurrin, telephone interview with author, July 7, 2010.

78. Lee McMurrin, "Educational Change: It Can Work to Your Advantage," *Theory into Practice* 20, no. 4 (1981): 265–266.

79. *Proceedings*, September 2, 1975.

80. McMurrin interview.

81. David Bennett, telephone interview with author, August 25, 2010.

82. Baruch interview; Doris Stacy, interview with author, Milwaukee, June 30, 2010.

83. David I. Bednarek, "McMurrin Offers Plan for Diversity," *Milwaukee Journal*, October 21, 1975, 1:5; Bednarek, "School Idea Rooted in Toledo," *Milwaukee Journal*, October 21, 1975, 2:1, 6; Rick Janka, "McMurrin Calls for Major Revamping," *Milwaukee Sentinel*, October 21, 1975; *Proceedings*, November 4, 1975; and "Policy Statements Passed by the Milwaukee Board of School Directors Relative to Racial Balance and Equality of Educational Opportunities," 1976, Radtke Papers, box 2, folder 20, and "Recommended September Plans for Providing Expanded Educational Opportunities and Initiating the First Phase of the School Desegregation," 1976, Radtke Papers, box 2, folders 5 and 25, and in other repositories.

84. *Proceedings*, February 3, 1976.

85. Ibid.

86. "Workable Plan," *Milwaukee Sentinel*, October 22, 1975, 1:16.

87. "McMurrin's Aim on Target," *Milwaukee Journal*, October 22, 1975, 1:16.

88. Ed Hinshaw, WTMJ–TV, March 9, 15, 17, and 22; June 23, 28, and 29; July 7 and 15; August 9; and December 29, 1976, and Carl Zimmerman, WITI–TV, May 3, 24, and 30, 1976, Radtke Papers, box 2, folder 5; Ed Hinshaw, WTMJ–TV, February 16 and 23, 1979, Radtke Papers, box 2, folder 7.

89. "Senator Criticizes Conta Plan," *Milwaukee Journal*, January 2, 1976, 2:1, 4. See also Milwaukee Teachers Education Association (MTEA), Minutes of the Special MTEA Building Representative Assembly, February 2, 1976, Hart Papers, box 1, folder 1.

90. Bennett, Stacy, and Todd interviews.

91. David I. Bednarek, "Suburbs Attracted by Magnet Concept," *Milwaukee Journal*, October 26, 1975, 1:1, 5.

92. Donald Pfarrer et al., "Reading, Riding, and Race: Public Opinion and School Segregation in Milwaukee County," Milwaukee: *Milwaukee Journal*, 1975, 1. Excerpts appear in the newspaper, but the citations here are from the complete study. The raw data are available in John H. Blexrud and Paul Tsao, eds., *Data Reference Book for Political, Desegregation, and Crime Studies in Milwaukee and Wisconsin, 1975–1976* (*Milwaukee Journal/Milwaukee Sentinel* and the University of Wisconsin–Milwaukee, 1977), 125–142.

93. Pfarrer et al., "Reading, Riding, and Race," 2–3.

94. Ibid., 18.

95. Ibid., 19–20.

96. Ibid., 22–24.

97. *Amos*, 113–129; David I. Bednarek, "Schools Told to Integrate," *Milwaukee Journal*, January 19, 1976, 1:1, 9. The school board officially acknowledged receipt of Judge Reynolds's decision on January 24, 1976, according to *Proceedings*, January 24, 1976.

98. *Proceedings*, April 15, 1976; Stacy interview.

99. Murphy and Pawasarat, "Why It Failed," 36–37.

100. *Amos*, 134–135.

101. David I. Bednarek, "Panel of 100 Suggested to Map Integration Plan," *Milwaukee Journal*, February 8, 1976, 1:1, 20; McMurrin interview; and Montgomery, "A Case Study of Political, Social, and Economic Forces," ii. The teacher representative spot was filled by the MTEA building representative (referred to as a union steward in other unions) in schools that elected representatives. MTEA President Guzniczak appointed the representative in the few buildings that did not hold elections. See "MTEA Fact Sheet" in Hart Papers, box 1, folder 1. A memo from MPS dated March 16, 1976, Hart Papers, box 1, folder 1, provides procedures for electing parents and community members.

102. Ian M. Harris, "The Committee of 100: Citizen Participation in Desegregation," unpublished report, Milwaukee Public Library, 1977, 5.

103. Ibid., 8.

104. Ibid., 8–9.
105. Stacy interview; Anthony Busalacchi, interview with author, Milwaukee, July 7, 2010; and Leon Todd, interview with author, Milwaukee, June 28, 2010.
106. Lorraine Radtke, "In My Opinion," Radtke Papers, box 2, folder 1. "Superior Ability" was the name of the program for gifted and talented students in some middle schools and high schools. It was succeeded by the Program for the Academically Talented (PAT) in the 1980s and honors classes at the high school level in the 1990s.
107. Quoted in "Integration Planning Begins Amid Complaints by Many," *Milwaukee Journal*, March 17, 1976, 2:1, 15. See also McMurrin, July 7, 2010. 108. Ralph Olive, "Gronouski Repeats Theme to Hamilton High Residents," *Milwaukee Journal*, March 20, 1976, 1:24.
109. "Integration Meetings Show Positive Spirit," *Milwaukee Sentinel*, March 31, 1976, 1:1, 8.
110. Ralph D. Olive, "Two Liberals Head Committee of 100," *Milwaukee Journal*, April 8, 1976, 2:1, 2.
111. Harris, "The Committee of 100," 9.
112. Ibid., 15–19.
113. Quoted in Miner, *Lessons from the Heartland*, 92.
114. John Semancik, interview with author, Milwaukee, June 5, 2011.
115. Memo from Hamilton Cluster Delegates to the Committee of 100 and the Board of School Directors, June 2, 1976, Hart Papers, box 1, folder 1.
116. "Hamilton Cluster to Quit C-100," *Milwaukee Sentinel*, April 5, 1976, 1:8.
117. David I. Bednarek, "Committee of 100 Opposes Appeal of Reynolds' Decision," *Milwaukee Journal*, April 7, 1976, 1:1, 4; Rick Janka, "Drop Appeal of Ruling, Committee of 100 Asks," *Milwaukee Sentinel*, April 7, 1976, 1:5. See also Harris, "The Committee of 100," 5–6.
118. Kathleen Hart, interview with author, Greendale, WI, August 23, 2010; "Gronouski OKs Delay on Deadline," *Milwaukee Journal*, April 9, 1976, 2: 1.
119. Pulaski Cluster Resolution, April 12, 1976, Hart Papers, box 1, folder 1.
120. Cluster plans from Custer, Pulaski, Riverside, South Division, Washington, and West Division are scattered in Hart Papers, box 1, folder 1. Some additional information is contained in folder 2, including the Madison cluster plan. Minutes from the Committee of 100 are available in folders 2–5. Minutes from the South Division Cluster are scattered in box 1, folders 1–4, including a South Division "Guide for Students, 1977–78" in folder 4. A detailed plan for Riverside's feeder schools called the "Four-Grade-Level and One Open Education Magnet Plan" can be found in People United for Integrated and Quality Education Papers, in possession of Robert Peterson, Milwaukee (hereafter cited as People United). Other documents in the collection call for bilingual education and an end to tracking.
121. David I. Bednarek, "McMurrin's Proposal Would Bus 7,500," *Milwaukee Journal*, April 14, 1976, 1:1, 4; Rick Janka, "Integration Formula Caution Earned," *Milwaukee Sentinel*, April 14, 1976, 1:5; and Marilyn Kucer, "Keep N. Division Open, Panel Asks," *Milwaukee Sentinel*, April 14, 1976, 1:1, 4.

122. Dougherty, *More Than One Struggle*, 29; Murphy and Pawasarat, "Why It Failed," 40.

123. "Program Descriptions: Options for Learning and Schools for the Transition," July 28, 1976, Hart Papers, box 1, folder 3; Montgomery, "A Case Study of Political, Social, and Economic Forces," 396–398; "Older Pupils have Role in School Integration,"*Milwaukee Sentinel*, August 17, 1976, 1: 12; and *Proceedings*, May 11, 1976.

124. "Faculty Integration," in A Collection of Papers Relating to the Desegregation/Integration of the Milwaukee Public Schools, Milwaukee Public Library Humanities Room, 1976; *Proceedings*, May 11, 1976. As chapter 3 indicated, MPS had racially segregated its teachers in the 1960s.

125. David I. Bednarek, "Clashes Plague School Board," *Milwaukee Journal*, May 30, 1976, 1:1, 19; Bednarek, "Reynolds Schedules Hearing on Proposal," *Milwaukee Journal*, May 25, 1976, 1:1, 4.

126. David I. Bednarek, "Judge Gets School Plan," *Milwaukee Journal*, May 24, 1976, 1:1, 12; Bednarek, "School Plan Withdrawn" or "Judge Rejects School Plan," *Milwaukee Journal*, June 9, 1976, 1:1, 9. (The title changed between editions.)

127. David I. Bednarek, "53 City Schools to Be Integrated," *Milwaukee Journal*, June 10, 1976, 1:1, 20; James Parks, "Board Lawyer Tastes Reynolds' Wrath," *Milwaukee Journal*, June 10, 1976, 1:20; and Michael Stolee, "The Milwaukee Desegregation Case," in Rury and Cassell, *Seeds of Crisis*, 252. See also Harris, "The Committee of 100," 11.

128. Montgomery, "A Case Study of Political, Social, and Economic Forces," 453–454.

129. Harris, "The Committee of 100," 12; Montgomery, "A Case Study of Political, Social, and Economic Forces," 441–517. This plan is not unlike Gousha's pairing plan, described earlier in this chapter. Map 9 shows the African American population in Milwaukee in 1975, map 10 shows the leagues, and map 11 for a draft of the distribution of elementary magnet schools within the zones. Original maps found in Office of the Superintendent of Schools, "Preliminary Recommendations for Increasing Educational Opportunities and Improving Racial Balance" (Milwaukee Public Schools, June 25, 1976, printed with corrections on July 15, 1976), 44–47, in John A. Gronouski Papers, 1953–1983, part 4, box 8, Wisconsin Historical Society Archives, Madison, WI (hereafter cited as Gronouski Papers). Additional copies are in part 4, box 9, and part 5, box unnumbered. An untitled and undated planning document in Gronouski Papers, part 4, box 9, provides a list of schools by league and possible sites for citywide magnet programs. There appear to be a few minor discrepancies between the planning document and the plan that was published in 1977, copies of which are in Hart Papers, box 2, folder 1. See map 10.

130. Lee McMurrin, "Perspectives on Busing," in untitled, unpublished manuscript in author's possession, 4.

131. Stolee, "The Milwaukee Desegregation Case," 252–253. See also Harris, "The Committee of 100," 12.

132. "Integration Through Educational Alternatives," 1976, Radtke Papers, box 2,

folder 9. See also "Magnet School Program," undated, in folder 11, and "Memorandum in Response to Court Order Requiring Defendants to Devise and Submit a Plan for Desegregating the Public School System," 1977, in folder 11.

133. *Proceedings*, June 1, 1976, and Steven Baruch, interview with author, Glendale, WI, July 9, 2010. Baruch was a human relations coordinator at Rufus King High School in 1978–79 and was one of the chief people assigned to prepare the staff for its transformation to a magnet school. He also spent one semester at North Division before going to MPS's human relations office, where he would be in charge of human relations curriculum.

134. David I. Bednarek, "New School Appeal Could Go to Voters," *Milwaukee Journal*, June 24, 1976, 1:1, 8; "Busalacchi Replies to Critics," *Milwaukee Sentinel*, July 24, 1976, 1:5; James Parks, "School Panel Unsure of Next Move," *Milwaukee Journal*, June 24, 1976, 1:1, 8; *Proceedings*, October 5, 1976; and Stolee, "The Milwaukee Desegregation Case," 247.

CHAPTER 3

1. David I. Bednarek, "Schools Hit Mark for Integration," *Milwaukee Journal*, September 8, 1976, 1:1, 5; Eileen Hammer, "Junior High Problems Few," *Milwaukee Sentinel*, 1:12; Damien Jaques, "A Day of 'Getting to Know You,'" *Milwaukee Journal*, September 8, 1976, 2:1, 5; "Many Laud Smoothness of First Day," *Milwaukee Journal*, September 8, 1976, 2:1, 12; and Stuart Wilk, "Integration Off to a Peaceful Start but Delays, Confusion Abound," *Milwaukee Sentinel*, September 8, 1976, 1:1, 13. Quotes from Rick Janka, "McMurrin Keeps Smiling," *Milwaukee Sentinel*, September 8, 1976, 1:13.

2. Quoted in *Forced Choice: The Milwaukee Plan; A Model for Northern School Desegregation*, VHS, produced and directed by Jones Cullinan (Milwaukee: Medusa Veritape, 1980).

3. Christine H. Rossell, "Is It the Busing or the Blacks?" *Urban Affairs Quarterly* 24, no. 1 (1988): 139–145. See David R. Morgan and Robert E. England, "Large District School Desegregation: A Preliminary Assessment of Techniques," *Social Science Quarterly* 63 (December 1982): 698–700; James E. Rosenbaum and Stefan Presser, "Voluntary Integration in a Magnet School," *The School Review* 86, no. 2 (February 1978): 156–186, for two other studies that show the relationship between length of a bus ride and white flight. Even proponents of magnet schools recognize that magnets are not enough to draw white students into the inner city. See McMillan, *Magnet Schools*, 23.

4. See Christine H. Rossell, *The Carrot or the Stick for School Desegregation Policy: Magnet Schools or Forced Busing* (Philadelphia: Temple University Press, 1990), especially 10–19, 115–126, 208, 211.

5. Belden Paulson, "White Flight and School Desegregation," November 3, 1977, Hart Papers, box 1, folder 1.

6. Maria Luce, "Supportive Data to Facilitate School Integration Planning for the City of Milwaukee," Center for Urban Community Development, University of Wisconsin–Extension, April 1976, 22–23, People United.

7. David I. Bednarek, "Panel Orders Talks on North Division," *Milwaukee Journal*, August 31, 1979, 2:1, 3.

8. "Older Pupils Have Role in Integration," *Milwaukee Sentinel*, August 17, 1976, 1:12. See map 12 for proposed high schools. Course descriptions for these courses and other specialized courses available in "High Schools Unlimited: Special Courses Available at Milwaukee's 15 Public High Schools," People United. Specialized courses were offered in art, business, English, foreign languages, home economics, industry, music, physical education, science, social studies, and technical education. Social studies course titles, for example, included Anthropology; Afro-American Heritage; the Corporation; Environmental Education; Hispano-American Culture, Language, and History; Indian American Culture; Minorities in American Society; Philosophy; Political Philosophies; Simulated Social Problems; Water, Air, and Man; Wisconsin History and Geography; and Women's Studies.

9. McMurrin, "Big City Rookie," 14.

10. "Older Pupils Have Role in Integration," *Milwaukee Sentinel*, August 17, 1976, 1:12.

11. Sampson, *Options, School Desegregation*, i. This is how the term *forced choice* originated. See chapter 6 for more information.

12. "Older Pupils Have Role in Integration," *Milwaukee Sentinel*, August 17, 1976, 1:12.

13. The Milwaukee School Board approved Superintendent McMurrin's plan to convert junior high schools to middle schools and end the use of six-year junior-senior high schools by September 1978 on April 6, 1977, according to *Proceedings*, April 6, 1977. However, fourteen of the district's eighteen middle schools were for only seventh- and eighth-graders until 1986, according to David I. Bednarek, "6th Graders Might Go to Middle School," *Milwaukee Journal*, November 6, 1985, 2:1.

14. "Older Pupils Have Role in Integration," *Milwaukee Sentinel*, August 17, 1976, 1:12; Office of the Deputy Superintendent, "Report to the Special Master on the First Phase of School Desegregation," Milwaukee Public Schools (October 8, 1976), Radtke Papers, box 2, folder 31. See LouAnn S. Dickson et al., *Focus on Fundamentals: A Longitudinal Study of Students Attending a Fundamental School* (Arlington, VA: Educational Research Service, 1993); Philip Jones, "All About Those New 'Fundamental' Public Schools, What They're Promising, and Why They're Catching On," *American School Board Journal* (1976): 24–31; and Larry Weber et al., "An Evaluation of Fundamental Schools," *Evaluation Review* 8, no. 5 (1984): 595–614, for more on fundamental schools.

15. "Older Pupils Have Role in Integration," *Milwaukee Sentinel*, August 17, 1976, 1:12; Office of the Superintendent of Schools, "League and Council Proposals for the Development of a Comprehensive Plan for Achieving Racial Balance in Milwaukee's Schools," Milwaukee Public Schools, November 15, 1976; "Preliminary Recommendations for Increasing Educational Opportunities and Improving Racial Balance," Milwaukee Public Schools, June 25, 1976, printed with corrections on July 15, 1976, 72–78, Gronouski Papers, part 4, box 8. See also Joseph M. Cronin, "City School Desegregation and the Creative Uses of Enrollment Decline," *Equity & Excellence in Education* 15, no. 1 (January 1977): 10–12.

16. Rick Janka, "Voluntary Plans Called Failures," *Milwaukee Sentinel*, July 28, 1976, 1:11.

17. Quoted in Keith Spore, "Voluntary Integration Plan Working, Most Parents Say," *Milwaukee Sentinel*, November 5, 1976, 1:1, 7.

18. Gregory E. Strong, "Metropolitan Desegregation: Administrative Practices and Procedures" (PhD diss., University of Wisconsin–Milwaukee, 1980), 75–82.

19. James Coulter, executive director, MTEA, to John Gronouski, November 17, 1976, Gronouski Papers, part 4, box 9. The substitute teachers could have been of any race.

20. Barbara Koppe, "Problems Still Plague Specialty Schools," *Milwaukee Journal*, April 12, 1977, 2:1, 4. The reporter kept the identities of the schools anonymous, probably to encourage teachers to speak freely.

21. Ibid.

22. Jeff Browne, "Busing Grows Complex for City Schools," *Milwaukee Journal*, August 17, 1976, 2:1, 5; Dan Patrinos, "Integration Gain Viewed as Loss for Victory School," *Milwaukee Sentinel*, August 21, 1976, 1:5, 7.

23. Arlo Coplin, interview with author, Greendale, WI, August 17, 2010.

24. David I. Bednarek, "Bus Firm Stumbles Over School Pact," *Milwaukee Journal*, 2:1, 2; "Bus Wait Gives 5 Year Old a 12 Hour Day," *Milwaukee Sentinel*, September 9, 1976, 1:1, 18; and "Schools Start Switch to Other Bus Firms," *Milwaukee Journal*, 1:1, 15.

25. "Bus Woes Ironed Out, Aides Hope," *Milwaukee Sentinel*, September 15, 1976, 1:5.

26. "Busing Costs Twice as High as Planned, *Milwaukee Sentinel*, September 24, 1976, 1:8; "Desegregation Planners Hit Snag," *Milwaukee Journal*, September 23, 1976, 2:1, 4.

27. *Proceedings*, December 7, 1976.

28. "Recommendations for the Milwaukee Public Schools Integration Plan," People United.

29. The communications and media center closed in 1977 when Marshall was awarded that specialty. Thus, there were a total of eight satellite centers in 1977–78. See *Proceedings*, February 24, 1977.

30. Kenneth R. Lamke, "Support Stays for Integration," *Milwaukee Sentinel*, April 5, 1977, 1:1, 9.

31. Ibid. The raw data are available in Blexrud and Tsao, *Data Reference Book*, 173–188.

32. Quoted in Rick Janka, "15 Hopefuls State Views on Schools," *Milwaukee Sentinel*, February 7, 1977, 1:5, 6.

33. Anthony S. Busalacchi, "Busalacchi Defends Appeal," *Milwaukee Sentinel*, March 9, 1977, 1:14.

34. Rick Janka, "15 Hopefuls State Views on Schools," *Milwaukee Sentinel*, February 7, 1977, 1:5, 6; "O'Neil Decries Forced Busing," *Milwaukee Sentinel*, March 29, 1977, 1:5; Lennox Samuels, "Says Integration Can't Be Forced," *Milwaukee Sentinel*, January 28, 1980.

35. Jeff Kartz, interview with author, Milwaukee, October 10, 2010.

36. Rick Janka and Marilyn Kucer, "Conservatives Gain School Seat," *Milwaukee Sentinel*, April 6, 1977, 1:1, 7.

37. "McMurrin Says Integration Won't Halt," *Milwaukee Sentinel*, May 25, 1977, 1:5.

38. Anthony Busalacchi, interview with author, Milwaukee, July 7, 2010; Doris Stacy, interview with author, Milwaukee, June 30, 2010; and Leon Todd, interview with author, Milwaukee, June 28, 2010.

39. *Brennan v. Armstrong*, 433 U.S. 672 (1977); Stolee, "The Milwaukee Desegregation Case," 247–248, 253.

40. *Armstrong v. Brennan*, 566 F.2d 1175 (7th Cir. 1977); *Milwaukee Sentinel*, August 23, 1977.

41. David I. Bednarek, "Board Delays Plan for Special Schools," *Milwaukee Journal*, October 26, 1977, 2: 1; Marilyn Kucer, "Schools Back Working on Integration," *Milwaukee Sentinel*, September 9, 1977, 1: 5, 14; Murphy and Pawasarat, "Why It Failed," 40; and "Schools Case Resolution Far Off," *Milwaukee Sentinel*, September 10, 1977, 1:5.

42. Rick Janka, "Teacher Strike Will Halt All School Bus Service," *Milwaukee Sentinel*, April 6, 1977, 1:5.

43. Rick Janka, "Bus Is a Vital Medium in School Integration," *Milwaukee Sentinel*, September 2, 1977, 1:5, 10.

44. Jeff Aikin, "School Bus Routes Shift Daily," *Milwaukee Sentinel*, September 24, 1977, 1:5.

45. "Accelerating Bus Costs Need Brake," *Milwaukee Sentinel*, March 22, 1978, 1:8; Louis Liebovich, "School Busing Costs Rise 58%," *Milwaukee Sentinel*, March 18, 1978, 1:5, 8; and Louis Liebovich and Bill Hurley, "Bus Firm Operates at Desegregation Sites," *Milwaukee Sentinel*, February 1, 1978, 1:5, 12.

46. See "City School Buses Need 100 Drivers," *Milwaukee Sentinel*, August 17, 1978, 1:5; Bill Hurley, "Serious Study Is the Specialty at Rufus King," *Milwaukee Sentinel*, September 6, 1978, 1:5; Rick Janka, "83,000 Attend School Start," *Milwaukee Sentinel*, September 6, 1978, 1:1, 12; Rick Janka, "Parents Not Aware of New Bus Routes," *Milwaukee Sentinel*, September 2, 1978, 1:5; and "Pupils Lose Bus Service," *Milwaukee Sentinel*, October 23, 1978, 1:4.

47. "Buses to Suburbs in Gear," *Milwaukee Sentinel*, September 7, 1977, 1:6; Rick Janka, "Specialties Preceded Court Order," *Milwaukee Sentinel*, August 31, 1977, 1:1, 16; Marilyn Kucer, "Some Are Calm, Some Cry as Kids Bear Busing Brunt," *Milwaukee Sentinel*, September 7, 1977, 1:7; and William Janz, "McMurrin Spreads the Cheerful Word," *Milwaukee Sentinel*, September 7, 1977, 1:10. Of course, one would expect such positive reports to run in a newspaper at the beginning of the school year.

48. "Board Backs More Pupil Transfers," *Milwaukee Sentinel*, February 8, 1978, 1:6.

49. David I. Bednarek, "Students Offer Insight," *Milwaukee Journal*, June 26, 1977, 1:1, 22.

50. Quoted in Rick Janka, "Watchful Army Alerted to School Trouble Spots," *Milwaukee Sentinel*, September 1, 1977, 1:5, 14. The monitoring board's organizational structure is explained in "Special Master's Monitoring Board," Gronouski Papers, part 4, box 9. Training materials and observation forms are in Gronouski Papers, part 4, box 9; Hart Papers, box 2, folders 3–4. See also Harris, "The Committee of 100," 14.

51. Robert Peterson, interview with author, Milwaukee, August 16, 2010.

52. "Activist Will Lead Milwaukee Teachers' Education Association," *Milwaukee Journal Sentinel*, May 22, 2011.

53. Quoted in Rick Janka, "Watchful Army Alerted to School Trouble Spots," *Milwaukee Sentinel*, September 1, 1977, 1:5, 14. A memo in the People United Papers dated April 6, 1976, from the Franklin Pierce School Advisory Committee to the Riverside cluster committee demanded a new multicultural curriculum, expansion of bilingual education, and an end to "tracking." According to the memo, 60 percent of Riverside's students were African American or Hispanic, but 90 percent of the students in the college-bound track were white. A duplicate copy is in Radtke Papers, box 2, folder 5. Evidence of internal segregation in magnet schools in other parts of the United States was reported in James E. Rosenbaum and Stefan Presser, "Voluntary Integration in a Magnet School," *The School Review* 86, no. 2 (February 1978): 156–186. Many scholarly articles have been written on the disproportionate representation of African Americans in special education. Daniel J. Losen and Gary Orfield, eds., *Racial Inequity in Special Education* (Cambridge, MA: Harvard Education Press, 2002) is one of the best collections of articles on the subject.

54. Robert Peterson interview. "Human relations" was the term used to describe activities that fostered racial tolerance.

55. Harris, "The Committee of 100," 15.

56. Gronouski Papers, part 4, box 9.

57. Robert Peterson interview.

58. Rick Janka, "Schools Work on '78 Plan," *Milwaukee Sentinel*, September 3, 1977, 1:5; Marilyn Kucer, "Schools Back Working on Integration," *Milwaukee Sentinel*, September 9, 1977, 1:5, 14.

59. Rick Janka, "Schools Work on '78 Plan," *Milwaukee Sentinel*, September 3, 1977, 1:5.

60. *Proceedings*, November 2 and 16, 1977.

61. McMurrin was especially proud of the German Immersion School, the support it had from the large German American community in Milwaukee, and the positive response from African American students enrolled at the school. See McMurrin, "Big City Rookie," 6.

62. *Proceedings*, November 2 and 16, 1977; January 9, 1979; January 8, 1984; and January 2, 1985; the MPS school selection guide, 2002–03 and 2010–11, author's possession. Vincent did not open until 1979, according to Rick Janka, "High School Starts from Scratch in Properly Rural Surroundings," *Milwaukee Sentinel*, August 29, 1979, 1:5, 16. I can find no references to the satellite centers after the 1977–78 school year, but the general feeling among people I interviewed is that they were no longer needed after Bay View and Lincoln high schools received programs in fall 1978. Custer had been floated as a north side technical school for years. In fact, the idea of establishing a second trade school in Milwaukee goes back to the 1930s. See Lamers, *Our Roots Grow Deep*, 41–43; *Proceedings*, April 7, 1931; October 3, 1933; and January 10, 1939.

63. *Proceedings*, November 2, 1978.

64. Bill Hurley, "Serious Study Is the Specialty at Rufus King," *Milwaukee Sentinel*, September 6, 1978, 1:5; and *Proceedings*, January 6, 1976, and February 24, 1977. The subject of admissions tests for magnet schools has been controversial from the 1970s until the present time. There have been periods in which no entrance examination was required. An exam is required for most students entering King as of this writing.

65. Rick Janka, "Black School Staff Fears Testifying, Judge Told," *Milwaukee Sentinel*, January 4, 1978, 1:1, 4; Rick Janka, "Black Teachers Placement Policy Charged," *Milwaukee Sentinel*, January 6, 1978, 1:5; and Rick Janka, "Integration Still Part of Fall School Plans," *Milwaukee Sentinel*, January 3, 1978, 1:5.

66. "Expert Says Board Acts Fostered Segregation," *Milwaukee Sentinel*, July 11, 1978, 1:5; "'Racism Hidden Between Lines,'" *Milwaukee Sentinel*, March 9, 1978, 1:5; and Stolee, "The Milwaukee Desegregation Case," 253.

67. Jeff Browne, "Desegregation Suit a History Lesson," *Milwaukee Journal*, January 12, 1978, 2:1, 5; Rick Janka, "Busing in '60s Criticized," *Milwaukee Sentinel*, January 13, 1978, 1:5.

68. Dougherty, *More Than One Struggle*, 163; miscellaneous witness statements in Barbee Papers, box 160, folders 19–20. The evidence from the remand trial fills fifty-five archives boxes, and the evidence from the original trial is in more than one hundred boxes.

69. Jeff Browne and David I. Bednarek, "Court Finds Intentional School Bias," *Milwaukee Journal*, June 1, 1978, 1:1, 14; Stolee, "The Milwaukee Desegregation Case," 253.

70. *Armstrong v. O'Connell*, 451 F. Supp. 817 (E.D. Wis. 1978); Stolee, "The Milwaukee Desegregation Case," 253–254.

71. David I. Bednarek, "McMurrin's Hope: End of Litigation," *Milwaukee Journal*, November 3, 1978, 2:2; Jeff Browne, "Desegregation Suit a History Lesson," *Milwaukee Journal*, January 12, 1978, 2:1, 5; "Final Order Entered in Discrimination Case," *Milwaukee Courier*, January 6, 1979, 1, 3; "School Board Offers to Settle," *Milwaukee Journal*, November 3, 1978, 2:2; and Rick Janka, "Teacher Desegregation Going Smoothly," *Milwaukee Sentinel*, September 1, 1978, 1:5.

72. Quoted in Jeff Browne, "New Monitor to Keep Order," *Milwaukee Journal*, August 1, 1978, 2:1, 5.

73. Luisa Ginnetti, "School Board Increases Pay for New Members," *Milwaukee Sentinel*, December 12, 1978, 1:1, 12; "OK School Board Bill; Fate Cloudy," *Milwaukee Sentinel*, March 29, 1978, 1:1; "School Board Lawsuit Muller Over Revamp," *Milwaukee Sentinel*, June 22, 1978, 1:5; and "Size of School Board to Dip; Appeal Denied," *Milwaukee Sentinel*, December 1, 1978, 1:5.

74. Rick Janka and Marilyn Kucer, "Board's Liberal Majority May Seek Full Integration," *Milwaukee Sentinel*, April 5, 1979, 1:1, 11.

75. *Armstrong v. Board of School Directors of the City of Milwaukee*, 471 F. Supp. 800 (E.D. Wis. 1979); David I. Bednarek, "Citywide Integration Ordered," *Milwaukee Journal*, February 8, 1979, 1:1, 12; "Desegregation Settlement Approved," *Milwaukee Community Journal*, May 9, 1979, 2.

76. L. C. Hammond (of Quarles & Brady) to Lee McMurrin, Thomas Linton, and all

members of the Milwaukee Board of School Directors, February 23, 1979, Radtke Papers, box 1, folder 1; "Integration Accord, Protest Coincide," *Milwaukee Sentinel*, May 5, 1979, 1:5; "Proposed Lincoln Closing Draws Fire," *Milwaukee Courier*, February 10, 1979, 1,3; and Stolee, "The Milwaukee Desegregation Case," 254–255.

77. *Armstrong v. Board of School Directors of the City of Milwaukee*.

78. Dahlk, *Against the Wind*, 329–331.

79. Jeff Browne, "McMurrin Appeals for OK of Settlement," *Milwaukee Journal*, February 24, 1979, 1:1, 7; Dahlk, *Against the Wind*, 332; and Murphy and Pawasarat, "Why It Failed," 39.

80. Luisa Ginnetti, "School Board Increases Pay for New Members," *Milwaukee Sentinel*, December 12, 1978, 1:1, 12; Joanne Huebner, "Community Rallies Against Lincoln Closing," *Milwaukee Sentinel*, July 25, 1978, 1:1, 6; Huebner, "Parents Seek Delay of 3 School Closings," *Milwaukee Sentinel*, August 5, 1978, 1:5; "Panel Opposes School Closing," *Milwaukee Sentinel*, December 8, 1978, 1:5; *Proceedings*, August 1, 1978; "Proposed Lincoln Closing Draws Fire," *Milwaukee Courier*, February 10, 1979, 1, 3.

81. *Proceedings*, March 30, 1982. See also *Proceedings*, April 3 and November 17, 1979, and January 2 and 10, 1980. *Proceedings*, January 4, 1983.

82. Jim Bednarek, "Board OKs Making West Citywide High School for Arts," *Milwaukee Sentinel*, January 5, 1984, 1:1, 13; *Proceedings*, January 6, 1981, and January 26, 1984.

83. See the MPS school selection guide, 2010–11.

84. *Proceedings*, January 4, 1983.

85. *Proceedings*, January 3, 1985. See also *Proceedings*, November 26, 1985.

86. Rick Janka, "McMurrin Urges Pupils Stay Put," *Milwaukee Sentinel*, February 8, 1978; *Proceedings*, January 4 and February 22, 1988; and Stolee, "The Milwaukee Desegregation Case," 255–256. Additional language immersion programs would eventually be created in German, Italian, Chinese, and American Sign Language.

87. David I. Bednarek, "City Showing the Way on Magnet Schools," *Milwaukee Journal*, February 8, 1981, 2:1, 9.

88. Marilyn Kucer, "Milwaukee Area Girls Shine in Computer Classes," *Milwaukee Sentinel*, September 28, 1982, 1:9.

89. Jerry Ressler, "Computers in Our Classrooms," *Milwaukee Sentinel*, April 4, 1984, 1:6.

90. "Word Processing Courses Here Popular," *Milwaukee Sentinel*, April 21, 1982, special section, 4.

91. "Business Education Program at Juneau in Class by Itself," *Milwaukee Sentinel*, November 9, 1985, 2:8

92. Bill Hubbard, "High School Program Prepares Graduates for Hospitality Industry," *Milwaukee Journal*, April 27, 1980, 9:4, 5.

93. Jim Bednarek, "College-Bound Programs Hailed by Students, Officials," *Milwaukee Sentinel*, August 25, 1983, 1:5, 15; McMurrin, "Perspectives on Busing," 9–11.

94. David I. Bednarek, "Popularity a Problem for School," *Milwaukee Journal*, January 10, 1985, 2:1, 6; Mary R. Ring and Ken Locke, "Move Immersed in Debate," January 19, 1985, 1:8.

95. Alan Borsuk, "Gambling on a Special School," *Milwaukee Journal*, March 1, 1985, 2:1, 5; Sandra Lindquist and Thomas M. Ganser, "Student Placement Fails to Make Grade," *Milwaukee Sentinel*, April 13, 1985, 1:8; David I. Bednarek, "Most Blacks, Whites Happy with Schools, Survey Says," *Milwaukee Journal*, June 6, 1985, 1: 1, 6.

96. Quoted in David I. Bednarek, "Magnet Schools Get $4 Million," *Milwaukee Journal*, October 7, 1985, 2:1.

97. Quoted in Jeff Cole, "Pupils Get Up Early to Take Class in City," *Milwaukee Sentinel*, November 4, 1985, 1:5.

98. Quoted in Maggie Menard, "Specialty Program's Students Are Cultivating Future Careers," *Milwaukee Sentinel*, October 21, 1980, 1:5.

99. Jim Bednarek, "U.S. Plans Forestry Program for Minorities and City School," *Milwaukee Sentinel*, March 12, 1984, 1:6.

100. Dorothy Austin, "Vincent's Specialty Is Growing," *Milwaukee Sentinel*, April 30, 1983, special section, 3, 22.

101. Lennox Samuels, "Stronger Technical Program Gets McMurrin's Support," *Milwaukee Sentinel*, November 26, 1980, 1:5; "Varied High School Program Not Without Its Problems," *Milwaukee Sentinel*, November 26, 1980, 1:1, 13.

102. "School Program Sets Sights Too Low, Physician Says," *Milwaukee Sentinel*, December 13, 1982, 1:6.

103. Michelle Derus, "Specialty Schools' Benefits Evaluated," *Milwaukee Sentinel*, August 3, 1982, 1:5.

104. David I. Bednarek, "Classrooms Are Not Fully Desegregated," *Milwaukee Journal*, December 9, 1980, 1:1, 10; Alan J. Borsuk, "Race Is Forgotten in Lively Chaos of a Grade-School Day," *Milwaukee Journal*, June 11, 1984, 2:1, 10. The percentages of desegregated elementary schools and classes, on the other hand, were 76.1 percent and 76.7 percent, respectively. The reason for the discrepancies in the middle and high schools is unknown. One possible explanation is that high school students and some middle school students are allowed to choose their own classes. Academically talented students, who happened to be white, may have chosen more rigorous classes, apart from the general population. Because most students pick the same classes as their friends and because most adolescents do not have friends outside their racial group, that would lead to self-segregation in classes. See Beverly Daniel Tatum, *"Why Are All the Black Kids Sitting Together in the Cafeteria?": A Psychologist Explains the Development of Racial Identity* (New York: Basic Books, 2003) for a stunning explanation of why many racially balanced schools may be voluntarily segregated internally.

105. Alan J. Borsuk, "Race Is Forgotten in Lively Chaos of a Grade-School Day," *Milwaukee Journal*, June 11, 1984, 1:1, 10. Running a second round of buses to take children home from school activities would have cost extra money.

106. Gregory D. Stanford, "Surface Harmony May Be Deceiving," *Milwaukee Journal*, June 13, 1984, 1:1, 6.

107. Milwaukee Public Schools, "Chapter 220 Enrollment," Milwaukee Public Schools, www2.milwaukee.k12.wi.us/supt/Chapter220_Enrollment.html. See Jim Bednarek, "Suburban Enrollment of City Students Triples," *Milwaukee Sentinel*, March 29, 1982, 1:10; "Wisconsin Legislature Assembly," John O. Norquist Papers, 1970–1988, box 21, folder 15, Milwaukee Manuscript Collection 200, Wisconsin Historical Society, Milwaukee Area Research Center, Golda Meir Library, University of Wisconsin–Milwaukee, for exact enrollment figures. See Barbara M. Wise, *Chapter 220: The Compromise to Integrate* (master's thesis, University of Wisconsin–Milwaukee, 2009) for the best history of Chapter 220. See Amy Stuart Wells and Robert L. Crain, "Where School Desegregation and School Choice Collide," in *School Choice and Diversity: What the Evidence Says*, ed. Janelle T. Scott (New York: Teachers College Press, 2005), 59–76, for similar programs in other states.

108. David I. Bednarek, "City, Suburbs Move Closer to Integration Agreement," *Milwaukee Journal*, February 2, 1984, 2:1, 6; Jim Bednarek, "Suburban Enrollment of City Students Triples," *Milwaukee Sentinel*, March 29, 1982, 1:10; Nancy Torner, "Greenfield Residents Divided on Plan to Join Integration," *Milwaukee Journal*, May 6, 1983, 2:3; and Michael O. Zahn, "Panel Backs Equal Access for All Students," *Milwaukee Journal*, March 13, 1980, Accent on the News:1.

109. David I. Bednarek, "School Board Acts to Boost Integration," *Milwaukee Journal*, October 27, 1983, 1:1, 14. See also "Board Rejects Integration Plan," *Milwaukee Sentinel*, April 3, 1979, 1:7; and "Integration Plan Urged," *Milwaukee Sentinel*, March 7, 1978, 1:7.

110. Janet Urquhart, "Whitnall Will Expand Integration Program," *Milwaukee Sentinel*, January 26, 1983, 1:12.

111. David I. Bednarek, "School Board Acts to Boost Integration," *Milwaukee Journal*, October 27, 1983, 1:1, 14.

112. Larry Sandler, "Nicolet Students Get View of City Courses," *Milwaukee Sentinel*, January 10, 1985, 1:6.

113. Craig Gilbert, "Heart of Wisconsin's GOP Can Be Found in Milwaukee's Suburbs," *Milwaukee Journal Sentinel*, April 1, 2012, blog post; Torben Lütjen, "20 Miles and a World Apart," *WI Magazine* 21, no. 3 (November 2012), www.wpri.org/WPRI/WI-Magazine/Volume-21No3/30-Miles-And-a-World -Apart.htm; and Scott Wittkopf, "Blame Waukesha: The GOP's Answer to Liberal Dane County Swings Elections to the Right," *Isthmus*, November 3, 2011, www.isthmus.com/isthmus/article.php?article=35114.

114. David I. Bednarek, "School Board Acts to Boost Integration," *Milwaukee Journal*, October 27, 1983, 1:1, 14.

115. Quoted in David I. Bednarek, "Many Teachers Tell of Attacks," *Milwaukee Journal*, November 28, 1983, 2:1, 4. Teachers who were employed in MPS prior to the implementation of the residency requirement in 1977 were allowed to live outside the city. See Mark C. Schug and M. Scott Niederjohn, "The Milwaukee Teacher Residency Requirement: Why It's Bad for Schools, and Why It Won't Go Away," *Wisconsin Policy Research Institute* 19, no. 5 (June 2006), 6–7.

116. Mary T. Wagner, "Prospect of Suit Irks Some Schools," *Milwaukee Journal*, February 5, 1980, Accent on the City:1; David I. Bednarek, "Candidates' Reaction to Critic Are Revealing," *Milwaukee Journal*, February 1, 1983: 2:1; Jim Bednarek, "All 6 Candidates Served on Board," *Milwaukee Sentinel*, February 11, 1983, 2:12; Jim Bednarek, "Eight Seek Four School Board Seats," *Milwaukee Sentinel*, April 2, 1983, 1:5; Jim Bednarek, "School Board Taking Charge of Integration," *Milwaukee Sentinel*, January 9, 1984, 1:6; Jim Bednarek, "Stacy Is Re-Elected to School Board Seat," *Milwaukee Sentinel*, April 6, 1983, 1:5; and Thomas and Carol Hoff, "Critical Vote on Schools," *Milwaukee Journal*, February 7, 1983, 1:10.

117. David I. Bednarek, "School Board Acts to Improve Education," *Milwaukee Journal*, October 27, 1983, 1:1, 14; David I. Bednarek, "Integration Poses Hard Choices," *Milwaukee Journal*, October 28, 1983, 2:1, 5; Jim Bednarek, "School Board Backs Plan for More Integration," *Milwaukee Sentinel*, October 27, 1983, 1:1, 7; Ernst-Ulrich Franzen, "Board Panel Backs Lawsuit Against Suburban Districts," *Milwaukee Sentinel*, August 17, 1982, 1:5; and *Proceedings*, October 26, 1983. MIRC continued to advocate for redistricting through 1985. See the *Sherman Park News*, especially vol. 14, no. 12 (December 1984), 17–18, SPCA Papers, box 8, folder 2, and vol. 15, no. 3 (March 1986), 5, in box 8, folder 3. Duplicate copies are in Hart Papers, box 1, folder 5.

118. "Board Jousts Over Integration," *Milwaukee Sentinel*, January 27, 1984, 1:6; Ruth Wilson, "School Official Upset Over Integration Story," *Milwaukee Journal*, February 5, 1984, 2:1,15; and Marie Rohde, "Tosa Specialty School Proposed by Board," *Milwaukee Journal*, January 16, 1984, 2:3.

119. Quoted in Dannial J. Conta, "Forced Integration Won't Solve Past Injustice," *Milwaukee Journal*, March 30, 1984, 1:13. See also Mary Dooley, "Merger Plan Surprises Officials," *Milwaukee Journal*, March 3, 1982, Accent on the City:1.

120. David I. Bednarek, "80% in Poll Back Voluntary Steps for Integration," *Milwaukee Journal*, April 22, 1984, 2:1, 10.

121. Quoted in "Some Blacks Criticize Integration Suit," *Milwaukee Sentinel*, July 9, 1984, 1:6. See also David I. Bednarek, "Desegregation Debate Pulls Ironic About-Face," *Milwaukee Journal*, March 25, 1984, 2:1, 8; Jeff Cole and Amy Rinard, "Integration Suit Accord Proposed," *Milwaukee Sentinel*, January 8, 1986, 1:1, 4. See Miner, *Lessons from the Heartland*, 204–205, for biographical information on Williams.

122. Dahlk, *Against the Wind*, 395; "Integration Proposals Run into More Opposition," *Milwaukee Journal*, June 19, 1984, 2:3; "School Remap Plan Must Be Sold," *Milwaukee Journal*, May 21, 1984, 1:14; and "Try Voluntary Integration," *Milwaukee Journal*, June 21, 1984, 1:14.

123. David I. Bednarek, "Integration Backed," *Milwaukee Journal*, February 7, 1984, 2:1, 5; "Two Board Back Integration Plan," *Milwaukee* Sentinel, February 8, 1984, 1:4; and "Voluntary Integration Plan OK'd," *Milwaukee Sentinel*, January 31, 1984, 1: 6.

124. Rick Romell, "Reaction to Suburban Integration Mixed," *Milwaukee Sentinel*, January 5, 1984, 1:6.

125. David I. Bednarek, "School Board Puts Off Plan to Sue Suburbs," *Milwaukee Journal*, February 9, 1984, 2:1, 6.

126. *Proceedings*, April 26, 1984; "School Board Has New Leader," *Milwaukee Journal*, April 28, 1984, Green Sheet, 4.

127. David I. Bednarek, "School District Shakeup Sought," *Milwaukee Journal*, May 11, 1984, 1:1, 8; Jim Bednarek, "Board Sets Deadline on Integration Plan," *Milwaukee Sentinel*, May 11, 1984, 1:1, 11; *Proceedings*, May 10, 1984; and Rick Romell, "Officials Disagree on Board's Intent," *Milwaukee Sentinel*, May 12, 1984, 1:5.

128. "5 Suburban Boards Oppose Mandatory School Integration," *Milwaukee Journal*, June 11, 1984, 2:3; David I. Bednarek, "Suit Won't Halt Talks, School Board Hopes," *Milwaukee Journal*, June 28, 1984, 2:1, 16; Jim Bednarek, "Suburbs Ask School Board to Keep Talks Going," *Milwaukee Sentinel*, June 21, 1984, 1:5; "Integration Proposals Run into More Opposition," *Milwaukee Journal*, June 19, 1984, 2:3; Ralph D. Olive, "Suburbs Dislike Reorganization," *Milwaukee Journal*, May 11, 1984, 1:1, 8; Rick Romell, "Integration Plan Is Final Offer, School Officials Say," *Milwaukee Sentinel*, May 16, 194, 1:10; Rick Romell, "Officials Disagree on Board's Intent," *Milwaukee Sentinel*, May 12, 1984, 1:5; Rick Romell, "Two School Boards Reject City School Integration Plan," *Milwaukee Sentinel*, June 19, 1984, 1:5; and "Try Voluntary Integration," *Milwaukee Journal*, June 21, 1984, 1:14.

129. Quoted in "Riley Sees Need in City Lawsuit," *Milwaukee Sentinel*, May 2, 1984, 1:6–7. See also David I. Bednarek, "School Board Will Again Weigh Integration Suit," *Milwaukee Journal*, June 25, 1984, 2:1, 3.

130. David I. Bednarek, "Suit Assails Dual System of Education," *Milwaukee Journal*, June 28, 1984, 1:1, 11; *Proceedings*, June 25, 1984; and Larry Sandler, "School Board to Sue Suburbs," *Milwaukee Sentinel*, June 28, 1984, 1:1, 15.

131. Michele Derus, "State, Suburbs Seek Dismissal of Integration Suit," *Milwaukee Sentinel*, September 1, 1984, 1:4; Rick Romell, "Integration Suit Similar to One in Kansas City," *Milwaukee Sentinel*, July 2, 1984, 1:5.

132. David I. Bednarek, "Board Would Welcome Proposal from Suburbs," *Milwaukee Journal*, November 18, 1985, 2:1; David I. Bednarek, "City, Suburban Schools Deep in Talks on Hiring, Lawsuit," *Milwaukee Journal*, June 18, 1985, 2:3; David I. Bednarek, "City, Suburbs Promote 2 School Plans," *Milwaukee Journal*, May 15, 1985, 2:1–2; David I. Bednarek, "Crushing Blow Delivered in Integration Case," *Milwaukee Journal*, May 7, 1985, 2:1–2; David I. Bednarek, "Desegregation Raises Power Issue," *Milwaukee Journal*, June 12, 1985, 1:1, 6; David I. Bednarek, "Integration Talks Reach Critical Stage," *Milwaukee Journal*, April 21, 1985, 1:1, 12; David I. Bednarek, "Marathon Talks on Integration Called Encouraging," *Milwaukee Journal*, April 28, 1985, 2:1, 4; David I. Bednarek, "School Boards in Suburbs Chanting 'No Deal,'" *Milwaukee Journal*, May 9, 1985, 2:1, 8; David I. Bednarek, "Study's Effect on Integration Suit Unclear," *Milwaukee Journal*, May 21, 1985, 2:1, 3; David I. Bednarek and M. I. Blackwell, "Suburbs Refuse to Accept Latest School-Suit Proposal," *Milwaukee Journal*, May 7, 1985, 1:1, 9; "Legislators Give Opinions on Integration at Hearing,"

Milwaukee Journal, May 29, 1985, 2:3; Ralph D. Olive, "Board Candidates All Oppose Forced Busing," *Milwaukee Journal*, February 18, 1985, 2:3; Amy Rabideau, "Shorewood Board Assails School Suit," *Milwaukee Journal*, June 12, 1985, 2:3; and Larry Sandler, "City Schools Must Choose Between Suit, Cooperation," *Milwaukee Sentinel*, May 17, 1985, 1:5. According to David I. Bednarek, "Suburbs Lose Bias Suit Ruling," *Milwaukee Journal*, April 30, 1985, 1:1, 9, MPS engaged in discussions with the school districts of Brown Deer, Cudahy, Elmbrook, Fox Point–Bayside, Franklin, Germantown, Glendale–Riverhills, Greendale, Greenfield, Hamilton, Maple Dale–Indian Hill, Menomonee Falls, Mequon–Thiensville, Muskego, New Berlin, Nicolet, Oak Creek–Franklin, Saint Francis, Shorewood, South Milwaukee, Wauwatosa, West Allis–West Milwaukee, Whitefish Bay, and Whitnall.

133. David I. Bednarek, "City, Suburban Schools Deep in Talks on Hiring, Lawsuit," *Milwaukee Journal*, June 18, 1985, 2:3; David I. Bednarek, "Integration Basics Intact," *Milwaukee Journal*, June 24, 1985, 2:1, 3; David I. Bednarek, "Is a Deal at Hand on Integration?," *Milwaukee Journal*, June 25, 1985, 2:1; David I. Bednarek, "Only Loose Ends Remain on New Integration Plan," *Milwaukee Journal*, June 21, 1985, 2:1; David I. Bednarek, "School Board Seeks Deal with Some Suburbs," *Milwaukee Journal*, June 19, 1985, 1:1, 10; and Amy Rabideau, "Shorewood Board Assails School Suit," *Milwaukee Journal*, June 12, 1985, 2:3.

134. Jeff Cole, "School Board OKs Agreement to Settle Desegregation Suit," *Milwaukee Sentinel*, March 26, 1986, 1:1, 14; *Proceedings*, July 23, 1987.

CHAPTER 4

1. Quoted in Marilyn Kucer, "Plaintiffs Recall Their Reasons for Filing School Suit in '65," *Milwaukee Sentinel*, January 20, 1976, 1:8.
2. Marilyn Kucer, "Plaintiffs Recall Their Reasons for Filing School Suit in '65," *Milwaukee Sentinel*, January 20, 1976, 1:8.
3. Quoted in Rick Janka, "Board Lines Up on Appeal Issue," *Milwaukee Sentinel*, January 20, 1976, 1:8.
4. Busalacchi interview.
5. Quoted in Rick Janka, "Catholics Work on Integration," *Milwaukee Sentinel*, July 4, 1977, 1:1, 22. See also Rick Janka and Marilyn Kucer, "Parents Choose School in 2nd Year Plan," *Milwaukee Sentinel*, March 12, 1977, 1:1, 8.
6. Walter Jones, "Rights Fighters Laud Decision," *Milwaukee Courier*, January 24, 1976, 1, 18.
7. "Maier Encourages Cooperation with Integration Order," *Milwaukee Journal*, January 22, 1976, 2:1, 10.
8. Quoted in "Makes My Blood Boil—Zablocki," *Milwaukee Sentinel*, January 20, 1976, 1:5, 7. Zablocki later urged cautious compliance with the judge's decision. See "Statement by Hon. Clement J. Zablocki on the Integration of the Milwaukee Public School System Submitted to the Office of the Special Master," April 1976, in A Collection of Papers Relating to the Desegregation/Integration of the Milwaukee Public Schools, Milwaukee Public Library, 1976.
9. Quoted in "Seraphim Criticizes Decision," *Milwaukee Journal*, January 23, 1976, 2:8.

10. Kenneth Lamke, "Lucey Favors Aid for Integration," *Milwaukee Sentinel*, January 22, 1976, 1:1, 20.

11. Keith Spore, "72 Percent in Survey Oppose Busing," *Milwaukee Sentinel*, January 31, 1976, 1:1, 6. The raw data are available in Blexrud and Tsao, *Data Reference Book*, 143–147. See pages 149–171 for similar data from a *Milwaukee Journal* poll, which included polling data on students.

12. Dorothy Peterson, "Busing Is Insanity," *Milwaukee Sentinel*, April 6, 1976, 1:18.

13. Rick Janka, "Latinos Hope School Plan Won't Ignore Their Needs," *Milwaukee Sentinel*, April 2, 1976, 1:11; Rick Janka, "Indians Reject Integration Role," *Milwaukee Sentinel*, April 23, 1976, 1:1; Gary C. Rummler, "Indians Resist Role in Integration Suit," *Milwaukee Journal*, April 23, 1976, 2:1.

14. "Sherman Park Poll Corrected," *Milwaukee Sentinel*, January 21, 1976, 1:8.

15. Keith Spore, "56% Back Suburb Integration Role," *Milwaukee Sentinel*, February 2, 1976, 1:1, 9; "Suburbanite View of City Changing," *Milwaukee Sentinel*, December 1, 1977, 1:16.

16. Dorothy Austin, "Reactions Vary Widely to Reynolds' Ruling," *Milwaukee Sentinel*, January 20, 1976, 1:6; "Citizens OK Integration, Strongly Oppose Busing," *Milwaukee Sentinel*, January 20, 1976, 1:8; and "PTA Group Opposed to Busing," *Milwaukee Sentinel*, January 29, 1976, 1:5.

17. Quoted in Donald Pfarrer, "Reynolds' Order Stirs Hopes, Fears, Doubts," *Milwaukee Journal*, January 29, 1976, 1:1, 12. The comment about the viaduct was a reference to Father Groppi's open-housing marches in the 1960s. See chapter 2.

18. Quoted in Eileen Hammer, "Quality Education Seen as Key," *Milwaukee Sentinel*, January 20, 1976, 1:8.

19. "Strong Integration Support in Area," *Milwaukee Courier*, April 3, 1976, 1, 18; Gregory Stanford, "School Board Hit for Dragging Feet," *Milwaukee Journal*, May 3, 1976, 2:3; and "Triple O Plans Survival Effort for Black Children, Parents," *Milwaukee Courier*, February 19, 1977, 2. The *Courier* articles should not be construed as to represent a majority of the black community, which was still sharply divided on the method to be used to achieve integration and whether integration was the goal.

20. Dan Carpenter, "Battle Won, but War Goes On," *Milwaukee Courier*, January 24, 1976, 1, 18; Eileen Hammer, "Quality Education Seen as Key," *Milwaukee Sentinel*, January 20, 1976, 1:8; and Walter Jones, "Rights Fighters Laud Decision," *Milwaukee Courier*, January 24, 1976, 1, 18.

21. "Bus Is Target at Hamilton," *Milwaukee Sentinel*, September 23, 1976, 1:1, 10; "Hamilton High Reconvenes After Brief Racial Incident," *Milwaukee Journal*, September 23, 1976, 2:1, 9.

22. Quoted in Ralph D. Olive, "School Tries to Keep Lid On," *Milwaukee Journal*, September 24, 1976, 2:1, 5. "Greasers" were working-class white males who greased back their hair with wax, gel, creams, tonics, or pomade. They typically wore white or black T-shirts, denim jeans, and denim or leather jackets. Some rode motorcycles, as in the film *Easy Rider* (1969). "Fonzie," a character from the Milwaukee-based television series *Happy Days*, is perhaps the most famous example of a greaser.

23. John Semancik, interview with author, Milwaukee, June 6, 2011.

24. Quoted in "White Students Stage Protest at Hamilton," *Milwaukee Journal*, September 30, 1983, 2:1, 4.

25. Arlo Coplin, interview with author, Greendale, WI, August 17, 2010.

26. Anonymous guidance counselor, interview with author, Milwaukee, August 19, 2010.

27. Scott Hirsch, interview with author, Milwaukee, May 13, 2011.

28. Semancik interview.

29. James Jones, interview with author, Greenfield, WI, August 23, 2010.

30. Jeff Kartz, interview with author, Milwaukee, October 10, 2010.

31. Dena Platow, interview with author, Milwaukee, January 24, 2011.

32. Hirsch interview.

33. Semancik interview.

34. Kenneth Knoll, interview with author, Milwaukee, June 11, 2011.

35. Quoted in "Their Three Choices: Fernwood," *Milwaukee Sentinel*, May 26, 1977, 1:5. Emphasis in the original.

36. Quoted in Mike Plemmons, "Half Hour Trip by Bus Is Cost of Integration," *Milwaukee Sentinel*, September 6, 1977, 1:5.

37. Quoted in Rick Janka, "End to Forced Transfers Urged," *Milwaukee Sentinel*, August 25, 1977, 1:5.

38. David I. Bednarek, "Integration Here Unusually Successful," *Milwaukee Journal*, July 22, 1977, 1:1, 5; "Integration Planning Begins Amid Complaints by Many," *Milwaukee Journal*, March 16, 1976, 1:1, 15; Robert H. Edelman, "Pupils More Negative on Race," *Milwaukee Sentinel*, April 17, 1979, 1:1, 12.

39. Grace M. Iacolucci, interview by Michael A. Gordon, June 22, 1989, Introduction and Abstract, 9, Milwaukee Public Schools Oral History Project, UW–Milwaukee Public Schools Oral History Project records, 1989–1990, UWM Archival Collection 82, Wisconsin Historical Society, Milwaukee Area Research Center, Golda Meir Library, University of Wisconsin–Milwaukee; Jeff Browne, "Narrower Integration Plan Favored by School Board," *Milwaukee Journal*, December 21, 1976, 1:1, 7; "Heartening Success at Washington High," *Milwaukee Sentinel*, May 9, 1978, 1:12; Sandy Wilson, "Integration Proud to Take Bow," *Milwaukee Sentinel*, May 8, 1978, 2:15.

40. Quoted in Miner, *Lessons from the Heartland*, 88.

41. Quoted in Miner, *Lessons from the Heartland*, 89.

42. David I. Bednarek, "McMurrin's Proposal Would Bus 7,500," *Milwaukee Journal*, April 14, 1976, 1:1, 5; "McMurrin Very Confident," *Milwaukee Sentinel*, April 15, 1976, 1:1–2.

43. Rick Janka, "Schools Work on '78 Plan," *Milwaukee Sentinel*, September 3, 1977, 1:5; Rick Janka, "Several Factors May Lessen Black Pupil Walkout Impact," *Milwaukee Sentinel*, September 20, 1977, 1:5; "School Buses Set to Roll; Firms Expect No Trouble," *Milwaukee Sentinel*, September 3, 1977, 1:5, 9; "WCLU Says Busing Is Not Discriminatory," *Milwaukee Sentinel*, August 27, 1977, 1:7. See "Fair Integration Means Equal Bussing," Hart Papers, box 2, folder 2, for a list of complaints about unequal busing.

44. "What Is People United?," People United.

45. Jeff Browne, "Black Pupils Suspended at a Higher Rate," *Milwaukee Journal*, February 10, 1978, 1:1, 13; "School Suspensions Attacked at Hearing," *Milwaukee Courier*, May 27, 1978, 1, 5; and "School System's Black Suspension Rate, One of the Nation's Highest, Prompts Hearing," *Milwaukee Courier*, May 13, 1978, 3.

46. "Do You Care About Suspensions?," People United.

47. See various documents in People United.

48. People United.

49. Robert Peterson, interview with author, Milwaukee, August 16, 2010.

50. Dougherty, *More Than One Struggle,* is the best explanation of the divisions within Milwaukee's African American community. Thomas Sugrue touches on similar themes at the national level by exploring the motivations of various civil rights advocates in *Sweet Land of Liberty: The Forgotten Struggle for Civil Rights in the North* (New York: Random House, 2008).

51. "Barbee Tells It Like It Is," *Milwaukee Courier*, March 13, 1976, 1,4; David I. Bednarek, Gronouski Turns to PTAs for Help on Integration," *Milwaukee Sentinel*, March 27, 1976, 1:1,24; and James Parks, "Black Role Pushed in Desegregation," *Milwaukee Journal*, March 21, 1976, 2:1,3.

52. David I. Bednarek, "Plan Foes Cheer Integration Appeal," *Milwaukee Journal*, June 9, 1979, 1:1, 26. See Miner, *Lessons from the Heartland*, 130–131, for biographical information on Mallory.

53. Quoted in Murphy and Pawasarat, "Why It Failed," 39.

54. Quoted in Joe Williams, "'White Benefit' Was Driving Force of Busing," *Milwaukee Journal Sentinel*, October 19, 1999. See also Miner, *Lessons from the Heartland*, 90–92.

55. Dahlk, *Against the Wind*, 347–357.

56. Radtke Papers, box 1, folder 4. This was a pattern that would continue into at least the early 1980s. See Howard L. Fuller, "The Impact of the Milwaukee Public School System's Desegregation Plan on Black Students and the Black Community (1976–1982)" (PhD diss., Marquette University, 1985), 151–153.

57. Milwaukee Board of School Directors, *Proceedings of the Board of School Directors* (Milwaukee: The Board of School Directors), August 2, 1977 (hereafter cited as *Proceedings*). A partial version of this list is located in Radtke Papers, box 1, folder 4.

58. Report from the Committee on Community and Advisory Group Relations to the Board of School Directors, August 2, 1977, in *Proceedings*, August 2, 1977; Radtke Papers, box 1, folder 4. See also *Milwaukee Journal*, August 5, 1977. As a side note, African American teachers also bore a disproportionate share of teacher transfers. See David I. Bednarek, "Integration of Teachers Slows Down," *Milwaukee Journal*, September 9, 1978, 2:1,11.

59. *Proceedings*, August 2, 1977.

60. Quoted in *Milwaukee Sentinel*, August 27, 1977.

61. Eileen Hammer, "Equal Busing Backed in Poll," *Milwaukee Sentinel*, September 1, 1977, 1:10.

62. Quoted in Ira Jean Hadnot, "Majority or Minority: Pupils Want Equality," *Milwaukee Sentinel*, December 25, 1978, 1:5,16. See also Jeff Browne, "School Lesson: Integration Takes Work," *Milwaukee Journal*, October 21, 1979, 2:1,8.

63. Hart Papers, box 1, folder 4.

64. Quoted in MPS Human Relations Update, Hart Papers, box 1, folder 4.

65. "About Bay View Today," The Bay View Historical Society, www.bayview historicalsociety.org/Bay%20View%20Today.html.

66. Human Relations Update, Hart Papers, box 1, folder 4.

67. Quoted in *Forced Choice: The Milwaukee Plan: A Model for Northern School Desegregation*, VHS, produced and directed by Jones Cullinan (Milwaukee: Medusa Veritape, 1980). See Bruce Murphy, "Forced Choices," *Milwaukee Magazine*, January 1982, 56–58, for a review of *Forced Choice*. According to the review, McMurrin would not allow the documentary to be shown in schools.

68. Quoted in *Forced Choice*.

69. Quoted in *Forced Choice*.

70. Quoted in *Forced Choice*.

71. David I. Bednarek, "City Showing the Way on Magnet Schools," *Milwaukee Journal*, February 8, 1981, 2:1, 9; David I. Bednarek, "Pupil Swaps Don't Please All," *Milwaukee Journal*, September 13, 1981; and *Forced Choice*.

72. Jim Bednarek, "Panel's View Questioned by McMurrin," *Milwaukee Sentinel*, May 25, 1983, 1:5, 10; "Public School Closings Regrettable, Necessary," *Milwaukee Sentinel*, January 8, 1983, 1:8.

73. Murphy and Pawasarat, "Why It Failed," 39–40.

74. David I. Bednarek, "Panel's Vote Indicates Desegregation Support," *Milwaukee Journal*, February 20, 1979, 2:1, 3; David M. Novick, "Lincoln High School 'Saved,'" *Milwaukee Courier*, August 5, 1978, 1, 4.

75. Marilyn Kucer, "School Closing Vote 'Well Orchestrated,'" *Milwaukee Sentinel*, August 3, 1978, 1:1, 7; Dean A. Showers, "Interest High in Schools to Be Closed," *Milwaukee Sentinel*, August 3, 1978, 1:5. See also "Haste Inadvisable in School Closings," *Milwaukee Sentinel*, July 1, 1978, 1:10. The program for grades six to eight was discontinued in fall 1978. See *Proceedings*, March 14, 1978.

76. See Dougherty, *More Than One Struggle*, chapter 7.

77. Lamers, *Our Roots Grow Deep*, 10–13, 153–159, 164–165; quoted in Jane B. Mace, "House of Horrors," *Milwaukee Sentinel*, May 29, 1973, 1:12.

78. Marilyn Kucer, "New North Division School Poses Racial Questions," *Milwaukee Sentinel*, April 14, 1973, 1:5, 14.

79. Barbara A. Koppe, "Walnut Site Picked for North Division," *Milwaukee Journal*, June 29, 1973, 1:1, 4; "Where Should North Division Go?" *Milwaukee Journal*, June 20, 1973, 1:24.

80. "5 Alarm Blaze Hits N. Division," *Milwaukee Sentinel*, March 5, 1976, 1:1; "North Division Ravaged by Fire," *Milwaukee Journal*, March 5, 1976, 1:1, 4.

81. David I. Bednarek, "North Fire May Cost $200,000," *Milwaukee Journal*, March 10, 1976, 1:1, 14.

82. "6,000 Attend Sessions to Help Plan Desegregation," *Milwaukee Courier*, March 20, 1976, 1, 8; David I. Bednarek, "Integrate New North: McMurrin," *Milwaukee Journal*, March 25, 1976, 1:1, 10; David I. Bednarek, "North Urged as Magnet," *Milwaukee Journal*, March 26, 1976, 2:1, 4; Dan Carpenter, "Decision on North Div. Expected by Mid-Month," *Milwaukee Courier*, April 10, 1976, 1, 8; "Integration Meetings Show Positive Spirit," *Milwaukee Journal*, March 31,

1976, 1:1, 8; "Parents Say Build New North, but Buses Must Roll Both Ways," March 27, 1976, 1, 18; and James Parks, "Black Role Pushed in Desegregation," *Milwaukee Journal*, March 22, 1976, 2:1, 3.

83. "Efforts to Save North Win Stay," *Milwaukee Courier*, April 3, 1976, 1, 18; Gregory D. Stanford, "Black Pupils Balk at Idea of Busing," *Milwaukee Journal*, January 29, 1976, 2:1.

84. "McMurrin Doubts Black Walkout," *Milwaukee Sentinel*, September 28, 1977, 1:5. Although Howard Fuller is often credited as the leader behind the movement to save North Division, Larry Harwell actually did a lot of the early work in the mid-1970s, prior to Fuller's rise to fame. See chapter 9 of Dahlk, *Against the Wind*, for more information.

85. David I. Bednarek, "School Plan Likely to Be Modified," *Milwaukee Journal*, June 29, 1976, 1:1, 6; Rick Janka, "McMurrin Cites Efforts for North Area Renewal," *Milwaukee Sentinel*, March 31, 1976, 1:5; and "McMurrin Suggests Busing North Pupils," *Milwaukee Journal*, March 20, 1976, 1:1, 24.

86. "Student March Triggers Meeting," *Milwaukee Sentinel*, May 5, 1979, 1:5.

87. Ira Jean Hadnot, "Pupils, Staff Explore North Division," *Milwaukee Sentinel*, September 6, 1978, 1:5; "Computers May Turn Students On," *Milwaukee Journal*, June 7, 1978, 2:1.

88. Rick Janka, "Chapter Closed on Gronouski's Special Master Role," *Milwaukee Sentinel*, September 2, 1978, 1:5; Ira Jean Hadnot, "Pupils, Staff Explore North Division," *Milwaukee Sentinel*, September 6, 1978, 1:5.

89. David I. Bednarek, "School Plans Mired in Confusion," *Milwaukee Journal*, January 24, 1978, 2:1, 4.

90. David I. Bednarek, "Whites Welcome Black School's Task," *Milwaukee Journal*, December 26, 1978, 2:1, 6.

91. David I. Bednarek, "Board Delays Plan for North Division," *Milwaukee Journal*, April 19, 1979, 2:2; David I. Bednarek, "New Board President Tells of Maier Snub," April 25, 1979, 2:1, 8; *Proceedings*, May 1, 1979; and "Student March Triggers Meeting," *Milwaukee Sentinel*, May 5, 1979, 1:5.

92. "North Division Plan Readied," *Milwaukee Journal*, March 21, 1979, 2:2. Marian McEvilly was the school board's chief sponsor of the new North Division. See David I. Bednarek, "Board Delays Plan for North Division," *Milwaukee Journal*, April 19, 1979, 2:2.

93. "500 Students Protest Board Action," *Milwaukee Community Journal*, May 9, 1979, 2.

94. Quoted in "Student March Triggers Meeting," *Milwaukee Sentinel*, May 5, 1979, 1:5. See also Rick Janka, "'Fed Up' After Plan for North," *Milwaukee Sentinel*, May 10, 1979, 1:1, 8.

95. Quoted in Milford Prewitt, "Teachers Join Students in North Protest," *Milwaukee Journal*, June 5, 1979, Accent on the City: 1, 4.

96. Quoted in Rick Janka, "'Fed Up' After Plan for North," *Milwaukee Sentinel*, May 10, 1979, 1:1, 8.

97. Quoted in David I. Bednarek, "North High an Example of Pitfalls," *Milwaukee Journal*, May 30, 1979, 2:1, 5.

98. Quoted in *Forced Choice*. Not surprisingly, McMurrin refused to discuss the

documentary with reporters, referring all questions to his assistant, Robert Tesch, who promised to include *Forced Choice* in the school system's human relations library. This never came to pass. WTMJ and WITI were interested in airing it, but it did not meet their technical requirements. The documentary did, however, receive private screenings in Milwaukee, Atlanta, Minneapolis, St. Louis, and Washington, DC. See Murphy, "Forced Choices." The use of "forced choice" is also heavily criticized in Howard Fuller's dissertation.

99. Dahlk, *Against the Wind*, 371–372.

100. Tom Bamberger, "The Education of Howard Fuller," *Milwaukee Magazine*, July, 1988, 56–59; Dougherty, *More Than One Struggle*, 173–176; and Miner, *Lessons from the Heartland*, 207–208.

101. Dahlk, *Against the Wind*, 371–372; Quoted in Rick Janka and Karen Rothe, "North Division Plan Is Last Straw: Blacks," *Milwaukee Sentinel*, July 31, 1979, 1:5, 8. See also Milford Prewitt, "Plan for North High Termed Part of White Conspiracy," *Milwaukee Journal*, June 12, 1979, Accent on the News:1, 4.

102. Quoted in William Murder, "N. Division Issue Settled From Board's View," *Milwaukee Courier*, September 1, 1979, 1, 11.

103. Quoted in Gary Rummler, "Shift in Southside Integration View Found," *Milwaukee Journal*, February 22, 1979, 2:1, 4. See David I. Bednarek, "North High to Be for Science," *Milwaukee Journal*, May 2, 1979, 2:1, 4; Nathan Conyers, "Some Pleased by Board Action," *Milwaukee Community Journal*, June 6, 1979, 2, 25, for more on Todd's advocacy for conversion of North Division to a citywide specialty.

104. Quoted in Rick Janka and Karen Rothe, "North Division Plan Is Last Straw: Blacks," *Milwaukee Sentinel*, July 31, 1979, 1:5, 8.

105. "Pupils Neglected, North Backer Says," *Milwaukee Sentinel*, August 15, 1979, 1:12. See also Fuller's dissertation; David I. Bednarek, "Foes in North High Disagreement Talk It Out," *Milwaukee Journal*, September 27, 1979, 2:5; and David I. Bednarek, "School Plan Called an Insult to Blacks," *Milwaukee Journal*, September 18, 1979, 2:3.

106. *Forced Choice*. Further evidence of this attitude can be found in David I. Bednarek, "School Officials May Forgo Plan, Quiz Board on Issues," *Milwaukee Journal*, March 7, 1978, 2:1, 4; Jeff Browne, "MacDowell Segregated, Parents Say," *Milwaukee Journal*, October 8, 1976, 2:1, 6; "MPS in Wonderland," *Milwaukee Courier*, May 27, 1978, 4; Delois Vann, "Blacks Shortchanged in Montessori Program," *Milwaukee Courier*, October 30, 1976, 1, 12; and Kevin J. Walker, "MacDowell Parents Fight Sept. Plans," *Milwaukee Courier*, March 11, 1978, 1. See also Howard Fuller's dissertation, "The Impact of the Milwaukee Public School System's Desegregation Plan on Black Students and the Black Community (1976–1982)."

107. Rick Janka and Karen Rothe, "North Division Plan Is Last Straw: Blacks," *Milwaukee Sentinel*, July 31, 1979, 1:5, 8.

108. Quoted in Lisa Smith, "North Students Vow Struggle," *Milwaukee Courier*, June 2, 1979, 4. See James Scott, "Never Will Accept This Unfair Burden," *Milwaukee Courier*, February 23, 1980, 4, for a similar opinion from another student.

109. "Carley to Lead North Division Panel," *Milwaukee Sentinel*, August 2, 1979, 1:5; "North Becomes a Specialty High School," *Milwaukee Community Journal*, May 5, 1979, 1, 2; "North Specialty Approval Prompts Walkout Protest," *Milwaukee Courier*, June 2, 1979, 1; and "Group Seeks to Block North Division Changes," *Milwaukee Sentinel*, August 4, 1979, 1:11.

110. David I. Bednarek, "North High Plan to Be Reviewed," *Milwaukee Journal*, August 4, 1979, 1:11; Karen Rothe, "North Rally Urged on Opening Day," *Milwaukee Sentinel*, August 31, 1979, 1:5.

111. "Busing Goes Smoothly as School Starts," *Milwaukee Journal*, September 4, 1979, 1:1, 3.

112. Rick Janka, "Group Joins North Battle," *Milwaukee Sentinel*, September 8, 1979, 1:5.

113. Quoted in Karen Rothe, "Pupils Walk Out at North Division to Rally for School," *Milwaukee Sentinel*, January 11, 1980, 1:5, 11.

114. Rick Janka, "Group Joins North Battle," *Milwaukee Sentinel*, September 8, 1979, 1:5; "Misstep on School Desegregation," *Milwaukee Journal*, June 13, 1979, 1:20.

115. "Teachers Group Opposes Shift," *Milwaukee Journal*, March 13, 1980, 1:18; "The Pangs of North Division High," *Milwaukee Journal*, August 8, 1979, 1:18; "Compromise at North," *Milwaukee Sentinel*, November 12, 1979, 1:12; Scott Anderson, "North Division 'Field Trips' Enrage Coalition," *Milwaukee Courier*, March 8, 1980, 1, 11; "Do We Have the Courage," *Milwaukee Courier*, March 8, 1980, 4; "Wanted: Black Candidates," *Milwaukee Courier*, January 10, 1981, 4; and "Here We Go Again," *Milwaukee Community Journal*, May 9, 1979, 5.

116. David I. Bednarek, "North Division Students Revel in the Glory," *Milwaukee Sentinel*, March 24, 1980, 2:1, 5; "North High Plan Faces Questions in Hearing," *Milwaukee Journal*, January 5, 1980, 1:9.

117. Quoted in Kevin Merida, "Legal Minds Gather to Fight North Division Plan," *Milwaukee Journal*, March 23, 1980, 2:7.

118. Dahlk, *Against the Wind*, 43; Kevin Merida, "Legal Minds Gather to Fight North Division Plan," *Milwaukee Journal*, March 23, 1980, 2:7.

119. Quoted in Dougherty, *More Than One Struggle*, 164. See also Dan Carpenter, "Barbee: Beware Phony Desegregation Plans," *Milwaukee Courier*, March 13, 1976, 1, 4, 7.

120. Quoted in Dougherty, *More Than One Struggle*, 186. James Meredith was the first African American to enroll at the University of Mississippi in 1962.

121. David I. Bednarek, "Death of North Plan Is Turning Point," *Milwaukee Journal*, April 20, 1980, 1:1, 9. See also David I. Bednarek, "800 Pupils Lose Bids for Nearby Schools," *Milwaukee Journal*, March 28, 1980, 2:1, 5.122. Lennox Samuels, "Board Drops North Specialty Plan," *Milwaukee Sentinel*, April 25, 1980, 1:1, 12; *Proceedings*, May 1, 1980, and February 24, 1981.

123. David I. Bednarek, "More Integration Rejected," *Milwaukee Journal*, May 2, 1980, 2:1, 6; David I. Bednarek, "School Board Kills North High Plan," *Milwaukee Journal*, April 25, 1980, 1:1, 16.

124. Quoted in David I. Bednarek, "Death of North Plan Is Turning Point," *Milwaukee Journal*, April 20, 1980, 1:1, 9.

125. David I. Bednarek, "More Integration Rejected," *Milwaukee Journal*, May 2, 1980, 2:1, 6.

126. David I. Bednarek, "Death of North Plan Is Turning Point," *Milwaukee Journal*, April 20, 1980, 1:1, 9; David I. Bednarek, "School Board to Reconsider Busing Plan," *Milwaukee Journal*, April 14, 1980, 1:1, 12.

127. Howard Fuller, "School Closings Discriminate Against Blacks," *Milwaukee Journal*, June 30, 1983, 1:17.

128. Wisconsin Legislative Audit Bureau, "The Chapter 220 Integration Aids Program," November 20, 1984, 16–17; ibid., 3–4.

129. Quoted in Murphy and Pawasarat, "Why It Failed," 40.

130. Larry Sandler, "Changes Sought in Integration Plan," *Milwaukee Sentinel*, February 2, 1985, 1:5.

131. Quoted in Jim Bednarek, "College-Bound Programs Hailed by Students, Officials," *Milwaukee Sentinel*, August 25, 1983, 1:5.

132. Quoted in Robert Anthony, "Dozens Call for End to Involuntary Busing," *Milwaukee Sentinel*, May 13, 1986, 1:1, 8. See also David I. Bednarek, "Parents' Answer to Busing: A Resounding 'No,'" *Milwaukee Journal*, May 13, 1986, 2:1–2.

133. McMurrin, "Perspectives on Busing," 7–8.

134. David I. Bednarek, "Alternatives to South Side Busing Will Be Sought," *Milwaukee Journal*, April 21, 1986, 1:1, 10; David I. Bednarek, "Busing Plan Opens Some Eyes," *Milwaukee Journal*, April 22, 1986, 1:1, 6; and David I. Bednarek, "Riley Bus Plan Changed," *Milwaukee Journal*, April 23, 1986, 1:1, 8.

135. James M. Abraham, "Woman Fights Busing," *Milwaukee Journal*, June 25, 1986, 2:1.

136. David I. Bednarek, "School Idea Popular, Problematic," *Milwaukee Journal*, June 10, 1986, 2:1–2; Alan J. Borsuk, "Black Educators Call for Shift of Power," *Milwaukee Journal*, June 9, 1986, 1:1, 12.

137. David I. Bednarek, "80% in Poll Back Voluntary Steps for Integration," *Milwaukee Journal*, April 22, 1984, 2:1, 10. The disparity between the 80 percent and 25 percent may indicate that these particular survey respondents favored integration only if their children did not have to ride buses. It may also indicate support for integration but opposition to tax-supported transportation. Either theory is consistent with opinions expressed in this chapter and previous chapters.

138. Gary G. Rummler, "School Integration Has Fewer Supporters," *Milwaukee Journal*, April 27, 1984, 1:1, 5.

139. Gary G. Rummler, "Opposition to Busing Easing, Poll Indicates," *Milwaukee Journal*, April 29, 1984, 1:1, 10.

140. Ronald S. Edari, *The Life Cycle, Segregation and White Attitudes Toward Busing* (Milwaukee: University of Wisconsin–Milwaukee, Urban Research Center, 1977), 1.

141. Ibid., 2–5.

142. Ibid., 7–8.

143. Gary Orfield, "Segregated Housing and Resegregation," in *Dismantling Desegregation: The Quiet Reversal of* Brown v. the Board of Education, ed. Gary Orfield, Susan E. Eaton, and the Harvard Project on School Desegregation, 315–317 (New York: The New Press, 1996). Sociologists Gregory Squires and

William Velez of UWM found a huge disparity in the loans made to home buyers in Milwaukee's all-white neighborhoods compared to those in black neighborhoods during the period 1983–1984. See Gregory D. Squires and William Velez, "Neighborhood Racial Composition and Mortgage Lending: City and Suburban Differences," *Journal of Urban Affairs* 9 (1987): 217–232.

144. David I. Bednarek, "Drop in Enrollment Is Biggest in History," *Milwaukee Journal*, October 21, 1977, 1:1, 6; David I. Bednarek, "Enrollment Loss May Set Record," *Milwaukee Journal*, October 5, 1977, 2:1, 4; David I. Bednarek, "Whites Become a Minority in City's Public Schools," *Milwaukee Journal*, December 4, 1978, 2:1, 3; "Enrollments Decline in Catholic Schools," *Milwaukee Journal*, October 12, 1977; J. S. Fuerst and Daniel Pupo, "Desegregated Schooling: The Milwaukee Experience," *Urban Education* 18, no. 2 (July 1983): 231–233; and Murphy and Pawasarat, "Why It Failed," 36, 43.

145. Ira Jean Hadnot, "Majority or Minority: Pupils Want Quality," *Milwaukee Sentinel*, December 25, 1978, 1:5, 16; Mark Levine and John Zipp, "A City at Risk," in Rury and Cassell, *Seeds of Crisis*, 54–55.

146. Murphy and Pawasarat, "Why It Failed," 36, 43. See also chapter 12 of Miner, *Lessons from the Heartland*.

147. Gregory D. Stanford, "Public Money for Private Pupils Asked," *Milwaukee Journal*, May 31, 1985, 2:3. See also Massey and Denton, *American Apartheid*, 71. The state government would authorize vouchers for Milwaukee students in the 1990s (see chapter 7).

148. Fuerst and Pupo, "Desegregated Schooling," 231, 239.

149. Ibid., 232.

150. Ibid., 233–234.

151. Ibid., 234–236.

152. Ibid., 236–237.

153. Quoted in Edward H. Blackwell, "In the Inner City," *Milwaukee Journal*, November 23, 1977, Accent on the News:1, 5.

154. Gregory D. Stanford and Edward H. Blackwell, "Still Victims, Blacks Insist," *Milwaukee Journal*, May 15, 1977, 1:1, 8. St. Leo's had been part of the Independent Community Schools (ICS) movement in the late 1960s and early 1970s. The ICS movement was a coalition of central-city Catholic and nonreligious schools that operated with private funding. The Catholic schools were motivated by an exodus of Catholic families from the central city and the need to find replacement students. They sought but were denied tuition vouchers from the state of Wisconsin. See Bill Dahlk, *Against the Wind*, chapter 8; Jules Modlinski and Esther Zaret, *The Federation of Independent Community Schools: An Alternative Urban School System* (Milwaukee: Marquette University, Division of Continuing Education, 1970); and Doreen H. Wilkinson, *Community Schools: Education for Change* (Boston: National Association of Independent Schools, 1973).

155. Jeff Browne, "Catholic School Holds Its Own," *Milwaukee Journal*, October 11, 1978, 2:12; Edward H. Blackwell, "St. Leo's First Year a Success," *Milwaukee Journal*, April 4, 1978, Accent on the City: 1, 3.

156. Murphy and Pawasarat, "Why It Failed," 43.

CHAPTER 5

1. Lauri Steel, Roger Levine, and the American Institute for Research, *Educational Innovation in Multiracial Contexts: The Growth of Magnet Schools in American Education* (Washington, DC: US Department of Education, 1994), 7–8. See chapter 7 of William Hayes, *The Progressive Education Movement: Is It Still a Factor in Today's Schools?* (Lanham, MD: Rowman & Littlefield Education, 2006) for an overview of *A Nation at Risk*.

2. Steel and Levine, *Educational Innovation*, 56–57.

3. Ibid., 16–20.

4. Ellen B. Goldring, "Perspectives on Magnet Schools," in *Handbook of Research on School Choice*, ed. Mark Berends et al. (New York: Routledge, 2009), 361–378; Claire Smrekar and Ellen Goldring, *School Choice in Urban America: Magnet Schools and the Pursuit of Equity* (New York: Teachers College Press, 1999), 7; and Steel and Levine, *Educational Innovation*, 15–30, 53.

5. William Lowe Boyd, "Choice Plans for Public Schools in the USA: Issues and Answers," *Local Government Policy Making* 18 (July 1993): 20–27.

6. Anysia P. Mayer, "Expanding Opportunities for High Academic Achievement: An International Baccalaureate Diploma Program in an Urban High School," *Journal of Advanced Academics* 19, no. 2 (Winter 2008): 202–235. See also Dale Ballou, "Magnet School Outcomes," in Berends's *Handbook*, 408–426. See chapter 5 of Darlene Leiding, *The Hows and Whys of Alternative Education: Schools Where Students Thrive* (Lanham, MD: Rowman & Littlefield Education, 2008) for more on magnet schools and student engagement in fine arts, technology, and Advanced Placement.

7. Office of the Superintendent of Public Instruction, Washington State Report Card, http://reportcard.ospi. k12.wa.us.

8. "2011–2012 School Profiles for High Schools," Houston Independent School District, www.houstonisd.org/Page/61439.

9. Dana Goldstein, "Bostonians Committed to School Diversity Haven't Given Up on Busing," *The Atlantic Cities*, October 10, 2012, www.theatlanticcities.com /politics/2012/10/bostonians-committed-school-diversity-havent-given-busing /3544.

10. Smrekar and Goldring, *School Choice in Urban America*, 26–30.

11. Ibid., 34–41. Quotes on pages 39–40.

12. "Best High School Rankings by State," *U.S. News & World Report*, www.usnews .com/education/best-high-schools. The three schools that ranked higher are three of Chicago's newer magnet schools, but they have enrollments that are less than half of Whitney Young's. Whitney Young is still the flagship magnet school.

13. City of Chicago, "[Whitney] Young Magnet High School," 2012 Illinois School Report Card, http://webprod.isbe.net/ereportcard/publicsite/getReport.aspx ?year=2012&code=1501629900764_e.pdf.

14. "Whitney M. Young High School Course Registration Guide, 2013–2014," Whitney M. Young Magnet High School, www.wyoung.org/pdf/planning _guide.pdf.

15. Whitney M. Young Magnet High School, www.wyoung.org.

16. United States Academic Decathlon, www.usad.org.

17. *Cheaters*, written and directed by John Stockwell, produced by Kevin Reidy and Gloria Jean Sykes, 108 min., Home Box Office, 2000.

18. Ian M. Harris, "Criteria for Evaluating School Desegregation in Milwaukee," *Journal of Negro Education* 52, no. 4 (Autumn 1983): 434.

19. George A. Mitchell and the Wisconsin Policy Research Institute, *An Evaluation of State-Financed School Integration in Metropolitan Milwaukee* (Milwaukee: Wisconsin Policy Research Institute, 1989), 6–8.

20. Ibid., 26–28.

21. Ibid., 34.

22. Ibid., 58, 65, 80.

23. Ibid., 63–65.

24. David Bednarek, "Are Dropouts Tied to Desegregation?" *Milwaukee Journal*, May 13, 1985, 2:1,2. See also David Bednarek, "School Budget Focuses on High Schools," *Milwaukee Journal*, May 16, 1985, 1:1,7.

25. Mitchell, *An Evaluation of State-Financed School Integration*, 84–104.

26. Ibid., 69.

27. Ibid., 66–68.

28. Ibid., 83.

29. Quoted in Alan J. Borsuk, "MPS Committee Recommends Expanding King," *Milwaukee Journal Sentinel*, June 11, 2009. See also "3 High Schools Seeing High Admissions Criteria; 15 Other MPS Schools to Require That Students Just Pass 8th Grade," *Milwaukee Journal Sentinel*, November 3, 1997.

30. Dahlk, *Against the Wind*, 422–423, 429–430; Dougherty, *More Than One Struggle*, 191. Jack Dougherty and other contemporary observers have suggested that business leaders liked the voucher scheme because it was a way to break up the public school system to bring in cheaper nonunion labor, which would lower taxes and create a better business climate. Thus, they worked with Fuller toward a common goal with completely different purposes in mind. See Dougherty, *More Than One Struggle*, 191–192; Doris Stacy, interview with author, Milwaukee, June 30, 2010; and Leon Todd, interview with author, Milwaukee, June 28, 2010.

31. David I. Bednarek, "State Will Look at All Area Schools," *Milwaukee Journal*, June 7, 1984, 1:1, 14. See also Robert Anthony, "Dozens Call for End to Involuntary Busing," *Milwaukee Sentinel*, May 13, 1986, 1:1, 8; David I. Bednarek, "Are Dropouts Tied to Desegregation?," *Milwaukee Journal*, May 13, 1985, 2:1; David I. Bednarek, "Blacks' Scores Up in Reading, Math, McMurrin Says," *Milwaukee Journal*, February 15, 1984, 1:1, 13; David I. Bednarek, "Desegregation Raises Issues of Power," *Milwaukee Journal*, June 12, 1985, 1:1, 6; David I. Bednarek, "Parents Answer to Busing: A Resounding 'No,'" *Milwaukee Journal*, May 13, 1986, 2:1, 2; Jeff Cole, "Plans Stress Local Control, Reaching Students Early," *Milwaukee Sentinel*, January 13, 1988, 1:14; Larry Sandler, "Changes Sought in Integration Plan," *Milwaukee Sentinel*, February 2, 1985, 1:5; and Larry Sandler, "'Pro-Choice' Emerges as Busing Buzzword," *Milwaukee Sentinel*, 1:5.

32. "Coverage of Blacks Criticized," *Milwaukee Journal*, February 22, 1987, B:4.

33. Jeff Cole, "Overseer Eyed for School Talks," *Milwaukee Sentinel*, March 13, 1987, 1:1, 13.

34. Polly Williams, "Voluntary Integration Still Desirable," *Milwaukee Journal*, July 24, 1987, A:9.

35. Dahlk, *Against the Wind*, 428.

36. Hayes, *The Progressive Education Movement*, 121–122; Jeffrey R. Henig, *Rethinking School Choice: Limits of the Market Metaphor* (Princeton, NJ: Princeton University Press, 1994), 6–7; Miner, *Lessons from the Heartland*, 166; Gayle Schmitz-Zien, "The Genesis of and Motivations for the Milwaukee Parental Choice Program, 1985–1995" (PhD diss., University of Wisconsin–Milwaukee, 2003), 41–45; and John F. Witte, *The Market Approach to Education: An Analysis of America's First Voucher Program* (Princeton, NJ: Princeton University Press, 2000), 11.

37. Henig, *Rethinking School Choice*, 64–65.

38. Ibid., 71–77, 125–127. See also John Chubb and Terry Moe, *Politics, Markets, and America's Schools* (Washington, DC: Brookings Institution, 1989). Bruce Fuller, "School Choice: Who Gains, Who Loses?" *Issues in Science and Technology* (Spring 1996): 61–67, provides a concise history of school choice nationally and in Milwaukee since 1989. Linda A. Renzulli and Lorraine Evans, "School Choice, Charter Schools, and White Flight," *Social Problems* 52, no. 3 (August 2005): 398–418, explains the possible segregative effects of charter and choice schools.

39. Only three ICS schools survived into the 1980s—Urban Day, Harambee, and Bruce-Guadalupe. See *Milwaukee Journal Sentinel*, December 26, 1995, and several other news articles and almost any scholarly work on ICS. The three schools were academically successful, according to Mitchell, *An Evaluation of State-Financed School Integration*, 73–74. See Russ Kava, "Milwaukee Parental Choice Program Information Paper," *Wisconsin Legislative Reference Bureau* (2009). Harambee closed in 2011 due to financial and academic problems. See Alan J. Borsuk, "A School They Deserve," *Milwaukee Journal Sentinel*, February 20, 2010; and Erin Richards, "Harambee Community School Remains Shuttered," *Milwaukee Journal Sentinel*, January 13, 2011.

40. See Governor Tommy Thompson's memoir, *Power to the People: An American State at Work* (New York: HarperCollins, 1996), 87–92, for Thompson's opinions on school choice.

41. Dave Hendrickson, "Youths' Reading Skills Deplored," *Milwaukee Journal*, March 5, 1987, B:1–2.

42. Quoted in Jeff Cole, "Schools Linked to Revitalization," *Milwaukee Sentinel*, June 17, 1987, 1:1, 11; "Rhetoric Conceals Real School Issues," *Milwaukee Sentinel*, March 11, 1987, 1:12.

43. "Caught in the Middle," *Milwaukee Sentinel*, June 18, 1987, 1:16; "Debate on Schools Evades Major Issues," *Milwaukee Journal*, March 10, 1987, A:6.

44. Jeff Cole, "Schools Linked to Revitalization," *Milwaukee Sentinel*, June 17, 1987, 1:1, 11.

45. David I. Bednarek, "School Test Results Divide Senior Class," *Milwaukee Journal*, March 29, 1987, B:1, 4.

46. David I. Bednarek, "Stacy to Face Mason for School Seat," *Milwaukee Journal*, February 18, 1987, B:5.

47. David I. Bednarek, "School Leadership Is a Hot Issue in Race," *Milwaukee Journal*, February 8, 1987.

48. David I. Bednarek, "Different Styles, Same Ideas," *Milwaukee Journal*, March 24, 1987, B:2.

49. "Candidate Focuses on Quality of Education," *Milwaukee Journal*, March 15, 1987, A:23.

50. "Candidate Rips Schools on Test Data," *Milwaukee Journal*, February 25, 1987, B:4.

51. David I. Bednarek, "City Voters Give Stacy, Schools Benefit of the Doubt," *Milwaukee Journal*, April 8, 1987, B:1, 3; "Mason's Good Showing Bodes Well for Blacks," *Milwaukee Sentinel*, April 9, 1987; and "Moderation Prevails in School Board Vote," *Milwaukee Journal*, April 9, 1987, 1:16.

52. "Schools Welcome Help from Committee," *Milwaukee Sentinel*, April 7, 1987, 1:6.

53. Quoted in George A. Mitchell, "McMurrin's Performance Adds Up to Failure," *Milwaukee Sentinel*, June 30, 1987, 1:14.

54. George A. Mitchell, "McMurrin's Performance Adds Up to Failure," *Milwaukee Sentinel*, June 30, 1987, 1:14.

55. "Caught in the Middle," *Milwaukee Sentinel*, June 18, 1987, 1:16; "McMurrin More Demands Attention," *Milwaukee Sentinel*, July 22, 1987, 1:10.

56. Miner, *Lessons from the Heartland*, 92–94.

57. David I. Bednarek, "All-Year School Here Could Begin in '88," *Milwaukee Journal*, February 11, 1987, B:1, 3; David I. Bednarek, "Board Rejects Tighter Entrance Rules," *Milwaukee Journal*, January 29, 1987, B:2; Grade Policy May Rise at Rufus King," *Milwaukee Journal*, January 21, 1987, B:2; Alan Borsuk, "Is the System Fair to Intelligent Kids?" *Milwaukee Journal*, August 3, 1984.

58. David I. Bednarek, "Tech's Success Creates Trouble for Plan to Build New School," *Milwaukee Journal*, July 20, 1987, B:1–2.

59. Quoted in Chester Sheard, "Chief Says School Board in Control," *Milwaukee Sentinel*, May 4, 1987, 1:5.

60. "McMurrin Says He's Tired of Complaints, Undecided About Leaving," *Milwaukee Sentinel*, July 6, 1987, 1:10.

61. "McMurrin Leaves a Solid Record," *Milwaukee Journal*, July 28, 1987, A:10; "Ohio District Plans Offer for McMurrin," *Milwaukee Journal*, July 24, 1987, B:1.

62. Quoted in "Board Applauds Departing McMurrin," *Milwaukee Sentinel*, July 30, 1987, 1:5. See also *Proceedings* , July 29, 1987.

63. Levine and Zipp, "A City at Risk," 43. See also Dougherty, *More Than One Struggle*, 187–188; Miner, *Lessons from the Heartland*, 114–116.

64. This shift in employment could be considered a negative side effect of the "spreading out" of Milwaukeeans (see chapter 2).

65. Dahlk, *Against the Wind*, 444–445; Levine and Zipp, "A City at Risk," 56.

66. Levine and Zipp, "A City at Risk," 43.

67. Tim Cuprisin, "Friends May Draw Poor Blacks Here," *Milwaukee Journal*, February 28, 1994, B:1, 8.

68. Dahlk, *Against the Wind*, 442–443.

69. "Student Turnover Troubles Schools," *Milwaukee Journal*, March 9, 1989, B:6.

70. Ibid.

71. Gregory D. Stanford, "So Far to Go After 20 Years," *Milwaukee Journal*, July 26, 1987, A:1, 16; Levine and Zipp, "A City at Risk," 61.

72. Gary C. Rummer, "Grim Proof of the Feminization of Poverty," *Milwaukee Journal*, November 21, 1982, B:1, 17.

73. Gregory D. Stanford, "So Far to Go After 20 Years," *Milwaukee Journal*, July 26, 1987, A:1, 16.

74. Quoted in Ira J. Hadnot, "Threats to the Black Family Call for Dramatic Response," *Milwaukee Journal*, January 12, 1992. See also Steven Walters, "Pregnancy Rate High for Black Teens," *Milwaukee Journal Sentinel*, January 11, 1992.

75. Quoted in Dahlk, *Against the Wind*, 446.

76. Quoted in Jason DeParle, *American Dream: Three Women, Ten Kids, and a Nation's Drive to End Welfare* (New York: Viking, 2004), 69.

77. Ira J. Hadnot, "Threats to the Black Family Call for Dramatic Response," *Milwaukee Journal*, January 12, 1992.

78. Greg J. Duncan and Jeanne Brooks-Gunn, eds., *Consequences of Growing Up Poor* (New York: Russell Sage, 1997); Meredith Phillips et al., "Family Background, Parenting Practices, and the Black-White Test Score Gap," in *Black-White Test Score Gap*, ed. Christopher Jencks and Meredith Phillips, 103–145 (Washington, DC: Brookings Institution Press, 1998); and Abigail and Stephan Thernstrom, *No Excuses: Closing the Racial Gap in Learning* (New York: Simon and Schuster, 2003).

79. See chapter 1 of Richard Rothstein, *Class and Schools: Using Social, Economic, and Educational Reform to Close the Black–White Achievement Gap* (Washington, DC: Economic Policy Institute, 2004).

80. Priscilla Ahlgren, "City Short on Experienced Teachers," *Milwaukee Journal*, October 1, 1989, B:1, 3.

81. Quoted in Dahlk, *Against the Wind*, 448.

82. Quoted in Jeff Cole, "Teachers Frustrated by Bureaucracy, Lack of Support," *Milwaukee Sentinel*, June 12, 1987, 1:1, 17. See David I. Bednarek, "City Teachers Have Less Job Satisfaction, Study Says," *Milwaukee Journal*, April 27, 1985, 2:5; and David I. Bednarek, "Suburban Teachers Seem Happier Lot," *Milwaukee Journal*, August 31, 1981, 1:1, 8, for earlier reports of teachers' dissatisfaction with their jobs.

83. Jeff Cole, "Special School Eyed for Disruptive Pupils," *Milwaukee Sentinel*, November 7, 1987, 1:1, 11.

84. Chuck Doherty et al., "Girl Who Reported Rape Fears New Attack at School," *Milwaukee Sentinel*, May 18, 1988, 1, 11; Priscilla Ahlgren, Jim Stingl, and Leonard Sykes Jr., "Girl, 13, Raped at School, 2 Classmates Held in Attack,"

Milwaukee Journal, May 17, 1988, A:1, 4; "Milwaukee Must Have Safer Schools," *Milwaukee Journal*, May 20, 1988, A:10; and Leonard Sykes Jr., Priscilla Ahlgren, and Joanne Weintraub, "Mother Says Raped Girl Will Remain in School," *Milwaukee Journal*, May 18, 1988, B:1, 7.

85. Jeff Cole, "Special School Eyed for Disruptive Pupils," *Milwaukee Sentinel*, November 7, 1987, 1:1, 11.

86. Alan J. Borsuk, "Dreams vs. Reality: Despite Gains, Blacks Still Lag in Education," *Milwaukee Journal*, September 14, 1986, A:1, 8

87. Quoted in Miner, *Lessons from the Heartland*, 124–126.

88. Jeff Cole, "City Flight Blamed on Schools," *Milwaukee Sentinel*, November 19, 1987, 1:1, 16.

89. Dahlk, *Against the Wind*, 455–457.

90. Ibid., 450–452; John M. Hagedorn, *People and Folks: Gangs, Crime, and the Underclass in a Rustbelt City* (Chicago: Lake View Press, 1988), 124–125, 142.

91. Quoted in Gregory D. Stanford, "Is Poverty at Root of Unrest?" *Milwaukee Journal*, May 13, 1983, 1:1, 10.

92. *Milwaukee Journal*, February 3, 1982.

93. Dahlk, *Against the Wind*, 453–455, 457. Hostility toward police peaked in 1981, when three white police officers beat Ernest Lacy, an African American, to death after taking him into custody. See chapter 11 of Miner, *Lessons from the Heartland*.

94. Quoted in Gregory D. Sanford, "Groppi: New Job, Old Fight," *Milwaukee Journal*, January 17, 1983, 1:1, 6.

95. Quoted in Eugene Kane, "Problem Lies with Youth, Speaker Says," *Milwaukee Journal*, September 22, 1983, Accent on the City:7.

96. David I. Bednarek, "Blacks Push School Plan," *Milwaukee Journal*, August 11, 1987, A:1, 8; Dahlk, *Against the Wind*, 477–478; Dougherty, *More Than One Struggle*, 189–190; "Black Leaders Want Own School District," *Milwaukee Journal*, August 12, 1987, A:1; and "Black School District Plan Too Risky," *Milwaukee Journal*, August 14, 1987, B:1.

97. Press release, Hart Papers, box 1, folder 6.

98. Jeff Cole, "New Separate School District Called Only Solution for Blacks," *Milwaukee Sentinel*, February 11, 1988, 1:10; Dahlk, *Against the Wind*, 482–485.

99. Tom Bamberger, "The Education of Howard Fuller," *Milwaukee Magazine*, July, 1988, 56–59; Fran Bauer, "Black School Idea Gains Favor," *Milwaukee Journal*, September 2, 1987, A:1, 15.

100. "Manifesto for New Directions in the Education of Black Children in the City of Milwaukee," Hart Papers, box 1, folder 6.

101. David I. Bednarek, "Blacks Push School Plan," *Milwaukee Journal*, August 11, 1987, A:1, 8; press release, Hart Papers, box 1, folder 6.

102. *Proceedings*, August 6, 1987.

103. Dahlk, *Against the Wind*, 469–471.

104. Fran Bauer, "Black School Idea Gains Favor," *Milwaukee Journal*, September 2, 1987, A:1, 15; David I. Bednarek, "Blacks, Whites Criticize School Resegregation Idea," *Milwaukee Journal*, August 17, 1987, B:1, 2; and Bill Hurley, "Black School District OK'd by Assembly," *Milwaukee Sentinel*, March 18, 1988, 1:1, 13.

105. Quoted in Jeffrey L. Katz and David I. Bednarek, "Black School District Rejected in Survey," *Milwaukee Journal*, September 28, 1987, A:1, 8.

106. Fran Bauer, "Black School Idea Gains Favor," *Milwaukee Journal*, September 2, 1987, A:1, 15.

107. Jeffrey L. Katz and David I. Bednarek, "Black School District Rejected in Survey," *Milwaukee Journal*, September 28, 1987, A:1, 8.

108. Bill Hurley, "Black School District OK'd by Assembly," *Milwaukee Sentinel*, March 18, 1988, 1:1, 13; Steve Schultze and David I. Bednarek, "Black District Clears One Hurdle," *Milwaukee Journal*, March 17, 1988, A:1, 7; "Separate District No Cure for Schools," *Milwaukee Journal*, March 18, 1988, A:8; Dahlk, *Against the Wind*, 486–487; Charles E. Freidrich, "Senators Scrap Black District," *Milwaukee Journal*, March 25, 1988, A:1, 13.

109. Jeff Cole, "Teachers Union Endorses Faison for Superintendent," *Milwaukee Sentinel*, December 9, 1987, 1:5; *Proceedings*, December 8, 1987; "School Chief Search Finds 30 Candidates," *Milwaukee Journal*, January 4, 1988, B: 1; Priscilla Ahlgren, "Top Candidate Wants School Job," *Milwaukee Journal*, April 29, 1988, A:1, 6.

110. Priscilla Ahlgren, "Top Candidate Wants School Job," *Milwaukee Journal*, April 29, 1988, A:1, 6. See also Priscilla Ahlgren, "School in Peterkin's District Uses Diverse, Innovative System," *Milwaukee Journal*, May 3, 1988. Mary Bills would be a staunch advocate for closing the achievement gap between white and African American students in the late 1980s and early 1990s. See chapter 17 of Dahlk, *Against the Wind*, for more information.

111. Jeff Cole, "Peterkin Named Superintendent of City Schools," *Milwaukee Sentinel*, May 7, 1988, 1:1, 5, 10; Jeff Cole, "Peterkin Appearances Well-Received," *Milwaukee Sentinel*, May 21, 1988, 1:5. See also Jeff Cole, "Schools Need Clear Goals, Peterkin Says," *Milwaukee Sentinel*, June 24, 1988, 1:5; and "Peterkin, Teachers Off to a Good Start," *Milwaukee Sentinel*, September 24, 1988, 1:6.

112. Quoted in Priscilla Ahlgren, "Peterkin Aims High," *Milwaukee Journal*, May 7, 1988, A:1, 9.113. "Decentralization: Why, How, and What Ends?" North Central Regional Educational Laboratory, last modified 1993, www.ncrel.org/sdrs /areas/issues/envrnmnt/go/93–1milw.htm. Various people and agencies have proposed a breakup of MPS from at least 1985 through 2010. See David I. Bednarek, "10 School Districts Suggested for City," *Milwaukee Journal*, June 6, 1985, 2:1–2; Kenneth R. Lamke and Gretchen Schuldt, "Grover Suggests Breaking MPS into 33 Districts," *Milwaukee Sentinel*, June 7, 1990, 1:5; and "MPS Given 2 Years, or Else," *Milwaukee Journal Sentinel*, January 21, 1998.

114. Jeff Cole, "Peterkin Named Superintendent of City Schools," *Milwaukee Sentinel*, May 7, 1988, 1:1, 5, 10; "Schools Need Clear Goals, Peterkin Says," *Milwaukee Sentinel*, June 24, 1988, 1:5.

115. Priscilla Ahlgren, "Board Member Questions Racial Equity of 6 School District Appointments," *Milwaukee Journal*, June 1, 1989, B:4; Priscilla Ahlgren, "Now It's Up to Peterkin to Put His Plan to Work," *Milwaukee Journal*, October 27, 1988, B:1, 4; Priscilla Ahlgren, "Peterkin Plan Gains Support," *Milwaukee Journal*, January 17, 1989, B:1, 4, Priscilla Ahlgren, "Peterkin to Seek Money as

School Reorganization Advances," *Milwaukee Journal*, October 22, 1988, B:7; Priscilla Ahlgren, "School Plan Follows Neighborhood Lines," *Milwaukee Journal*, January 8, 1989, B:1–2; Jeff Cole, "Overhaul of Schools Presented," *Milwaukee Sentinel*, November 22, 1988, 1:1, 4; Jeff Cole, "Peterkin Sees Combination Neighborhood-Specialty Schools," *Milwaukee Sentinel*, 1:5; "Decentralization: Why, How, and What Ends?"; "Peterkin Plan Wins Quick Backing," *Milwaukee Journal*, October 20, 1988, B:2; Paula A. Poda, "Promise Is Seen in Management Plan for Schools," *Milwaukee Sentinel*, 1:6; and Jim Stingl, "5 Endorsed to Lead School Regions," *Milwaukee Journal*, May 16, 1989, B:7.

116. McKenzie Group, "Options for Organizing the Milwaukee Public Schools" (Milwaukee: Milwaukee Public Schools, August 15, 1988), 16–19, 32; *Proceedings*, January 25, 1989.

117. Priscilla Ahlgren, "Now It's Up to Peterkin to Put His Plan to Work," *Milwaukee Journal*, October 27, 1988, B:1, 4; Dahlk, *Against the Wind*, 497; "Decentralization: Why, How, and What Ends?"; and Gretchen Schuldt, "Board Member Raps School 'Zones' Plan," *Milwaukee Sentinel*, February 13, 1990, 1:5.

118. George A. Mitchell and the Wisconsin Policy Research Institute, *An Evaluation of State-Financed School Integration in Metropolitan Milwaukee* (Milwaukee: Wisconsin Policy Research Institute, 1989), 51.

119. See also Jeff Cole, "Integration Plan Gets Failing Grade," *Milwaukee Sentinel*, June 27, 1989, 1:1, 9; Section III of Mitchell, *An Evaluation of State-Financed School Integration*.

120. Priscilla Ahlgren, "High School Grades Down Again," *Milwaukee Journal*, September 27, 1989, A:1, 8; Gretchen Schuldt, "Attendance Still Dropping at MPS, Figures Show," *Milwaukee Sentinel*, February 10, 1990; "Suspension Report Merits Serious Study," *Milwaukee Sentinel*, August 16, 1989, 1:10. See also Priscilla Ahlgren, "Peterkin Takes Aim at Troublemakers," *Milwaukee Journal*, November 3, 1989, A:1–2.

121. Priscilla Ahlgren, "Choice Plan Learns from Other Tries," *Milwaukee Sentinel*, March 25, 1990; Priscilla Ahlgren, "Consultant's Plan Would Target Weakest Schools," *Milwaukee Journal*, February 12, 1990, A:1, 4; Priscilla Ahlgren, "School Plan: Less Busing, More Choice," *Milwaukee Journal*, February 11, 1990, A:1, 26; Priscilla Ahlgren, "School Plan Puts Onus on Principals, Staff," *Milwaukee Journal*, February 13, 1990, B:1, 4; and Jeff Cole, "Choice Plan May Help Bad Schools," *Milwaukee Sentinel*, April 10, 1989, 1:5.

122. Priscilla Ahlgren, "Pupils, Parents Race for Seats in Specialty School," *Milwaukee Journal*, January 30, 1989, B:1, 5.

123. Quoted in Gretchen Schuldt, "'Willie Plan' for Schools Criticized at Hearing," *Milwaukee Sentinel*, February 28, 1990, 1: 5.

124. Gretchen Schuldt, "'Willie Plan' for Schools Criticized at Hearing," *Milwaukee Sentinel*, February 28, 1990, 1: 5.

125. Priscilla Ahlgren, "Schools Near Home a Tough Assignment," *Milwaukee Journal*, March 21, 1990, B:1, 5.

126. Priscilla Ahlgren, "Peterkin Asks to Scrap Much of Willie Plan," *Milwaukee Journal*, May 20, 1990, A:1, 28; Priscilla Ahlgren, "School Plan a Beginning,

Board Agrees," *Milwaukee Journal*, February 16, 1990, B:1, 4; Priscilla Ahlgren, "Stacy Calls on Peterkin to Scrap Assignment Plan," *Milwaukee Journal*, May 9, 1990, B:1, 4, 20, 21, 1990; Dahlk, *Against the Wind*, 498–500; Jim Stingl, "Hearing Reveals Distrust of Attendance Plan," *Milwaukee Journal*, February 28, 1990; Jim Stingl, "School Board Presses for Changes in Student Assignment Proposal," *Milwaukee Journal*, April 10, 1990; and David E. Umhoefer, "Aldermen Want Say in School Plan," *Milwaukee Journal*, March 1, 1990, B:1, 9.

127. Quoted in Priscilla Ahlgren, "Peterkin Asks to Scrap Much of Willie Plan," *Milwaukee Journal*, May 20, 1990, A:1, 28.

128. Quoted in Priscilla Ahlgren, "Observers Wait for Proof of Peterkin's School Reform," *Milwaukee Journal*, April 1, 1990, A:1, 18.

129. "Can the Boys Be Saved?" *Newsweek*, October 15, 1990, 67. See also *USA Today*, October 11, 1990; *Washington Post*, February 15, 1991. Additional statistics are in Priscilla Ahlgren, "'D+' Image a Reflection of Truancy," *Milwaukee Journal*, October 21, 1990, A:1, 26; Priscilla Ahlgren, "Peterkin Funnels Money to Classrooms," *Milwaukee Journal*, May 23, 1990, B:1, 3; and Gretchen Schuldt, "Many Minorities Fail at MPS Schools," *Milwaukee Sentinel*, May 23, 1990, 1:1, 13.

130. Quoted in "Can the Boys Be Saved?" See also Priscilla Ahlgren, "Plan Pays Parents to Help Kids," *Milwaukee Journal*, October 11, 1990, B:1, 5; Priscilla Ahlgren, "Stacy Says Begel Oversteps Bounds, Should Be Reviewed," *Milwaukee Journal*, March 20, 1990, B:1.

131. Kevin Johnson, "A Bold Experiment in Educating Black Males," *USA Today*, October 11, 1990.

132. Quoted in Charles Whitaker, "Do Black Males Need Special Schools?" *Ebony*, March 1991, 18.

133. Quoted in "Can the Boys Be Saved?"

134. Quoted in Kevin Johnson, "A Bold Experiment in Educating Black Males," *USA Today*, October 11, 1990.

135. "African-American Immersion Schools Aim to Help Failing Students," *Christian Science Monitor,* June 14, 1991, 10; Priscilla Ahlgren, "Immersion Schools Not Just for Boys," *Milwaukee Journal*, August 9, 1991; "Can the Boys Be Saved?"; Dahlk, *Against the Wind*, 501–506, 581; and Dan Parks, "MPS Board Okays Change to Malcolm X," *Milwaukee Sentinel*, February 25, 1993, A:5. See also *Proceedings*, March 22 and June 27, 1989; September 26, 1990; and December 18, 1991.

136. Gretchen Schuldt, "Peterkin Quitting to Take Harvard Job," *Milwaukee Sentinel*, November 20, 1990, 1:1, 6; *Proceedings*, November 20, 1990. Peterkin's letter of resignation is in *Proceedings*, May 29, 1991.

137. Dahlk, *Against the Wind*, 507.

138. Ibid., 508–509.

139. "Four Milwaukee Middle Schools Want to Merge into Two," *Milwaukee Journal Sentinel*, January 11, 2007; *Proceedings*, November 30, 2006, and January 25 and February 22, 2007.

140. "North Division High School to Make a Comeback in 2010," *Milwaukee Journal Sentinel*, March 26, 2009; *Proceedings*, November 20, 2006, and June 29, 2007;

and "School Options Are Multiplying" *Milwaukee Journal Sentinel*, April 17, 2007.

141. "12 Milwaukee High Schools Identified as Low Performers," *Milwaukee Journal Sentinel*, April 11, 2011; "Federal Funds Could Help with North Division Overhaul," *Milwaukee Journal Sentinel*, March 12, 2010.

142. Priscilla Ahlgren, "Broad Experience Drives Interest in Fuller," *Milwaukee Journal*, February, 2, 1991, B:1, 4; Murphy and Pawasarat, "Why It Failed," 45–46; Gretchen Schuldt, "Two Seek School Board's At-Large Seat," *Milwaukee Sentinel*, March 21, 1991, 1:11; Jim Stingl, "Fuller Pushed for Top Job," *Milwaukee Journal*, February 22, 1991, A:1, 14; and Steven Walters, "2 Push to Make Fuller Eligible for MPS Post," *Milwaukee Sentinel*, March 8, 1991, 1:5. Additional background information in Dahlk, *Against the Wind*, 556–557.

143. "McGriff's Departure Leaves Gap," *Milwaukee Journal*, March 27, 1991, A:1, 10; "MPS Loses; Slim Pickings Exist," *Milwaukee Sentinel*, March 28, 1991, 1:10; "All MPS Board Needs Now Is Rubber Stamp," *Milwaukee Sentinel*, April 20, 1991, 1:6; Richard P. Jones, "Hurdle to Fuller's Candidacy About to Fall," *Milwaukee Journal*, April 19, 1991; Jones, "Senate Approves Waiver for Fuller," *Milwaukee Journal*, April 18, 1991; Steven Walters, "Assembly Okays Bill on MPS," *Milwaukee Sentinel*, March 18, 1991, 1:1; and Steven Walters and Jeff Cole, "Fuller Gets the Go-Ahead to Seek MPS Job," *Milwaukee Sentinel*, April 19, 1991, 1:7.

144. Priscilla Ahlgren, "50% in Poll Support Fuller for School Superintendent," *Milwaukee Sentinel*, April 17, 1991; Priscilla Ahlgren, "Prominent Blacks Urge Swift Action on School Job," *Milwaukee Journal*, March 21, 1991, A:1, 6; Jeff Bentoff, "Ament Endorses Fuller as MPS Superintendent," *Milwaukee Sentinel*, February 27, 1991, 1:8; "Fuller Finds Support Among North Students," *Milwaukee Journal*, April 23, 1991, B:5; Kenneth R. Lamke, "Teachers Favor Further Search," *Milwaukee Sentinel*, April 22, 1991, 1:1, 9; and Leonard Sykes Jr., "Mayor Backs Fuller's Ideas for Schools," *Milwaukee Journal*, May 23, 1991, B:1, 5.

145. Priscilla Ahlgren, "Decision Nearer on Selection," *Milwaukee Journal*, May 14, 1991, B:1 ,5; Priscilla Ahlgren, "Superintendent Finalists Narrowed to 2," *Milwaukee Journal*, May 15, 1991, B:1, 5; "Candidate to Be Revealed Next Week," *Milwaukee Journal*, May 16, 1991, B:8; *Milwaukee Sentinel*, April 23 and May 7 and 12–14, 1991; and Celeste Williams, "Other Competitors Likely for School Job," *Milwaukee Journal*, May 4, 1991, A:22. See also *Proceedings*, November 29 and December 10, 1990; February 20 and 25, 1991; and March 6, 1991.

146. Priscilla Ahlgren and Leonard Sykes Jr., "Exultant Fuller at Head of the Class," *Milwaukee Journal*, May 30, 1991, B:1; Paula A. Poda, "New School Chief Approved Unanimously," *Milwaukee Sentinel*, May 30, 1991, 1:1, 4. See also *Proceedings*, June 26, 1991.

147. Mark J. Rochester, "Peterburs Leaves with Books in Order," *Milwaukee Journal*, July 8, 1991, B:7.

148. Wisconsin Advisory Committee to the United States Civil Rights Commission, "Impact of School Desegregation in Milwaukee Public Schools on Quality Education for Minorities . . . 15 Years Later," August 1992 (hereafter cited as Wisconsin Advisory Committee).

149. Ibid., 2.

150. Ibid., 6–7.

151. Ibid., 8.

152. Priscilla Ahlgren, "Dismal Report No Help, Mitchell Says," *Milwaukee Journal*, April 23, 1991, B:1, 5. See also Celeste Williams, "Saving the Kids," *Milwaukee Journal*, November 17–21, 24, 1991.

153. Wisconsin Advisory Committee, 7.

154. "Parents Give Public Schools Passing Grade," *Milwaukee Community Journal*, September 26, 1990, 1, 10.

155. Wisconsin Advisory Committee, 11–12.

156. Quoted in Mark J. Rochester, "Fuller Won't Keep Begel in Cabinet Post," *Milwaukee Journal*, June 18, 1991, B:5. See also Paula Poda, "Major Kindergarten Expansion Sought," *Milwaukee Sentinel*, June 19, 1991, A:1, 10.

157. Priscilla Ahlgren, "Fuller: More Power to Schools," *Milwaukee Journal*, May 19, 1991, A:1, 24; "Fuller Ready to Give More Power to the Schools," *Milwaukee Journal*, June 30, 1991; "Decentralization: Why, How, and What Ends?"; and Dahlk, *Against the Wind*, 556.

158. Priscilla Ahlgren, "92 Administrative Jobs May Be Cut," *Milwaukee Journal*, June 19, 1991, B:4; "Fuller Fears Not, Clips Layers of Bureaucracy," *Milwaukee Sentinel*, June 22, 1991, A:6; Paula Poda, "Major Kindergarten Expansion Sought," *Milwaukee Sentinel*, June 19, 1991, A:10; and Mark J. Rochester, "Board Sees Most of Budget Fuller's Way," *Milwaukee Journal*, June 20, 1991, B:1, 7.

159. Priscilla Ahlgren, "23 Tech Students Suspended for Brawl," *Milwaukee Journal*, November 13, 1991, A:1, 12; Priscilla Ahlgren, "Fuller Faces Risks in Discipline Plan," *Milwaukee Journal*, October 11, 1991, B:1, 5; Priscilla Ahlgren, "Fuller Names New Principal for Marshall," *Milwaukee Journal*, October 19, 1991, A:1, 20; Priscilla Ahlgren, "Fuller Offers Do-or-Die Way to Fix Schools," *Milwaukee Journal*, August 6, 1991, A:1, 7; Priscilla Ahlgren, "Fuller Says Staff Must Be Responsible for Enforcing Rules," *Milwaukee Journal*, October 15, 1991, B:5; Priscilla Ahlgren, "Principals Supporting Expulsion," *Milwaukee Journal*, November 14, 1991; "Good First Steps to Dealing with Disrupters," *Milwaukee Journal*, November 15, 1991, A:8; Erin Knoche and Tina Burnside, "Fuller Vows to Crack Down on Rowdiness in Schools," *Milwaukee Sentinel*, November 16, 1991, A:1, 7; "Manuel Mendoza and Celeste Williams, "Principal at South Division Wants Unruly Students Ousted," *Milwaukee Journal*, November 1, 1991, A:1, 4; Dan Parks, "MPS Teachers Rap Disruptions," *Milwaukee Sentinel*, November 7, 1992, A:5, 7; Paula A. Poda, "More Study Sought on Fuller Proposals," *Milwaukee Sentinel*, August 7, 1991, A:5; Mark J. Rochester and Priscilla Ahlgren, "Young Pupils to Get Tougher Rules," *Milwaukee Journal*, February 6, 1992, B:1, 7; Lori Skalitzky and Jan Uebehelrr, "Marshall Not the Only School with Problems, Fuller Says," *Milwaukee Sentinel*, October 21, 1991, A:7; "Tougher Discipline so Students Can Learn," *Milwaukee Journal*, February 10, 1992; and "When Street Gangs Disrupt Job Fair, Crackdown Is Imperative," *Milwaukee Sentinel*, November 19, 1991, A:10. Also Howard Fuller, telephone interview with author, August 30, 2010.

160. Wisconsin Advisory Committee, 12.

161. Priscilla Ahlgren, "Board Rejects Charter Schools," *Milwaukee Journal*, December 19, 1991; Priscilla Ahlgren, "Fuller Offers Do-or-Die Way to Fix Schools," *Milwaukee Journal*, August 6, 1991, A:1, 7; Priscilla Ahlgren, "New Leader Cites Need to Cooperate," *Milwaukee Journal*, August 14, 1991, B:1, 2; Priscilla Ahlgren and Mark J. Rochester, "Fuller's School-Closing Plan Draws Fire," *Milwaukee Journal*, December 17, 1991, B:1, 5; "Closing 'Failing' Schools Ignores Host of Other Factors," *Milwaukee Journal*, December 14, 1992; Paula A. Poda, "More Study Sought on Fuller Proposals," *Milwaukee Sentinel*, August 7, 1991, A:5; and Paula A. Poda and Rick Romell, "Power Over Failing Schools Sought," *Milwaukee Sentinel*, December 17, 1991, A:5–6.

162. Priscilla Ahlgren, "Fuller Facing a Job That Just Got Tougher," *Milwaukee Journal*, December 22, 1991, B:1, 3; Priscilla Ahlgren, "Fuller's Reform Will Be Tested in the Coming Year," *Milwaukee Journal*, December 29, 1991, B:1, 5; Priscilla Ahlgren and Mark J. Rochester, "Fuller's School-Closing Plan Draws Fire," *Milwaukee Journal*, December 17, 1991; and Tannette Johnson-Elie, "Teachers Meet with Fuller," *Milwaukee Sentinel*, February 5, 1991, A:5.

163. Priscilla Ahlgren, "Budget Seeks Equity in Per-Pupil Funding," *Milwaukee Journal*, May 5, 1992, A:1, 7; "Fuller's Challenge Cuts Right to the Soul," *Milwaukee Journal*, March, 20, 1993, B:4; Priscilla Ahlgren, "In the End, MPS Budget Must Be Proved in Classroom," *Milwaukee Journal*, B:5; "Property Tax Showdown Tonight," *Milwaukee Journal*, June 30, 1991, B:1, 6; and "School Board Achieves Goal of Cutting Tax Rate," *Milwaukee Journal*, July 1, 1992, A:1, 14.

164. Priscilla Ahlgren, "Poor Schools Get Less School Money," *Milwaukee Journal*, April 17, 1992, B:1–2.

165. Priscilla Ahlgren, "600 Protestors Assail Fuller on Budget Plan," *Milwaukee Journal*, June 10, 1992, B:1–2; Priscilla Ahlgren, "Budget Seeks Equity in Per-Pupil Funding," *Milwaukee Journal*, May 5, 1992, A:1, 7; Priscilla Ahlgren, "Equality Plan Brings Fears of Mediocrity for All Schools," *Milwaukee Journal*, May 26, 1991, B:1, 5; Priscilla Ahlgren, "Frustrated Students, Others Plead with Fuller Against Fund Reallocation," *Milwaukee Journal*, May 27, 1991, B:1–2; Paula A. Poda and Gretchen Schuldt, "Fuller Raps Mayor's Comments," *Milwaukee Sentinel*, July 3, 1992; and "School Budget Hits Bull's-Eye," *Milwaukee Journal*, July 2, 1992.

166. Dan Parks, "MPS Budget Equals Change," *Milwaukee Sentinel*, July 25, 1992, A:1, 9.

167. Quoted in Manuel Mendoza, "Fuller's Board Appeal Isn't Attractive to Anyone," *Milwaukee Sentinel*, March 18, 1991.

168. Paula A. Poda, "Plan Backed to Cut School Bus Routes," *Milwaukee Sentinel*, November 12, 1991, A:5; Mark J. Rochester, "Board Rejects Proposal on Gay Issues," *Milwaukee Journal*, November 21, 1991, B:1, 5.

169. Quoted in Paula A. Poda, "Plan Would Narrow School Facilities Gap," *Milwaukee Sentinel*, February 26, 1992, A:1, 8. See also Priscilla Ahlgren, "Forum Has Questions on School Building Plan," *Milwaukee Journal*, October 18, 1992;

Priscilla Ahlgren, "Fuller Promises Radical Change," *Milwaukee Journal*, March 2, 1992, B:1; Priscilla Ahlgren, "Fuller's Building Plan Would Cost $474.3 Million," September 20, 1992, B:1, 5; Priscilla Ahlgren, "School Plan Would Top $1 Billion," *Milwaukee Journal*, September 29, 1992; Priscilla Ahlgren, "Schools Plan Would Boost Tax Bills," *Milwaukee Journal*, February 26, 1992, A:1, 12; Kenneth R. Lamke, "Norquist Doubts Referendum on School Building Would Pass," *Milwaukee Sentinel*, January 9, 1992, A:11; Paula A. Poda, "Fuller Plan Stirs Split on Board," *Milwaukee Sentinel*, March 4, 1992, A:5; Gretchen Schuldt, "Norquist Backs Fuller on Reorganization," April 2, 1992, A:5; and Leonard Sykes Jr. and Priscilla Ahlgren, "Aldermen Urge Fuller to Phase in Building," *Milwaukee Journal*, October 6, 1992, B:5.

170. Priscilla Ahlgren, "Schools Plan Would Boost Tax Bills," *Milwaukee Journal*, February 26, 1992, A:1, 12.

171. See articles in *Milwaukee Journal*, June 6, September 27, October 30, November 3 and 5, and December 6–7, 12, and 24, 1992; January 6, 8, 12, 14, 19, 24, and 31, and February 3–4 and 7–8, 1993; *Milwaukee Sentinel*, March 4–5, 24, and 31, April 23, June 9, September 21, 24, and 30, October 23 and 26, November 6 and 20, and December 1, 4, 9, and 25, 1992; January 2, 18, 21, 23, and 25, and February 2, 4, 10–13, and 15, 1993.

172. Quoted in Paula A. Poda, "Plan Would Narrow School Facilities Gap," *Milwaukee Sentinel*, February 26, 1992, A:1, 8.

173. Jeff Browne, "Support Soft on School Plan," *Milwaukee Journal*, February 7, 1993; Jerry Goldstein, "Broader Base Must Ungird Public School Funding," *Milwaukee Journal*, December 7, 1993, A:10; and Karen Herzog, "Poll Shows Most Blacks Back Plan," *Milwaukee Sentinel*, January 23, 1993, A:14.

174. Priscilla Ahlgren, "'No' Votes Resound," *Milwaukee Journal*, February 17, 1993, A:1, 8; Dan Parks, "MPS Resurrects Plan to Close Failing Schools," *Milwaukee Sentinel*, February 18, 1993, A:1, 11.

175. See articles in *Milwaukee Journal*, April 22, August 22, September 14 and 19, October 10, 14, and 17, 1993; January 16 and 20, February 1 and 24, March 16, April 8, 16, and 25–26, May 3, July 15, August 3 and 22, October 24, November 27, and December 12, 1994; *Milwaukee Journal Sentinel*, February 24, March 6 and 16, April 24–25, and June 28, 1995; and *Milwaukee Sentinel*, December 18, 1992; March 26 and August 1 and 23, 1994; January 24, 1995; Curtis Lawrence, "Fuller Vows to Enforce MPS Standards," *Milwaukee Journal*, August 25, 1994; Curtis Lawrence, "Schools Challenged to Improve," *Milwaukee Journal*, August 19, 1994, B:1, 5.

176. Dahlk, *Against the Wind*, 571–574.

177. Curtis Lawrence, "Forum to Focus on Limits on Black Teachers," *Milwaukee Journal*, September 27, 1993; Curtis Lawrence, "Taking Up the Gauntlet Union," *Milwaukee Journal Sentinel*, November 21, 1995; Mark J. Rochester, "Flexibility Sought on Black Teachers," *Milwaukee Journal*, May 6, 1992, B:1, 7; Gregory Stanford, "Teacher Union Seeks Foul Deal," *Milwaukee Journal*, March 24, 1993, A:13; and Michael R. Zahn, "Black Schools Found to Defy Racial Formula," March 19, 1992, B:3.

178. Priscilla Ahlgren, "Fuller Announces Panel to Set New Course for North

Division," *Milwaukee Journal*, April 17, 1992, B:2; Priscilla Ahlgren, "Panel Watches North Division Open," *Milwaukee Journal*, August 24, 1992, B:1; Curtis Lawrence, "Taking Up the Gauntlet Union," *Milwaukee Journal Sentinel*, November 21, 1995; Paula A. Poda, "North Division Principal Says He's Been Fired by Fuller," *Milwaukee Sentinel*, April 17, 1992, A:1, 8; and Paula A. Poda, "North Division's Students Say Austin's Firing Hurts School," *Milwaukee Sentinel*, April 28, 1992.

179. "South Division Assistant to Lead North Division," *Milwaukee Journal*, June 5, 1993.

180. Curtis Lawrence, "Taking Up the Gauntlet Union," *Milwaukee Journal Sentinel*, November 21, 1995.

181. Dahlk, *Against the Wind*, 585.

182. Daniel McGroarty, "Teacher Knows Best," *National Review* 47 (1995): 62–64; Wisconsin Advisory Committee, 12, 22–23.

183. Daynel L. Hooker, "Anti-Privatization Candidates Win," *Milwaukee Journal Sentinel*, April 5, 1995; Daynel L. Hooker, "Teachers Union Spent $40,000 on Candidates," *Milwaukee Journal Sentinel*, April 7, 1995; Daynel L. Hooker, "Fuller Consults Allies on Next Move," *Milwaukee Journal Sentinel*, April 16, 1995; Curtis Lawrence, "School Board Leader to Give Up Top Seat," *Milwaukee Journal Sentinel*, April 11, 1995; and Curtis Lawrence and Daynel L. Hooker, "Governor, Others Back Fuller," *Milwaukee Journal Sentinel*, April 12, 1995.

184. Quoted in Daynel L. Hooker, "Fuller Resigns," *Milwaukee Journal Sentinel*, April 19, 1995. See also *Proceedings*, April 18, 1995.

CHAPTER 6

1. Brunno V. Mano, "Charter School Politics," in *Choice and Competition in American Education*, ed. Paul E. Peterson (Lanham, MD: Rowman & Littlefield, 2006), 161.

2. Miner, *Lessons from the Heartland*, 230.

3. Ibid., 227.

4. Janet D. Mulvey et al., *Blurring the Lines: Charter, Public, Private and Religious Schools Coming Together* (Charlotte, NC: Information Age, 2010), 3. See also chapter 4 of Darlene Leiding, *The Hows and Whys of Alternative Education: Schools Where Students Thrive* (Lanham, MD: Rowman & Littlefield Education, 2008). See Tom Loveless and Katharyn Field, "Perspectives on Charter Schools," in *Handbook of Research on School Choice*, ed. Mark Berends et al. (New York: Routledge, 2009), 99–114, for the best review of the current literature on charter schools. These works and those in the next few notes are the most recent studies of charter schools.

5. Preston Green, "Charter School Law," in Berends et al., *Handbook*, 142–145.

6. Mulvey et al., *Blurring the Lines,* 1–6.

7. Green, "Charter School Law," 145–148.

8. Miner, *Lessons from the Heartland*, 229; Erin Richards, "Milwaukee Among Tops in Nation for Charter School Enrollment," *Milwaukee Journal Sentinel*, November 14, 2012.

9. Dahlk, *Against the Wind*, 599–603; Matthew E. Vick, "The Effects of Charter

Schools, Race, Socioeconomics, and Teacher Characteristics in Wisconsin's Urban School Districts" (PhD diss., University of Wisconsin–Milwaukee, 2009), 46–47.

10. Miner, *Lessons from the Heartland*, 229.

11. See William Lowe Boyd and Herbert J. Walberg, eds., *Choice in Education: Potential and Problems* (Berkeley, CA: McCutchan, 1990) for an early collection of articles written mostly by classic conservative educators who support choice in the broad sense of the word, including charter schools, school choice, open enrollment, and magnet schools. The introduction directly references *A Nation at Risk* and hypothesizes that choice and competition are the solutions to improving schools.

12. See Bryan C. Hassel, "Charter Schools: Mom and Pops or Corporate Design," Jay Matthews, "Contracting Out: The Story Behind Philadelphia's Edison Contract," and Terry M. Moe, "A Union by Any Other Name," in *Choice and Competition in American Education*, ed. Paul E. Peterson (Lanham, MD: Rowman & Littlefield, 2006).

13. R. Kenneth Godwin, "Sinking Swann: Public School Choice and the Resegregation of Charlotte's Public Schools," *Review of Policy Research* 23, no. 5 (2006): 983–997; Kevin G. Welner and Kenneth R. Howe, "Steering Toward Separation: The Policy and Legal Implications of 'Counseling' Special Education Students Away from Charter Schools," in *School Choice and Diversity: What the Evidence Says*, ed. Janelle T. Scott (New York: Teachers College Press, 2005), 93–111.

14. Barbara Miner, "Do Milwaukee's Children Deserve Art and Music Classes?," *Milwaukee Journal Sentinel*, January 5, 2013.

15. Hamilton Lankford and James Wyckoff, "Why Are Schools Racially Segregated?: Implications for School Choice Policies," in Scott, *School Choice and Diversity*, 9–26; Jordan Rickles and Paul M. Ong, "The Integrating (and Segregating) Effect of Charter, Magnet, and Traditional Elementary Schools: The Case of Five California Metropolitan Areas," *California Politics & Policy* 9, no. 1 (June 2005): 16–38; W. David Stevens et al., "Barriers to Access: High School Choice Processes in Chicago," in *School Choice and School Improvement*, ed. Mark Berends et al. (Cambridge, MA: Harvard Education Press, 2011), 125–145; and Ron Zimmer et al., "Charter Schools: Do They Cream Skim, Increasing Student Segregation?" in Berends et al., *School Choice*, 215–232. See also "Extensive Lit Review Shows More School Choice = More Segregation," *10th Period*, February 9, 2012, http://10thperiod.blogspot.com/2012/02/extensive-lit-review-shows-more-school.html.

16. Gary Orfield, "Forward," in *Choice Without Equity: Charter School Segregation and the Need for Civil Rights Standards*, by Erica Frankenberg, Genevieve Siegel Hawley, and Jia Wang (Los Angeles: Civil Rights Project, 2010), 1–2.

17. Caroline M. Hoxby, "Do Vouchers and Charters Push Public Schools to Improve?" in Peterson, *Choice and Competition*, 194–205, especially 200.

18. Julian R. Betts, "The Competitive Effects of Charter Schools on Traditional Public Schools," in Peterson, *Choice and Competition*, 195–207, especially pages 206–207; Stéphane Lavertu and John Witte, "The Impact of Milwaukee Charter Schools on Student Achievement," *Issues in Governance Studies* 23 (March

2009); Erin Richards, "Studies Show No Big Advantage for Charter Schools," *Milwaukee Journal Sentinel*, July 29, 2010; Becky Vevea, "Charters Score No Better than MPS," *Milwaukee Journal Sentinel*, December 17, 2010; and Bettie Teasly, "Charter School Outcomes," in Peterson, *Choice and Competition*, 209–226, especially 223–224.

19. William G. Howell et al., "The Impact of Vouchers on Student Performance," in Peterson, *Choice and Competition*, 183. See also chapter 7 of Leiding, *The Hows and Whys of Alternative Education*.

20. Miner, *Lessons from the Heartland*, 162.

21. *The Lynde and Harry Bradley Foundation 2011 Annual Report*, Bradley Foundation, www.bradleyfdn.org/pdfs/Reports2011/2011AnnualReport.pdf, and the related financial report at www.bradleyfdn.org/pdfs/Reports2011 /2011AnnualReport.pdf.

22. Daniel Bice et al., "From Local Roots, Bradley Foundation Builds Conservative Empire," *Milwaukee Journal Sentinel*, November 19, 2011; John J. Miller, "Strategic Investment in Ideas: How Two Foundations Reshaped America" (Washington, DC: The Philanthropy Roundtable, 2003), 34–40; and Miner, *Lessons from the Heartland*, 160–164.

23. Quoted in Miller, "Strategic Investment in Ideas," 36.

24. John Chubb and Terry Moe, *Politics, Markets, and America's Schools* (Washington, DC: Brookings Institution, 1989); Miner, *Lessons from the Heartland*, 41–42. According to Miner, the Bradley Foundation is second only to the Walton Family Foundation (the Walmart family) in its monetary support for privatized education. See Miner, *Lessons from the Heartland*, 209.

25. Richard J. Herrnstein and Charles Murray, *The Bell Curve: Intelligence and Class Structure in American Life* (New York: Free Press, 1994); Miner, *Lessons from the Heartland*, 164–166.

26. Miller, "Strategic Investment in Ideas," 44; "PAVE History," PAVE: Excellence from the Boardroom to the Classroom, www.pave.org/About-Us/PAVE -History.htm.

27. Thompson, *Power to the People*, 93.

28. Mikel Holt, *Not Yet "Free at Last": The Unfinished Business of the Civil Rights Movement—Our Battle for School Choice* (Oakland: Institute for Contemporary Studies Press, 2000), 57–58.

29. Dave Daley, "Committee Backs Plan to Help Needy Pay for Private School," *Milwaukee Journal*, March 8, 1990, A:16; Alex Molnar, "Educational Vouchers: A Review of the Research," Center for Education Research, Analysis and Innovation, University of Wisconsin–Milwaukee, October 1999; Steve Schultze and Priscilla Ahlgren, "School Choice Empowers Poor, Lawmaker Says," *Milwaukee Sentinel*, March 23, 1990, B:1, 7; Thompson, *Power to the People*, 99–100; and Wisconsin Legislative Audit Bureau, "An Evaluation: The Milwaukee Parental Choice Program," February 2000, 3, 12–13.

30. Alan J. Borsuk, "Compromise on Vouchers," *Milwaukee Journal Sentinel*, June 2, 2009; Alan J. Borsuk, "Fuller Backs New Choice Regulation," *Milwaukee Journal Sentinel*, March 27, 2009; and Wisconsin Department of Public Instruction,

Summary of Wisconsin Act 28 Final 2009–11 Budget with Vetoes: Provisions Related to Elementary and Secondary Education and State Agency Operation (Madison: Wisconsin Department of Public Instruction, July 2009), 20.

31. Miner, *Lessons from the Heartland*, 156–160, 174–175; Erin Richards, "Wisconsin Told to Boost Oversight of Voucher Schools' Disability Rolls," *Milwaukee Journal Sentinel*, May 2, 2013.

32. Miner, *Lessons from the Heartland*, 247.

33. The Urban Institute, *Private School Participants in Federal Programs Under the No Child Left Behind Act and the Individuals with Disabilities Act: Private School and Public School District Representatives* (Washington, DC: US Department of Education, 2007). See Miner, *Lessons from the Heartland*, 238–242, for an interpretation of how No Child Left Behind affected public and private schools in Milwaukee.

34. Alan J. Borsuk, "Fairness Is in the Eye of the Beholder," *Milwaukee Journal Sentinel*, December 7, 2008; Alan J. Borsuk, "Milwaukee Makes Gain, Wants More, in School Voucher Funding," *Milwaukee Journal Sentinel*, June 14, 2009; Tom Brokaw, "Your Kids, Our Schools, Tough Choices," *Dateline* television broadcast, Prod. Elise Pearlstein, NBC, October 29, 2000; Robert M. Costrell, "Who Gains, Who Loses?: The Fiscal Impact of the Milwaukee Parental Choice Program," *Education Next* 9, no. 1 (2009): 68–69; "Fix the Flaw First," *Milwaukee Journal Sentinel*, March 7, 2011; Erin Richards, "MPS 'Voucher Tax' Statement OK'd," *Milwaukee Journal Sentinel*, September 22, 2011; David E. Umhoefer and Priscilla Ahlgren, "Abolish Chapter 220, Norquist Says," *Milwaukee Journal*, April 4, 1990, A:1, 6; and Wisconsin Legislative Audit Bureau, "An Evaluation," 21–24.

35. Priscilla Ahlgren, "Academy Quits School Choice," *Milwaukee Journal*, January 7, 1991, B:1, 7; Lindsay Fiori, "Fewer Students, Same Money," *Racine Journal Times*, June 2, 2013; Miner, *Lessons from the Heartland*, 170; and Dominque Paul Noth, "Angry Citizens Rising Up Against Vouch Tax Scam," *Milwaukee Labor Press*, February 15, 2013, www. milwaukeelabor.org/in_the_news/article .cfm?n_id=00323.

36. Thompson, *Power to the People*, 103; Joe Williams, "Schools Interested in Choice," *Milwaukee Journal Sentinel*, July 3, 1995, B:1, 7; and Witte, *The Market Approach to Education*, 56.

37. Paul Peterson and Chad Noyes, "School Choice in Milwaukee," in *New Schools for a New Century: The Redesign of Urban Education*, ed. Diane Ravitch and Joseph P. Viteritti (New Haven: Yale University Press, 1997), 140, 144.

38. Richard P. Jones, "Choice Plan Adds Church School Option," *Milwaukee Journal*, January 15, 1995, 1:1, 14; Richard P. Jones, "Court Temporarily Bars Religious School Choice," *Milwaukee Journal Sentinel*, August 28, 1995; Amy Rinard, "Doyle Should Defend Choice, Williams Says," *Milwaukee Journal Sentinel*, August 10, 1995; Amy Rinard, "Religious School Choice Advances," *Milwaukee Journal Sentinel*, June 22, 1995; and Gregory Stanford, "Unlikely Alliance for School Choice," *Milwaukee Journal Sentinel*, July 23, 1995. See also Miner, *Lessons from the Heartland*, 200–201.

39. Craig Gilbert, "Bradley Charity Spreads Wealth Wide," *Milwaukee Journal*, June 30, 1991; "Messmer Fights Rejection," *Milwaukee Journal*, June 14, 1992; Tannette Johnson-Elie, "Business Leaders Give to Choice Effort," *Milwaukee Journal Sentinel*, August 20, 1995, D:1, 7; Mary Beth Murphy, "School Choice Plan Spurs Flood of Interest," *Milwaukee Sentinel*, June 12, 1992, A:1, 9; Dan Parks, "Choice Plan Is Touted as Best for the Poor," *Milwaukee Sentinel*, November 13, 1992, A:15; and Paula A. Poda, "School Choice Program," *Milwaukee Sentinel*, August 4, 1992, special section on education, 14–15.

40. Eldon Knoche, "Expansion of Choice Supported," *Milwaukee Sentinel*, February 18, 1995.

41. Manuel Mendoza, "MICAH, North Division Announce Partnership," *Milwaukee Journal*, November 30, 1990, B:1, 5; Marie Rohde, "Bills Letter Angers Officials," *Milwaukee Journal*, October 23, 1990, B:6; and David E. Umhoefer and Priscilla Ahlgren, "Abolish Chapter 220, Norquist Says," *Milwaukee Journal*, April 4, 1990, A:1, 6.

42. Quoted in Priscilla Ahlgren and Leonard Sykes Jr., "Mayor Reaffirms Support for School Choice Plans," *Milwaukee Journal*, January 2, 1992, B:1, 7.

43. Daniel L. Hooker, "Fuller Publicly Backs School Choice," *Milwaukee Journal Sentinel*, May 9, 1995, and Miner, *Lessons from the Heartland*, 207.

44. Quoted in "Rift Seen in Support of Choice," *Milwaukee Journal Sentinel*, September 10, 1995. See also Curtis Lawrence, "Choice Supporters Will Have to Unite," *Milwaukee Journal*, January 15, 1995; Curtis Lawrence, "Legislators Defend Vote Against Choice Expansion," *Milwaukee Journal Sentinel*, July 12, 1995, B:3.

45. Quoted in Miner, *Lessons from the Heartland*, 205.

46. Ibid., 204.

47. Daniel Bice, "$150,000 Raised," *Milwaukee Journal Sentinel*, December 1, 1995; Miner, *Lessons from the Heartland*, 202–203; and Thompson, *Power to the People*, 109. See Gayle Schmitz-Zien, "The Genesis of and Motivations for the Milwaukee Parental Choice Program, 1985–1995" (PhD diss., University of Wisconsin–Milwaukee, 2003), 20–33, for the complete legal history.

48. Dahlk, *Against the Wind*, 603–606; Miner, *Lessons from the Heartland*, 210–211. See chapter 5 of R. Kenneth Godwin and Frank R. Kemerer, *School Choice Tradeoffs: Liberty, Equality, and Diversity* (Austin: University of Texas Press, 2002), for a legal history of the Milwaukee and Cleveland cases. John J. Peterburs, "An Analysis of the Milwaukee Parental Choice Program in Light of the First Amendment Establishment Clause Federal Supreme Court Cases" (PhD diss., Marquette University, 1998) is the best legal analysis of Wisconsin's voucher program. Peterburs was MPS's secretary-business in the 1980s and early 1990s (the last one in MPS) and was responsible for overseeing the lawsuit against the suburbs (see chapter 5). He may be considered the best legal expert on school choice and metropolitan integration in Milwaukee. 49. Alan Borsuk, Sarah Carr, and Leonard Sykes Jr., "Inside School Choice: 15 Years of Vouchers," *Milwaukee Journal Sentinel*, June 12–18, 2005. Two years later, a more scientific report indicated that parents with high economic status were more likely to be

involved in their children's lives, more likely to choose successful schools, and more likely to be involved in those schools. See David Dodenhoff, "Fixing the Milwaukee Public Schools: The Limits of Parent-Driven Reform," *Wisconsin Policy Research Institute Report* 20, no. 8 (October 2007).

50. Alan J. Borsuk, "Fighting Closes Voucher School," *Milwaukee Journal Sentinel*, January, 26, 2005; Alan J. Borsuk, "State Orders Private School Out of Choice Program," January 28, 2005; and Sarah Carr, "Ex-Voucher School Shut for 2 Weeks," *Milwaukee Journal Sentinel*, February 1, 2005.

51. Sarah Carr, "Louis Tucker Voucher School Will Close," *Milwaukee Journal Sentinel*, February 25, 2005; Sarah Carr, "State Seeks Fraud Inquiry into 2 Voucher Schools," *Milwaukee Journal Sentinel*, February 11, 2005.

52. Sarah Carr, "Northside High Ousted from Voucher Program," *Milwaukee Journal Sentinel*, January 25, 2006.

53. Alan J. Borsuk, "Scrutiny Heightens in Voucher Program," *Milwaukee Journal Sentinel*, October 18, 2005.

54. Sarah Carr, "Teachers Paid from Sale of Mercedes," *Milwaukee Journal Sentinel*, December 17, 2005. "Mandella" is one of several spelling errors in voucher schools, which makes writing a history of them confusing.

55. Quoted in Alan Borsuk, Sarah Carr, and Leonard Sykes Jr., "Inside School Choice: 15 Years of Vouchers," *Milwaukee Journal Sentinel*, June 16, 2005.

56. Alan J. Borsuk, "Another School Booted from Choice," *Milwaukee Journal Sentinel*, January 28, 2006.

57. Jessica McBride and Joe Williams, "Judge Sentences Choice School's CEO, a Convicted Rapist, for Tax Fraud," *Milwaukee Journal*, May 4, 2000.

58. Joe Williams, "School Closed After City Finds Building, Fire Violations," *Milwaukee Journal Sentinel*, November 12, 1999; Joe Williams, "School Shut Because of Building Troubles to Reopen at YMCA," *Milwaukee Journal Sentinel*, November 25, 1999.

59. Sarah Carr, "Alex's Academics to Resume Teaching Once It Has a New Home," *Milwaukee Journal Sentinel*, September 4, 2003; Sarah Carr, "Evicted Choice School Was Investigated by DA," *Milwaukee Journal Sentinel*, June 12, 2003; and Sarah Carr, "Who Cleans Up Problem Choice Schools?," *Milwaukee Journal Sentinel*, September 15, 2003.

60. Stacy Forster and Patrick Marley, "Voucher Deal Passes," *Milwaukee Journal Sentinel*, March 3, 2006.

61. Alan J. Borsuk, "Voucher Schools Put to the Test," *Milwaukee Journal Sentinel*, April 23, 2006. The law, as it was written at the time, required schools to gain accreditation but did not require them to maintain accreditation. See Erin Richards, "2 Voucher Schools Got State Money after Losing Accreditation," *Milwaukee Journal Sentinel*, March 13, 2013. See Alan J. Borsuk, "Education Struggle Goes on for Howard Fuller," *Milwaukee Journal Sentinel*, May 11, 2013, for a summary of Fuller's activities between 1995 and 2013.

62. Tom Held, "Bradley Grants Welcomed," *Milwaukee Journal Sentinel*, July 13, 2006; Miner, *Lessons from the Heartland*, 209.

63. "Senate OK'd Budget Goes to Walker," *Milwaukee Journal Sentinel*, June 16, 2011.

64. Alan J. Borsuk, "MPS Gets a Tax Surprise," *Milwaukee Journal Sentinel*, October 24, 2006; Alan J. Borsuk, "Shift in Voucher Funding Sought," *Milwaukee Journal Sentinel*, June 13, 2007; Alan J. Borsuk, "Vouchers to Pass $100 Million Mark," *Milwaukee Journal Sentinel*, November 21, 2006; Sarah Carr, "State Aid to MPS to Fall Short," *Milwaukee Journal Sentinel*, July 14, 2006; and Stacy Walters and Stacy Forster, "Doyle Wants State to Pay for Added School Choice," *Milwaukee Journal Sentinel*, February 7, 2007.

65. "Nearly All Wisconsin Schools See a Drop in Aid," *Milwaukee Journal Sentinel*, October 14, 2011.

66. See chapter 16 of Miner, *Lessons from the Heartland*, for stories about budget cuts.

67. Alan J. Borsuk, "Difficult Years Ahead for MPS," *Milwaukee Journal Sentinel*, June 5, 2007; Alan J. Borsuk, "Next Year, MPS Budget Just Grows Tougher," *Milwaukee Journal Sentinel*, November 14, 2007; and James E. Causey, "Milwaukee Public Schools District's Financial Hole Makes Everything Harder," *Milwaukee Journal Sentinel*, October 5, 2008. See also Karen Herzog, "Schools Get Funding-Cut Detail," *Milwaukee Journal Sentinel*, July 2, 2011; Erin Richards, "Milwaukee Teachers Won't Give Up More," *Milwaukee Journal Sentinel*, July 29, 2011; Erin Richards, "Teachers Reject Pay Concession," *Milwaukee Journal Sentinel*, April 4, 2012; Jason Stein and Karen Herzog, "Property Tax Cuts Likely for Most School Districts," *Milwaukee Journal Sentinel*, June 28, 2011; and Tom Tolan and Erin Richards, "School Levies Decrease Statewide," *Milwaukee Journal Sentinel*, November 16, 2011.

68. Alan J. Borsuk, "Compromise on Vouchers," *Milwaukee Journal Sentinel*, June 2, 2009; Alan J. Borsuk, "Fuller Backs New Choice Regulation," *Milwaukee Journal Sentinel*, March 27, 2009; Wisconsin Department of Public Instruction, *Summary of Wisconsin Act 28 Final 2009–11 Budget with Vetoes*, 19; Amy Hetzner and Erin Richards, "Schools Testing Fuels a Debate," *Milwaukee Journal Sentinel*, April 8, 2011.

69. Hoxby, "Do Vouchers and Charters Push," 194–205, especially 200.

70. Jay P. Greene and Ryan H. Marsh, *The Effect of Milwaukee's Parental Choice Program on Student Achievement in Milwaukee Public Schools* (Fayetteville: University of Arkansas, March 2009).

71. Martin Carnoy et al., *Vouchers and Public School Performance: A Case Study of the Milwaukee Parental Choice Program* (Washington, DC: The Economic Policy Institute, 2007).

72. "Wisconsin's Information Network for Successful Schools (WINSS)," Wisconsin Department of Public Instruction, http://data.dpi.state.wi.us/data.

73. Howell et al., "The Impact of Vouchers," 183–193; Patrick J. Wolf et al., "School Vouchers in the Nation's Capital," in Berends, *School Choice*, 17–34.

74. Priscilla Ahlgren, "Enrollment in Choice Has Doubled," *Milwaukee Journal*, October 3, 1991, A:1, 21; Priscilla Ahlgren, "Scores Aren't Up Under School Choice," *Milwaukee Journal*, November 21, 1991, A:1, 7; Alan Borsuk, "Study Echoes MPS, Voucher Findings," *Milwaukee Journal Sentinel*, May 27, 2008; and Erin Richards, "Voucher Schools' Graduation Rates Top MPS in Study;

Officials Question Accuracy of Findings," *Milwaukee Journal Sentinel*, February 2, 2010.

75. Alan Borsuk, "No Big Difference Found in MPS, Voucher School Results," *Milwaukee Journal Sentinel*, March 26, 2009; Martin Carnoy, "School Vouchers: Examining the Evidence" (Washington, DC: The Economic Policy Institute, 2001); "Choice Schools Not Outperforming MPS," *Milwaukee Journal Sentinel*, March 29, 2011; David Figlio, "Voucher Outcomes," in Berends, *Handbook*, 321–337, especially 336; Johnnie M. Johnson, "School Choice and Urban Reform: A Case Study of Milwaukee's Parental Choice Program and Black Student Achievement" (PhD diss., University of Wisconsin–Milwaukee, 2004); Erin Richards, *Voucher vs. MPS Students New Data Shows Similar Academic Results, Milwaukee Journal Sentinel*, April 8, 2010; "School Choice Shapes Educational Landscape," *Milwaukee Journal Sentinel*, November 29, 2009; "The Story Behind School Choice Study," *Milwaukee Journal Sentinel*, May 28, 2011; Wisconsin Legislative Audit Bureau, "Test Score Data for Pupils in the Milwaukee Parental Choice Program," September 2008, August 2009, and August 2010; and Patrick J. Wolf, *The Comprehensive Longitudinal Evaluation of the Milwaukee Parental Choice Program: Summary of Fourth Year Reports* (Fayetteville: University of Arkansas, March 2011).

76. "2010–11 Wisconsin Student Assessment System Results," Wisconsin Department of Public Instruction, http://dpi.wi.gov/oea/pdf/mcpc-wsasrslts.pdf.

77. "Board Members Rap School-Choice Plan," *Milwaukee Journal*, January 12, 1989; "School Choice Program Shuts Out Disabled, Federal Complaint Says," *Milwaukee Journal Sentinel*, June 7, 2011.

78. Erin Richards, "Proficiency Drops at Voucher Schools, MPS with New Test Scoring," *Milwaukee Journal Sentinel*, October 24, 2012; Erin Richards, "Wisconsin Voucher Students Lag in State Tests," *Milwaukee Journal Sentinel*, April 23, 2013.

79. Alan J. Borsuk, "Scores Show Voucher Schools Need Accountability," *Milwaukee Journal Sentinel*, December 1, 2012.

80. Mary Jo Cleaver and Scott Eagleburger, *Public School Open Enrollment in Wisconsin 2003–04 and 2004–05: A Report to the Governor and the Legislature* (Madison: Wisconsin Department of Public Instruction, 2007), i; Tom Heinen, "Legislators, Educators Offer New School Plan," *Milwaukee Journal Sentinel*, April 15, 1997. See also "Public School Open Enrollment," Wisconsin Department of Instruction, http://dpi.wi.gov/sms/psctoc.html.

81. Amy Hetzner, "More Students Cross District Lines," *Milwaukee Journal Sentinel*, February 1, 2009.

82. Cleaver and Eagleburger, *Public School Open Enrollment*, iii; Tom Kertscher, "MPS Loses Big in Open Enrollment," *Milwaukee Journal Sentinel*, September 10, 2005. See Ann E. Smejkal, "The Effects of Open Enrollment on Highly Impacted Small Wisconsin School Districts and the Leadership Response" (PhD diss., University of Wisconsin–Milwaukee, 2010) for the only systematic study of the academic and financial effects of open enrollment on school districts.

83. Greg J. Borowski, "MPS Opts to Open Choice Plan to Whites," *Milwaukee Journal Sentinel*, April 29, 1999; Gary Rummler, "MPS Policies, Few Openings Limit Transfers," *Milwaukee Journal Sentinel*, May 11, 1998; Joe Williams, "Benson Says Open Enrollment Is for All," *Milwaukee Journal Sentinel*, July 28, 1998; Joe Williams, "MPS Will Fight Open Enrollment," *Milwaukee Journal Sentinel*, August 12, 1998; Joe Williams, "Pact Lets Students Enroll in Suburbs," *Milwaukee Journal Sentinel*, February 13, 1999; and Joe Williams, "White Parents Challenge Racial Restrictions of Open Enrollment," *Milwaukee Journal Sentinel*, April 19, 1999.

84. Alan J. Borsuk, "Report Find That Mostly White Students Used Open Enrollment," *Milwaukee Journal Sentinel*, September 29, 1999.

85. Alan J. Borsuk, "A New Picture of Public Schools," *Milwaukee Journal Sentinel*, October 17, 2003; Alan J. Borsuk, "MPS Enrollment Declines but Less Than Predicted," *Milwaukee Journal Sentinel*, October 8, 2005. See also Alan J. Borsuk, "The Face of Milwaukee Public Schools Is Changing," *Milwaukee Journal Sentinel*, October 26, 2007; Alan J. Borsuk, "Pupil Transfer Rights Clarified," *Milwaukee Journal Sentinel*, December 21, 2007; and Alan J. Borsuk, "Segregation in U.S. Schools Rising," *Milwaukee Journal Sentinel*, September 16, 2007.

86. Quoted in Alan J. Borsuk, "MPS Watches Students Hop the Border," *Milwaukee Journal Sentinel*, February 5, 2011.

87. Alan J. Borsuk, "MPS Watches Students Hop the Border," *Milwaukee Journal Sentinel*, February 5, 2011. See Amy Hetzner, "More Students Cross District Lines," *Milwaukee Journal Sentinel*, February 1, 2009, for additional statistics.

88. "Neighbors Seek to Revive Bay View High School," *Milwaukee Journal Sentinel*, August 15, 2011.

89. Quoted in Alan J. Borsuk, "MPS Watches Students Hop the Border," *Milwaukee Journal Sentinel*, February 5, 2011; "Wisconsin's Information Network for Successful Schools (WINSS)," Wisconsin Department of Public Instruction, http://data.dpi.state.wi.us/data.

90. Amy Hetzner, "Doors Closed to Some Special Education Students," *Milwaukee Journal Sentinel*, September 22, 2003; Amy Hetzner, "Open Enrollment Gives Disabled More Options," *Milwaukee Journal Sentinel*, December 18, 2006; Amy Hetzner, "Special Education Not So Open," *Milwaukee Journal Sentinel*, February 19, 2001; and Amy Hetzner, "Special Education Rules May Change," *Milwaukee Journal Sentinel*, June 19, 2004.

91. Alan J. Borsuk, "Students Continue to Leave MPS," *Milwaukee Journal Sentinel*, November 24, 2012. See also Alan J. Borsuk, "MPS Watches Students Hop the Border," *Milwaukee Journal Sentinel*, February 5, 2011; Erin Richards, "Fewer Students in MPS Schools," *Milwaukee Journal Sentinel*, October 13, 2011.

92. Joe Williams, "MPS Plans Neighborhood School for North Side," *Milwaukee Journal Sentinel*, May 20, 1998; Dahlk, *Against the Wind*, 607–609.

93. Eugene Kane, "Admissions Plan Fails Student," *Milwaukee Journal Sentinel*, August 31, 1997; Curtis Lawrence, "Attendance OK'd as Enrollment Criteria," *Milwaukee Journal Sentinel*, June 27, 1996; Curtis Lawrence, "Split on MPS

Board Widens with Changes in Policies," *Milwaukee Journal Sentinel*, July 1, 1996; Miner, *Lessons from the Heartland*, 220–225; Gregory Stanford, "MPS Admissions Standards Invite Trouble," *Milwaukee Journal Sentinel*, August 25, 1997; Gregory Stanford, "Rufus King's Risky Reform Bares Watching," *Milwaukee Journal Sentinel*, August 5, 1997; Joe Williams, "3 High Schools Setting Higher Admissions Criteria," *Milwaukee Journal Sentinel*, November 3, 1997; Joe Williams, "MPS Seeks Admissions Standards," *Milwaukee Journal Sentinel*, August 27, 1997; Joe Williams, "More than 430 Apply to Rufus King," *Milwaukee Journal Sentinel*, November 28, 1997; and Joe Williams, "More Schools to Set Requirements," *Milwaukee Journal Sentinel*, August 25, 1998.

94. Quoted in Miner, *Lessons from the Heartland*, 218.

95. "Neighborhood School Plan OK'd," *Milwaukee Journal Sentinel*, December 18, 1997.

96. Alan J. Borsuk and Joe Williams, "Math Figures Heavily in Board Races," *Milwaukee Journal Sentinel*, February 15, 1999; Alan J. Borsuk and Joe Williams, "MPS Election Indicates Drumbeat for Change," *Milwaukee Journal Sentinel*, April 7, 1999; Joe Williams, "All 5 Union Allies Fall in MPS Races," *Milwaukee Journal Sentinel*, April 7, 1999; Joe Williams, "Campaign Spending in Citywide MPS Race Tops $100,000," *Milwaukee Journal Sentinel*, March 30, 1999; Joe Williams, "Election Means Big Changes for MPS," *Milwaukee Journal Sentinel*, April 8, 1999; and Joe Williams, "MPS Race Intrigues Nation, if Not Voters," *Milwaukee Journal Sentinel*, April 4, 1999.

97. Jack Norman, "Voting in Gardner-Taylor Race Is Racially Polarized," *Milwaukee Journal Sentinel*, April 11, 1999.

98. Greg J. Borowski, "MPS Opts to Open Choice Plans to Whites," *Milwaukee Journal Sentinel*, April 29, 199; Miner, *Lessons from the Heartland*, 226; and Joe Williams, "MPS Endorses School Choice Plan," *Milwaukee Journal Sentinel*, May 14, 1999.

99. Dahlk, *Against the Wind*, 616–620.

100. Steven Walters, "Plan to Cut MPS Busing Joins Budget," *Milwaukee Journal Sentinel*, June 9, 1999; Steven Walters and Joe Williams, "MPS Reform Plan May Face Referendum," *Milwaukee Journal Sentinel*, June 23, 1999; Joe Williams, "Legislators Reach Deal to End MPS' Mandatory Busing," *Milwaukee Journal Sentinel*, June 8, 1999; and "Segregation Coming Back in State's Schools, Study Says," *Milwaukee Journal Sentinel*. See also Dahlk, *Against the Wind*, 606–609.

101. Joe Williams, "Stop MPS Busing, Lawmakers Say," *Milwaukee Journal Sentinel*, May 25, 1999.

102. Alan J. Borsuk and Joe Williams, "Area Residents Oppose Busing for Integration, Poll Finds," *Milwaukee Journal Sentinel*, October 18, 1999; Gregory Stanford, "Black Community Must Ask Who's Driving the School," *Milwaukee Journal Sentinel*, October 24, 1999; and Gregory Stanford, "Reaping Busing Plan's Bitter Harvest," *Milwaukee Journal Sentinel*, October 20, 1999.

103. Dennis Chapman and Joe Williams, "Education Measures Key to State Budget Deal," *Milwaukee Journal Sentinel*, October 5, 1999, Steven Walters and Joe

Williams, "Thompson Clears Way for Ending Busing," *Milwaukee Journal Sentinel*, October 26, 1999; Felicia Thomas-Lynn, "Segregation Ruins Neighborhood Schools, Expert Says," *Milwaukee Journal Sentinel*, September 12, 2000; and Anneliese Dickman, "The Implications of Eliminating Busing: Considerations at the End of an Era," with Emily Van Dunk (Milwaukee: The Public Policy Forum, November 1999).

104. *Proceedings*, May 30 and August 24, 2000; Alan J. Borsuk, "MPS Plan Leaves Room for Choices," *Milwaukee Journal Sentinel*, August 14, 2000; Alan J. Borsuk, "MPS Takes a Page from Korté's Book," *Milwaukee Journal Sentinel*, August 29, 2000; Alan J. Borsuk, "School Plan Wins Board's Approval 8–0," *Milwaukee Journal Sentinel*, August 25, 2000; Alan J. Borsuk and Mark Johnson, "MPS Takes Overhaul to Neighborhoods," *Milwaukee Journal Sentinel*, August 21, 2000; and "Public Seems to Accept MPS Plan," *Milwaukee Journal Sentinel*, August 22, 2000.

105. Alan J. Borsuk, "MPS Plan Emphasizes Neighborhood, K–8 Schools," *Milwaukee Journal Sentinel*, August 15, 2000; Wisconsin Legislative Council Staff, "Information Memorandum 99-7, Milwaukee Public Schools Neighborhood School Initiative (1999 Wisconsin Act 9)," December 6, 1999. See also Dahlk, *Against the Wind*, 609–612.

106. Alan J. Borsuk, "Initiatives Rapidly Reshaping MPS," *Milwaukee Journal Sentinel*, January 23, 2004; "MPS to Shut 2 Middle Schools," *Milwaukee Journal Sentinel*, December 22, 2004.

107. Alan J. Borsuk, "Parents Still Prefer Distant MPS Schools," *Milwaukee Journal Sentinel*, July 12, 2001.

108. Alan J. Borsuk, "MPS in Gear to Bus Fewer Students," *Milwaukee Journal Sentinel*, August 23, 2001.

109. Alan J. Borsuk, "Korte Prepared to Quit," *Milwaukee Journal Sentinel*, May 3, 2001; Alan J. Borsuk, "MPS Board Passes on Electing Korte Ally," *Milwaukee Journal Sentinel*, May 4, 2001; and Alan J. Borsuk and Sam Schulhofer-Wohl, "Voters Shake Up School Board," *Milwaukee Journal Sentinel*, April 4, 2001.

110. Alan J. Borsuk, "Board Will Discuss Korte's Job Status at Meeting Thursday," *Milwaukee Journal Sentinel*, June 26, 2001; Alan J. Borsuk and Sam Schulhofer-Wohl, "MPS Reform, Korte's Job in Jeopardy," *Milwaukee Journal Sentinel*, April 15, 2001.

111. Dahlk, *Against the Wind*, 620.

112. Steven Walters, "State ACT Scores Again Best in Nation," *Milwaukee Journal Sentinel*, August 17, 2000; Alan J. Borsuk, "MPS Graduates Just 56% of Class," *Milwaukee Journal Sentinel*, March 11, 2000; Alan J. Borsuk, "9th Grade Is 'Parking Lot' for Thousands of MPS Kids," *Milwaukee Journal Sentinel*, April 16, 2000; and Sam Schulhofer-Wohl, "Report Shows Gap in Graduation Rates," *Milwaukee Journal Sentinel*, November 14, 2001.

113. Alan J. Borsuk, "Citing School Board, MPS Chief Quitting," *Milwaukee Journal Sentinel*, June 15, 2002; Alan J. Borsuk, "Korte Had Enough After Performance Review Meeting," *Milwaukee Journal Sentinel*, June 16, 2002; Sam Schulhofer-Wohl and Tom Held, "Admirers, Critics Generally Agree That Job Is a Tough

One," *Milwaukee Journal Sentinel*, June 15, 2002; and Gregory Stanford, "MPS Takes One on the Chin," *Milwaukee Journal Sentinel*, June 15, 2002.

114. Alan J. Borsuk and Vikki Ortiz, "Andrekopoulos Gets School Chief Job," *Milwaukee Journal Sentinel*, August 23, 2002; Alan J. Borsuk and Vikki Ortiz, "Full of Energy, New MPS Chief Ready to Tackle District's Problems," *Milwaukee Journal Sentinel*, August 24, 2002. See also *Proceedings*, August 22, 2002.

115. Alan J. Borsuk, "MPS Ready to Shake Up System to Make Most of Tight Budget," *Milwaukee Journal Sentinel*, December 9, 2003; Alan J. Borsuk, "Mission Not Yet Accomplished," *Milwaukee Journal Sentinel*, August 25, 2003. See also *Proceedings*, August 28, 2003.

116. Sarah Carr, "MPS Overhauls Enrollment Process," *Milwaukee Journal Sentinel*, October 19, 2004.

117. Alan J. Borsuk, "Building Program on Track in MPS," *Milwaukee Journal Sentinel*, July 8, 2003; "MPS Seeks to Drop Plans for New School," *Milwaukee Journal Sentinel*, September 10, 2003; Amy Hetzner, "Some Fear Busing Cuts Put Students in Harm's Way," *Milwaukee Journal Sentinel*, October 13, 2003; and Gregory Stanford, "What Drives MPS Spending," *Milwaukee Journal Sentinel*, December 10, 2003.

118. Dave Umhoefer and Alan J. Borsuk, "Subtraction by Addition, Part 1 of 3" *Milwaukee Journal Sentinel*, August 17, 2008.

119. Ibid., August 18, 2008.

120. Quoted in ibid, August 17, 2008.

121. Ibid, August 17, 2008.

122. Rick Romell, "Proposal Would Close 3 Schools," *Milwaukee Journal Sentinel*, November 14, 2011.

123. Dave Umhoefer and Alan J. Borsuk, "Subtraction by Addition, Part 1 of 3" *Milwaukee Journal Sentinel*, August 17, 2008.

124. Quoted in Ibid., Part 2 of 3, August 18, 2008. 126. Ibid., August 18, 2008.

125. Ibid., Part 3 of 3, August 19, 2008.

126. Ibid., Part 3 of 3, August 19, 2008.

127. Alan J. Borsuk, "MPS Committee Recommends Expanding King," *Milwaukee Journal Sentinel*, June 11, 2009; *Proceedings*, June 25, 2009.

128. Alan J. Borsuk, "Four More MPS Schools Marked for Closing in Fall," *Milwaukee Journal Sentinel*, February 3, 2005; Alan J. Borsuk, "4 MPS Schools Chosen for Closure," *Milwaukee Journal Sentinel*, October 21, 2005.

129. Georgia Pabst, "Facing an Uncertain Future," *Milwaukee Journal Sentinel*, November 5, 2005; *Proceedings*, June 25, 2005.

130. Quoted in Dave Umhoefer and Alan J. Borsuk, "Subtraction by Addition," *Milwaukee Journal Sentinel*, August 17, 2008.

131. Several books have been written on the small schools movement. Thomas B. Gregory and Gerald R. Smith, *High Schools as Communities: The Small School Reconsidered* (Bloomington, IN: Phi Delta Kappa, 1987) was one of the first. Recent works include Tim L. Adsit, *Small Schools, Education, and the Importance of Community: Pathways to Improvement and a Sustainable Future* (Lanham, MD: Rowman & Littlefield Education, 2011); William Ayers et al., eds., *Simple Justice: The Challenge of Small Schools* (New York: Teachers College

Press, 2000); Gilberto Q. Conchas and Louie F. Rodriguez, *Small Schools and Urban Youth: Using the Power of School Culture to Engage Students* (Thousand Oaks, CA: Corwin Press, 2008); Evans Clinchy, ed., *Creating New Schools: How Small Schools Are Changing American Education* (New York: Teachers College Press, 2000); Jay Feldman et al., *Choosing Small: The Essential Guide to Successful High School Conversion* (San Francisco: Jossey-Bass, 2006); and Thomas Toch, *High Schools on a Human Scale: How Small Schools Can Transform American Education* (Boston: Beacon Press, 2003). See also Alain Jehlen and Cynthia Kopkowski, "Is Smaller Better?," *NEA Today*, February 2006, www .nea.org/home/12214.htm; and Sema Shah et al., "Building a Districtwide Small Schools Movement," Annenberg Institute for School Reform at Brown University, April 2009, http://annenberginstitute.org/pdf/Mott_Oakland_high.pdf.

132. Sarah Carr, "Smaller High Schools Seen as Challenge, Opportunity," *Milwaukee Journal Sentinel*, April 25, 2003.

133. "Gates Foundation to Give Millions to N.Y. Schools," *Milwaukee Journal Sentinel*, September 18, 2003.

134. Sarah Carr, "MPS Calls for Creating 45 'Small' High Schools," *Milwaukee Journal Sentinel*, February 22, 2003; Sarah Carr, "MPS Hope in Small High Schools," *Milwaukee Journal Sentinel*, June 15, 2006. See also Sarah Carr, "Baltimore Thinks 'Small' in Revamp of High Schools," *Milwaukee Journal Sentinel*, March 23, 2003.

135. Nahal Toosi, "Gates Foundation Gives Millions to MPS," *Milwaukee Journal Sentinel*, July 15, 2003.

136. Sarah Carr, "Change Comes, but Changing Perceptions Isn't So Easy," *Milwaukee Journal Sentinel*, November 3, 2003; *Proceedings*, April 22 and May 27, 2004.

137. Sarah Carr, "Dramatic Reconfiguration at MPS Endorsed," *Milwaukee Journal Sentinel,* November 12, 2003. See also Alan J. Borsuk, "Small High Schools Would Mean Big Changes for MPS," *Milwaukee Journal Sentinel*, November 15, 2003.

138. Quoted in Sarah Carr, "Teachers Hope New, Smaller Schools Will Make the Difference," *Milwaukee Journal Sentinel*, September 2, 2004.

139. Sarah Carr, "At Some New MPS High Schools, A-B-Seas and a Haven from Bullies," *Milwaukee Journal Sentinel*, August 1, 2005.

140. Alan J. Borsuk, "MPS Report Finds Continued Crowding in 9th Grade," *Milwaukee Journal Sentinel*, December 13, 2005.

141. Sarah Carr, "At Some New MPS High Schools, A-B-Seas and a Haven from Bullies," *Milwaukee Journal Sentinel*, August 1, 2005.

142. Alan J. Borsuk, "School Conceived in Idealism, Closed in Sadness," *Milwaukee Journal Sentinel*, May 30, 2010; Sarah Carr, "Schools Deal with Shrinking Pains," *Milwaukee Journal Sentinel*, November 12, 2005; and Erin Richards, "Charter School Faces Closing Despite Pleas of Students, Staff," *Milwaukee Journal Sentinel*, January 27, 2011. See also Alan J. Borsuk, "MPS Attendance Slips," *Milwaukee Journal Sentinel*, November 27, 2007; and Erin Richards, "Good City Schools Scarce," *Milwaukee Journal Sentinel*, May 27, 2010.

143. Alan J. Borsuk, "Small Schools Under Microscope," *Milwaukee Journal Sentinel*,

October 12, 2007. See Sarah Carr, "The Struggle to Keep Milwaukee Schools Safe," *Milwaukee Journal Sentinel*, May 6–9, 2007, for more on the increase in violence in MPS.

144. *Bully*, written by Lee Hirsch and Cynthia Owen, directed by Lee Hirsch, produced by the Bully Project, 2011; Erin Richards, "MPS' Alliance Charter School Gets 2-Year Reprieve," *Milwaukee Journal Sentinel*, March 9, 2010; and Erin Richards, "MPS Panel to Debate Future of Alliance Charter School," *Milwaukee Journal Sentinel*, March 8, 2010.

145. Alan J. Borsuk, "Maasai Institute Closes," *Milwaukee Journal Sentinel*, June 26, 2008.

146. Erin Richards, "Free Condom Plan Clears MPS Panel," *Milwaukee Journal Sentinel*, December 9, 2010; Erin Richards, "MPS Plan Targets Weakest Schools," *Milwaukee Journal Sentinel*, March 12, 2010; and Becky Vevea, "MPS' Vel Phillips School Is Targeted for Closure," *Milwaukee Journal Sentinel*, December 15, 2010.

147. Alan J. Borsuk, "School Conceived in Idealism, Closed in Sadness," *Milwaukee Journal Sentinel*, May 30, 2010.

148. Alan J. Borsuk, "Fights, Financial Trouble Blamed for School's Demise," *Milwaukee Journal Sentinel*, October 19, 2006; Alan J. Borsuk and Erin Richards, "MPS High School Ordered Closed," *Milwaukee Journal Sentinel*, October 18, 2006; and *Proceedings*, October 19, 2006.

149. Sarah Carr, "Board Split on School," *Milwaukee Journal Sentinel*, June 27, 2006.

150. Alan J. Borsuk, "Hardin Signals Her Departure," *Milwaukee Journal Sentinel*, March 12, 2009; Alan J. Borsuk, "North Division Makes Comeback," *Milwaukee Journal Sentinel*, March 27, 2009; and *Proceedings*, October 23, 2008, and March 26, 2009.

151. Erin Richards, "Funds Could Help North Division," *Milwaukee Journal Sentinel*, March 12, 2010.

152. Sarah Carr, "Grants Revoked for Two of MPS's Small High Schools," *Milwaukee Journal Sentinel*, March 10, 2006.

153. Erin Richards, "MPS Plan Targets Weakest Schools," *Milwaukee Journal Sentinel*, March 12, 2010.

154. Sarah Carr, "Grants Revoked at Two of MPS's Small High Schools," *Milwaukee Journal Sentinel*, March 10, 2006; Erin Richards, "MPS Agrees to Close, Merge, Move Schools," *Milwaukee Journal Sentinel*, April 1, 2011; Erin Richards, "12 Schools Cited for Low Test Results," *Milwaukee Journal Sentinel*, April 11, 2011; and *Proceedings*, April 21, 2011.

155. Alan J. Borsuk, "MPS Panel Votes to Pull School's Charter," *Milwaukee Journal Sentinel*, April 9, 2008; *Proceedings*, April 24, 2008.

156. Alan J. Borsuk, "Two Small MPS High Schools Might Close," *Milwaukee Journal Sentinel*, January 12, 2009; Dani McClain, "High School Seeks New Quarters," *Milwaukee Journal Sentinel*, September 20, 2008; and *Proceedings*, October 23, 2008, and January 29 and February 26, 2009. See also Linda Spice, "Milwaukee Officers Respond to High School Fight," *Milwaukee Journal Sentinel*, November 25, 2008.

157. Erin Richards, "MPS Plan Targets Weakest Schools," *Milwaukee Journal Sentinel*, March 12, 2010.

158. Erin Richards, "MPS Board Overhauls Schools Lineup for Next Year," *Milwaukee Journal Sentinel*, December 13, 2011; Erin Richards, "MPS Considers Closing Some Schools, Expanding Others," *Milwaukee Journal Sentinel*, December 5, 2011.

159. Erin Richards, "MPS Plan Targets Weakest Schools," *Milwaukee Journal Sentinel*, March 12, 2010; Erin Richards, "Contraceptives at High Schools," *Milwaukee Journal Sentinel*, December 9, 2009; and *Proceedings*, December 17, 2009.

160. Erin Richards, "Principal of High-Achieving MPS High School Steps Down," *Milwaukee Journal Sentinel*, February 16, 2011.

161. Quoted in Alan J. Borsuk, "Making the Grade? Inside MPS High Schools," *Milwaukee Journal Sentinel*, June 11, 2006.

162. Alan J. Borsuk, "Making the Grade? Inside MPS High Schools, Part 1 of 4" *Milwaukee Journal Sentinel*, June 11, 2006.

163. Alan J. Borsuk, "Making the Grade? Inside MPS High Schools, Part 2 of 4" *Milwaukee Journal Sentinel*, June 12, 2006.

164. Alan J. Borsuk, "Making the Grade? Inside MPS High Schools, Part 2 of 4" *Milwaukee Journal Sentinel*, parts 3 and 4, June 13 and 14, 2006.

165. Ibid., June 11, 2006.

166. "A Candid Conversation with Gregory Thornton" and "Thornton Promises Big Changes for MPS," *Milwaukee Journal Sentinel*, July 11, 2010; Alan J. Borsuk, "Making the Grade? Inside MPS High Schools," *Milwaukee Journal Sentinel*, June 11, 2006; Erin Richards, "It's Day One for MPS' New Leader," *Milwaukee Journal Sentinel*, July 2, 2010; and Erin Richards, "Thornton Voted New MPS Chief," *Milwaukee Journal Sentinel*, January 23, 2010. See also Dahlk, *Against the Wind*, 609–612.

167. Alan J. Borsuk, "School Conceived in Idealism, Closed in Sadness," *Milwaukee Journal Sentinel*, May 30, 2010.

168. Erin Richards, "Parents Fret About MPS Mixing Ages," *Milwaukee Journal Sentinel*, July 19, 2010.

169. Alan J. Borsuk, "MPS Has Plans for Marshall Building," *Milwaukee Journal Sentinel*, January 27, 2009; Alan J. Borsuk, "Two Small MPS High Schools Might Close," *Milwaukee Journal Sentinel*, January 12, 2009; Erin Richards, "Panel Votes on Charter Schools," *Milwaukee Journal Sentinel*, March 12, 2009; and *Proceedings*, October 23, 2008.

170. Erin Richards, "Failing Schools Chase U.S. Grants," *Milwaukee Journal Sentinel*, July 7, 2010; Erin Richards, "MPS Agrees to Close, Merge, Move Schools," *Milwaukee Journal Sentinel*, April 1, 2011; Erin Richards, "MPS Lists Cutback Proposals," *Milwaukee Journal Sentinel*, March 19 and 20, 2011; Erin Richards, "Moved Principal Could Be Manager," *Milwaukee Journal Sentinel*, July 26, 2011; and Erin Richards, "Parents Fret About Mixing Ages," *Milwaukee Journal Sentinel*, July 19, 2010.

171. *Proceedings*, April 22, 2014.

172. Alan J. Borsuk, "What Will It Take to Improve Bay View High School's Reputation?," *Milwaukee Journal Sentinel*, October 20, 2012; Jesse Garza, "12 Arrested After Melee at Bay View High School," *Milwaukee Journal Sentinel*, February 6, 2012; Ryan Haggerty, "Bay View Student Stabbed 3 Times on Bus," *Milwaukee Journal Sentinel*, November 12, 2010; Erin Richards, "Bay View to Get New Principal . . . Again?" *Milwaukee Journal Sentinel*, March 27, 2012; and Erin Richards, "Neighbors Seek to Revive Bay View High," *Milwaukee Journal Sentinel*, August 16, 2011.

173. Jay Bullock, "Don't Ignore Strides Made at Bay View High," *Milwaukee Journal Sentinel*, April 17, 2012; Daniel Slapczynski, "How to Fix Bay View High," *Milwaukee Journal Sentinel*, April 10, 2012.

174. Erin Richards, "School Board Approves Major Changes to Bay View High School," *Milwaukee Journal Sentinel*, February 1, 2013.

175. "Long-Range Facilities Master Plan," Milwaukee Public Schools, November 2011, 32; Erin Richards, "MPS Considers Future of Buildings," *Milwaukee Journal Sentinel*, September 20, 2011. The traditional middle schools were cut back to four by 2013. See MPS school selection guide, 2013–14.

176. "Long-Range Facilities Master Plan," 74–75; Erin Richards, "MPS Considers Future of Buildings," *Milwaukee Journal Sentinel*, September 20, 2011.

177. See MPS high school list, http://mpsportal.milwaukee.k12.wi.us/portal/server .pt/comm/high_schools/327.

178. See MPS school selection guide, 2011–12, 2012–13, and 2013–14; Hamilton High School budget, in author's possession.

179. See MPS school selection guide, 2011–12, 2012–13, and 2013–14.

CHAPTER 7

1. The Madison protests were covered by every major media outlet in the United States. See Mary Jo Buhle and Paul Buhle, *It Started in Wisconsin: Dispatches from the Front Lines of the New Labor Protest* (London: Verso: 2011) for a book-length work. See also chapter 25 of Miner, *Lessons from the Heartland*. See Jason Stein and Patrick Marley, "Walker Plan Limits State Unions," *Milwaukee Journal Sentinel*, February 11, 2011, for one of many printed news articles.

2. political articles, nbc26, "Walker 'Divide and Conquer,'" www.youtube.com /watch?v=K1S_Pxw2n-U.

3. See sources in note 1. The protests were also documented through several YouTube videos. See "Wis. union workers, legislators clash," *CBSNewsOnline*, www.youtube.com/watch?v=_uScx1DqtTc; Henry Bloggit, "30,000 in Madison Protest Gov. Walker's Union Busting (Feb 16, 2011)," MSNBC, www.youtube.com /watch?v=SVKNvB8_LKk; and mediagirrl9, "A Guided Tour of the Protest Encampment Inside the Wisconsin State Capitol in Madison," www.youtube .com/watch?v=pOv6S4aACx8. See boredjoewo, "Governor Walker and Koch brother phonecall [sic]," www.youtube.com/watch?v=O7nRjwvUfWM, for Walker's involvement with the Koch brothers. See "The Other Story: Home Made Uprising in Madison Wisconsin," *Russia Today*, www.youtube.com/watch ?v=1mI—Ar8Ry0, for international coverage, and "Wisconsin Protesters Get Pizza Donations," Associated Press, www.youtube.com/watch?v=7mBJgV7wdLc,

for the pizza story. The *Milwaukee Journal Sentinel* and every other Wisconsin newspaper gave in-depth coverage of the protests.

4. Jason Stein, Patrick Marley, and Steve Schultze, "Day 3: Dems Flee," *Milwaukee Journal Sentinel*, February 18, 2011 and innumerable other articles.

5. Jason Stein, Patrick Marley, and Lee Bergquist, "Walker Wins; Battle Shifts," *Milwaukee Journal Sentinel*, March 11, 2011.

6. Patrick Marely, "Assembly OKs Budget with Income Taxes, Sweeping Changes," *Milwaukee Journal Sentinel*, June 19, 2013.

7. Alan J. Borsuk, "New State Budget Continues to Support Some Bad Voucher Schools," *Milwaukee Journal Sentinel*, June 22, 2013; Aaron Cadle, "Milwaukee's Voucher Schools Need to Clean House," *Milwaukee Journal Sentinel*, May 16, 2013; and "Evidence Doesn't Support Choice Program Expansion," *Milwaukee Journal Sentinel*, April 30, 2013.

8. National School Boards Association, "State Voucher Programs," www.nsba.org /Advocacy/Key-Issues/SchoolVouchers/VoucherStrategyCenter/State-Voucher -Programs.pdf; National School Boards Association, "Charter Schools," 12, www.nsba.org/Advocacy/2012-NSBA-Annual-Conference-Advocacy-Handouts /Charter-Schools-Finding-out-the-Facts.pdf.

9. National Alliance for Public Charter Schools, "Public Charter Schools and Teachers Unions," www.publiccharters.org/editor/files/NAPCS%20Documents / PublicCharterSchoolsandTeachersUnions.pdf.

10. Some books that support this theory include Jim Carl, *Freedom of Choice: Vouchers in American Education* (Santa Barbara, CA: ABC-CLIO, 2011); Bill Fletcher, *"They're Bankrupting Us! and 20 Other Myths About Unions* (Boston: Beacon Press, 2012); Mary Lee Smith et al., *Political Spectacle and the Fate of American Schools* (New York: Routledge, 2004); and Lois Weiner, *The Future of Our Schools: Teachers Unions and Social Justice* (Chicago: Haymarket Books, 2012).

11. Quoted in Patrick Marley, "Past School Voucher Advocate Rips Gov. Walker's Plan," *Milwaukee Journal Sentinel*, May 16, 2013.

12. Barry Schwartz, *The Paradox of Choice* (New York: HarperCollins, 2004), 1–3.

13. Ibid., 202, 209.

14. Ibid., 106–107.

15. Ibid., 104.

16. Chester Finn, *We Must Take Charge: Our Schools and Our Future* (New York: The Free Press, 1991); Jay P. Greene, "The Business Model," *Education Next* 2, no. 2 (Summer 2002); Diane Ravitch, *The Death and Life of the Great American School System: How Testing and Choice Are Undermining Education* (New York: Basic Books, 2010), especially chapter 5; and "Testing Our Schools," *Frontline*, 20:7 (March 28, 2002), www.youtube.com/watch?v=X2UGOUGsqVM.

17. Erin Richards, "MPS Scores Near Bottom in National Test," *Milwaukee Journal Sentinel*, December 7, 2011. Detailed reports are available at *The Nation's Report Card*, www.nationsreportcard.gov.

18. Erin Richards, "State, MPS Post Improved High School Graduation Rates," *Milwaukee Journal Sentinel*, May 17, 2012.

19. Samuel Casey Carter, *No Excuses: Lessons from 21 High-Performing, High-Poverty*

Schools (Washington, DC: Heritage Foundation, 2001); Chester Hartman, ed., *Poverty & Race in America: The Emerging Agenda* (Lanham, MD: Rowman & Littlefield Education, 2006); Laura Lippman et al., *Urban Schools: The Challenge of Location and Poverty* (Washington, DC: National Center for Education Statistics, Office of Educational Research and Improvement, July 1996); Susan B. Neuman, *Changing the Odds for Children at Risk: Seven Essential Principles of Educational Programs That Break the Cycle of Poverty* (Westport, CT: Praeger, 2009); Susan B. Neuman, ed., *Educating the Other America: Top Experts Tackle Poverty, Literacy, and Achievement in Our Schools* (Baltimore: Paul H. Brookes Pub., 2008); and Beth Lindsay Templeton, *Understanding Poverty in the Classroom: Changing Perceptions for Student Success* (Lanham, MD: Rowman & Littlefield Education, 2011) are some of the recent books on this topic.

20. Bill Glauber and Ben Poston, "Milwaukee Now Fourth Poorest City in Nation," *Milwaukee Journal Sentinel*, September 28, 2010.

21. There are an abundance of studies on the relationship between family background and educational achievement. Some of the recent ones, from both ends of the political spectrum, include Daniele Checchi, *The Economics of Education: Human Capital, Family Background and Inequality* (Cambridge: Cambridge University Press, 2006); Dalton Conley and Karen Albright, eds., *After the Bell: Family Background, Public Policy and Educational Success* (London: Routledge, 2004); W. Norton Grubb, *The Money Myth: School Resources, Outcomes, and Equity* (New York: Russell Sage Foundation, 2009); and Timothy M. Smeeding et al., *Persistence, Privilege, and Parenting: The Comparative Study of Intergenerational Mobility* (New York: Russell Sage Foundation, 2011).

22. Erin Richards, "MPS Wants to Even Out Special Ed," *Milwaukee Journal Sentinel*, November 23, 2009.

23. "Best High Schools in Wisconsin," *U.S. News & World Report*, www.usnews.com/education/best-high-schools/wisconsin.

24. Quoted in Erin Richards, "MPS Wants to Even Out Special Ed," *Milwaukee Journal Sentinel*, November 23, 2009.

BIBLIOGRAPHY

ARCHIVAL COLLECTIONS

Aukofer, Frank A., Papers, 1957–2000. Milwaukee Manuscript Collection 16. Wisconsin Historical Society. Milwaukee Area Research Center. Golda Meir Library. University of Wisconsin–Milwaukee.

Barbee, Lloyd A., Papers, 1933–1982. Milwaukee Manuscript Collection 16 and Milwaukee Micro Collection 42. Wisconsin Historical Society. Milwaukee Area Research Center. Golda Meir Library. University of Wisconsin–Milwaukee.

Barnhill, Helen I., Papers, 1963–1965. Milwaukee Manuscript Collection 4. Wisconsin Historical Society. Milwaukee Area Research Center. Golda Meir Library. University of Wisconsin–Milwaukee.

Birmingham, Carol. "A Chronology of the Desegregation of Milwaukee Public Schools, 1963–1976, with Emphasis on the Course of the De Facto Segregation Suit and Addendum." Submitted to Frank Zeidler, May 17, 1983. Milwaukee Public Library, July 15, 1996.

A Collection of Papers Relating to the Desegregation/Integration of the Milwaukee Public Schools. Milwaukee Public Library Humanities Room, 1976.

Gronouski, John A., Papers, 1953–1983. Wisconsin Historical Society Archives. Madison, WI.

Harris, Ian M. "The Committee of 100: Citizen Participation in Desegregation." Unpublished report, Milwaukee Public Library, 1977.

Hart, Kathleen Mary. Milwaukee Public Schools Desegregation Collection, 1975–1987. UWM Manuscript Collection 90, Golda Meir Library, University of Wisconsin–Milwaukee.

Milwaukee Urban League Records, 1919–1979. Milwaukee Manuscript Collection EZ. Wisconsin Historical Society. Milwaukee Area Research Center. Golda Meir Library. University of Wisconsin–Milwaukee.

Norquist, John O., Papers, 1970–1988. Milwaukee Manuscript Collection 200. Wisconsin Historical Society. Milwaukee Area Research Center. Golda Meir Library. University of Wisconsin–Milwaukee.

People United for Integrated and Quality Education Papers. In possession of Robert Peterson, Milwaukee, WI.

Radtke, Lorraine, Papers, 1947–1981. UWM Manuscript Collection 64. Wisconsin Historical Society. Milwaukee Area Research Center. Golda Meir Library. University of Wisconsin–Milwaukee.

Sherman Park Community Association. Sherman Park Community Association Records. UWM Manuscript Collection 72. Wisconsin Historical Society. Milwaukee Area Research Center. Golda Meir Library. University of Wisconsin–Milwaukee.

Sherman Park News in Sherman Park Community Association. Sherman Park

Community Association Records. UWM Manuscript Collection 72. Wisconsin Historical Society. Milwaukee Area Research Center. Golda Meir Library. University of Wisconsin–Milwaukee.

BOOKS

Adsit, Tim L. *Small Schools, Education, and the Importance of Community: Pathways to Improvement and a Sustainable Future*. Lanham, MD: Rowman & Littlefield Education, 2011.

Alexander, William M., and Paul S. George. *The Exemplary Middle School*. New York: CBS College Publishing, 1981.

Alkebulan, Paul. *Survival Pending Revolution: The History of the Black Panther Party*. Tuscaloosa: University of Alabama Press, 2007.

Angus, David L., and Jeffrey E. Mirel. *The Failed Promise of the American High School, 1890–1995*. New York: Teachers College, Columbia University, 1999.

Arrow, Kenneth Joseph. *Social Choice and Individual Values*. 2nd ed. New York: Wiley, 1963.

Aukofer, Frank A. *City with a Chance*. Milwaukee: Bruce Pub., 1968.

Ayers, William, et al., eds. *Simple Justice: The Challenge of Small Schools*. New York: Teachers College Press, 2000.

Baugh, Joyce A. *The Detroit School Busing Case:* Milliken v. Bradley *and the Controversy Over Desegregation*. Lawrence: University Press of Kansas, 2011.

Berends, Mark, et al., eds. *Handbook of Research on School Choice*. New York: Routledge, 2009.

Black, Duncan. *Theory of Committees and Elections*. Cambridge: Cambridge University Press, 1958.

Bonner, John. *Introduction to the Theory of Social Choice*. Baltimore: Johns Hopkins University Press, 1986.

Boyd, William Lowe, and Herbert J. Walberg, eds. *Choice in Education: Potential and Problems*. Berkeley, CA: McCutchan Pub. Corp., 1990.

Brown, Elmer Ellsworth. *The Making of Our Middle Schools: An Account of the Development of Secondary Education in the United States*. New York: Longmans, Green, and Co., 1903.

Bruce, William George, ed. *History of Milwaukee, City and County*. Chicago: S.J. Clarke, 1922. Buchanan, James M. *Choice, Contract, and Constitutions*. Indianapolis: Liberty Fund, 2001.

Buchanan, James M., and Gordon Tullock. *The Calculus of Consent: Logical Foundations of Constitutional Democracy*. Ann Arbor: University of Michigan Press, 1962.

Buhle, Mary Jo, and Paul Buhle. *It Started in Wisconsin: Dispatches from the Front Lines of the New Labor Protest*. London: Verso, 2011.

Callaway, Rolland L. *The Milwaukee Public Schools: A Chronological History, 1836–1986*. With Steven Baruch. Thiensville, WI: Caritas Communications, 2008. CD-ROM.

Carl, Jim. *Freedom of Choice: Vouchers in American Education*. Santa Barbara: ABC-CLIO, 2011.

Chubb, John, and Terry Moe. *Politics, Markets, and America's Schools*. Washington, DC: Brookings Institution, 1989.

Chudacoff, Howard P., and Judith E. Smith. *The Evolution of American Urban Society*. 5th ed. Upper Saddle River, NJ: Prentice Hall, 2000.

Clinchy, Evans, ed., *Creating New Schools: How Small Schools Are Changing American Education*. New York: Teachers College Press, 2000.

Conchas, Gilberto Q., and Louie F. Rodriguez. *Small Schools and Urban Youth: Using the Power of School Culture to Engage Students*. Thousand Oaks, CA: Corwin Press, 2008.

Conrad, Howard Louis, ed. *History of Milwaukee County from Its First Settlers to the Year 1895*. Chicago: American Biographical Publishing, 1895.

Cookson, Peter W., and Barbara L. Schneider. *Transforming Schools*. New York: Garland, 1995.

Dahlk, Bill. *Against the Wind: African Americans and the Schools in Milwaukee, 1963–2002*. Milwaukee: Marquette University Press, 2010.

Danford, John W. *Roots of Freedom: A Primer on Modern Liberty*. Wilmington, DE: ISI Books, 2000.

Danns, Dionne. *Something Better for Our Children: Black Organizing in Chicago Public Schools, 1963–71*. New York: Routledge, 2003.

Davis, R. W., ed. *The Origins of Modern Freedom in the West*. Stanford, CA: Stanford University Press, 1995.

d'Avray, D. L. *Medieval Religious Rationalities: A Weberian Analysis*. Cambridge: Cambridge University Press, 2010.

———. *Rationalities in History: A Weberian Essay in Comparison*. Cambridge: Cambridge University Press, 2010.

Dickson, LouAnn S., et al. *Focus on Fundamentals: A Longitudinal Study of Students Attending a Fundamental School*. Arlington, VA: Educational Research Service, 1993.

Donnelly, Patrick. *History of Milwaukee Public Schools*. Milwaukee: Evening Wisconsin Company, 1892.

Dougherty, Jack. *More Than One Struggle: The Evolution of Black School Reform in Milwaukee*. Chapel Hill: University of North Carolina Press, 2004.

Douglas, Davison M. *School Busing: Constitutional and Political Developments*. Vol. 2, *The Public Debate over Busing and Attempts to Restrict Its Use*. New York: Garland Publishing, Inc., 1994.

Downs, Anthony. *An Economic Theory of Democracy*. New York: Harper, 1957.

Duncan, Greg J., and Jeanne Brooks-Gunn, eds. *Consequences of Growing Up Poor*. New York: Russell Sage, 1997.

Dunn, Joshua M., and Martin R. West, eds. *From Schoolhouse to Courthouse: The Judiciary's Role in American Education*. Washington, DC: Thomas B. Fordham Institute, Brookings Institution Press, 2009.

Edari, Ronald S. *The Life Cycle, Segregation and White Attitudes Toward Busing*. Milwaukee: University of Wisconsin–Milwaukee, Urban Research Center, 1977.

Ehrlander, Mary F. *Equal Educational Opportunity: Brown's Elusive Mandate*. New York: LFB Scholarly Publishing, 2002.

Elster, Jon, ed. *Rational Choice*. Oxford: Basil Blackwell, 1986.

Feldman, Jay, et al. *Choosing Small: The Essential Guide to Successful High School Conversion*. San Francisco: Jossey-Bass, 2006.

Finn, Chester. *We Must Take Charge: Our Schools and Our Future*. New York: The Free Press, 1991.

Fischer, David Hackett. *Liberty and Freedom*. Oxford: Oxford University Press, 2005.

Fletcher, Bill. *"They're Bankrupting Us! and 20 Other Myths about Unions*. Boston: Beacon Press, 2012.

Foner, Eric. *The Story of American Freedom*. New York: W.W. Norton, 1998.

Formisano, Ronald. *Boston Against Busing: Race, Class, and Ethnicity in the 1960s and 1970s*. Chapel Hill: University of North Carolina Press, 1991.

Formisano, Ronald P., and Constance K. Burns, eds. *Boston, 1700–1980: The Evolution of Urban Politics*. Westport, CT: Greenwood Press, 1984.

Foss-Mollan, Kate. *Hard Water: Politics and Water Supply in Milwaukee, 1870–1995*. West Lafayette, IN: Purdue University Press, 2001.

Franciosi, Robert J. *The Rise and Fall of American Public Schools: The Political Economy of Public Education in the Twentieth Century*. Westport, CT: Praeger Publishers, 2004.

Friedman, Murray, Roger Meltzer, and Charles Miller, eds. *New Perspectives on School Integration*. Philadelphia: Fortress Press, 1979.

Godwin, R. Kenneth, and Frank R. Kemerer. *School Choice Tradeoffs: Liberty, Equality, and Diversity*. Austin: University of Texas Press, 2002.

Gregory, John G. *History of Milwaukee, Wisconsin*. Chicago: S.J. Clarke, 1931.

Gregory, Thomas B., and Gerald R. Smith. *High Schools as Communities: The Small School Reconsidered*. Bloomington, IN: Phi Delta Kappa, 1987.

Grizzell, Emit Duncan. *Origin and Development of the High School in New England Before 1865*. New York: MacMillan, 1923.

Gruberg, Martin. *A Case Study in U.S. Urban Leadership: The Incumbency of Milwaukee Mayor Henry Maier*. Aldershot, Hants, England: Avebury, 1996.

Gurda, John. *The Making of Milwaukee*. 3rd ed. Milwaukee: Milwaukee County Historical Society, 2008.

Hagedorn, John M. *People and Folks: Gangs, Crime and the Underclass in a Rustbelt City*. Chicago: Lake View Press, 1988.

Hayes, Edward J. *Busing and Desegregation: The Real Truth*. Springfield, IL: Charles C. Thomas, 1981.

Hayes, William. *The Progressive Education Movement: Is It Still a Factor in Today's Schools?* Lanham, MD: Rowman & Littlefield Education, 2006.

Heckelman, Jac C., et al., eds. *Public Choice Interpretations of American Economic History*. Norwell, MA: Kluwer Academic, 2000.

Henig, Jeffrey R. *Rethinking School Choice: Limits of the Market Metaphor*. Princeton: Princeton University Press, 1994.

Herrick, Mary J. *The Chicago Schools: A Social and Political History*. Beverly Hills, CA: Sage Publications, 1971.

Herrnstein, Richard J., and Charles Murray. *The Bell Curve: Intelligence and Class Structure in American Life*. New York: Free Press, 1994.

Hill, Lance. *The Deacons for Defense: Armed Resistance and the Civil Rights Movement*. Chapel Hill: University of North Carolina Press, 2004.

Hirsch, Arnold R. *Making the Second Ghetto: Race and Housing in Chicago, 1940–1960*. Cambridge: Cambridge University Press, 1983. Reprint, Chicago: The University of Chicago Press, 1998.

Holmes, Pauline. *A Tercentenary History of the Boston Public Latin School, 1635–1935*. Cambridge, MA: Harvard University Press, 1935. Reprint, Westport, CT: Greenwood Press, 1970.

Holt, Mikel. *Not Yet "Free at Last": The Unfinished Business of the Civil Rights Movement—Our Battle for School Choice*. Oakland, CA: ICS Press, 2000.

Huyler, Jerome. *Locke in America: The Moral Philosophy of the Founding Era*. Lawrence: University Press of Kansas, 1995.

Jackson, Kenneth T. *Crabgrass Frontier: The Suburbanization of the United States*. New York: Oxford University Press, 1985.

Jacobs, Gregory S. *Getting Around* Brown. Columbus: University of Ohio Press, 1998.

Jacobson, Matthew Frye. *Whiteness of a Different Color: European Immigrants and the Alchemy of Race*. Cambridge, MA: Harvard University Press, 1998.

Jencks, Christopher, and Meredith Phillips, eds. *Black-White Test Score Gap*. Washington, DC: Brookings Institution Press, 1998.

Jones, Patrick D. *The Selma of the North: Civil Rights Insurgency in Milwaukee*. Cambridge, MA: Harvard University Press, 2009.

Joseph, Peniel E. *Waiting 'Til the Midnight Hour: A Narrative History of Black Power in America*. New York: Holt, 2006.

Kammen, Michael. *Spheres of Liberty: Changing Perceptions of Liberty in American Culture*. Madison: University of Wisconsin Press, 1986.

Kincheloe, Joe L., and Kecia Hayes. *Teaching City Kids: Understanding and Appreciating Them*. New York: Peter Lang, 2007.

King, Richard H. *Civil Rights and the Idea of Freedom*. Athens: University of Georgia Press, 1996.

Kirp, David L., et al. *Race, Housing, and the Soul of Suburbia*. New Brunswick, NJ: Rutgers University Press, 1995.

Kluger, Richard. *Simple Justice: The History of* Brown v. Board of Education *and Black America's Struggle for Equality*. New York: Knopf, 1976.

Krug, Edward A. *The Shaping of the American High School, 1880–1920*. Madison: University of Wisconsin Press, 1969.

Kruse, Kevin M. *White Flight: Atlanta and the Making of Modern Conservatism*. Princeton, NJ: Princeton University Press, 2005.

Lamers, William M. *Our Roots Grow Deep*. 2nd ed. Milwaukee: Milwaukee Board of School Directors, 1974.

Leiding, Darlene. *The Hows and Whys of Alternative Education: Schools Where Students Thrive*. Lanham, MD: Rowman & Littlefield Education, 2008.

Levine, Daniel U., and Robert J. Havinghurst, eds. *The Future of Big-City Schools: Desegregation Policies and Magnet Alternatives*. Berkeley, CA: McCutchan Publishing, 1977.

Locke, Michael. *Power and Politics in the School System: A Guidebook*. London: Routledge & Kegan Paul, Ltd., 1974.

Losen, Daniel J., and Gary Orfield, eds. *Racial Inequity in Special Education*. Cambridge, MA: Harvard Education Press, 2002.

Lukas, J. Anthony. *Common Ground: A Turbulent Decade in the Lives of Three American Families*. New York: Knopf, 1985.

Marson, Philip. *Breeder of Democracy*. Cambridge, MA: Schenkman Publishing, 1963.

Mason, Alpheus Thomas, and Richard H. Leach. *In Quest of Freedom: American Political Thought and Practice*. Englewood Cliffs, NJ: Prentice-Hall, 1972.

Massey, Douglas, and Nancy Denton. *American Apartheid: Segregation and the Making of the Underclass*. Cambridge, MA: Harvard University Press, 1993.

McCarthy, John M. *Making Milwaukee Mightier: Planning and the Politics of Growth, 1910–1960*. DeKalb: Northern Illinois University Press, 2009.

McLean, Iain, and Arnold B. Urken, eds. *Classics of Social Choice*. Ann Arbor: University of Michigan Press, 1995.

McMillan, Charles B. *Magnet Schools: An Approach to Voluntary Desegregation*. Bloomington, IN: Phi Delta Kappa Educational Foundation, 1980.

McMurrin, Lee. Untitled unpublished manuscript, author's possession.

Merritt, Edwin T., ed. *Magnet and Specialized Schools of the Future: A Focus on Change*. Lanham, MD: Scarecrow Education, 2005.

Metcalf, George R. *From Little Rock to Boston: The History of School Desegregation*. Westport, CT: Greenwood Press, 1983.

Meyer, Stephen. *"Stalin over Wisconsin": The Making and Unmaking of Militant Unionism, 1900–1950*. New Brunswick, NJ: Rutgers University Press, 1992.

Miner, Barbara J. *Lessons from the Heartland: A Turbulent Half Century of Public Education in an Iconic American City*. New York: The New Press, 2013.

Mirel, Jeffrey. *The Rise and Fall of an Urban School System: Detroit, 1907–81*. Ann Arbor: The University of Michigan Press, 1993.

Mitchell, George A., and the Wisconsin Policy Research Institute. *An Evaluation of State-Financed School Integration in Metropolitan Milwaukee*. Milwaukee: Wisconsin Policy Research Institute, 1989.

Modlinski, Jules, and Esther Zaret. *The Federation of Independent Community Schools: An Alternative Urban School System*. Milwaukee, 1970.

Mondale, Sarah, and Sarah B. Patton, eds. *School: The Story of American Public Education*. Boston: Beacon Press, 2001.

Olson, Mancur, Jr., *The Logic of Collective Action: Public Goods and the Theory of Groups*. Cambridge, MA: Harvard University Press, 1965.

O'Reilly, Charles T., et al. *The People of the Inner Core—North*. New York: LePlay Research, 1974.

Orfield, Gary. *Must We Bus?: Segregated Schools and National Policy*. Washington, DC: The Brookings Institution, 1978.

Orfield, Gary, Susan E. Eaton, and the Harvard Project on School Desegregation, eds. *Dismantling Desegregation: The Quiet Reversal of Brown v. the Board of Education*. New York: The New Press, 1996.

Patterson, James T. Brown v. Board of Education: *A Civil Rights Milestone and Its Troubled Legacy*. Oxford: Oxford University Press, 2001.

Pereles, Jas. M. *Historical Sketch: The Milwaukee School Board, 1845–1895*. Milwaukee, 1895.

Peterson, Paul E., ed. *Choice and Competition in American Education*. Lanham, MD: Rowman & Littlefield Publishers, 2006.

Powell, John. A., Gavin Kearney, and Vina Kay, eds. *In Pursuit of a Dream Deferred: Linking Housing & Education Policy*. New York: Peter Lang, 2001.

Pride, Richard A., and J. David Woodard. *The Burden of Busing: The Politics of Desegregation in Nashville, Tennessee*. Knoxville: The University of Tennessee Press, 1985.

Quinby, Lee. *Freedom, Foucault, and the Subject of America*. Boston: Northeastern University Press, 1991.

Ravitch, Diane. *The Death and Life of the Great American School System: How Testing and Choice Are Undermining Education*. New York: Basic Books, 2010.

———. *The Great School Wars: A History of the New York City Public Schools*. Rev. ed. Baltimore: Johns Hopkins University Press, 2000.

———. *The Troubled Crusade: American Education, 1945–1980*. New York: Basic Books, 1983.

Ravitch, Diane, and Joseph P. Viteritti, eds. *New Schools for a New Century: The Redesign of Urban Education*. New Haven, CT: Yale University Press, 1997.

Reese, William J. *The Origins of the American High School*. New Haven, CT: Yale University Press, 1995.

Rosenbloom, David H., and Rosemary O'Leary. *Public Administration and Law*. New York: M. Dekker, 1997.

Rossell, Christine H. *The Carrot or the Stick for School Desegregation Policy: Magnet Schools or Forced Busing*. Philadelphia: Temple University Press, 1990.

Rothstein, Richard. *Class and Schools: Using Social, Economic, and Educational Reform to Close the Black-White Achievement Gap*. Washington, DC: Economic Policy Institute, 2004.

Rury, John L., and Frank A. Cassell, eds. *Seeds of Crisis: Public Schooling in Milwaukee Since 1920*. Madison: University of Wisconsin Press, 1993.

Schofield, Norman. *Architects of Political Change: Constitutional Quandaries and Social Choice Theory*. Cambridge: Cambridge University Press, 2006.

Schueler, D. H. *Milwaukee Public Schools: Historical Sketch*. Milwaukee, 1904.

Schwartz, Barry. *The Paradox of Choice*. New York: HarperCollins, 2004.

Scott, Janelle T., ed. *School Choice and Diversity: What the Evidence Says*. New York: Teachers College Press, 2005.

Seligman, Amanda I. *Block by Block: Neighborhoods and Public Policy on Chicago's West Side*. Chicago: University of Chicago Press, 2005.

Shuffelton, Frank, ed. *The American Enlightenment*. Rochester, NY: University of Rochester Press, 1993.

Smith, Mary Lee, et al. *Political Spectacle and the Fate of American Schools*. New York: Routledge, 2004.

Smrekar, Claire, and Ellen Goldring. *School Choice in Urban America: Magnet*

Schools and the Pursuit of Equity. New York: Teachers College Press, 1999.

Spring, Joel H. *The American School, 1642–1996*. 4th ed. New York: McGraw-Hill, 1997.

Stephan, Walter G., and Joe R. Feagin, eds. *School Desegregation: Past, Present, and Future*. New York: Plenum Press, 1980.

Still, Bayrd. *Milwaukee: The History of a City*. Madison: State Historical Society of Wisconsin, 1940.

Stivers, Richard. *The Illusion of Freedom and Equality*. Albany: State University of New York Press, 2008.

Sugrue, Thomas J. *The Origins of the Urban Crisis: Race and Inequality in Postwar Detroit*. Princeton, NJ: Princeton University Press, 1996.

———. *Sweet Land of Liberty: The Forgotten Struggle for Civil Rights in the North*. New York: Random House, 2008.

Tanzilo, Robert. *Historic Milwaukee Public Schoolhouses*. Charleston, SC: The History Press, 2012.

Tatum, Beverly Daniel. *"Why Are All the Black Kids Sitting Together in the Cafeteria?": A Psychologist Explains the Development of Racial Identity*. New York: Basic Books, 2003.

Taylor, Clarence. *Knocking at Our Own Door: Milton A. Galamison and the Struggle to Integrate New York City Schools*. New York: Columbia University Press, 1997.

Taylor, Steven J. L. *Desegregation in Boston and Buffalo: The Influence of Local Leaders*. Albany: State University of New York Press, 1998.

Thayer, V. T. *Formative Ideas in American Education: From the Colonial Period to the Present*. New York and Toronto: Dodd, Mead & Co., 1965.

Theoharis, Jeanne. "'I'd Rather Go to School in the South': How Boston's School Desegregation Complicates the Civil Rights Paradigm." In *Freedom North: Black Freedom Struggles Outside the South, 1940–1980*, edited by Jeanne Theoharis and Komozi Woodard. New York: Palgrave Macmillan, 2003.

Thernstrom, Abigail, and Stephan Thernstrom. *No Excuses: Closing the Racial Gap in Learning*. New York: Simon and Schuster, 2003.

Thompson, Tommy. *Power to the People: An American State at Work*. New York: HarperCollins, 1996.

Toch, Thomas. *High Schools on a Human Scale: How Small Schools Can Transform American Education*. Boston: Beacon Press, 2003.

Tozer, Steven E., Paul C. Violas, and Guy Sense. *School and Society: Historical and Contemporary Perspectives*. 6th ed. New York: McGraw-Hill, 2009.

Trotter, Joe William, Jr. *Black Milwaukee: The Making of an Industrial Proletariat, 1915–1945*. Urbana: University of Illinois Press, 2007.

Tyack, David B. *The One Best System: A History of American Urban Education*. Cambridge, MA: Harvard University Press, 1974 .

Vassar, Rena L. *Social History of American Education*. Chicago: Rand McNally, 1965.

Walker, Decker F., and Jonas F. Soltis. *Curriculum and Aims*. New York: Teachers College Press and Columbia University, 2004.

Warner, W. Lloyd, Robert Havighurst, and Martin Loeb. *Who Shall Be Educated?* New York: Harper and Brothers, 1944.

Weinberg, Meyer. *Race and Place: A Legal History of the Neighborhood School.* Washington, DC: US Government Printing Office, 1967.

Weiner, Lois. *The Future of Our Schools: Teachers Unions and Social Justice.* Chicago: Haymarket Books, 2012.

Wells, Robert W. *This Is Milwaukee.* Garden City, NY: Doubleday, 1970.

Welter, Rush. *Popular Education and Democratic Thought in America.* New York: Columbia University Press, 1962.

Wenzel, Michael. *My Life in Milwaukee Public Schools: Kindergarten to Retirement.* AuthorHouse, 2005.

The Western Historical Company. *History of Milwaukee, Wisconsin, from Pre-Historic Times to the Present Date, Embracing a Summary Sketch of the Native Tribes, and an Exhaustive Record of Men and Events for the Past Century; Describing the City, Its Commercial, Religious, Educational and Benevolent Institutions, Its Government, Courts, Press, and Public Affairs; and Including Nearly Four Thousand Biographical Sketches of Pioneers and Citizens.* Chicago: The Western Historical Company, 1881.

Whipple, Leon. *The Story of Civil Liberty in the United States.* New York: Vanguard Press, 1927. Reprint, New York: Da Capo Press, 1970.

Wilkinson, Doreen H. *Community Schools: Education for Change.* Boston: National Association of Independent Schools, 1973.

Wilkinson, J. Harvie, III. *From Brown to Bakke: The Supreme Court and School Integration, 1954–1978.* New York: Oxford University Press, 1979.

Witte, John F. *The Market Approach to Education: An Analysis of America's First Voucher Program.* Princeton, NJ: Princeton University Press, 2000.

Wood, Gordon S. *The Idea of America: Reflections on the Birth of the United States.* New York: Penguin Press, 2011.

FILMS

Cullinan, Jones. *Forced Choice: The Milwaukee Plan; A Model for Northern School Desegregation.* VHS. Produced and directed by Jones Cullinan. Milwaukee: Medusa Veritape, 1980.

Hirsch, Lee, and Cynthia Owen. *Bully.* Directed by Lee Hirsch. Produced by the Bully Project, 2011.

Stockwell, John. *Cheaters.* Directed by John Stockwell. Produced by Kevin Reidy and Gloria Jean Sykes. Home Box Office, 2000.

"Testing Our Schools." *Frontline,* 20:7 (March 28, 2002).

WEBSITES

"2011–2012 School Profiles for High Schools." Houston Independent School District. www.houstonisd.org/Page/61439.

"2012 Texas NCLB Report Card Campus Report." Texas Education Agency. http://ritter.tea.state.tx.us/perfreport/nclb/2012/campus.srch.html.

"About Bay View Today." The Bay View Historical Society. www.bayviewhistoricalsociety.org/Bay%20View%20Today.html.

"American FactFinder." Bureau of the Census. http://factfinder2.census.gov.

"Best High School Rankings by State." *U.S. News & World Report*. www.usnews.com /education/best-high-schools.

Boston Latin School. www.bls.org.

Bronx High School of Science. www.bxscience.edu.

City of Boston. www.cityofboston.gov/archivesandrecords/ deseg-era.xml.

"Education: Sarah Roberts vs. Boston." The Massachusetts Historical Society. www.masshist.org/longroad/02education/roberts.htm.

"Enrollment Public School Reports, 2011–12." Pennsylvania Department of Education. www.education.state.pa.us/portal/server.pt/community/enrollment /7407/public_school_enrollment_reports/620541.

Magnet Schools of America. www.magnet.edu.

"McCarver Elementary School." Tacoma Public Schools. www.tacoma.k12.wa.us /Schools/es/Pages/McCarver.aspx.

Milwaukee Neighborhoods Photos and Maps, 1885–1992. Milwaukee: Golda Meir Library, 2007. www4.uwm.edu/libraries/digilib/Milwaukee/ index.cfm.

National Alliance for Public Charter Schools. www.publiccharters.org.

National School Boards Association. http://nsba.org.

"Publicly Funded School Voucher Programs." National Conference of State Legislators. www.ncsl.org/issues-research/educ/school-choice-vouchers.aspx.

"School and District Profiles." Massachusetts Department of Elementary and Secondary Education (ESE). http://profiles.doe.mass.edu.

"School Vouchers: Issues and Arguments." School Choices. 1998. www.school choices.org/roo/vouchers.htm.

United States Academic Decathlon. www.usad.org.

"Washington State Report Card." Office of Superintendent of Public Instruction. http://reportcard.ospi.k12.wa.us.

Whitney M. Young Magnet High School. www.wyoung.org.

"Wisconsin Governor John W. Reynolds." The National Governors Association. www.nga.org/cms/home/governors/past-governors-bios/page_wisconsin/col2 -content/main-content-list/title_reynolds_john.html.

"Wisconsin's Information Network for Successful Schools (WINSS)." Wisconsin Department of Public Instruction. http://data.dpi.state.wi.us/data.

MAGAZINE AND JOURNAL ARTICLES
USED AS PRIMARY SOURCES

"Can the Boys Be Saved?" *Newsweek*, October 15, 1990. Also appearing in *USA Today*, October 11, 1990, and *Washington Post*, February 15, 1991.

Goldstein, Dana. "Bostonians Committed to School Diversity Haven't Given Up on Busing." *The Atlantic Cities,* October 10, 2012. www.theatlanticcities.com /politics/2012/10/bostonians-committed-school-diversity-havent-given -busing/3544.

McGroarty, Daniel. "Teacher Knows Best." *National Review* 47 (1995): 62–64.

McMurrin, Lee. "Educational Change: It Can Work to Your Advantage." *Theory into Practice* 20, no. 4 (1981): 264–268.

Murphy, Bruce. "Forced Choices." *Milwaukee Magazine*, January 1982, 56–58.

Whitaker, Charles. "Do Black Males Need Special Schools?" *Ebony*, March 1991, 18.

MAGAZINE AND JOURNAL ARTICLES
USED AS SECONDARY SOURCES

André-Bechely, Lois. "Finding Space and Managing Distance: Public School Choice in an Urban California District." *Urban Studies* 44, no. 7 (June 2007): 1355–1376.

Archbald, Douglas A. "School Choice, Magnet Schools, and the Liberation Model: An Empirical Study." *Sociology of Education* 77 (October 2004): 283–310.

Bamberger, Tom. "The Education of Howard Fuller." *Milwaukee Magazine*, July 1988, 56–59.

Boyd, William Lowe. "Choice Plans for Public Schools in the USA: Issues and Answers." *Local Government Policy Making* 18 (July 1993): 20–27.

Brandstetter, John, and Charles R. Foster. "Quality Integrated Education in Houston's Magnet Schools." *Phi Delta Kappan* 57, no. 8 (April 1976): 502–506.

Bush, Lawson V., Hansel Burley, and Tonia Causey-Bush. "Magnet Schools: Desegregation or Resegregation? Students' Voices from Inside the Walls." *American Secondary Education* 29, no. 3 (2001): 33–50.

Charne, Irvin B. "The Milwaukee Cases." *Marquette Law Review* 89 (2005): 83–85.

Chen, Grace. "What Is a Magnet School?" *Public School Review*, December 4, 2007. http://publicschoolreview.com/articles/2.

Cohen, Sol. "The Industrial Education Movement." *American Quarterly* 28, no. 1 (1968): 95–110.

Conneely, Nancy. "After PICS: Making the Case for Socioeconomic Integration." *Texas Journal of Civil Liberties and Civil Rights* 12, no. 1 (2008): 95–125.

Costrell, Robert M. "Who Gains, Who Loses?: The Fiscal Impact of the Milwaukee Parental Choice Program." *Education Next* 9, no. 1 (2009): 62–69.

Cronin, Joseph M. "City School Desegregation and the Creative Uses of Enrollment Decline." *Equity & Excellence in Education* 15, no. 1 (January 1977): 10–12.

Foss-Mollan, Kate. "Waiting for Water: Service Discrimination and Polish Neighborhoods in Milwaukee, 1870–1910." *Michigan Historical Review* 25, no. 2 (1999): 29–46.

Fuerst, J. S., and Daniel Pupo. "Desegregated Schooling: The Milwaukee Experience." *Urban Education* 18, no. 2 (July 1983): 229–244.

Fuller, Bruce. "School Choice: Who Gains, Who Loses?" *Issues in Science and Technology* (Spring 1996): 61–67.

Gelber, Scott. "'The Crux and the Magic': The Political History of Boston Magnet Schools, 1968–1989." *Equity & Excellence in Education* 41, no. 4 (December 2008): 453–466.

Godwin, R. Kenneth, et al. "Sinking Swann: Public School Choice and the Resegregation of Charlotte's Public Schools." *Review of Policy Research* 23, no. 5 (2006): 983–997.

Gordon, William M. "The Implementation of Desegregation Plans Since *Brown*." *The Journal of Negro Education* 63, no. 3 (Summer 1994): 310–322.

Gore, Elaine Clift. "A Place to Belong: Student Agency in the Social Capital of a Magnet School." *Journal of Curriculum and Supervision* 20, no. 4 (2005): 271–297.

Greene, Jay P. "The Business Model." *Education Next* 2, no. 2 (Summer 2002).

Harris, Ian M. "Criteria for Evaluating School Desegregation in Milwaukee." *Journal of Negro Education* 52, no. 4 (Autumn 1983): 423–435.

Hellman, Walter. "Early NYC High School Physics and Development of the Science Magnet School." *The Physics Teacher* 43 (2005): 598–601.

Hendrie, Caroline. "Houston Reaches for Diversity Without Quotas." *Education Week* 17, no. 39 (1998): 11.

Henig, Jeffrey R. "Choice in Public Schools: An Analysis of Transfer Requests Among Magnet Schools." *Social Science Quarterly* 71, no. 1 (March 1990): 68–82.

———. "Choice, Race, and Public Schools: The Adoption and Implementation of a Magnet Program." *Journal of Urban Affairs* 11, no. 3 (1989): 243–259.

Jehlen, Alain, and Cynthia Kopkowski. "Is Smaller Better?" *NEA Today,* February 2006. www.nea.org/home/12214.htm.

Jones, Philip. "All about Those New 'Fundamental' Public Schools, What They're Promising, and Why They're Catching On." *American School Board Journal* (1976): 24–31.

The JBHE Foundation. "Almost No Blacks at Many of the Nation's Highest-Rated Public High Schools." *The Journal of Blacks in Higher Education*, no. 41 (Autumn 2003): 60–62.

Kantor, Harvey. "Choosing a Vocation: The Origins and Transformation of Vocational Guidance in California, 1910–1930." *History of Education Quarterly* 26, no. 3 (Fall 1986): 351–365.

Lavertu, Stéphane, and John Witte. "The Impact of Milwaukee Charter Schools on Student Achievement." *Issues in Governance Studies,* no. 23 (March 2009), 1–10.

Leahy, Stephen M. "Polish American Reaction to Civil Rights in Milwaukee, 1963 to 1965." *Polish American Studies* 63, no. 1 (2006): 35–56.

Mayer, Anysia P. "Expanding Opportunities for High Academic Achievement: An International Baccalaureate Diploma Program in an Urban High School." *Journal of Advanced Academics* 19, no. 2 (Winter 2008): 202–235.

McMillan, Charles B. "Magnet Education in Boston." *Phi Delta Kappan* 59, no. 3 (November 1977): 158–163.

Morgan, David R., and Robert E. England. "Large District School Desegregation: A Preliminary Assessment of Techniques." *Social Science Quarterly* 63 (December 1982): 688–700.

Morris, Jerome E., and Ellen Goldring. "Are Magnet Schools More Equitable? An Analysis of the Disciplinary Rates of African American and White Students in Cincinnati Magnet and Nonmagnet Schools." *Equity & Excellence in Education* 32, no. 3 (December 1999): 59–65.

"Most Believe Integration Improved Education for Black Students, Poll Finds." *Black Issues in Higher Education* 21, no. 7 (May 20, 2004): 12.

Murphy, Bruce, and John Pawasarat. "Why It Failed: Desegregation 10 Years Later." *Milwaukee Magazine*, September 1986, 36–46.

Nelson, Adam R. *The Elusive Ideal: Equal Educational Opportunity and the Federal Role in Boston's Public Schools, 1950–1985.* Chicago: University of Chicago Press, 2005.

Orfield, Gary. "Public Opinion and School Desegregation." *Teachers College Record* 96 (1995): 654–669.

Renzulli, Linda A., and Lorraine Evans. "School Choice, Charter Schools, and White Flight." *Social Problems* 52, no. 3 (August 2005): 398–418.

Rickles, Jordan, and Paul M. Ong. "The Integrating (and Segregating) Effect of Charter, Magnet, and Traditional Elementary Schools: The Case of Five California Metropolitan Areas." *California Politics and Policy* 9, no. 1 (June 2005): 16–38.

Rose, Harold M. "The Development of an Urban Subsystem: The Case of the Negro Ghetto." *Annals of the Association of American Geographers* 60, no. 1 (1970): 1–17.

Rosenbaum, James E., and Stefan Presser. "Voluntary Integration in a Magnet School." *The School Review* 86, no. 2 (February 1978): 156–186.

Rossell, Christine H. "Controlled-Choice Desegregation Plans: Not Enough Choice, Too Much Control?" *Urban Affairs Review* 31, no. 1 (1995): 43–76.

———. "The Desegregation Efficiency of Magnet Schools." *Urban Affairs Review* 38, no. 5 (May 2003): 697–725.

———. "Is It the Busing or the Blacks?" *Urban Affairs Quarterly* 24, no. 1 (1988): 139–145.

———. "Magnet Schools as a Desegregation Tool: The Importance of Contextual Factors in Explaining Their Success." *Urban Education* 14, no. 3 (October 1979): 303–320.

———. "Whatever Happened to . . . Magnet Schools?" *Education Next* 5, no. 2 (Spring 2005): 46–47.

Rossell, Christine H., and David J. Armor. "The Effectiveness of School Desegregation Plans, 1968–1991." *American Politics Quarterly* 24, no. 3 (1996): 267–302.

Saporito, Salvatore, and Deenesh Sohoni. "Mapping Educational Inequality: Concentrations of Poverty among Poor and Minority Students in Public Schools." *Social Forces* 85, no. 3 (2007): 1227–1253.

Schug, Mark C., and M. Scott Niederjohn. "The Milwaukee Teacher Residency Requirement: Why It's Bad for Schools, and Why It Won't Go Away." *Wisconsin Policy Research Institute* 19, no. 5 (June 2006), 1–25.

Selig, Ralph. "The Educational Bastion of the Bronx: The Uniqueness of the Bronx High School of Science." *Bronx County Historical Society Journal* 34, no. 1 (1997): 1–3.

Sergienko, Alex. "How a Small City in the Pacific Northwest Invented Magnet Schools." *Education Next* 5, no. 2 (Spring 2005): 49.

Shah, Sema, et al. "Building a Districtwide Small Schools Movement." Annenberg Institute for School Reform at Brown University (April 2009). http://annenberginstitute.org/pdf/Mott_Oakland_high.pdf.

Simonsen, Judith A. "The Third Ward: Symbol of Ethnic Identity." *Milwaukee History* 10, no. 2 (1987): 61–76.

Sitkoff, Harvard. "Segregation, Desegregation, Resegregation: African American Education; A Guide to the Literature." *Magazine of History* 15, no. 20 (Winter 2001): 6–13.

Slotten, Hugh R. "Science, Education, and Antebellum Reform: The Case of Alexander Dallas Bache." *History of Education Quarterly* 31, no. 3 (Fall 1991): 323–342.

Squires, Gregory D., and William Velez. "Neighborhood Racial Composition and Mortgage Lending: City and Suburban Differences." *Journal of Urban Affairs* 9 (1987): 217–232.

Staiger, Annegret. "Whiteness as Giftedness: Racial Formation at an Urban High School." *Social Problems* 51, no. 3 (2004): 161–181.

Weber, Larry, et al. "An Evaluation of Fundamental Schools." *Evaluation Review* 8, no. 5 (1984): 595–614.

West, Kimberly C. "A Desegregation Tool That Backfired: Magnet Schools and Classroom Segregation." *The Yale Law Journal* 103, no. 8 (June 1994): 2567–2592.

Wilson, William H. "Desegregation of the Hamilton Park School, 1955–1975." *Southwestern Historical Quarterly* 95, no. 1 (1991): 42–63.

Wolkomir, Richard. "The Winning Equation at 'P.S. IQ': Bright Kids, Good Teachers, Hard Work." *Smithsonian* 16, no. 2 (1985): 80–89.

Wraga, William G. "A Progressive Legacy Squandered: The *Cardinal Principles* Report Reconsidered." *History of Education Quarterly* 41, no. 4 (Winter 2001): 494–519.

REPORTS AND LEGAL DOCUMENTS

A+ Schools. "2009 Report to Community of Public School Progress in Pittsburgh." www.aplusschools.org/pdf/cspr09/A+Intro[1].pdf.

———. "2010 Report to Community of Public School Progress in Pittsburgh." www.aplusschools.org/pdf/cspr10/ A+2010-front.pdf.

Academy for Educational Development. *Quality Education in Milwaukee's Future: Recommendations to the Citizens Advisory Committee to Comprehensive Survey of Milwaukee Public Schools and the Milwaukee Board of School Directors*. New York: Academy for Educational Development, 1967.

Barbee, Lloyd A., and Irvin B. Charne. "Milwaukee School Desegregation Federal Court Litigation." Wisconsin Bar Association. www.wisbar.org/AM/Template.cfm?Section=Home&TEMPLATE=/CM/ContentDisplay.cfm&CONTENTID=52530.

Blexrud, John H., and Paul Tsao, eds. *Data Reference Book for Political, Desegregation, and Crime Studies in Milwaukee and Wisconsin, 1975-1976*. Milwaukee Journal/Milwaukee Sentinel and the University of Wisconsin–Milwaukee, 1977.

Boston Public Schools. "MCAS Individual School Results." www.bostonpublicschools.org/files/MCAS%20School%20Results%201998–2007.pdf.

———. "Report on Achievement Gap: The State of Student Subgroups Performance: 2008 Performance by Improvement." www.bostonpublicschools.org/files/Boston%20Spring%202009%20MCAS%20Results%20Summary.pdf.

Buffalo Public Schools. "2009–10 Accountability Status for Buffalo Schools, as of March 2010." www.buffaloschools.org/SharedAccountability.cfm?subpage=46152.

Carnoy, Martin. "School Vouchers: Examining the Evidence." Washington, DC: The Economic Policy Institute, 2001.

Carnoy, Martin, et al. "Vouchers and Public School Performance: A Case Study of the Milwaukee Parental Choice Program." Washington, DC: The Economic Policy Institute, 2007.

City of Chicago. "[Whitney] Young Magnet High School." 2012 Illinois School Report Card. Chicago: City of Chicago, 2012. http://webprod.isbe.net /ereportcard/publicsite/getReport.aspx?year=2012&code=1501629900764 _e.pdf.

Dodenhoff, David. "Fixing the Milwaukee Public Schools: The Limits of Parent-Driven Reform." *Wisconsin Policy Research Institute Report* 20, no. 8 (October 2007), 1–16.

Find Law for Legal Professionals. "U.S. Constitution: Fourteenth Amendment." http://supreme.lp.findlaw.com/constitution/amendment14/25.html.

Gill, Brian, et al. "Assessing the Performance of Public Schools in Pittsburgh." RAND Education. Working paper, December 2, 2005. www.rand.org/content /dam/rand/pubs/working_papers/2005/RAND_WR315–1.pdf.

Gillespie, Mark. "Americans Want Integrated Schools, but Oppose School Busing." *Gallup News Service*, September 27, 1999. www.gallup.com/poll/3577/Americans -Want-Integrated-Schools-Oppose-School-Busing.aspx.

Illinois State Board of Education. "City of Chicago SD 299, 2009–10 School Year Report Card District Summary." http://webprod1.isbe.net/ereportcard /publicsite/getReport.aspx?year=2010&code=150162990ds_e.html.

Luce, Maria. "Supportive Data to Facilitate School Integration Planning for the City of Milwaukee." Center for Urban Community Development, University of Wisconsin–Extension, April 1976.

McKenzie Group. "Options for Organizing the Milwaukee Public Schools." Milwaukee: Milwaukee Public Schools, August 15, 1988.

Miller, John J. "Strategic Investment in Ideas: How Two Foundations Reshaped America." Washington, DC: The Philanthropy Roundtable, 2003.

Milwaukee Board of School Directors. *Proceedings of the Board of School Directors.* Milwaukee: The Board of School Directors.

Milwaukee Public Schools. "Chapter 220 Enrollment." www2.milwaukee.k12.wi.us /supt/Chapter220_ Enrollment.html.

———. "A Plan for Improvement of Milwaukee's School Operations." Believed to have been written in 1967. In author's possession.

———. "Long-Range Facilities Master Plan," November 2011.

Milwaukee Public Schools Office of Research and Evaluation. District and School Report Cards. http://www2.milwaukee.k12.wi.us/acctrep/mpsrc.html.

Milwaukee Urban Atlas Population Characteristics. Milwaukee: Milwaukee Public Library, 2003. http://city.milwaukee.gov/ImageLibrary/Groups/cityDCD /planning/data/pdfs/UrbanAtlasPopulation.pdf.

Molnar, Alex. "Educational Vouchers: A Review of the Research." Center for Education Research, Analysis and Innovation, University of Wisconsin–Milwaukee, October 1999.

"New York Magnet Schools." *Public School Review*. www.publicschoolreview.com /state_magnets/stateid/NY.

North Central Regional Educational Laboratory. "Decentralization: Why, How, and What Ends?" Last modified 1993. www.ncrel.org/sdrs/areas/issues /envrnmnt/go93-1milw.htm.

Office of the Superintendent. "Policies and Procedures Relating to Pupil Transportation." Milwaukee: Milwaukee Public Schools.

Office of the Superintendent. "Report of School District Changes in Central Area of Milwaukee 1943–1953–1963." Milwaukee: Milwaukee Public Schools, January 1964.

Office of the Superintendent of Public Instruction. "Washington State Report Card." http://reportcard.ospi.k12.wa.us.

Ohio Department of Education. "Cincinnati Public Schools 2009–2010 Year Report Card." www.ode.state.oh.us/reportcardfiles/2009–2010/DIST/043752.pdf.

Palay, Miriam G. *Census Facts: Milwaukee Areas and Neighborhoods, 1970–1980 Statistics Compared*. Milwaukee: University of Wisconsin–Milwaukee and University of Wisconsin–Extension, 1984.

———. *Census Update, City of Milwaukee, 1975*. Milwaukee: Milwaukee Urban Observatory, 1977.

———. *Chapter 220, Student Exchanges Between City and Suburb: The Milwaukee Experience*. Milwaukee: Milwaukee Urban Observatory, 1978.

Pfarrer, Donald, et al. "Reading, Riding, and Race: Public Opinion and School Segregation in Milwaukee County." *Milwaukee Journal*, 1975. Pittsburgh Public Schools. "2011–12 Options and Offerings Guide." www.pps.k12.pa.us /1431105115023673/lib/1431105115023673/ PPS_Offerings_and_Opps_Guide2.pdf.

Sampson, Pamela J. "Forward" [sic] by Miriam G. Palay and Lois Quinn. *Options, School Desegregation*. Milwaukee: Milwaukee Urban Observatory, University of Wisconsin–Milwaukee, 1976.

Special Committee to the Shorewood School Board. Peter Barry, Chairman. *Report of the Special Committee Established by the Shorewood School Board to Prepare an Analysis of the Educational, Financial, Legal, and Community Implications of the Proposed Merger of the Schools in Whitefish Bay, Shorewood, and Certain Areas in Milwaukee*. April 7, 1975.

Texas Education Agency. "2009–2010 School Report Card." www.tea.state.tx.us /perfreport/src/2010/campus.srch.html.

US Commission on Civil Rights. *School Desegregation in Tacoma, Washington: A Staff Report of the U.S. Commission on Civil Rights*. Washington, DC: The Commission on Civil Rights, 1979.

US District Court (Wisconsin: Eastern District). *Craig Amos [and Other] Plaintiffs v. Board of School Directors of the City of Milwaukee (and Others) Defendants: Decision and Order / John W. Reynolds Presiding*. Milwaukee: The Court, 1976.

The Urban Institute. "Private School Participants in Federal Programs Under the No Child Left Behind Act and the Individuals with Disabilities Act: Private School and Public School District Representatives." Washington, DC: US Department of Education, 2007.

Wisconsin Advisory Committee to the United States Civil Rights Commission. "Impact of School Desegregation in Milwaukee Public Schools on Quality Education for Minorities. . . . 15 Years Later." August 1992. United States Commission on Civil Rights. Wisconsin Advisory Committee

Wisconsin Department of Public Instruction. "2010–11 Wisconsin Student Assessment System Results." http://dpi.wi.gov/oea/pdf/mcpc- wsasrslts.pdf.

Wisconsin Department of Public Instruction. "Public School Open Enrollment." http://dpi.wi.gov/sms/psctoc.html.

Wisconsin Legislative Audit Bureau. "An Evaluation: The Milwaukee Parental Choice Program." February 2000. Madison, WI: The Wisconsin Legislative Audit Bureau.

———. "Test Score Data for Pupils in the Milwaukee Parental Choice Program." September 2008, August 2009, August 2010, and August 2011.

Wolf, Patrick J. "The Comprehensive Longitudinal Evaluation of the Milwaukee Parental Choice Program: Summary of Fourth-Year Reports." Fayetteville: University of Arkansas, March 2011.

PUBLISHED REPORTS USED AS SECONDARY SOURCES

Dickman, Anneliese. "The Implications of Eliminating Busing: Considerations at the End of an Era." With Emily Van Dunk. The Public Policy Forum, November 1999.

Frankenberg, Erica, and Genevieve Siegel-Hawley. "The Forgotten Choice?: Rethinking Magnet Schools in a Changing Landscape; A Report to Magnet Schools of America." The Civil Rights Project, November 2008. Los Angeles: UCLA.

Greene, Jay P., and Ryan H. Marsh. "The Effect of Milwaukee's Parental Choice Program on Student Achievement in Milwaukee Public Schools." Fayetteville: University of Arkansas, March 2009.

Kava, Russ. "Milwaukee Parental Choice Program Information Paper." Madison, WI: Wisconsin Legislative Reference Bureau, 2009.

Steel, Lauri, Roger Levine, and the American Institute for Research. *Educational Innovation in Multiracial Contexts: The Growth of Magnet Schools in American Education.* Washington, DC: US Department of Education, 1994.

US Department of Commerce: Economics and Statistics Administration. US Bureau of the Census. *School Enrollment in the United States—Social and Economic Characteristics of Students.* By Amie Jamieson, Andrea Curry, and Gladys Martinez. www.census.gov/prod/2001pubs/ p20-533.pdf.

US Department of Education. National Center for Educational Statistics: Institute of Education Sciences. *1.5 Million Homeschooled Students in the United States in 2007.* NCES 2009–030. Washington, DC: US Government Printing Office, 2009. http://nces.ed.gov/pubs2009/2009030.pdf.

THESES AND DISSERTATIONS

Báez, Luis Antonio. "From Transformative School Goals to Assimilationist and Remedial Bilingual Education: A Critical Review of Key Precedent-Setting

Hispanic Bilingual Litigation Decided by Federal Courts Between 1974 and 1983." PhD diss., University of Wisconsin–Milwaukee, 1995.

Baruch, Steven A. "Factors Affecting the Process of Curriculum Formation in the Milwaukee Public Schools, July 1955 to June 1976." PhD diss., University of Wisconsin–Milwaukee, 1982.

Beyer, Steven. "Factors in the School Environment Associated with Student Achievement in Science." PhD diss., Columbia University Teachers College, 1990.

Carman, Greg J. "Wall of Exclusion: The Persistence of Residential Racial Segregation in Metropolitan Milwaukee." PhD diss., University of Wisconsin–Milwaukee, 2010.

Dahlk, William John. "The Black Educational Reform Movement in Milwaukee, 1963–1975." Master's thesis, University of Wisconsin–Milwaukee, 1990.

DeMarco, Marcella. "Magnet Programs in the Pittsburgh Schools: Development to Implementation, 1977 through 1982." PhD diss., University of Pittsburgh, 1983.

Duax, Timothy C. T. "The Impact of Nonselective Magnet Schools on a Predominately Black Neighborhood." PhD diss., University of Wisconsin–Milwaukee, 1988.

Ferrell, James Adrian. "A Magnet School and Desegregation: A Case Study of Booker T. Washington High School, 1975–1980." PhD diss., Oklahoma State University, 2008.

Fuller, Howard L. "The Impact of the Milwaukee Public School System's Desegregation Plan on Black Students and the Black Community (1976–1982)." PhD diss., Marquette University, 1985.

Goddard, Caroline Katie. "Lloyd A. Barbee and the Fight for Desegregation in the Milwaukee Public School System." Master's thesis, University of Wisconsin–Milwaukee, 1985.

Johnson, Johnnie M. "School Choice and Urban Reform: A Case Study of Milwaukee's Parental Choice Program and Black Student Achievement." PhD diss., University of Wisconsin–Milwaukee, 2004.

Mercer, Louis R. "'In Order to Form a More Complete Society': Black Students' Efforts Towards Educational Decolonization in Chicago and Milwaukee, 1968." Master's thesis, University of Wisconsin–Milwaukee, 2012.

Montgomery, Theodore V., Jr. "A Case Study of Political, Social, and Economic Forces Which Affected the Planning of School Desegregation, Milwaukee, 1976." PhD diss., University of Wisconsin–Milwaukee, 1984.

Santacroce, Phyllis M. "Rediscovering the Role of the State: Housing Policy and Practice in Milwaukee, Wisconsin, 1900–1970." PhD diss., University of Wisconsin–Milwaukee, 2009.

Schmitz-Zien, Gayle. "The Genesis of and Motivations for the Milwaukee Parental Choice Program, 1985–1995." PhD diss., University of Wisconsin–Milwaukee, 2003.

Smejkal, Ann E. "The Effects of Open Enrollment on Highly Impacted Small Wisconsin School Districts and the Leadership Response." PhD diss., University of Wisconsin–Milwaukee, 2010.

Smuckler, Nancy Sidon. "Chapter 220: A Study of the Academic Achievement of Minority Interdistrict Transfer Pupils." PhD diss., University of Wisconsin–Milwaukee, 1984.

Spurlin, Paul Merrill. "Montesquieu in America, 1760–1801." Master's thesis, Johns Hopkins University, 1940; New York: Octagon Books, 1969.

Straus, Ryane McAuliffe. "Reconstructing Magnet Schools: Social Construction and the Demise of Desegregation." PhD diss., University of California–Irvine, 2005.

Strong, Gregory E. "Metropolitan Desegregation: Administrative Practices and Procedures." PhD diss., University of Wisconsin–Milwaukee, 1980.

Vargas-Harrison, Juana Alejandrina. "A History of Hispanic Bilingual Education in Milwaukee's Public Schools: People, Policies, and Programs, 1969–1988." PhD diss., University of Wisconsin–Milwaukee, 1995.

Voigt, Cathy J. "A History of the Magnet Schools in the City of St. Louis, 1976–1980." PhD diss., Saint Louis University, 1982.

Wise, Barbara M. "Chapter 220: The Compromise to Integrate." Master's thesis, University of Wisconsin–Milwaukee, 2009.

ACKNOWLEDGMENTS

Writing a book is no easy task, but it is less hard when you have a good team of people behind you. I am fortunate enough to have a great team behind me. I started my initial research in 1997, took a break for a while, and then went to graduate school for twelve years. I wrote papers on a lot of subjects, but I always returned to schools. My list of supporters grew with each passing year that I worked on this project, which began as my dissertation. They say you should write what you know, so I suppose it makes sense that a high school teacher from Milwaukee would write a history of educational options in Wisconsin's largest city. But I never could have done it without my team.

I must first thank the staff of Hamilton High School in Milwaukee. My first experience at Hamilton was in 1989 when I enrolled there as a thirteen-year-old freshman. I did not know it at the time, but Hamilton and Washington High School were the first two high schools to be integrated in 1976 through Milwaukee's magnet school program. I lived in the Hamilton neighborhood, so I was not required to enroll in the school's word processing and marketing specialty. But many of my friends took those classes. Coincidentally, my best friend at the time lived in the Pulaski High School neighborhood but attended Washington, where he was enrolled in the computer specialty program. I had great teachers at Hamilton, and many of them became role models for my own teaching career. I went back to Hamilton in 1998 to complete my student teaching and was hired there at the end of the year when one of my former teachers was promoted to the district office. I made many friends in my fifteen years at Hamilton, and I thank them for all the encouragement they have given me in teaching and in completing this project. Several Hamilton staff members volunteered to give interviews, and I am grateful for their participation.

There are several UWM faculty to whom I owe my thanks. Michael Gordon read a twenty-four-page version of my dissertation when I was an undergraduate in his senior seminar. He later encouraged me to apply for the history department's doctoral program. Glen Jeansonne was my

master's advisor and was kind enough to take a position on my dissertation committee. Glen encourages students to write papers that are interesting and informative and that others will read, rather than something
that will only sit on a library shelf. I was also extremely lucky to have
Amanda Seligman as my doctoral advisor. Amanda is a person of many
talents—scholar, teacher, mentor. She expects the best from her students
and always encourages them to set high goals. As a part-time student,
I relied on Amanda to be my eyes and ears. Amanda always kept me
abreast of books to read, conferences at which to present, university and
department events to attend, and changes in the graduate program. She
also read my dissertation several times across many years and provided
me with useful feedback that was crucial for turning my work into a book.
Amanda did all that despite an extremely busy schedule involving family,
publication deadlines, and committee work and other university activities. Amanda also listens very deliberately to student concerns, demon-
strates concern about my personal life, and has memorized a startling
quantity of arcane facts about me. Academia would be a better place if
more students had advisors like Amanda.

Three former school board members, three former superintendents,
three former members of the Committee of 100, and several past and
current Milwaukee Public Schools staff members granted me interviews.
They welcomed me into their homes and lent a firsthand perspective not
revealed in primary sources. Former superintendent Dr. Lee McMurrin
and Milwaukee Teacher Education Association President Robert Peterson shared their private papers with me and suggested other sources. I
am especially indebted to Dr. Lynn Krebs, formerly of Milwaukee Public Schools, who introduced me to former school board president Doris
Stacy and former human relations specialist Dr. Steven Baruch. Dr.
Baruch finished *The Milwaukee Public Schools: A Chronological History,
1836–1986* for Rolland Callaway. Their work is essential for researching
school board policy.

Several people guided me to source material or provided advice. The
archives staff at UWM's Golda Meir library were constantly retrieving
boxes for me. They can find whatever a researcher needs and always do so
in a pleasant manner. The staff of the Humanities room in the Milwaukee
Public Library also did an amazing job and found materials for me that I
did not know existed. Gene Jones and his staff in the Milwaukee Public

School's Office of Board Governance do a wonderful job of keeping district records organized. Catherine Capellaro at the Wisconsin Historical Society Press is a wonderful editor. She did a lot of tedious work and provided some sound advice on word choice and formatting.

I also give my thanks to my friends and family, especially Leah, who always provides me with encouragement to fulfill my dreams. I respect and admire you so much as a teacher, friend, and companion. Finally, my brother, Dave, is not only a great guy and terrific brother; he is also my editor and proofreader. Having a professional copy editor in the family is a nice asset for anyone who does any kind of writing. Dave has read almost everything I have written, and I would never have reached this plateau without him. Thanks, man.

INDEX

Page numbers in *italics* refer to map illustrations.

ABOUT THE AUTHOR

Jim Nelsen is a high school social studies teacher in Milwaukee. He currently works at Golda Meir School, a public magnet school for college-bound students in grades 3 through 12. As a lifelong resident of Milwaukee, he finds the history of the city fascinating, from its early days in the mid-nineteenth century to the modern challenges of urban life today. As a teacher, he enjoys researching the history of education from colonial times to the present. He has a PhD in urban history from the University of Wisconsin–Milwaukee. When not teaching or researching, he enjoys volunteering with youth groups, exploring his city, and following his beloved Milwaukee Brewers baseball team.